ANCIENT EGYPTIAN PRISONER STATUES

MATERIAL AND VISUAL CULTURE
OF ANCIENT EGYPT

Series Editors
Joshua A. Roberson
Christina Geisen

NUMBER EIGHT

ANCIENT EGYPTIAN PRISONER STATUES:
FRAGMENTS OF THE LATE OLD KINGDOM

ANCIENT EGYPTIAN PRISONER STATUES
FRAGMENTS OF THE LATE OLD KINGDOM

Tara Prakash

LOCKWOOD PRESS
COLUMBUS, GEORGIA
2022

ANCIENT EGYPTIAN PRISONER STATUES
FRAGMENTS OF THE LATE OLD KINGDOM

Copyright © 2022 by Lockwood Press

All rights reserved. No part of this work may be reproduced or transmitted in any form or by any means, electronic or mechanical, including photocopying and recording, or by means of any information storage or retrieval system, except as may be expressly permitted by the 1976 Copyright Act or in writing from the publisher. Requests for permission should be addressed in writing to Lockwood Press, PO Box 1080, Columbus, GA 31901 USA.

ISBN: 978-1-948488-87-7

Cover design by Susanne Wilhelm. Cover image: A reconstructed prisoner statue probably from the pyramid complex of Pepi II in Saqqara; Sixth Dynasty. New York, MMA 64.260. Photograph: The Metropolitan Museum of Art, New York, Louis V. Bell Fund, 1964.

Cataloguing-in-Publication Data

Names: Prakash, Tara, author.
Title: The ancient Egyptian prisoner statues : art and culture in the late Old Kingdom / Tara Prakash.
Other titles: Material and visual culture of ancient Egypt ; 8.
Description: Columbus : Lockwood Press, 2022. | Series: Material and visual culture of ancient Egypt ; 8 | Includes bibliographical references and index.
Identifiers: LCCN 2022030984 (print) | LCCN 2022030985 (ebook) | ISBN 9781948488877 (hardcover) | ISBN 9781948488884 (adobe pdf)
Subjects: LCSH: Sculpture, Egyptian. | Prisoners in art.
Classification: LCC NB75 .P735 2022 (print) | LCC NB75 (ebook) | DDC 732/.8--dc23/eng/20220715
LC record available at https://lccn.loc.gov/2022030984
LC ebook record available at https://lccn.loc.gov/2022030985

This paper meets the requirements of ANSI/NISO Z39.48-1992 (Permanence of Paper).

Contents

Acknowledgements	vii
List of Figures	ix
List of Tables	xii
Abbreviations	xiii
Chronology	xv

Chapter 1. Introduction — 1

    1.1. The Context — 2
    1.2. The Iconography — 7
    1.3. Precursors and Related Representations — 12
    1.4. A Reexamination — 19

Chapter 2. The Evolution of the Prisoner Statues during the Late Old Kingdom — 23

    2.1. Egypt during the Late Old Kingdom — 24
    2.2. The Prisoner Statues — 33
    2.3. Changes and Similarities among the Prisoner Statues — 53
    2.4. The Prisoner Statues as Symbols of Kingship — 56

Chapter 3. Expressiveness and Ethnicity: The Prisoner Statue Heads — 61

    3.1. The Prisoner Statue Heads — 63
    3.2. The Expressiveness of the Prisoner Statues and the Late Old Kingdom Style — 78
    3.3. The Ethnicity of the Prisoner Statues — 83
    3.4. Egypt's Interactions with Foreigners during the Old Kingdom — 90
    3.5. The Prisoner Statues' Style and Ethnicity in the Context of the Late Old Kingdom — 102

Chapter 4. The Prisoner Statues and the Pyramid Complex — 105

    4.1. The Late Old Kingdom Pyramid Complex — 106
    4.2. Architectural Developments and the Findspots of the Prisoner Statues — 110
    4.3. The Relief Decoration — 128
    4.4. The Sculptural Decoration — 134
    4.5. The Original Placement of the Prisoner Statues and the Decorative Program — 138
    4.6. The Embellishment of the Late Old Kingdom Pyramid Complex — 141

Chapter 5. The Treatment of the Prisoner Statues and the Question of Ritualized Destruction — 145

    5.1. Previous Arguments concerning the Condition of the Prisoner Statues — 146
    5.2. The Condition of the Prisoner Statues — 148
    5.3. Execration Figurines during the Old Kingdom — 161
    5.4. The Ritualized Context of the Pepi I and Pepi II Prisoner Statues — 165

5.5. Rituals and Ritualization in the Late Old Kingdom Pyramid Complex   173

Chapter 6. Conclusion   177

Appendix. The Unprovenanced Prisoner Statues   183

A.1. The Prisoner Statues from the Diniacopoulos Collection   183
A.2. A Prisoner Statue Head in Brussels   186
A.3. Unidentified Prisoner Statues in Egypt   188
A.4. A Wrongly Identified Head in Los Angeles   190

Bibliography   193
Subject Index   215

Acknowledgments

This book would not have been possible without the help and support of many different individuals and institutions. It grew out of my PhD dissertation, which I completed in 2017 at the Institute of Fine Arts, New York University, and is a much revised and expanded version of my initial study on the prisoner statues. I would like to thank my dissertation advisor, David O'Connor, and the members of my committee, Ann Macy Roth, Ogden Goelet, and Marsha Hill, who provided endless advice and support throughout both the dissertation process and far beyond it.

My research was generously supported by a fellowship from the American Research Center in Egypt (funded by the U.S. Department of State Bureau of Educational and Cultural Affairs), a Francis Haskell Memorial Fund scholarship from the Burlington Magazine, and several grants from the Institute of Fine Arts and New York University. Portions of the book were written while I was a postdoctoral fellow in the Department of Near Eastern Studies at The Johns Hopkins University, an Andrew W. Mellon Research Fellow in the Department of Egyptian Art at the Metropolitan Museum of Art, and the W. Benson Harer Egyptology Scholar in Residence at California State University, San Bernardino. My sincere thanks go to these institutions and all of my friends and colleagues within them for their support and help.

I am indebted to Philippe Collombert and the Mission archéologique franco-suisse de Saqqâra (MAFS) for graciously permitting me to use all of the MAFS' archival records on the Pepi I prisoner statues and for inviting me to join the team in 2015 so that I could study and document the unpublished fragments in their storeroom. I am also grateful to the Supreme Council of Antiquities for granting me permission to conduct my research in Egypt. Throughout this project, I visited many museums and archives, and I would like to acknowledge the various curators, directors, and archivists who welcomed me to their institutions and assisted me. I am also grateful to those institutions for allowing me to publish the materials that I collected during my visits. In this regard, my sincere thanks go to Isadora Rogger and the Musée d'ethnographie in Neuchâtel; Patrizia Piacentini, Christian Orsenigo, and the Egyptological Library and Archives at the Università degli Studi di Milano; Mahmud El Halwagy and the Egyptian Museum in Cairo; Assayed el Banna and the Suez National Museum; Dr. Sanaa and the Luxor Museum; Nadia Khider and the Alexandria National Museum; Tarek Tawfiq and the Grand Egyptian Museum; the Military Museum at the Cairo Citadel; Emad Khadter and the Imhotep Museum in Saqqara; Mohamed Hassan Abdel Fattah and the SCA Documentation Center; Nadine Cherpion and the Institut français d'archéologie orientale; Luc Delvaux and the Musées Royaux d'Art et d'Histoire, Brussels; Klaus Finneiser and the Ägyptisches Museum und Papyrussammlung, Berlin; the Department of Ancient Egypt & Sudan at the British Museum; Cat Warsi and the Griffith Institute, University of Oxford; Edward Bleiburg, Yekaterina Barbash, and the Brooklyn Museum; Sheldon Cheek and the Image of the Black Archive & Library at the Hutchins Center, Harvard University; Denise Doxey and the Museum of Fine Arts in Boston; and Nancy Thomas and the Los Angeles County Museum of Art.

The scope of this book would not have been possible without the help of numerous individuals who aided me in locating prisoner statue fragments and archival records, and I appreciate all who answered my inquiries and emails. I am indebted to Mohamed Megahed for generously sharing his research with me and for all of the interesting conversations on Djedkare. I am also grateful to conservators Anna Serotta and Ann Heywood, Metropolitan Museum of Art, and Michele Marincola, Institute of Fine Arts, for teaching me more about the qualities of limestone and discussing the condition of the prisoner statues with me. Indeed, my thanks go to all of my colleagues who have discussed the prisoner statues with me over the years. Niv Allon, Kate Liszka, Marion Mazzone, Barry Stiefel, Mary Beth Heston, Mary Trent, and Brigit Ferguson graciously read portions of this book and provided valuable feedback. Moreover, I am indebted to two anonymous reviewers who read chapters at an early phase and provided useful commentary that enabled me to reimagine the manuscript in extremely productive and beneficial ways. Christina Geisen and Joshua Roberson were enthusiastic about this book from the start, and I am grateful to them and Billie Jean Collins for guiding it through the publication process. I would also like to thank my colleagues at the College of Charleston for all of their encouragement and support.

I am very lucky to be surrounded by incredible friends and family, who have always been willing to listen to me talk about the prisoner statues and have provided constant inspiration and reassurance. This is particularly true for Sheela Prakash and Jason Barr, who may have had to hear about the prisoner statues the most! Finally, I am so thankful to my mother and father for all that they taught me and have done for me. I dedicate this book to them.

List of Figures

Figure 1.1. The pyramid complex of Unas with the pyramids of South Saqqara and Dahshur in the background. 1

Figure 1.2. Reconstructed prisoner statue probably from the pyramid complex of Pepi II. New York, MMA 64.260. 2

Figure 1.3. Old Kingdom pyramid complexes and royal funerary monuments from Giza to Saqqara. 5

Figure 1.4. Reconstructed prisoner statue probably from the pyramid complex of Pepi II. New York, MMA 47.2. 8

Figure 1.5. Ramses III smiting a group of foreigners on the south wing of the first pylon of his mortuary temple at Medinet Habu. 8

Figure 1.6. Trampling scene on an arm panel from a throne of Thutmose IV. New York, MMA 30.8.45a–c. 9

Figure 1.7. Door socket in the form of a trussed prisoner. Philadelphia, Penn Museum, E3959. 13

Figure 1.8. Console with two connecting heads of prisoners from the Step Pyramid of Djoser. Alexandria, Alexandria National Museum JE 49613. 14

Figure 1.9. Two architectural consoles of foreign prisoners from the Eastern High Gate at Medinet Habu. 15

Figure 1.10. Statue base/offering table with the heads and hands of foreigners emerging. Cairo, Egyptian Museum CG 755/JE 28831. 16

Figure 1.11. Wooden figurine of a bound captive from the mortuary temple of Raneferef. Cairo, Egyptian Museum JE 98182(a). 17

Figure 1.12. Wooden (execration?) figurine from the tomb of Senedjemib Mehi. Boston, MFA 13.3459. 18

Figure 2.1. Prisoner statue fragment from the valley temple of Niuserre. Berlin, ÄM 17913. 33

Figure 2.2. Statue of Ramses VI "smiting" a Libyan. Luxor, Luxor Museum J.902. 34

Figure 2.3. Prisoner statue fragment (SCA no. 2232) from the mortuary temple of Djedkare-Isesi. 36

Figure 2.4. Prisoner statue fragment (SCA no. 2244) from the mortuary temple of Djedkare-Isesi. 36

Figure 2.5. Prisoner statue fragment from the mortuary temple of Unas in Saqqara. 37

Figure 2.6. Prisoner statue bust from the mortuary temple of Teti. Saqqara, Imhotep Museum JE 40047. 39

Figure 2.7. Drawing of a prisoner statue fragment (Bloc 64) from the mortuary temple of Teti. 40

Figure 2.8. Prisoner statues from the pyramid complex of Pepi I in Saqqara following the 1968–1969 excavation season. 42

Figure 2.9. Prisoner statue fragment (PP 56) from the pyramid complex of Pepi I. 43

Figure 2.10. Prisoner statue fragment (PP 59) from the pyramid complex of Pepi I. 43

Figure 2.11. Prisoner statue fragment (PP 46) from the pyramid complex of Pepi I. 43

Figure 2.12. Prisoner statue fragment (PP 41) from the pyramid complex of Pepi I. 43

Figure 2.13. Prisoner statue fragment (PP 45) from the pyramid complex of Pepi I. 43

Figure 2.14. Prisoner statue body (PP 1) from the pyramid complex of Pepi I. 45

Figure 2.15. Prisoner statue body (PP 2) from the pyramid complex of Pepi I. 46

List of Figures

Figure 2.16. Prisoner statue body and head (PP 3 and 23) from the pyramid complex of Pepi I.   47
Figure 2.17. Prisoner statue fragments (PP 4) from the pyramid complex of Pepi I.   48
Figure 2.18. Prisoner statue fragment (PP 6) from the pyramid complex of Pepi I.   49
Figure 2.19. Prisoner statue fragment (PP 14) from the pyramid complex of Pepi I.   49
Figure 2.20. Prisoner statue fragment (PP 8) from the pyramid complex of Pepi I.   49
Figure 2.21. Prisoner statue fragment (PP 29) from the pyramid complex of Pepi I.   49
Figure 2.22. Reconstructed prisoner statue from the pyramid complex of Pepi II. Cairo, GEM 1101.   51
Figure 2.23. Reconstructed prisoner statue from the pyramid complex of Pepi II. Suez, Suez National Museum JE 51729.   52
Figure 2.24. Prisoner statue fragment from the pyramid complex of Pepi II. Cairo, Egyptian Museum JE 45782.   53

Figure 3.1. Prisoner statue head from the valley temple of Niuserre. Berlin, ÄM 17912.   63
Figure 3.2. Prisoner statue bust (SCA no. 2233) from the mortuary temple of Djedkare-Isesi.   64
Figure 3.3. Prisoner statue head fragment from the mortuary temple of Djedkare-Isesi.   64
Figure 3.4. Prisoner statue head (PP 32) from the pyramid complex of Pepi I.   65
Figure 3.5. Prisoner statue head (PP 18) from the pyramid complex of Pepi I.   65
Figure 3.6. Prisoner statue head and body fragment (PP 16) from the pyramid complex of Pepi I.   67
Figure 3.7. Prisoner statue head (PP 17) from the pyramid complex of Pepi I.   67
Figure 3.8. Prisoner statue head (PP 19) from the pyramid complex of Pepi I.   67
Figure 3.9. Prisoner statue head (PP 20) from the pyramid complex of Pepi I.   67
Figure 3.10. Prisoner statue head (PP 21) from the pyramid complex of Pepi I.   67
Figure 3.11. Prisoner statue head (PP 22) from the pyramid complex of Pepi I.   67
Figure 3.12. Prisoner statue head (PP 23) from the pyramid complex of Pepi I.   67
Figure 3.13. Prisoner statue head (PP 60) from the pyramid complex of Pepi I.   67
Figure 3.14. Prisoner statue head from the pyramid complex of Pepi II. Cairo, Egyptian Museum JE 45781.   72
Figure 3.15. Prisoner statue head from the pyramid complex of Pepi II. Cairo, Egyptian Museum JE 57202.   72
Figure 3.16. Prisoner statue head from the pyramid complex of Pepi II. Cairo, National Military Museum JE 51730.   72
Figure 3.17. Prisoner statue head from the pyramid complex of Pepi II. Cairo, National Military Museum JE 51731.   72
Figure 3.18. Prisoner statue bust from the pyramid complex of Pepi II.   72
Figure 3.19. Prisoner statue bust from the pyramid complex of Pepi II.   72
Figure 3.20. Prisoner statue bust from the pyramid complex of Pepi II.   73
Figure 3.21. Prisoner statue head from the pyramid complex of Pepi II.   73
Figure 3.22. Prisoner statue head from the pyramid complex of Pepi II.   73
Figure 3.23. Prisoner statue head from the pyramid complex of Pepi II.   73
Figure 3.24. Prisoner statue head fragments from the pyramid complex of Pepi II.   73
Figure 3.25. Statue of the high official Demedji and his wife Henutsen. New York, MMA 51.37.   80
Figure 3.26. Kneeling statuette of Pepi I. Brooklyn, Brooklyn Museum 39.121.   80
Figure 3.27. A stereotypical Nubian, Asiatic, and Libyan from a relief that decorated the bottom of the causeway of Sahure.   85
Figure 3.28. Egypt and its surroundings with important Old Kingdom sites.   91

List of Figures   xi

Figure 4.1. Schematic plan of the pyramid complex of Sahure.   107
Figure 4.2. Valley temple of Sahure.   109
Figure 4.3. Mortuary temple of Sahure.   109
Figure 4.4. Valley temple of Niuserre.   112
Figure 4.5. Mortuary temple of Niuserre.   113
Figure 4.6. Mortuary temple of Djedkare-Isesi.   114
Figure 4.7. Photograph of Hussein's excavations in the mortuary temple of Djedkare-Isesi showing
            a prisoner statue fragment.   116
Figure 4.8. Mortuary temple of Unas.   118
Figure 4.9. Valley temple of Unas.   118
Figure 4.10. Mortuary temple of Teti.   119
Figure 4.11. Mortuary temple of Pepi I.   122
Figure 4.12. Valley temple of Pepi II.   124
Figure 4.13. Mortuary temple of Pepi II.   125
Figure 4.14. Schematic plan of the pyramid complex of Pepi II and environs with approximate
             findspots of prisoner statue fragments highlighted.   126
Figure 4.15. Relief fragments from a smiting scene in the open court of the mortuary temple of
             Sahure.   129
Figure 4.16. Relief fragments from a trampling scene at the end of the causeway of Niuserre.   131
Figure 4.17. Relief fragments from a scene of the king smiting a Libyan from the transverse
             corridor of the mortuary temple of Pepi II.   133
Figure 4.18. Relief fragments from a smiting scene from the rear vestibule of the mortuary
             temple of Pepi II.   134

Figure 5.1. Prisoner statue fragment (PP 66) from the pyramid complex of Pepi I.   155
Figure 5.2. Cairo, GEM 1101 (left) and Suez, Suez National Museum JE 51729 (right) from the
            pyramid complex of Pepi II at an earlier stage of reconstruction.   158
Figure 5.3. Execration figurines from Cemetery 2000 (western) in Giza. Boston, MFA 07.1025.   163
Figure 5.4. Votive statue for the governor Khnumemhet featuring a bound foreign prisoner.
            Luxor, Luxor Museum J.906.   169

Figure A.1. Reconstructed prisoner statue probably from the pyramid complex of Pepi II. London,
            BM EA 75198.   185
Figure A.2. Prisoner statue head probably from the pyramid complex of Pepi II. Brussels, Musées
            Royaux d'Art et d'Histoire E.07967.   187
Figure A.3. Limestone head of a late Old Kingdom high official. Los Angeles, LACMA 47.12.   190

List of Tables

Table 1. Division of Pepi I prisoner statue head fragments based on their hairstyle.	68
Table 2. Division of Pepi I prisoner statue head fragments based on their face shape.	69
Table 3. Division of Pepi I prisoner statue head fragments based on their brows.	69
Table 4. Division of Pepi I prisoner statue head fragments based on their eyes.	69
Table 5. Division of Pepi I prisoner statue head fragments based on their noses.	70
Table 6. Division of Pepi I prisoner statue head fragments based on their mouths.	70
Table 7. Division of Pepi I prisoner statue head fragments based on their beards.	71
Table 8. Types of facial features and hairstyles among the Pepi I prisoner statue heads.	71
Table 9. Division of Pepi II prisoner statue fragments based on their hairstyle.	74
Table 10. Subdivision of short and tiered hairstyle (Type 4) for the Pepi II prisoner statue fragments.	74
Table 11. Division of Pepi II prisoner statue fragments based on their face shape.	75
Table 12. Division of Pepi II prisoner statue fragments based on their brows.	75
Table 13. Division of Pepi II prisoner statue fragments based on their eyes.	75
Table 14. Division of Pepi II prisoner statue fragments based on their noses.	76
Table 15. Division of Pepi II prisoner statue fragments based on their mouths.	76
Table 16. Presence of a philtrum for the Pepi II prisoner statue heads that have this area preserved.	76
Table 17. Division of Pepi II prisoner statue fragments based on their beards.	77
Table 18. Types of facial features and hairstyles among the Pepi II prisoner statue heads.	77
Table 19. Summary of the evidence and conclusions for intentional damage to the prisoner statues.	149

Supplementary Material

A supplementary Open Access catalogue of all material available on the prisoner statues can be found online at: https://doi.org/10.5913/2022877

Abbreviations

ÄAT	Ägypten und Altes Testament
AAWWien	Anzeiger der österreichischen Akademie der Wissenschaften in Wien, Philosophisch-Historische Klasse
AegHelv	Aegyptiaca Helvetica
AfO	*Archiv für Orientforschung*
ÄgAbh	Ägyptologische Abhandlungen
AOAT	Alter Orient und Altes Testament
ASAE	*Annales du Service des Antiquités de l'Égypte*
ASAE-Suppl.	Supplément aux Annales du Service des Antiquités de l'Égypte
AulÆg-Stud	Aula Ægyptiaca – Studia
BACE	*Bulletin of the Australian Centre for Egyptology*
BASOR	*Bulletin of the American Schools of Oriental Research*
BeitrÄg	Beiträge zur Ägyptologie
BIE	*Bulletin de l'Institut d'Égypte*
BiEtud	Bibliothèque d'étude
BIFAO	*Bulletin de l'Institut français d'archéologie orientale*
BMMA	*The Metropolitan Museum of Art Bulletin*
BMPES	British Museum Publications on Egypt and Sudan
BMSAES	*British Museum Studies in Ancient Egypt and Sudan*
BN	Bibliothèque nationale
BSEG	*Bulletin de la Société d'égyptologie de Genève*
BSFE	*Bulletin de la Société française d'égyptologie*
CASAE	Cahiers. Supplément aux ASAE
CdE	*Chronique d'Égypte*
CGC	Catalogue général du musée du Caire
CHANE	Culture and History of the Ancient Near East
CRAIBL	*Comptes rendus de l'Académie des inscriptions et belles-lettres*
CRIPEL	*Cahiers de recherches de l'Institut de papyrologie et égyptologie de Lille*
DÖAWW	Denkschriften der österreichischen Akademie der Wissenschaften Wien
DOG	Deutschen Orient-Gesellschaft zu Berlin
ENiM	*Égypte nilotique et méditerranéenne*
ERA	Egyptian Research Account
FIFAO	Fouilles de l'Institut français d'archéologie orientale
FouillesSaqq	Fouilles à Saqqarah, Service des Antiquités de l'Égypte
GM	*Göttinger Miszellen*
GOF	Göttinger Orientforschungen
HÄB	Hildesheimer Ägyptologische Beiträge
HdO	Handbook of Oriental Studies: Section 1, Ancient Near East
HES	Harvard Egyptological Studies

IFAO	Institut français d'archéologie orientale
JARCE	*Journal of the American Research Center in Egypt*
JEA	*Journal of Egyptian Archaeology*
JESHO	*Journal of the Economic and Social History of the Orient*
JNES	*Journal of Near Eastern Studies*
KAW	Kulturgeschichte der Antiken Welt
LÄ	*Lexikon der Ägyptologie*
MAFS	Mission archéologique franco-suisse de Saqqâra (Previously Mission archéologique française de Saqqâra)
MÄS	Münchner Ägyptologische Studien
MÄU	Münchner Ägyptologische Untersuchungen
Menes	Menes: Studien zur Kultur und Sprache der ägyptischen Frühzeit und des Alten Reiches
MDAIK	*Mitteilungen des Deutschen Archäologischen Instituts, Abteilung Kairo*
MDOG	*Mitteilungen der Deutschen Orient-Gesellschaft zu Berlin*
MEES	Memoir of the Egypt Exploration Society
MIFAO	Mémoires publiés par les membres de l'Institut français d'archéologie orientale
MMAEE	The Metropolitan Museum of Art Egyptian Expedition
MMJ	*Metropolitan Museum Journal*
MoTA	Ministry of Tourism and Antiquities
MVCAE	Material and Visual Culture of Ancient Egypt
NEA	*Near Eastern Archaeology*
OBO	Orbis Biblicus et Orientalis
OIP	Oriental Institute Publications
OIS	Oriental Institute Seminars
OLA	Orientalia Lovaniensia Analecta
OrMonsp	Orientalia Monspeliensia
PAe	Probleme der Ägyptologie
PM	Bertha Porter and Rosalind L. B. Moss, *Topographical Bibliography of Ancient Egyptian Hieroglyphic Texts, Reliefs, and Paintings*, 8 vols. Oxford: Clarendon, 1960–.
RACE	Reports of the Australian Centre for Egyptology
RAPH	Recherches d'archéologie, de philologie et d'histoire
RdE	*Revue d'Égyptologie*
RGRW	Religions in the Graeco-Roman World
SAE	Service des Antiquités de l'Égypte
SAK	*Studien zur altägyptischen Kultur*
SAOC	Studies in Ancient Oriental Civilization
SCA	Supreme Council of Antiquities
SDAIK	Sonderschrift des deutschen archäologischen Instituts, Abteilung Kairo
Urk.	Kurt Sethe et al. *Urkunden des ägyptischen Altertums*, 8 vols. Leipzig: Hinrich, 1903–1957.
UUÅ	Uppsala Universitets Årsskrift
WAW	Writings from the Ancient World
WVDOG	Wissenschaftliche Veröffentlichungen der deutschen Orient-Gesellschaft
ZÄS	*Zeitschrift für ägyptische Sprache und Altertumskunde*

Chronology

Modified from Hornung, Krauss, and Warburton, *Ancient Egyptian Chronology*, 490–95. All dates are BCE and approximate.

Early Dynastic period	2900–2593
Old Kingdom	2592–2153
Dynasty 3	2592–2544
Dynasty 4	2543–2436
Snefru	2543–2510
Khufu	2509–2483
Radjedef	2482–2475
Khafre	2472–2448
Menkaure	2447–2442
Shepseskaf	2441–2436
Dynasty 5	2435–2306
Userkaf	2435–2429
Sahure	2428–2416
Neferirkare	2415–2405
Raneferef	2404
Shepseskare	2403
Niuserre	2402–2374
Menkauhor	2373–2366
Djedkare-Isesi	2365–2322
Unas	2321–2306
Dynasty 6	2305–2153
Teti	2305–2279
Userkare	?–?
Pepi I	2276–2228
Merenre	2227–2217
Pepi II	2216–2153
First Intermediate period	2118–1980
Middle Kingdom	1980–1760
Second Intermediate period	1759–1539
New Kingdom	1539–1077
Third Intermediate period	1076–723
Late period	722–332

Chapter 1
Introduction

The pyramids of Giza are perhaps the most iconic relics of ancient Egypt. Many people can easily picture the massive triangular forms, solidly standing against the desert backdrop, even if they have never visited Giza in person. These pyramids were the funerary monuments of the Fourth Dynasty pharaohs Khufu, Khafre, and Menkaure. Their enormous size, which still impresses travelers today, testifies to the power of these kings and the prosperity of Egypt during the height of the Old Kingdom, in the middle of the third millennium BCE.

What often surprises visitors is that each pyramid is not an independent structure. It was a part of a larger complex, which included multiple temples and spanned hundreds of meters across the desert. Equally surprising is the view from the Giza plateau: on a clear day, one can spot numerous other pyramids dotting the horizon. Khufu, Khafre, and Menkaure were not the only kings who built pyramids. For the remainder of the Old Kingdom, which included the Fifth and Sixth Dynasties, royal funerary monuments continued to be pyramid complexes (fig. 1.1).

The late Old Kingdom pyramids are not nearly as well preserved as those of the Fourth Dynasty. But originally, these complexes would have been extremely impressive monuments, primarily because of their lavish decoration rather than the size of the pyramids, which were smaller and more standardized. The temples in the late Old Kingdom complexes were paved with expensive stones, including black basalt and

Figure 1.1. The pyramid complex of Unas with the pyramids of South Saqqara and Dahshur in the background.

Figure 1.2. A reconstructed prisoner statue probably from the pyramid complex of Pepi II in Saqqara; Sixth Dynasty. New York, MMA 64.260. Photograph: The Metropolitan Museum of Art, New York, Louis V. Bell Fund, 1964.

white alabaster, and the walls were covered in finely carved, painted reliefs. The temples were also filled with statuary, much of which depicted the king. Additionally, a new type of statue appeared at this time and was a major component of the late Old Kingdom pyramid complex. Modern scholars refer to these statues as prisoner statues (fig. 1.2).

The ancient Egyptians clearly recognized the prisoner statues as a distinct genre of statuary. The statues all depict foreign male captives kneeling with their arms bound behind their backs, are nearly life-size, were carved from limestone, and were exclusive to the royal pyramid complex. At the same time, the prisoner statues changed dramatically over the course of the late Old Kingdom, and each king's prisoner statues differed in important ways from those of his predecessors. For example, the number of prisoner statues within each complex increased over time, from only a handful to dozens. Their placement within the complex also shifted from monument to monument. Additionally, their treatment and the way that the prisoner statues functioned in relation to the other decoration and the ritual life of the pyramid complex developed in significant ways. While the earliest statues were innovative, three-dimensional architectural decoration that was meant to stand in the monument permanently, the later statues were intentionally broken as a part of ritual performance.

The changes one finds among the prisoner statues relate to broader developments that were contemporaneously occurring in late Old Kingdom society, religion, art, and culture. The prisoner statues reflect a new conception of kingship and ethnicity. They illustrate some of the ways that each king, with the help of his high officials and artists, redesigned the pyramid complex to suit his needs and priorities better. Overall, they demonstrate the dynamism of the late Old Kingdom. The Fourth Dynasty tends to overshadow the Fifth and Sixth; much of the world knows of the Giza pyramids while few nonspecialists are familiar with the late Old Kingdom pyramids. But the late Old Kingdom was an incredibly important period of ancient Egyptian history. During this time, Egypt cemented its dominant status within the ancient Near East, and the political, social, and belief systems that would form the backbone of the country throughout pharaonic history were articulated. To understand ancient Egyptian history, one must look to the late Old Kingdom, and to understand fully the late Old Kingdom, one must consider the prisoner statues.

1.1. The Context

The Old Kingdom (ca. 2592–2153 BCE) consists of the Third Dynasty (ca. 2592–2544 BCE), the Fourth Dynasty (ca. 2543–2436 BCE), the Fifth Dynasty (ca. 2435–2306 BCE), and the Sixth Dynasty (ca. 2305–2153

BCE).¹ The prisoner statues first appeared during the reign of Niuserre (ca. 2403–2374 BCE) in the middle of the Fifth Dynasty. The Fifth Dynasty marks the beginning of the late Old Kingdom, and there are multiple ways that this period differed from what had come before. The power of the king was at its height during the Fourth Dynasty. The king was essentially a god on earth and at the apex of an extremely stratified society. Moreover, the administration was heavily centralized: it was situated in Memphis, which was the capital throughout the Old Kingdom, and largely consisted of the royal family.²

The composition of the administration and bureaucratic elite changed in the Fifth Dynasty. State positions were opened up to officials of nonroyal background, who nevertheless still remained closely tied to the royal family. This led to the proliferation of a distinct elite class that largely ran the country on behalf of the king, and to a growing complexity of the state.³ The new and more distanced relationship between the elite and the king was also reflected in the location of high officials' tombs, which were no longer in

---

1. Absolute dates follow Erik Hornung, Rolf Krauss, and David A. Warburton, ed., *Ancient Egyptian Chronology*, HdO 83 (Leiden: Brill, 2006). However, I differ from them in including the Third Dynasty in the Old Kingdom and in ending the Old Kingdom with Pepi II. While most Egyptologists recognize the Third Dynasty as initiating the Old Kingdom, when exactly the period came to an end continues to be a matter of debate. The First Intermediate period began when the central government lost control of the country and the provincial governors, or nomarchs, became fully independent. Some scholars believe that the provinces still recognized the Eighth Dynasty kings, who continued to rule from Memphis, as overlords and thus include them in the Old Kingdom. However, these kings were significantly weaker and more ephemeral than the Sixth Dynasty kings, and it seems unlikely that they held full power throughout the country. Effectively, the Old Kingdom came to an end after the reign of Pepi II even though the Eighth Dynasty kings still had some influence outside the capital and the country had not yet completely fragmented into the First Intermediate period. In other words, the Eighth Dynasty is best understood as a transitory period between the Old Kingdom and the First Intermediate period. I discuss some reasons for the decline of the Old Kingdom in ch. 2, but in this regard, see further Miroslav Bárta, *Analyzing Collapse: The Rise and Fall of the Old Kingdom* (Cairo: The American University in Cairo Press, 2019); Renate Müller-Wollerman, "Krisenfaktoren im ägyptischen Staat des Ausgehenden Alten Reichs" (PhD diss., University of Tübingen, 1986); Ellen Morris, "Ancient Egyptian Exceptionalism: Fragility, Flexibility and the Art of Not Collapsing," in *The Evolution of Fragility: Setting the Terms*, ed. Norman Yoffee (Cambridge: McDonald Institute for Archaeological Research, 2019), 76–83; Michel Baud, "The Old Kingdom," in *A Companion to Ancient Egypt*, vol. 1, ed. Alan B. Lloyd (Chichester: Wiley-Blackwell, 2010), 78–80; and Jaromir Malek, *In the Shadow of the Pyramids: Egypt during the Old Kingdom* (Norman: University of Oklahoma Press, 1986), 117–20. Regarding Old Kingdom chronology, see further Miroslav Verner, "The System of Dating in the Old Kingdom," in *Chronology and Archaeology in Ancient Egypt (The Third Millennium B.C.)*, ed. Hana Vymazalová and Miroslav Bárta (Prague: Czech Institute of Egyptology, 2008), 23–43; Miroslav Bárta, "Radiocarbon Dates for the Old Kingdom and their Correspondences," in *Radiocarbon and the Chronologies of Ancient Egypt*, ed. Andrew J. Shortland and C. Bronk Ramsey (Oxford: Oxbow, 2013), 218–23; Michel Baud, "Ménès, la mémoire monarchique et la chronologie du IIIᵉ millénaire," *Archéo-Nil* 9 (1999): 109–47; and Michel Baud, "The Relative Chronology of Dynasties 6 and 8," in Hornung, Krauss, and Warburton, 144–58. Concerning the controversial and possibly nonexistent Seventh Dynasty and the Eighth Dynasty, see Miroslav Bárta, "Kings, Viziers, and Courtiers: Executive Power in the Third Millennium B.C.," in *Ancient Egyptian Administration*, ed. Juan Carlos Moreno García, HdO 104 (Leiden: Brill, 2013), 173 and Hratch Papazian, "The State of Egypt in the Eighth Dynasty," in *Towards a New History for the Egyptian Old Kingdom: Perspectives on the Pyramid Age*, ed. Peter Der Manuelian and Thomas Schneider, HES 1 (Leiden: Brill, 2015), 393–428.

2. Concerning the capital and royal residence during the Old Kingdom, see Miroslav Verner, "Several Thoughts on the Old Kingdom Residence," in *Studies Dedicated to the Memory of Eva Pardey*, ed. Miroslav Bárta and Hella Küllmer (Prague: Charles University, 2013), 119–22 and Miroslav Verner, *Abusir: The Necropolis of the Sons of the Sun* (Cairo: American University in Cairo, 2017), 1–12. Regarding the administration during the Fourth Dynasty, see Bárta, "Kings," 162–65.

3. Miroslav Bárta, "Egyptian Kingship during the Old Kingdom," in *Experiencing Power, Generating Authority: Cosmos, Politics, and the Ideology of Kingship in Ancient Egypt and Mesopotamia*, ed. Jane A. Hill, Philip Jones, and Antonio J. Morales (Philadelphia: University of Pennsylvania Museum of Archaeology and Anthropology, 2013), 257–83; Bárta, "Kings," 165–66; Miroslav Bárta, "Architectural Innovations in the Development of the Non-Royal Tomb during the Reign of Nyuserra," in *Structure and Significance: Thoughts on Ancient Egyptian Architecture*, ed. Peter Jánosi (Vienna: Österreichische Akademie der Wissenschaften, 2005), 118; Nigel Strudwick, *The Administration of Egypt in the Old Kingdom: The Highest Titles and*

Giza, in the shadow of the pyramid of the king whom they had served. While the early Fifth Dynasty kings, beginning with Sahure, built their pyramid complexes at Abusir, most contemporary officials constructed their tombs a few miles away in Saqqara. Nigel Strudwick has questioned whether this separation between royal and private tombs was the result of a deliberate attempt to emphasize the division between the king and the elite.[4]

Additionally, the role of high officials outside Memphis became more prominent as the state's involvement with the provinces increased.[5] However, the Memphite region continued to be the unequivocal center of the country. And the king continued to be the undisputed leader of Egypt, even if the divide between him and his uppermost subjects had lessened.[6] In addition to a pyramid complex, the components of which I describe below, beginning in the Fifth Dynasty, each king also built an independent sun temple.[7] The exact meanings of the Fifth Dynasty sun temples are disputed, but these temples undoubtedly had a connection to the king's funerary cult and major symbolic and economic functions.[8] Additionally, the sun temples are one sign of the rise of solar religion and the sun god in the early Fifth Dynasty. During this time, the kings legitimized themselves through their piety to the gods, especially the sun god.[9]

Further major changes in ancient Egyptian society and administration occurred during the reign of Niuserre, when the prisoner statues first appeared, and I discuss these in the next chapter. Following Niuserre, at least five other late Old Kingdom pharaohs, including Djedkare-Isesi (ca. 2365–2322 BCE), Unas (ca. 2321–2306 BCE), Teti (ca. 2305–2279 BCE), Pepi I (ca. 2276–2228 BCE), and Pepi II (ca. 2216–2153 BCE), also commissioned prisoner statues for their pyramid complexes (fig. 1.3).[10] Over the second half of the Fifth Dynasty and the Sixth Dynasty, the elite continued to rise in prominence and power and the authority of the king gradually declined. At the same time, the number of prisoner statues in each king's monument increased. These developments were related; the prisoner statues were one way that kings could distinguish themselves from the elite. In this way, the greater popularity of the prisoner statues reflects the changing role of the king and nature of kingship at the end of the Old Kingdom.

Their Holders (London: KPI, 1985), 337–39; and Nigel Strudwick, *Texts from the Pyramid Age*, ed. Ronald Leprohon, WAW 16 (Atlanta: Society of Biblical Literature, 2005), 8.

4. Strudwick, *Administration*, 345.

5. Juan Carlos Moreno García, "The Territorial Administration of the Kingdom in the Third Millennium," in Moreno García, *Ancient Egyptian Administration*, 107–21; and Bárta, "Kings," 167 and 170–71. See also Leslie Anne Warden, "Centralized Taxation during the Old Kingdom," in Der Manuelian and Schneider, *Towards a New History*, 479–88.

6. See further Verner, *Abusir*, 35–50 and Miroslav Bárta, "'Abusir Paradigm' and the Beginning of the Fifth Dynasty," in *The Pyramids: Between Life and Death; Proceedings of the Workshop Held at Uppsala University, Uppsala, May 31st–June 1st, 2012*, ed. Irmgard Hein, Nils Billing, and Erika Meyer-Dietrich (Uppsala: Uppsala University, 2016), 51–74.

7. The sun temples of six Fifth Dynasty kings are referenced in textual records, but only two actual complexes have been discovered: that of Userkaf in north Abusir and that of Niuserre in Abu Ghurob.

8. A recent and comprehensive study of the sun temples is Massimiliano Nuzzolo, *The Fifth Dynasty Sun Temples: Kingship, Architecture and Religion in Third Millennium BC Egypt* (Prague: Charles University, 2018).

9. Toby Wilkinson, *Royal Annals of Ancient Egypt: The Palermo Stone and Its Associated Fragments* (London: Kegan Paul International, 2000), 148.

10. Future excavations could reveal prisoner statue fragments in other late Old Kingdom pyramid complexes. Currently, there are no indications that Merenre, who had a relatively short reign, had prisoner statues. While his mortuary temple has yet to be fully excavated and consequently, it remains possible that prisoner statue fragments will still be discovered from here (or that unprovenanced examples actually come from this complex), some of the relief decoration had been left unfinished, suggesting that the king died before his monument was completed (Mark Lehner, *The Complete Pyramids* [London: Thames & Hudson, 2008], 160–61). For this reason, it is possible that his artists never had an opportunity to carve prisoner statues. The pyramid of Menkauhor, who ruled for only eight years between Niuserre and Djedkare, has yet to be located (Lehner, *Complete Pyramids*, 153 and 165). Therefore, it also remains uncertain whether or not he had prisoner statues.

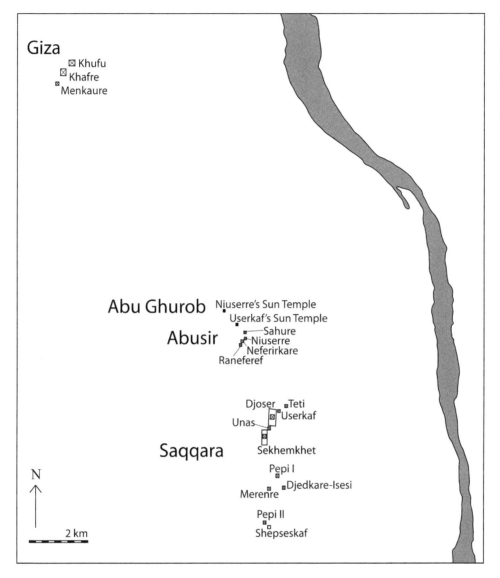

Figure 1.3. Old Kingdom pyramid complexes and royal funerary monuments from Giza to Saqqara. Modified from Lehner, *Complete Pyramids*, 9–10.

The standard pyramid complex had four main elements that were aligned along an east–west axis.[11] First, the pyramid itself was farthest to the west and marked the king's tomb. The funerary apartments, including the burial chamber, were carved out of the bedrock underneath the pyramid and accessed by a long descending corridor whose entrance was on the north face of the pyramid.[12] Second, a temple was directly adjacent to the east side of the pyramid: Egyptologists variously refer to this as the mortuary, funerary, pyramid, or upper temple. Third, a second temple, which is now known as the valley temple, was located to the east and at the edge of cultivation. Finally a long, usually covered causeway connected the temples and led from the cultivation toward the pyramid in the desert. While these elements were reproduced with remarkable consistency, the plan of each element could vary widely; I discuss this further in chapter 4.

---

11. For an overview of the ancient Egyptian pyramids, see Lehner.
12. Khufu's pyramid at Giza is an exception: his funerary apartments were built into the pyramid's masonry.

There was also a fifth element, whose function is unknown, that was regularly part of the pyramid complex. This was a small satellite pyramid, and according to Mark Lehner, it may have been associated with the king's *ka*.[13] The ancient Egyptians believed a person's self consisted of multiple parts.[14] One of the most important components was the *ka*, which is best translated as "life force." This life force was generic and shared; its original source was the creator god, and it was transferred down from generation to generation. A person acquired their *ka* at birth, and, if properly maintained, it would last forever.

Related to this was the royal *ka*, which was unique to kings. It linked each new king to his ancestors and the gods. In this way, it gave a king legitimacy. It also was an element of the king's divine power. The king himself was human and mortal, but he inhabited a divine office that the gods bestowed on him. Thus the pharaoh had a dual nature; he was a human being that embodied divinity while he was on the throne, partly via the royal *ka*.[15]

Yet conceptions of kingship were not stagnant.[16] As I mentioned above, the role of the king and his position vis-à-vis society fluctuated. At different points in Egyptian history, the divinity or the humanity of a king could be more or less prevalent. For example, certain kings deified themselves while still alive. Some scholars have questioned whether this might have been the case for the early Fourth Dynasty kings.[17] Certainly, the divinity of the king seems to have been particularly prominent at that time before it began to diminish over the rest of the Old Kingdom.[18] I consider the evidence for and implications of this diminishment of kingship in the next chapter.

When the king died, he became a god himself. During the late Old Kingdom, the royal funerary monument was to be the king's eternal home following his successful transition to the afterlife. The complex was critical to this important process and the king's continued survival in the afterlife. Its architecture, rituals, and decorative program all played roles in this and enabled it. Indeed, to consider the monument's decoration, which included its statuary and the painted reliefs that covered the walls of the temples and causeway, as simply decoration is misleading.[19] While they did serve to embellish and further beautify the architectural structures, they also did much more than this. The statuary, including the prisoner statues, and reliefs were replete with their own symbolisms and functions, and they added to the overall efficacy of the complex. Moreover, not only did they benefit the deceased king, but they also benefited the living

---

13. Lehner, *Complete Pyramids*, 18. See further Dieter Arnold, "Royal Cult Complexes of the Old and Middle Kingdoms," in *Temples of Ancient Egypt*, ed. Byron Shafer (Ithaca, NY: Cornell University Press, 1997), 70.

14. See further Willeke Wendrich, "Identity and Personhood," in *Egyptian Archaeology*, ed. Willeke Wendrich (Chichester: Wiley-Blackwell, 2010), 200–219. A detailed study of the *ka* is Eberhard Kusber, "Der altägyptische Ka – 'Seele' oder 'Persönlichkeit'?" (PhD Diss., University of Tübingen, 2005).

15. Lanny Bell, "Luxor Temple and the Cult of the Royal Ka," *JNES* 44 (1985): 251–94; David O'Connor and David P. Silverman, ed., *Ancient Egyptian Kingship*, PAe 9 (Leiden: Brill, 1995); and Jonathan Winnerman, "Rethinking the Royal *Ka*," (PhD Diss., The University of Chicago, 2018).

16. Concerning kingship during the Old Kingdom, see Hratch Papazian, "Perspectives on the Cult of Pharaoh during the Third Millennium BC: A Chronological Overview," in Vymazalová and Bartá, *Chronology and Archaeology*, 61–80; John Baines, "Kingship before Literature: The World of the King in the Old Kingdom," in *Selbstverständnis und Realität: Akten des Symposiums zur ägyptischen Königsideologie in Mainz 15.–17.6.1995*, ed. Rolf Gundlach and Christine Raedler (Wiesbaden: Harrassowitz, 1997), 125–74; Janet Richards, "Kingship and Legitimation," in Wendrich, *Egyptian Archaeology*, 55–84; and Bárta, "Egyptian Kingship," 257–83.

17. See further Nuzzolo, *Fifth Dynasty Sun Temples*, 39–45.

18. Nuzzolo, 32–73.

19. Regarding the term "decoration" in ancient Egypt, see further Jan Assmann, "Preservation and Presentation of Self in Ancient Egyptian Portraiture," in *Studies in Honor of William Kelly Simpson*, vol. 1, ed. Peter Der Manuelian (Boston: Museum of Fine Arts, 1996), 56 and William Kelly Simpson, "Egyptian Sculpture and Two-Dimensional Representation as Propaganda," *JEA* 68 (1982): 266–67.

king and kingship itself, as did many of the rituals and cult that took place inside the complex. In this way, the pyramid complex was a monument for kingship and not simply a structure for the afterlife.

The prisoner statues vividly illustrate important ways that each king's pyramid complex could change; in chapter 4 I examine how the architecture and decoration developed, while in chapter 5 I consider how the ritualized context of the prisoner statues evolved. The late Old Kingdom pyramid complex was not a static monument that each king copied from his predecessors. Rather its architecture, decoration, and rituals could be shifted and adapted according to the wishes or needs of the reigning king and his architects and artists.

1.2. The Iconography

The prisoner statues depict male captives, who are on their knees, sitting back on their heels with their arms bound behind their backs at the elbows and their hands held in fists on either side of their bodies (fig. 1.4). The statues, which are all limestone, are approximately two-thirds life-size and consistently uninscribed. Their bodies are homogenous, and they all wear short kilts. But based on their varying facial features and hairstyles, which I discuss in detail in chapter 3, they clearly portray a variety of different non-Egyptians.

In their form, these statues exemplify a particular ancient Egyptian motif that I designate the kneeling bound captive motif. This motif was extremely common. One regularly finds it on temple walls, in tomb paintings and reliefs, on statue bases, and in palatial decoration. It adorned objects from the king's daily life, such as his throne, sandals, and jewelry, and the belongings of other members of the royal family and elite high officials. Because of its presence on so many structures and objects, this popular iconography must have literally surrounded the ancient Egyptians.[20]

Despite its commonness, it was replete with significance and meaning.[21] The captives depicted in this motif were often foreigners.[22] According to the Egyptian belief system, the foreign was both alien and aberrant. Within the Egyptian hierarchal concept of the cosmos, the foreigner ranked under the Egyptian

---

20. There is also a hieroglyphic sign, namely, Gardiner A13, that represents a kneeling bound captive (see Alan Gardiner, *Egyptian Grammar*, 3rd rev. ed. [Oxford: Griffith Institute, 1957], 443).

21. Regarding the ancient Egyptian ideology of foreigners and this motif, see recently Flora Brook Anthony, *Foreigners in Ancient Egypt: Theban Tomb Paintings from the Early Eighteenth Dynasty (1550–1372 BC)* (London: Bloomsbury, 2017); Yvan Koenig, "The Image of the Foreigner in the Magical Texts of Ancient Egypt," in *Moving Across Borders: Foreign Relations, Religion and Cultural Interactions in the Ancient Mediterranean*, ed. Panagiotis Kousoulis and Konstantinos Magliveras, OLA 159 (Leuven: Peeters, 2007), 223–38; Gerald Moers, "'Unter den Sohlen Pharaos': Fremdheit und Alterität im pharaonischen Ägypten," in *Abgrenzung, Eingrenzung: Komparatistische Studien zur Dialektik kultureller Identitätsbildung*, ed. Frank Lauterbach, Fritz Paul, and Ulrike-Christine Sander (Göttingen: Vandenhoeck & Ruprecht, 2004), 81–160; Gerald Moers, "The World and the Geography of Otherness in Pharaonic Egypt," in *Geography and Ethnography: Perceptions of the World in Pre-Modern Societies*, ed. Kurt Raaflaub and Richard Talbert (Malden, MA: Wiley-Blackwell, 2010), 169–81; David O'Connor, "Egypt's Views of 'Others,'" in *"Never Had the Like Occurred": Egypt's View of Its Past*, ed. John Tait (London: UCL Press, 2003), 155–85; David O'Connor and Stephen Quirke, "Introduction: Mapping the Unknown in Ancient Egypt," in *Mysterious Lands*, ed. David O'Connor and Stephen Quirke (London: UCL Press, 2003), 1–21; Ann Macy Roth, "Representing the Other: Non-Egyptians in Pharaonic Iconography," in *A Companion to Ancient Egyptian Art*, ed. Melinda Hartwig (Chichester: Wiley-Blackwell, 2014), 155–74; and Thomas Schneider, "Foreigners in Egypt: Archaeological Evidence and Cultural Context," in Wendrich, *Egyptian Archaeology*, 143–63.

22. While the depiction of foreigners in this motif originally seems to have been restricted to the royal domain, by the First Intermediate period the use of this iconography had become more widespread and flexible (Roth, "Representing the Other," 162–63).

Figure 1.4. Reconstructed prisoner statue probably from the pyramid complex of Pepi II in Saqqara; Sixth Dynasty. New York, MMA 47.2. Photograph: The Metropolitan Museum of Art, New York, Fletcher Fund, 1947.

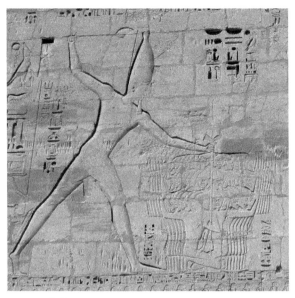

Figure 1.5. Ramses III smiting a group of foreigners on the south wing of the first pylon of his funerary temple at Medinet Habu; Twentieth Dynasty, New Kingdom.

and only above, or sometimes on par with, the natural world. While at least during certain periods, the Egyptians recognized foreigners as products of the creator god, like all else, and thus necessarily possessing intrinsic positive qualities, the different-ness of the foreign Other was a constant, potential threat to the Egyptian world.[23] A rebellious foreigner, who refused to accept his subordinate position, was a symbol of negative and malevolent forces, and he was regularly likened to criminals, dangerous animals, and demons.[24]

One of the king's primary responsibilities was to defeat and contain these threatening beings, thus maintaining the stability of the world.[25] This was of utmost importance in Egyptian ideology, and the king was often depicted in the act of annihilating rebels or symbols of evil, who usually took the form of foreigners. For example, in smiting scenes, the pharaoh strides forward with a weapon raised overhead in

---

23. These positive sentiments are best expressed during the Amarna period in the Great Hymn to the Aten (see William Kelly Simpson, ed., *The Literature of Ancient Egypt: An Anthology of Stories, Instructions, Stelae, Autobiographies, and Poetry*, 3rd ed. [New Haven: Yale University Press, 2003], 278–83).

24. Rebellious foreigners and bound captives in Egyptian iconography are nearly always male. Important and rare exceptions to this are the handful of scenes during the mid-Eighteenth Dynasty of queens smiting and trampling female enemies (see further Uroš Matić, "'Her Striking but Cold Beauty': Gender and Violence in Depictions of Queen Nefertiti Smiting the Enemies," in *Archaeologies of Gender and Violence*, ed. Uroš Matić and Bo Jensen [Oxford: Oxbow, 2017], 103–21). These parallel typical scenes of the king dominating male foreigners.

25. John Baines, "Kingship, Definition of Culture, and Legitimation," in O'Connor and Silverman, *Ancient Egyptian Kingship*, 11–12.

Figure 1.6. Trampling scene on an arm panel from a throne of Thutmose IV from his tomb in the Valley of the Kings; Eighteenth Dynasty, New Kingdom. Wood; H. 26 cm, W. 30 cm. New York, MMA 30.8.45a–c. Photograph: The Metropolitan Museum of Art, New York, Theodore M. Davis Collection, Bequest of Theodore M. Davis, 1915.

order to execute the one or more foreign enemies who are in his grasp (fig. 1.5).[26] In other scenes, the king takes the form of a sphinx or griffin and tramples foreign enemies (fig. 1.6). This imagery, like all imagery in ancient Egypt, had a magical capacity: by depicting the king defeating his enemies, the Egyptians guaranteed that the king would continually do so. The image created the reality. In this way, such imagery was both apotropaic and effective.[27]

Even when the king was not included, his presence was implied. The defeated foreigner, epitomized in the bound captive motif and the freestanding prisoner statues, referenced the overarching power of the Egyptian pharaoh and his ability to overturn and contain adverse forces and all threats to Egypt. He was

---

26. For the smiting scene, see further Emma Swan Hall, *The Pharaoh Smites His Enemy: A Comparative Study*, MÄS 44 (Munich: Deutscher Kunstverlag, 1986) and Sylvia Schoske, "Das Erschlagen der Feinde: Ikonographie und Stilistik der Feindvernichtung im alten Ägypten," (PhD diss., University of Heidelberg, 1994).

27. Robert K. Ritner, *The Mechanics of Ancient Egyptian Magical Practice*, SAOC 54 (Chicago: Oriental Institute of the University of Chicago, 1993), 113–36.

solely responsible for the foreigners' submission and defeat. The bound captive motif was integral to royal ideology, and it was apotropaic and magically effective in the same way as smiting and trampling scenes. Moreover, placing such imagery, including the prisoner statues, in the king's pyramid complex ensured that he would continue to perform this important duty and be a potent king in the afterlife.

The king was ultimately responsible for maintaining order and supremacy in light of potential threats or disruptions from any origin. Indeed, Egyptians, like foreigners, could also rebel and threaten the Egyptian world, thus aligning themselves with foreigners and malicious forces.[28] Criminals and rebels could be any ethnicity. However, while this was an important aspect of the ancient Egyptian belief system and royal ideology, the iconography rarely featured defeated Egyptians, as I discuss further in chapter 3.

Instead the Egyptian artists usually employed stereotypical ethnic categories when representing the king's enemies. These belie the diversity of the various ethnic and cultural groups who actually inhabited the regions that surrounded Egypt. In reality, Egyptian foreign relations were complex.[29] Foreigners constituted an unavoidable population with whom the Egyptians dealt on a regular basis, both at home and abroad, and ideology did not dictate the nature of these interactions.[30] For example, in his studies on Egyptian and Nubian ethnic identities and interactions in colonial Lower Nubia, Stuart Tyson Smith has showed that despite the ideology of separation and Otherness, Egyptians and Nubians interacted and even intermarried; additionally, while some Nubians became acculturated to Egyptian society, others remained more "Nubian."[31] Throughout the pharaonic period, large numbers of foreigners entered Egypt and underwent varying degrees of acculturation. Indeed, it was possible for a foreigner to become so integrated into Egyptian society that he could rise, seemingly with no overt opposition, to extremely prestigious offices during the height of Egyptian power, such as the New Kingdom vizier Abd'el.[32] Just as a rebellious Egyptian could be grouped together with foreigners, a well-behaved (i.e., accepting and assimilated) foreigner could "become" Egyptian. But these boundaries were undoubtedly fluid; the degree to which an individual foreigner identified with, or others identified him with, his ethnicity and native culture certainly varied from situation to situation.

The Egyptians recognized the diversity of the lands and peoples that surrounded them, as the many specific foreign toponyms that they used demonstrate.[33] But conceptually and visually, the Egyptians

---

28. Nathalie Beaux, "Enemies étrangers et malfaiteurs egyptiens: La signification du chatiment au pilori," *BIFAO* 91 (1991): 40–53; Koenig, "Image of the Foreigner," 223–38; and O'Connor, "Egypt's Views of 'Others.'"

29. Recent overviews include Pearce Paul Creasman and Richard H. Wilkinson, ed., *Pharaoh's Land and Beyond: Ancient Egypt and Its Neighbors* (Oxford: Oxford University Press, 2017) and Toby Wilkinson, ed., *The Egyptian World* (London: Routledge, 2007). I discuss Egypt's interactions with its neighbors during the Old Kingdom in ch. 3.

30. However, Peter Brand and Mario Liverani have convincingly argued that ideology did play a notable role in the way that the Egyptians approached issues of foreign relations on a state level (Peter Brand, "Ideological Imperatives: Irrational Factors in Egyptian–Hittite Relations under Ramesses II," in Kousoulis and Magliveras, *Moving across Borders*, 15–33 and Mario Liverani, *Prestige and Interest: International Relations in the Near East ca. 1600–1100 B.C.* [Padua: Sargon, 1990]). Concerning the dichotomy between Egypt's idealistic worldview and their actual diplomatic relations during the New Kingdom, see also William J. Murnane, "Imperial Egypt and the Limits of Power," in *Amarna Diplomacy: The Beginnings of International Relations*, ed. Raymond Cohen and Raymond Westbrook (Baltimore: Johns Hopkins University Press, 2000), 101–11 and Nadav Na'aman, "The Egyptian–Canaanite Correspondence," in Cohen and Westbrook, 125–38.

31. Stuart Tyson Smith, "Ethnicity and Culture," in Wilkinson, *The Egyptian World*, 230–38 and Stuart Tyson Smith, *Wretched Kush: Ethnic Identities and Boundaries in Egypt's Nubian Empire* (London: Routledge, 2003).

32. For Abd'el, see Schneider, "Foreigners in Egypt," 155; S. T. Smith, "Ethnicity and Culture," 231; and Alain-Pierre Zivie, *Decouverte à Saqqarah: Le vizir oublié* (Paris: Seuil, 1990).

33. Julien Cooper, *Toponymy on the Periphery: Placenames of the Eastern Desert, Red Sea, and South Sinai in Egyptian Documents from the Early Dynastic until the End of the New Kingdom*, PAe 39 (Boston: Brill, 2020); Karola Zibelius-Chen, *Afrikanische Orts- und Völkernamen in hieroglyphischen und hieratischen Texten* (Wiesbaden: Reichert, 1972); and Holger

categorized the outside world into broader types. During the Old Kingdom, the primary categories of foreigners that the Egyptians depicted were Nubians, who lived in Nubia to the south of Egypt; Libyans, who inhabited the Western Desert; and Asiatics, who came from the Levant. Each category was given particular clothing, facial features, and accoutrements, which I detail in chapter 3. In this way, one can easily distinguish Nubians, Libyans, and Asiatics in Old Kingdom art. Furthermore, the Egyptians tended to associate these groups with particular cardinal directions: Nubians were from the south and Asiatics were from the north. Although the Libyans actually lived to the west of Egypt, the Egyptians often classified them as Northerners, sometimes intermingling them with Asiatics.

As I discuss in chapter 3, the earlier prisoner statues follow these artistic conventions. The artists used stereotypical attributes to represent Nubians and Asiatics.[34] However, by the reign of Pepi I, this had changed. The prisoner statues of Pepi I and Pepi II depict imaginary foreigners, whose faces are all distinct from one another. In this way, they give the impression that the king has defeated all possible foreigners, not simply Nubians, Libyans, and Asiatics. This artistic change reflects a new conception of ethnicity and foreignness and coincides with changes in the nature of Egyptian foreign affairs that occurred in the Sixth Dynasty. At this time, new cultural groups emerged in Nubia, Egyptians began engaging more directly with foreigners and foreign goods, and there seems to have been an overall greater interest in and concern with foreigners and foreignness in Egypt. The Egyptian world was more complex in the Sixth Dynasty, and the change in the contemporary prisoner statues' ethnicity is a reflection of and a reaction to this.

Both the stereotypes and the later prisoner statues were essentially symbols of Otherness and the broad world that extended in all directions but was always under the king's authority. While none of this imagery was divorced from historical reality, the Egyptian belief system heavily informed it, and the modern scholar cannot depend on foreigner imagery to reconstruct historical interactions and events. It is true that some of this imagery is more overtly stereotypical than other examples. Indeed, Antonio Loprieno has demonstrated that in Egyptian texts and literature, the Egyptian treatment of foreigners was alternatively informed by an ideological, stereotypical, and negative construction of foreign identity (*topos*) in contrast to a more realistic, individualistic, and positive approach (*mimesis*).[35] Other scholars have identified a similar dichotomy in Egyptian artistic treatments of the foreigner.[36] However, there is a constant tension between veracity and ideology in all Egyptian representations of the foreign. For example, mimetic scenes of tribute in New Kingdom tomb chapels often include the specific and seemingly accurate characteristics and trade goods associated with different foreign cultures, yet they also transformed impartial trade between Egypt and foreign powers into ideological scenes of homage, in which the foreign powers recognized an Egyptian overlord. *Topos* and *mimesis* existed side by side. The purpose of foreigner imagery was never to record historical reality; instead it reveals more about the beliefs and attitudes of the ancient Egyptians and how they visualized identity.[37]

Kockelmann, "Die Fremdvölkerlisten in den Soubassements der ptolemäisch-römischen Heiligtümer: Feindnamen und Feindvernichtungsrituale im Tempel zwischen Tradition und Wandel," in *Von Meroe bis Indien: Fremdvölkerlisten und nubische Gabenträger in den griechisch-römischen Tempeln*, ed. Holger Kockelmann and Alexa Rickert (Wiesbaden: Harrassowitz, 2015), 3–141.

34. There are no clearly identifiable Libyans, but this could be a result of the incomplete archaeological record. I discuss this further in ch. 3.

35. Antonio Loprieno, *Topos und Mimesis: Zum Ausländer in der ägyptischen Literatur*, ÄgAbh 48 (Wiesbaden: Harrassowitz, 1988).

36. For example, O'Connor, "Egypt's Views of 'Others'" and Anthony, *Foreigners in Ancient Egypt*.

37. Concerning ethnic identity and approaches to its study in Egyptology, see Uroš Matić, *Ethnic Identities in the Land of the Pharaohs: Past and Present Approaches in Egyptology*, Cambridge Elements (Cambridge: Cambridge University Press,

1.3. Precursors and Related Representations

While the bound captive motif was extremely common in ancient Egypt from the predynastic period down to Greco-Roman times, especially in relief and painting, the prisoner statues are unique. Their large scale, material, freestanding nature, and exclusive use in royal pyramid complexes distinguish them. The prisoner statues are variations of the bound captive motif, but they also belong to a recognizable genre of ancient Egyptian statuary. Their occurrence and development over time in at least six different pyramid complexes emphasizes that the Egyptians viewed the statues as a particular, well-defined type that could be utilized, if the pharaoh desired and had the necessary time and resources, in the decorative program of the royal funerary monument. At present, the only known examples date to the Fifth and Sixth Dynasties.[38] Although the pharaohs of the Middle Kingdom reestablished multiple Old Kingdom practices and traditions, including that of building pyramid complexes as their royal funerary monuments, there is no evidence of any Middle Kingdom prisoner statues.[39] The Twelfth Dynasty king Senusret I was the first Middle Kingdom king to attempt to recreate the Old Kingdom pyramid complex on a full scale with all of its essential parts. In doing this, he clearly followed the models of the late Fifth and the Sixth Dynasties.[40] However, no prisoner statues have been discovered at his complex. On the other hand, there were significantly more statues of the king himself at this complex than at any of the late Old Kingdom complexes.[41] The statue program of Montuhotep II, the founder of the Middle Kingdom, may have influenced Senusret I more than the program of the late Old Kingdom kings, and Senusret I may have decided to dedicate his resources to producing statues of himself, rather than statues of his enemies.[42] It seems possible that his successors, who moved further away from the late Old Kingdom traditions, then followed his model in this regard.[43] Perhaps the Middle Kingdom kings found the subject matter too dangerous and magically charged or preferred not to devote resources to large-scale statues of despicable enemies. The

---

2020). But note important and pertinent criticism and bibliographic additions in Aaron de Souza's review of this book in *JARCE* 57 (2021): 347–51.

38. Dieter Arnold mistakenly referenced Third and Twelfth Dynasty prisoner statues in an early publication (Dieter Arnold, "Rituale und Pyramidentempel," *MDAIK* 33 [1977]: 7). It seems likely that he merged the evidence for the prisoner statues with that for architectural consoles featuring the heads of foreign captives, which I describe below. These consoles were certainly used in the Step Pyramid, and early scholars erroneously dated unprovenanced examples to the Middle Kingdom (e.g., see Ludwig Borchardt, *Statuen und Statuetten von Königen und Privatleuten im Museum von Kairo*, 6 vols., CGC [Berlin: Reichdruckerei, 1911–1936), 2:14, cat. no. 396 and 4:87, cat. no. 1196). Indeed in later publications, Arnold did not list any Third or Twelfth Dynasty prisoner statues (Dieter Arnold, "Old Kingdom Statues in their Architectural Settings," in *Egyptian Art in the Age of the Pyramids*, ed. Dorothea Arnold, Krzysztof Grzymski, and Christiane Ziegler [New York: The Metropolitan Museum of Art, 1999], 42 and Di. Arnold, "Royal Cult Complexes," 268 n. 128).

39. Given the great concern and interest in the Old Kingdom that the Middle Kingdom kings had, it seems quite possible that they or their high officials were aware of the prisoner statues. Certainly, some Middle Kingdom Egyptians, such as the priests living in the mortuary temple of Pepi I, who were there by royal order, must have encountered prisoner statue fragments; I discuss the later activity at the late Old Kingdom pyramids, including that during the Middle Kingdom, further in ch. 5.

40. Dieter Arnold, *The Pyramid of Senwosret I*, MMAEE 22, The South Cemeteries of Lisht 1 (New York: The Metropolitan Museum of Art, 1988), 17.

41. Di. Arnold, 18–22 and 56; see also Karin Dohrmann, "Arbeitsorganisation, Produktionsverfahren und Werktechnik – eine Analyse der Sitzstatuen Sesostris' I. aus Lischt" (PhD diss., Georg-August-Universität Göttingen, 2004).

42. For the statuary of Montuhotep II from his funerary monument, see further Rita Freed, "Sculpture of the Middle Kingdom," in Lloyd, *Companion to Ancient Egypt*, 887.

43. Concerning the later Middle Kingdom pyramid complexes in comparison to the Old Kingdom ones, see Dieter Arnold, "Architecture: Building for Eternity across Egypt," in *Ancient Egypt Transformed: The Middle Kingdom*, ed. Adela Oppenheim et al. (New York: The Metropolitan Museum of Art, 2015), 14 and Lehner, *Complete Pyramids*, 174.

lack of prisoner statues could also reflect changes in funerary beliefs. Regardless of the reasons, erecting prisoner statues seems to have been a tradition that the Middle Kingdom pharaohs did not resume, and the available evidence suggests that the genre was strictly a late Old Kingdom royal trend.[44]

The prisoner statues were not the first three-dimensional depictions of bound captives in ancient Egypt. Small figurines, which seem to have functioned as votives, are known as far back as the predynastic and the protodynastic periods.[45] An early large-scale, three-dimensional depiction of a prisoner is a door socket that James Quibell discovered at the site of Hierakonpolis (fig. 1.7).[46] This dolerite sculpture depicts a foreign prisoner who lies on his belly with his arms and legs trussed behind his back. His head projects from the schematic body, and a hole, which originally held the pivot of the door, is positioned between his elbows. Symbolically, the original pivot would seem to have represented a pole to which the prisoner was bound, and each time the door was opened or closed the prisoner was metaphorically tortured with the pivot driven deeper and deeper into his body.[47] In this way, the symbolism of the imagery was reinforced through active manipulation. The door socket is also an early example of the way in which three-dimensional foreigner

Figure 1.7. Door socket in the form of a trussed prisoner from Hierakonpolis; First Dynasty, Early Dynastic period. Dolerite; H. 19 cm, W. 53 cm, L. 77.5 cm. Philadelphia, Penn Museum, E3959. Photograph courtesy of the Penn Museum.

---

44. However, the Middle Kingdom pyramids are in worse condition than the Old Kingdom ones. Thus, one must allow for the hypothetical possibility that there were originally Middle Kingdom prisoner statues of which no traces remain.

45. Such figurines have been found at the sites of Tell el-Farkha, Abydos, and Hierakonpolis (Krzysztof M. Cialowicz, "The Early Dynastic Administrative-Cultic Centre at Tell el-Farkha," *BMSAES* 13 [2009]: 92–93 and figs. 17 and 27; Krzysztof M. Cialowicz, "The Predynastic/Early Dynastic Period at Tell el-Farkha," in *Before the Pyramids: The Origins of Egyptian Civilization*, ed. Emily Teeter [Chicago: Oriental Institute of the University of Chicago, 2011], 59; and Ritner, *Mechanics*, 116). Moreover, in the main deposit at Hierakonpolis, James Quibell discovered a large number of ivory objects, including several fragments of bound captives that originally had been attached to another item, probably an article of temple furniture (James Quibell, *Hierakonpolis*, part 1, ERA 4 [London: Quaritch, 1900], 7 and pls. 11 and 12 and James Quibell and F. W. Green, *Hierakonpolis*, part 2, ERA 5 [London: Quaritch, 1900], 37). Unprovenanced examples of predynastic or protodynastic bound captive figurines include Basel, Antikenmuseum und Sammlung Ludwig BSAe SSOM 924 and Berlin, ÄM 13808. For these, see Hermann A. Schlögl, "1. Mann mit auf dem Rücken gefesselten Armen," in *Höhenflug und Absturz: Wilhelm Dieudonné Stieler (1888–1912), Ägyptenreisender, Sammler und Luftfahrtpionier*, ed. Noëlle Gmür Brianza and Elisabeth Staehelin (Basel: Stiftung fur ein Schweizerisches Orient-Museum, 2006), cat. no. 1; Heinrich Schäfer, "Neue Alterümer der 'New Race' aus Negadeh," *ZÄS* 34 (1896): 158–61; Alexander Scharff, *Die Altertümer der Vor- und Frühzeit Ägyptens*, vol. 2 (Berlin: Curtius, 1929), 34; and Jacques Vandier, *Manuel d'archéologie égyptienne*, 6 vols. (Paris: Picard, 1952–1978), 1:433–34.

46. Philadelphia, University Museum, Penn E3959. See further Bernard Bothmer, "On Realism in Egyptian Funerary Sculpture of the Old Kingdom," in *Egyptian Art: Selected Writings of Bernard V. Bothmer*, ed. Madeleine Cody, Paul Stanwick, and Marsha Hill (New York: Oxford University Press, 2004), 388 and fig. 25.27; Diana Craig Patch, *Dawn of Egyptian Art* (New York: The Metropolitan Museum of Art, 2011), 156, 257, and cat. no. 134; Quibell, *Hierakonpolis 1*, 6 and pl. 3; Quibell and Green, *Hierakonpolis 2*, 36; and Ritner, *Mechanics*, 117–18.

47. The position of the pivot recalls later statues of men bound to poles (e.g., Berlin, ÄM 22577; Brussels, Royal Museums of Art and History E.08241; and Marseille, Musée Borely 493; see further Beaux, "Enemies étrangers").

Figure 1.8. Console with two connecting heads of prisoners from the Step Pyramid of Djoser in Saqqara; Third Dynasty. Black granite; H. 26 cm, W. 46 cm, D. 21 cm. Alexandria, Alexandria National Museum JE 49613. Photograph: Tara Prakash, courtesy of the Alexandria National Museum.

imagery could be integrated into architectural contexts, serving to simultaneously embellish the building and magically protect it.

By the Third Dynasty or perhaps slightly earlier, foreigners decorated other architectural elements. Archaeologists discovered consoles with projecting high relief heads of foreign enemies at the Step Pyramid complex of King Djoser, the first king of the Third Dynasty (fig. 1.8).[48] Other unprovenanced examples seem to date to roughly the same time period based on stylistic grounds.[49] These consoles are analogous to statue bases that feature the bodies of foreigners, and some of the Third Dynasty consoles may have instead functioned as statue bases.[50] Such architectural consoles and statue bases are known throughout ancient Egyptian history (figs. 1.9 and 1.10).[51] They were manifestations of royal domination. Only statues of the king or aggressive deities who were closely associated with the king were

---

48. Alexandria, Alexandria National Museum JE 49613 and Cairo, Egyptian Museum TR 18/2/26/5 A–B. See Cecil Firth, "Preliminary Report on the Excavations at Saqqara (1925–1926)," *ASAE* 26 (1926): 99 and pl. 4b and Cecil Firth and James Quibell, *The Step Pyramid*, 2 vols., Excavations at Saqqara (Cairo: Institut français d'archéologie orientale, 1935), 1:14, 66, 75, 113, 115, and 2:pl. 57.

49. Some possibilities include Cairo, Egyptian Museum CG 396; Cairo, Egyptian Museum CG 1165/ JE 32013; Suez, Suez National Museum JE 40291; and London, Petrie Museum UC 14884. More uncertain possibilities include London, Petrie Museum UC 14885 and Los Angeles, LACMA 50.18.1, though the directionality of the heads in this last block is unusual and suggests that it is a later piece in an archaizing style. For further discussion on all of these heads, see Borchardt, *Statuen und Statuetten* 2:14, cat. no. 396 and 4:87, cat. no. 1196; Bothmer, "On Realism," 374–78; Hans Gerhard Evers, *Staat aus dem Stein: Denkmäler, Geschichte und Bedeutung der ägyptischen Plastik während des Mittleren Reichs* (Munich: Bruckmann, 1929), 91–93 and Abb. 47–50; *Illustrated Handbook of the Los Angeles County Museum of Art* (Los Angeles: Los Angeles County Museum of Art, 1965), 19 (note here that the interpretation of the heads as female is incorrect); Anthea Page, *Egyptian Sculpture: Archaic to Saite, From the Petrie Collection* (Warminster: Aris & Phillips, 1976), 2–3, cat. no. 2 and 3; Quibell, *Hierakonpolis*, 6; Donald Spanel, *Through Ancient Eyes: Egyptian Portraiture* (Birmingham: Birmingham Museum of Art, 1988), 70, cat. no. 14; Vandier, *Manuel*, 3:246 n. 3 and pl. 86.3 and 4; and Miroslav Verner, "Les statuettes de prisonniers en bois d'Abousir," *RdE* 36 (1985): 146. On the other hand, Miroslav Verner dates Cairo, Egyptian Museum JE 60538 to the reign of Khufu because of its architectural context (Verner, 146). It had been reused in a monumental gate at Tanis (M. Pierre Montet, *Les constructions et les tombeau de Chéchanq III à Tanis*, La nécropole royale de Tanis 3, Fouilles de Tanis [Paris: Typographie Protat Frères, 1960], 37–38 and pls. 8, 21, and 22 and M. Pierre Montet, "Les fouilles de Tanis: En 1933 et 1934," *Kemi* 5 [1935–1937]: 1–8 and pls. 1–6). However, based on its style and scale, a Fourth Dynasty date is highly unlikely. Rather, a date in the Rameside period, which the archaeology equally supports, is more probable.

50. Firth, "Preliminary Report," 99; Firth and Quibell, *The Step Pyramid*, 1:14 and 67 and 2:vi; and Dietrich Wildung, "4. Gefangenenköpfe," in *Götter Pharaonen*, ed. Dietrich Wildung and Günter Grimm (Essen: Villa Hügel e. V., 1978), cat. no. 4.

51. See further Dietrich Wildung, "Der König Ägyptens als Herr der Welt? Ein seltener ikonographischer Typus der Königsplastik des Neuen Reiches," *AfO* 24 (1973): 108–16; Carol Andrews, "Pharaoh Trampler of Egypt's Enemies, A New Amuletic Form," in *Ancient Egypt, the Aegean, and the Near East: Studies in Honour of Martha Rhoads Bell*, vol. 1, ed. Jack Phillips (San Antonio: Van Siclen, 1997), 39–42; Ritner, *Mechanics*, 119–36; and Joshua A. Roberson, "The Trampled Foe: Two New Examples of a Rare Amuletic Form," *JEA* 96 (2010): 119–22.

Figure 1.9. Two architectural consoles of foreign prisoners from the Eastern High Gate at Medinet Habu; Twentieth Dynasty, New Kingdom.

placed on top of bases with three-dimensional foreigners.[52] In this way, the king, through his image or the image of his agent, perpetually interacted with, trampled, and thus destroyed the malevolent forces

---

52. Andrews, "Pharaoh," 40; Sylvia Schoske and Dietrich Wildung, *Gott und Götter im alten Ägypten* (Mainz am Rhein: von Zabern, 1993), 156–68, cat. no. 107 and 108; Dietrich Wildung, "The Image of the Nubian in Egyptian Art," in *Sudan:*

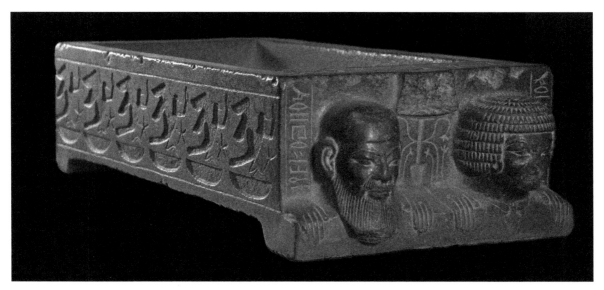

Figure 1.10. Statue base/offering table with the heads and hands of an Asiatic (left) and Nubian (right) emerging, from Medinet Habu; Twentieth Dynasty, New Kingdom. Granite; H. 19 cm, W. 36 cm, L. 81 cm. Cairo, Egyptian Museum CG 755/JE 28831. Photograph courtesy of the Egyptian Museum.

beneath his feet. For the architectural consoles, the foreigners' bodies were metaphorically trapped, prostrate, in the stone itself, from which their heads emerged (fig. 1.9). The monument, as a royal symbol and product, was an agent of the king, and the foreigner was forever squeezed, consumed, and disarmed within the royal architecture. Additionally, this message could be reinforced with further two-dimensional or three-dimensional imagery of the king set above the consoles or with open space in which the living king could appear and stand atop the foreigners' heads and bodies.[53]

Nine wooden statuettes from the Fifth Dynasty pyramid complex of Niuserre's predecessor King Raneferef (ca. 2404 BCE) originally functioned in the same way (fig. 1.11).[54] Raneferef came to the throne following the death of his father, King Neferirkare (ca. 2415–2405 BCE), but Raneferef only reigned for a year or two before his premature death.[55] His brother Niuserre was responsible for completing his pyramid complex, and seemingly as a result of this, there are some major differences between Raneferef's complex and the other Fifth Dynasty ones, as I discuss in chapter 4. In 1984, Miroslav Verner and the Czech Institute of Egyptology discovered nine figurines, which range between 14 and 28 cm high, of kneeling bound cap-

---

Ancient Kingdoms of the Nile, ed. Dietrich Wildung, trans. Peter Der Manuelian and Kathleen Guillaume (Paris: Flammarion, 1997), 156, cat. no. 161; and Wildung, "König Ägyptens," 113–14.

53. The best examples of this can still be found on the walls of Ramses III's mortuary temple at Medinet Habu, which dates to the New Kingdom (Uvo Hölscher, *The Mortuary Temple of Ramses III*, part 1, trans. Diederika Seele, The Excavation of Medinet Habu 3, OIP 54 [Chicago: University of Chicago Press, 1941], 40–41 and pl. 3; Uvo Hölscher, *Das Hohe Tor von Medinet Habu: Eine Baugeschichtliche Untersuchung*, WVDOG 12 [Leipzig: Hinrich, 1910], 43; and Uvo Hölscher, *The Mortuary Temple of Ramses III*, part 2, trans. Elizabeth Hauser, The Excavation of Medinet Habu 4, OIP 55 [Chicago: University of Chicago Press, 1951], 5–6).

54. Cairo, Egyptian Museum JE 98182(a–i); see especially Hana Benešovská, "Statues from the Pyramid Complex of King Raneferef," in *The Pyramid Complex of Raneferef: The Archaeology*, ed. Miroslav Verner, Abusir 9 (Prague: Czech Institute of Egyptology, 2006), 407–17 and Verner, "Statuettes de prisonniers," 145–52.

55. See further Verner, *Abusir*, 111–41.

tives in Raneferef's mortuary temple. These figurines have often been falsely described as prisoner statues, but they are carved from wood, not limestone, and they are significantly smaller than the prisoner statues. Perhaps most importantly, they were not freestanding but were originally part of ritual furniture, as is indicated by the tenons that emerge from them and their archaeological context; differences between the figurines themselves suggest that they probably belonged to two different statue naoi or bases.[56]

Although Raneferef's figurines are not prisoner statues, it is possible that there was a close connection between Raneferef's figurines and the earliest prisoner statues since Niuserre was responsible for the construction of most of Raneferef's pyramid complex. Raneferef's smaller, cheaper, and multifunctional figurines might have been understood as quick substitutes for the prisoner statues Niuserre commissioned for himself.[57] Or Niuserre might have derived inspiration from Raneferef's figurines, but as I described above, defeated foreign rebels could decorate statue bases and in this way, the Raneferef figurines are traditional. While Niuserre's artists were likely aware of some of the three-dimensional precursors that I have mentioned here, Niuserre's prisoner statues were innovative; no statue of the king stood above them. The prisoner statues appeared during a period of significant artistic experimentation, as I argue in chapter 4. They were part of a Fifth Dynasty trend of transferring two-dimensional motifs from the walls of the pyramid complex into freestanding statues. The Hierakonpolis door socket and the Third Dynasty architectural consoles set a precedent for the use of three-dimensional foreign captive elements as architectural decoration (figs. 1.7 and 1.8). However, it is only at the pyramid complex of Niuserre that the kneeling bound captive motif became a type of architectural decoration.

Figure 1.11. Wooden figurine of a bound Asiatic captive from the mortuary temple of Raneferef in Abusir; Fifth Dynasty. Cairo, Egyptian Museum JE 98182(a). H. 15.5 cm, W. 5.9 cm. Photograph courtesy of the Egyptian Museum.

The Raneferef figurines are not the only late Old Kingdom artifacts that have been incorrectly called prisoner statues. William Stevenson Smith described five figurines that George Reisner excavated from

---

56. My arguments regarding the Raneferef bound captive figurines are expanded in Tara Prakash, "Reconsidering the Bound Captive Statuary from the Pyramid Complex of Raneferef," *JARCE* 54 (2018): 137–59.

57. Niuserre did take shortcuts in constructing and decorating Raneferef's mortuary temple. For example, he used mudbrick rather than stone building blocks, and decorated faience inlays and tablets of Egyptian Blue seem to have functioned as a cheaper, quicker substitute for the missing relief decoration. For the mortuary temple in general, see Miroslav Verner, ed., *The Pyramid Complex of Raneferef: The Archaeology*, Abusir 9 (Prague: Czech Institute of Egyptology, 2006). For the inlays, see also Renata Landgráfová, *Faience Inlays from the Funerary Temple of King Raneferef: Ranreferef's Substitute Decoration Programme*, Abusir 14 (Prague: Czech Institute of Egyptology, 2006) and Renata Landgráfová, "The Function of the Faience Inlays in the Funerary Temple of Raneferef at Abusir," in *The Old Kingdom Art and Archaeology: Proceedings of the Conference Held in Prague, May 31–June 4, 2004*, ed. Miroslav Bárta (Prague: Czech Institute of Egyptology, 2006), 203–8.

Figure 1.12. Wooden (execration?) figurine from the tomb of Senedjemib Mehi (G 2378 A) in Giza; Sixth Dynasty. H. 9 cm. Boston, MFA 13.3459. Photograph © 2021 Museum of Fine Arts, Boston.

the tomb complex of the vizier and chief architect, Senedjemib Mehi, as nonroyal versions of the prisoner statues (fig. 1.12).[58] The Senedjemib family was a prominent elite family during the late Old Kingdom. Senedjemib Mehi specifically served the late Fifth Dynasty pharaoh Unas. His tomb, which was part of a large family funerary complex, stood at the northwest corner of the Great Pyramid of Khufu in Giza, on the eastern edge of the western cemetery. The figurines, which are roughly executed and vary slightly in size, averaging about 10 cm in height, represent the bound captive motif.[59] Because of this, in addition to traces of what may be red pigment on the bodies of at least one and possibly three of them and their burial in a private cemetery, the Senedjemib Mehi figurines are most likely execration figurines.[60]

Execration figurines have frequently been compared to the prisoner statues, but there are notable differences between the two genres, as I discuss in chapter 5. Execration figurines are rough human representations with cursing formulas, or execration texts, written on them.[61] They functioned similarly to voodoo dolls in that the figurines acted as magical substitutes for the intended victims and could be mistreated in numerous ways, including broken, buried, or bound with cords or rope, during execration rituals. Execration figurines, which were often depicted in the kneeling bound captive motif, ranged in crudeness from highly abstracted forms to fairly well executed statuettes. However, the execration formulas written upon their bodies demarcates

---

58. William Stevenson Smith, *Ancient Egypt as Represented in the Museum of Fine Arts, Boston* (Boston: Museum of Fine Arts, 1960), 55–56 and William Stevenson Smith, *A History of Egyptian Sculpture and Painting in the Old Kingdom* (New York: Hacker Art Books, 1978), 58, 90 and pl. 23 (Smith incorrectly gives the Boston figurines' accession numbers as 13458 and 13459 here). The figurines are Boston, MFA 13.3458 and 13.3459 and Cairo, Egyptian Museum JE 44614–44616. Reisner was working as part of the Harvard University – Boston Museum of Fine Arts Expedition. See also George A. Reisner, "New Acquisitions of the Egyptian Department: A Family of Builders of the Sixth Dynasty, about 2600 B. C.," *Museum of Fine Arts Bulletin* 11 (1913): 62. Concerning the Senedjemib mastaba complex, see Edward Brovarski, *The Senedjemib Complex Part I: The Mastabas of Senedjemib Inti (G 2370), Khnumenti (G 2374), and Senedjemib Mehi (G 2378)*, Giza Mastabas 7 (Boston: Museum of Fine Arts, 2001).

59. Boston, MFA 13.3458 and 13.3459 (fig. 1.12) are 9 cm, and Cairo, Egyptian Museum JE 44614–44616 are 10 cm.

60. I first made this argument in Prakash, "Reconsidering," 152–53. See also Georges Posener, *Cinq figurines d'envoûtement*, BiEtud 101 (Cairo: Institut français d'archéologie orientale, 1987), 2 and Christoffer Theis, *Magie und Raum: Der magische Schutz ausgewählter Räume im alten Ägypten nebst einem Vergleich zu angrenzenden Kulturbereichen*, Oriental Religions in Antiquity 13 (Tübingen: Mohr Siebeck, 2014), 711, but note Theis's Fourth Dynasty date is most likely wrong.

61. See further Ritner, *Mechanics*, 136–80 and Christoffer Theis, "Ächtungstexte," in *Das Wissenschaftliche Bibellexikon im Internet*, Deutsche Bibel Gesellschaft, http://www.bibelwissenschaft.de/stichwort/12613.

the genre, linking these figurines with other execration texts, which also could be written on pots, and strongly differentiating them from the prisoner statues and other examples of the bound captive motif.[62] During the Old Kingdom, execration rituals most commonly took place in private cemeteries and the only examples of bound captive imagery coming from an elite context were execration figurines.

1.4. A Reexamination

The prisoner statues have never fully been published following their discovery, and the little commentary that does exist is largely speculative and tends to be based on only a fraction of the statues and incomplete information. Moreover, although multiple pharaohs repeatedly used the statues over the course of almost three hundred years, there has been a proclivity in previous scholarship, probably due in part to the cursory publication of the statues, to discuss them as though they were fixed in their form, placement, treatment, and meaning. For example, the location of the prisoner statues within the pyramid complex has been debated as though all six pharaohs set them in the same part of each complex.[63]

As the first comprehensive study of the prisoner statues, this book demonstrates that the genre changed significantly over time. Conclusions for statues from one complex do not necessarily apply to statues from another. Furthermore, these changes reflect broader developments that were contemporaneously occurring during the late Old Kingdom. The prisoner statues were part of a complex period when many things were shifting, including the role of the king, ritual activity, foreign interactions, and artistic styles. These did not occur independent from one another, and thus they cannot be independently studied. Here I consider the prisoner statues in relation to history, religion, art, and architecture, and in this way, this is a book about the late Old Kingdom.

My observations and conclusions on the prisoner statues are based on direct study of the statues and archival documents, as well as the published excavation reports. The current location of each statue fragment is noted in the digital catalogue, which details all of the fragments that I was able to securely locate.[64] Throughout this book, I reference the fragments by their museum or storeroom inventory number (if known) and/or the catalogue (C) number that I have assigned them. The vast majority of the fragments remain in archaeological storerooms in Egypt.[65] Additionally, there are nearly a dozen fragments and reconstructed prisoner statues in museum collections in the United States, Europe, and Egypt. Archival research supplemented my direct study of fragments, and I have compiled a significant photographic corpus. Additionally, I located excavation journals, unpublished manuscripts, notes, and letters that provide further information on the prisoner statues and their discovery. Using all of these materials, this book considers the prisoner statues thematically, with each chapter addressing particular issues that are central to the statues. It is focused on the excavated remains, but I briefly address several unprovenanced prisoner statues in the appendix.

---

62. Not all execration figurines were provided with text. In these cases, the treatment and context of the figurines may indicate their role in execration rituals. See Ritner, *Mechanics,* 135 n. 611 for examples.

63. I discuss the original placement of the prisoner statues, including the previous theories for this, in ch. 4.

64. https://doi.org/10.5913/2022877

65. Most of the fragments are in a storeroom in Saqqara under the control of the Supreme Council of Antiquities (SCA). Unfortunately, this storeroom has remained closed to scholars since 2011. Therefore, at the time of publication it was still impossible for me to directly study those fragments. About half of the fragments from the pyramid complex of Pepi I are in the storeroom of the Mission archéologique franco-suisse de Saqqâra (MAFS), and I was able to record and photograph these unpublished pieces.

The next chapter situates the prisoner statues within the history and society of the late Old Kingdom and elucidates their development, focusing primarily on their bodies. Despite the cohesion of the prisoner statue genre, I show that the statues varied from complex to complex, including in their number, size, form, and stylistic features. Overall, the statues were symbols of royal authority, and they were one of the many ways that these late Old Kingdom kings tried to assert their power and distinguish themselves from the growing number of influential, elite high officials. In this way, they reflect the nature of the late Old Kingdom, a period when concepts of kingship were rapidly changing and the kings themselves were experimenting with means to express this.

Chapter 3 focuses more closely on the heads of all of the excavated prisoner statues. Multiple scholars have described the prisoner statues' faces as unusually individualistic, expressive, and emotive, setting them apart from contemporary Egyptian statuary. Some scholars have gone so far as to describe the prisoner statue heads as portraits or realistic representations of foreigners. However, the heads of the prisoner statues are not realistic anomalies or portraits. Instead, they reflect the appearance and development of the so-called Second Style, or the late Old Kingdom style, a more expressive style, which was dominant throughout ancient Egypt by the end of the Old Kingdom. The facial features of the later prisoner statues also convey a new conception of Otherness. While the earlier prisoner statues more clearly depict specific ethnic stereotypes, with ethnic markers that correspond to those employed for foreigners in Old Kingdom two-dimensional representations, the statues from the complexes of Pepi I and Pepi II do not depict real ethnicities; instead they represent an array of imaginary foreigners. The artists of these two kings mixed and matched facial features and hairstyles among the heads from each complex to produce a wide range of individualized non-Egyptian characters. This change reflects a new understanding of ethnic and cultural identity that arose as Egypt's interactions with foreigners became increasingly commonplace and complex in the Sixth Dynasty.

Chapter 4 examines the critical question of where inside the pyramid complex the prisoner statues had originally been set. The statues clearly were an important element of the complex, representing a significant use of resources and labor. But none of the excavated fragments were discovered in situ. For this reason, the placement of the prisoner statues and their relationship to the rest of the decorative program has been uncertain. My reexamination of the archaeological evidence indicates that the location of the prisoner statues within each pyramid complex changed over time. Furthermore, it is clear that the statues were closely related to reliefs of triumph and domination. They appeared during a period of experimentation, when kings and their officials were transferring traditional two-dimensional themes into three-dimensional statues. Indeed, the important developments in the prisoner statues and the decorative program of the late Old Kingdom pyramid complex indicates that these monuments were much less standardized and creatively stagnant than many scholars have assumed.

A particularly difficult question concerns whether the prisoner statues were ritually broken or attacked. This is the subject of chapter 5. A complete statue has yet to be excavated; they have only ever been found in fragments. This, along with their poorly preserved condition, has led scholars to suggest that they may have been intentionally damaged. However, my analysis shows that the treatment of the statues, and consequently their function and the Egyptians' understanding of them, also changed over time. Large back pillars demonstrate that the earliest statues were not carved with any intention of active manipulation or destruction; rather, they were three-dimensional decorative elements. However, the prisoner statues from the pyramid complex of Pepi I were methodically decapitated as part of their original function, while the prisoner statues from the pyramid complex of Pepi II, which represent yet another change, were not decapitated but instead were violently smashed.

To what extent and in what capacity was this damage to the Pepi I and Pepi II prisoner statues ritualistic? The rest of chapter 5 revolves around these questions. The prisoner statues of both kings were part of a ritualized context that served to benefit the pharaoh, but the significance of the destructive action developed along with the change in the nature of the action itself. This indicates that the ritual life of the late Old Kingdom pyramid complex was itself dynamic.

Chapter 6 reviews and integrates my conclusions concerning the major developments in the prisoner statues' original location, form, style, ethnicity, and treatment at each pyramid complex that I put forward throughout this book. The changes were part of broader changes that occurred during the late Old Kingdom, and I consider the role that the king, his high officials and architects, and the statues' artists had in initiating and implementing them. While the king was largely responsible for making certain decisions, such as on the number of statues to commission, the artists had more agency in other aspects of the statues, including how the statues' foreignness was depicted. Ultimately, the prisoner statues were the products of conversations and collaboration between multiple individuals. In this way, chapter 6 calls attention to new lines of inquiry that this book makes possible. The following is intended to be an introduction to the prisoner statues and their historical context; I hope that it will stimulate future studies on topics as diverse as the functioning of the late Old Kingdom pyramid complex, the working processes of Old Kingdom artists, and the cultural memory of the prisoner statues and the pyramid complex.

Chapter 2
The Evolution of the Prisoner Statues during the Late Old Kingdom

The late Old Kingdom was a dynamic period of Egyptian history when major shifts in religion, society, state administration, and kingship occurred. The role of the king gradually diminished while the status of those around him rose. It is against this backdrop that the prisoner statues appeared. The mid-Fifth Dynasty and the reign of Niuserre was a turning point in many ways, as I discuss in this chapter, and numerous innovations took place at this time. The prisoner statues were among these.

Five other late Old Kingdom pharaohs commissioned prisoner statues following Niuserre, namely, Djedkare-Isesi, Unas, Teti, Pepi I, and Pepi II. However, each king's statues looked different from those of his predecessors. For example, over time the position of the statues became more naturalistic and expressive. The large back pillars that were features of the earliest prisoner statues disappeared, and the artists began carving the backs of the statues. By the reign of Pepi II, the backs were not only depicted but also naturalistically modeled. At the same time, the number of prisoner statues seems to have increased in the reign of Pepi I and again in the reign of Pepi II, who had dozens of statues in his monument. The statues were symbols of royal authority, and they were one of the many ways that these Sixth Dynasty kings tried to assert their power and distinguish themselves from the growing number of powerful, elite high officials.

In the following section, I review the primary historical developments that took place during the Fifth and Sixth Dynasties in order to contextualize the prisoner statues, which I then introduce in the subsequent section. This second section presents the history of the prisoner statues' excavation and the features of their bodies.[1] The developments in regard to the statues' form, stylistic features, and number are articulated in the third section of this chapter. Moreover, while the statues clearly changed over time, there were also variations among the statues within a single complex, and I also consider these. This is particularly the case for the statues of Pepi I, and the differences between these statues provide some insight into the priorities and agency of this king's artists. Indeed, there were certain aspects of these statues, such as the bonds around their arms, that apparently did not need to be uniform and thus the artists chose how to represent them. Finally, in the last section of this chapter I return to the question of historical context by considering the prisoner statues' first appearance and evolution over time in light of the broader events that occurred during the Fifth and Sixth Dynasties in Egypt.

---

1. The heads and facial features of the prisoner statues are the focus of ch. 3.

2.1. Egypt during the Late Old Kingdom

By the beginning of the Fifth Dynasty, the composition of the ancient Egyptian administration was changing.[2] Government offices, which had previously been limited and held by members of the royal family, were increasing, diversifying, and being given to nonroyal individuals. This led to a more complex administrative system and a distinct elite class of high officials with resources and influence. The state also had new interest in the provinces; there was increased building activity throughout the country and a sustained effort to gain control of local agricultural production and the country's economy. As Egyptian society grew in complexity, the conception of the king and kingship shifted as well. The king's identification with the sun god and divine status declined. Instead, the idea that he was the son of the sun god became paramount.[3]

The Fifth Dynasty began with the pharaoh Userkaf. This king built his pyramid complex in Saqqara, at the northeast corner of the Step Pyramid of Djoser, the founder of the Old Kingdom (fig. 1.3). This location seems to have been an attempt on the part of Userkaf to align himself with Djoser and thus enforce his legitimacy, which may have been threatened by his not being of fully royal blood.[4] Userkaf's other main building project may have also been an effort to legitimize himself, namely, by emphasizing the king's relationship with the sun god, but it initiated a new tradition as well: at the site of Abusir, Userkaf constructed a sun temple (fig. 1.3). The following five kings, with the exception of the ephemeral pharaoh Shepseskare, also had sun temples according to textual records, although only the complexes of Userkaf and Niuserre, which is located nearby in Abu Ghurob, have been discovered. Scholars still debate the purpose and function of the sun temples, but they clearly were associated with the cult of the king, as well as the sun god, and each king's sun temple functioned together with his pyramid complex, with the monuments complementing each other in meaning and symbolism.[5] Moreover, the sun temples illustrate the importance of the solar cult to the Fifth Dynasty kings.

Userkaf's successor was Sahure, who initiated another new tradition. He constructed his pyramid complex at Abusir (fig. 1.3). This site continued to function as the royal necropolis for most of the remaining kings of the Fifth Dynasty, including Sahure's successors Neferirkare and Raneferef, who both died before their complexes were completed. Raneferef was Neferirkare's son, and he only reigned for a year or two; following his premature death, his brother Niuserre succeeded him.[6]

The earliest pyramid complex in which prisoner statue fragments were found is that of Niuserre.[7] Deep changes in Egyptian society, administration, and economics, which would profoundly affect the rest of the Old Kingdom, characterized Niuserre's long reign.[8] For example, beginning around this time, the number

---

2. For an overview of the early Fifth Dynasty, see Verner, *Abusir*, 35–50 and Miroslav Verner, *Sons of the Sun: Rise and Decline of the Fifth Dynasty* (Prague: Czech Institute of Egyptology, 2014), 29–75 and 240–44. See also references in n. 3 in ch. 1.1.

3. Nuzzolo, *Fifth Dynasty Sun Temples*, 47.

4. Verner, *Abusir*, 47.

5. For the sun temples, see further Nuzzolo, *Fifth Dynasty Sun Temples*.

6. The ephemeral king Shepseskare probably ruled for a very short time between Raneferef and Niuserre (see further Miroslav Verner, "Who Was Shepseskare, and When Did He Reign?" in *Abusir and Saqqara in the Year 2000*, ed. Miroslav Bárta and Jaromír Krejčí [Prague: Oriental Institute of the Academy of Sciences of the Czech Republic, 2000], 581–602).

7. Concerning the reign of Niuserre, see further Bárta, *Analyzing Collapse*, 123–49.

8. Some changes likely had already begun during the reign of Niuserre's father, Neferirkare (Klaus Baer, *Rank and Title in the Old Kingdom: The Structure of the Egyptian Administration in the Fifth and Sixth Dynasties* [Chicago: University of Chicago Press, 1960], 296–301; Baud, "The Old Kingdom," 75; Peter Jánosi, "The Tombs of Officials: Houses of Eternity," in Arnold, Grzymski, and Ziegler, *Egyptian Art*, 34; and Strudwick, *Administration*, 337). For a helpful, concise overview of the

of titles that high-ranking officials held increased; Miroslav Bárta has interpreted this as signaling a royal attempt to stem the increasing independence of the growing elite class by concentrating duties and power into the hands of fewer men, thus reducing the number of high officials. Presumably as a result, the wealth of individual officials also increased enormously.[9] Additionally, many offices at various levels of the state administration seem to have become hereditary around the time of Niuserre's reign.[10]

By the middle of the Fifth Dynasty, the state's interest in the provinces and their efforts to exert control over more remote areas had further increased; this trend would continue for the rest of the Old Kingdom.[11] Thus, Niuserre or his successor, Djedkare-Isesi, created the office of "Overseer of Upper Egypt," though the extent to which the early holders of this title actually were present in the provinces is debatable, as they were clearly connected to the central administration, being buried, and presumably residing, in the capital.[12]

Niuserre was a prolific builder, and he undertook an enormous amount of construction during his reign.[13] Not only did he build his own monuments, including his pyramid complex at Abusir and sun temple at Abu Ghurab, but he completed the largely unfinished pyramid complexes of his father Neferirkare, his mother Khentkawes II, and his brother Raneferef. In order to save resources, he positioned his pyramid and mortuary temple near the northeast corner of Neferirkare's pyramid and took over Neferirkare's valley temple and causeway foundation as his own (fig. 1.3).[14] Niuserre's mortuary temple included a number of architectural innovations, which I detail in chapter 4. At Raneferef's complex, little had been completed before this king's death, and Niuserre and his high officials came up with several creative cost-saving solutions. Moreover, while rebuilding his mother's complex, Niuserre had a satellite pyramid installed, which, prior to this point, had been exclusively employed for kings' funerary monuments.[15] The incredible amount of production and building during Niuserre's reign led to a creative atmosphere that enabled important artistic developments, including the prisoner statues.[16]

Around the same time, significant changes occurred in nonroyal funerary architecture as well. For example, new types of tombs emerged, such as family tombs, which may reflect the new trend toward hereditary administrative offices.[17] The size of tombs belonging to the highest-ranking officials also substantially increased, with a greater number of rooms, more relief decoration with new scene types, and increasing

---

increasing bureaucratic complexity that occurred throughout the Fifth Dynasty, particularly in regard to social, economic, and administrative changes, see Christopher Eyre, "Weni's Career and Old Kingdom Historiography," in *The Unbroken Reed: Studies in the Culture and Heritage of Ancient Egypt in Honour of A. F. Shore*, ed. Christopher Eyre, Anthony Leahy, and Lisa Montagno Leahy (London: Egypt Exploration Society, 1994), 107–24.

9. Bárta, "Architectural Innovations," 117–19 and Bárta, "Egyptian Kingship," 271.

10. Bárta, "Architectural Innovations," 116–17 and Bárta, "Kings," 166 and 168–69.

11. Concerning developments in the provincial administration during the Old Kingdom, see further Eva Martin-Pardey, *Untersuchungen zur ägyptischen Provinzialverwaltung bis zum Ende des Alten Reiches* (Hildesheim: Gerstenberg, 1976).

12. Bárta, "Architectural Innovations," 119; Bárta, "Egyptian Kingship," 272; Bárta, "Kings," 171; Edward Brovarski, "Overseers of Upper Egypt in the Old to Middle Kingdoms," *ZÄS* 140 (2013): 91–92; Naguib Kanawati, *Governmental Reforms in Old Kingdom Egypt* (Warminster: Aris & Phillips, 1980), 15; and Moreno García, "Territorial Administration," 118–19.

13. In this regard, see further Jaromír Krejčí, "Nyuserra Revisited," in *Abusir and Saqqara in the Year 2010*, vol. 2, ed. Miroslav Bárta, Filip Coppens, and Jaromír Krejčí (Prague: Czech Institute of Egyptology, 2011), 518–29.

14. Miroslav Verner has suggested that Niuserre may have also chosen this location, adjacent to his father's pyramid, in order to enhance his legitimacy since he did not directly succeed his father (Verner, *Abusir*, 72–73).

15. Bárta, "Architectural Innovations," 106; Peter Jánosi, "The Reconstruction and Evaluation of the Pyramid Complex of Queen Khentkaus," in *The Pyramid Complex of Khentkaus*, ed. Miroslav Verner, Abusir 3 (Prague: Czech Institute of Egyptology, 1995), 160 and 163; and Verner, *Abusir*, 184.

16. I return to this idea in ch. 4.

17. Bárta, "Architectural Innovations," 106–17 and Bárta, "Egyptian Kingship," 269. Regarding changes in elite tomb dec-

numbers of cult statues. The vizier Ptahshepses was one of the wealthiest and most powerful high officials during this period. He married Princess Khamerernebty, who was likely a daughter of Niuserre. Indeed, Niuserre seems to have married off a number of his daughters to elite high officials; during the early Fifth Dynasty this practice was less common, but in the mid-Fifth Dynasty it increased and then continued into the Sixth Dynasty.[18] Ptahshepses's tomb, which marked a turning point in elite funerary architecture, was the largest private funerary monument in the Old Kingdom. In it, Ptahshepses adopted a number of elements that had previously been royal prerogatives, including a monumental columned portico; a statue room with three niches; a large, open court; and a saddle ceiling over the burial chamber. Many of these features continued to be employed and adapted in the tombs of other elite officials. Ptahshepses also seems to have been the first high official to have a true autobiography in his tomb.[19]

Niuserre's successor was Menkauhor, whose tomb has yet to be identified.[20] Rather, Djedkare-Isesi is the next known king to make use of prisoner statues. Djedkare may have been the son of Niuserre, or possibly Menkauhor, and the central administration continued as it had under Niuserre with certain organizational and titular changes.[21] The state's growing interest in the provinces continued as well, and increasing numbers of officials were buried outside of the capital in the regions that they governed.[22] Moreover, new types of elite autobiographies appeared that seem to signal this class' increasing independence.[23]

Most significantly, Djedkare was the first king of the Fifth Dynasty who did not build a sun temple.[24] Indeed, his reign marks the end of this practice, which had dominated and, in many ways, defined the nature of the earlier Fifth Dynasty. Multiple scholars have debated the reasons for this seemingly sudden change.[25] According to Jaromir Malek, the reasons were economical rather than ideological, with the system no longer being able to sustain the construction and endowment of sun temples and royal funerary monuments during a single reign.[26] However, while economic concerns may have been a factor, it seems unlikely that this was the only, or even the primary, reason that the kings stopped building sun temples. Indeed, the cessation of sun temples must be considered in light of other changes during the reign of Djed-

---

oration, see also John Burn, "An Ecological Approach to Determine the Potential Influence that the Pyramid Texts has upon the Sixth Dynasty Tomb Decorations," in Bárta, Coppens, and Krejčí, *Abusir and Saqqara...2010*, 233–45.

18. Michel Baud, *Famille royale et pouvoir sous l'Ancien Empire égyptien*, 2 vols., BiEtud 126 (Cairo: Institut français d'archéologique orientale, 1999), 1:368–71 and Miroslav Bárta and Veronika Dulíková, "Divine and Terrestrial: The Rhetoric of Power in Ancient Egypt (The Case of Nyuserra)," in *Royal versus Divine Authority: Acquisition, Legitimization and Renewal of Power*, ed. Filip Coppens, Jiří Janák, and Hana Vymazalová (Wiesbaden: Harrassowitz, 2015), 36–41.

19. Bárta, "Architectural Innovations," 106–20; Bárta, "Egyptian Kingship," 268–69; Jánosi, "Tombs of Officials," 34–36; Nicole Kloth, *Die (auto-) biographischen Inschriften des ägyptischen Alten Reiches: Untersuchungen zu Phraseologie und Entwicklung* (Hamburg: Buske, 2002), 284–85; Jaromír Krejčí, *The Architecture of the Mastaba of Ptahshepses*, Abusir 11 (Prague: Czech Institute of Egyptology, 2009); and Verner, *Abusir*, 158–80. I prefer to call these biographical texts that were written in high officials' tombs autobiographies rather than biographies. Although the tomb owner likely did not write the text himself, he undoubtedly had some role in its composition, and the term autobiography better reflects this. In general concerning Old Kingdom autobiographies, see Strudwick, *Texts*, 42–46.

20. See further Verner, *Abusir*, 27 and Miroslav Verner, *The Pyramids*, trans. Steven Randall (Cairo: American University of Cairo Press, 2001), 227–29.

21. Strudwick, *Administration*, 339–40. Concerning the Fifth Dynasty royal lineage, see Verner, *Abusir*, 91–111.

22. Bárta, "Kings," 171; Kanawati, *Governmental Reforms*, 128; and Strudwick, *Texts*, 9.

23. Kloth, *(Auto-) biographischen Inschriften*, 283–85 and Richards, "Kingship and Legitimation," 67–68.

24. This is with the exception of the ephemeral king Shepseskare, for whom no monuments of any kind are attested.

25. In addition to those arguments mentioned below, other recent discussions include Nuzzolo, *Fifth Dynasty Sun Temples*, 490–504 and Racheli Shalomi-Hen, "The Dawn of Osiris and the Dusk of the Sun-Temples: Religious History at the End of the Fifth Dynasty," in Der Manuelian and Schneider, *Towards a New History*, 462.

26. Malek, *In the Shadow*, 108.

kare, particularly his decision to construct his pyramid complex in South Saqqara rather than in Abusir, where most of his predecessors had built their own monuments, and the contemporaneous appearance of the god Osiris, whose religious influence would only increase after Djedkare. Thus, the end of the sun temples seems to be closely tied to gradual religious changes during the late Fifth Dynasty. Miroslav Verner has rightly noted that multiple factors were likely involved, including changing social conditions and practical reasons, in addition to religion.[27]

Djedkare's decision to not build a sun temple and to move his pyramid complex did not reflect a rejection of these institutions and the Abusir cults. Indeed, he had multiple family members, including his daughter and eldest son, buried in Abusir. Moreover, the Abusir papyri indicate that this king paid close attention to the funerary complexes and sun temples at Abusir, as he reconstructed monuments and reorganized cults.[28]

Djedkare's successor, Unas, was the last king of the Fifth Dynasty, and he also erected prisoner statues in his pyramid complex, which he built in Saqqara near the southern side of Djoser's Step Pyramid complex (figs. 1.1 and 1.3). While Unas may have been Djedkare's son, other scholars have suggested that he was a relatively weak ruler, who did not have a strong claim to the throne and needed to strengthen his legitimacy in various ways, including by placing his pyramid complex close to Djoser's.[29] The independence and influence of select elite families seems to have continued to increase during his reign, and Unas may have sought to reconsolidate the central government since there are no known high officials who were buried in the provinces at this time.[30]

The religious changes that had first begun during the late Fifth Dynasty became more apparent during Unas's reign, particularly with the appearance of the Pyramid Texts on the walls of the funerary apartments inside this king's pyramid.[31] This collection of religious texts, which were inscribed on the inner walls of all subsequent Old Kingdom kings' pyramids, reflect ancient Egyptian afterlife beliefs. Although they include solar and stellar references, the relatively new Osirian religion is dominant, and thus they epitomize the decline in the prominence of the sun god and the rise of Osiris, a god of death and resurrection, within the funerary realm. This development was apparent in other contemporaneous changes as well, including the end of the construction of royal sun temples under Djedkare and various royal and private names, such as those of the kings Menkauhor and Unas, which do not reference Re, the primary sun god.[32]

---

27. Verner, *Abusir*, 256–57.

28. Paule Posener-Kriéger, Miroslav Verner, and Hana Vymazalová, *The Pyramid Complex of Raneferef: The Papyrus Archive*, Abusir 10 (Prague: Czech Institute of Egyptology, 2006), 334–35 and Verner, *Abusir*, 198–216.

29. Verner, 29.

30. Bárta, "Architectural Innovations," 117; Bárta, "Kings," 172; Kanawati, *Governmental Reforms*, 128; and Verner, *Abusir*, 311.

31. In regard to the Pyramid Texts, see further James P. Allen, *The Ancient Egyptian Pyramid Texts*, 2nd ed., ed. Peter Der Manuelian, WAW 38 (Atlanta: SBL Press, 2015); James P. Allen, "The Cosmology of the Pyramid Texts," in Simpson, *Religion and Philosophy*, 1–28; and James P. Allen, "Reading a Pyramid," in *Hommages à Jean Leclant*, vol. 1, ed. Catherine Berger, Gisèle Clerc, and Nicolas Grimal (Cairo: Institut français d'archéologie orientale, 1994), 5–28. Alternative interpretations include Harold M. Hays, *The Organization of the Pyramid Texts: Typology and Disposition*, PAe 31 (Leiden: Brill, 2012); Harold M. Hays, "Unreading the Pyramids," *BIFAO* 109 (2009): 195–220; Antonio J. Morales, "From Voice to Papyrus to Wall: *Verschriftung* and *Verschriftlichung* in the Old Kingdom Pyramid Texts," in *Understanding Material Text Cultures*, ed. Markus Hilgert (Berlin: de Gruyter, 2016), 69–130; and Massimiliano Nuzzolo, "Royal Architecture and Pyramid Texts: Some Remarks on 'Kingship' in the III Millennium B.C.," in *Recent Discoveries and Latest Researches in Egyptology: Proceedings of the First Neapolitan Congress of Egyptology, Naples, June 18th–20th 2008*, ed. Francesco Raffaele, Massimiliano Nuzzolo, and Ilaria Incordino (Wiesbaden: Harrassowitz, 2010), 177–97.

32. Baud, "The Old Kingdom," 74 and Naguib Kanawati, *Conspiracies in the Egyptian Palace: Unis to Pepy I* (London:

The origins of Osiris and his earliest appearance are a matter of debate.[33] Although numerous scholars have argued that there may be Fourth Dynasty references to this new god, the more securely dated occurrences of his name are from the middle of the Fifth Dynasty, including in the tomb of Ptahshepses, which I described above. Regardless of their date, the initial attestations of Osiris seem to have appeared in private contexts rather than royal ones, as the earliest royal attestation dates to the reign of Djedkare; Osiris was named and possibly depicted in this king's mortuary temple. But it was not until the reign of Unas that Osiris became a prominent deity, as the Pyramid Texts demonstrate. Therefore, the emergence of Osiris and the resulting religious developments that this signaled were another important change that occurred in the middle of the Fifth Dynasty.

Because Osiris was present prior to the reign of Unas, it seems unlikely that his prominence in the Pyramid Texts indicates a sudden change in religious beliefs at the end of the Fifth Dynasty. Rather the Pyramid Texts appear to reflect a change in practices and traditions associated with religion. Indeed, Harold Hays has argued that the Pyramid Texts drew on an older body of literature that was accessible to both royal and elite individuals throughout the late Old Kingdom, when both classes shared common funerary beliefs and access to the afterlife. At the end of the Fifth Dynasty and the beginning of the Sixth Dynasty, the kings began to inscribe their pyramids with Pyramid Texts as a means of social distinction, monumentalizing and entextualizing what had previously been ritual scripts, and thus turning them into a type of visual decoration that was solely the reserve of the king.[34] While this certainly reflects a continuing religious development, the appearance of the Pyramid Texts during the reign of Unas also signals a shift in social organization and the relationship between the king and the elite class at the end of the Fifth Dynasty.

With the start of the Sixth Dynasty, a number of important trends intensified, and these would come to characterize the entire dynasty.[35] The religious changes that had begun in the middle of the Fifth Dynasty fully crystallized, with the use of the Pyramid Texts becoming standard practice for kings and eventually spreading to royal women as well. This coincides with a proliferation of uses of writing and monumental applications of texts in both royal and nonroyal contexts.[36] Moreover, increasing attention was devoted to the subterranean areas of elite tombs, with these rooms now being decorated.[37] However, despite the

---

Routledge, 2003), 144–46; cf. Mark Smith, *Following Osiris: Perspectives on the Osirian Afterlife from Four Millennia* (Oxford: Oxford University Press, 2017), 127–29, who has questioned the connection between the rise of Osiris and the decline of Re.

33. See recently Smith, 107–33; Baud, *Famille royale*, 2:517–18; Harold M. Hays, "The Death of the Democratisation of the Afterlife," in *Old Kingdom, New Perspectives: Egyptian Art and Archaeology 2750–2150 BC*, ed. Nigel Strudwick and Helen Strudwick (Oxford: Oxbow, 2011), 120–23; Bernard Mathieu, "Mais qui est donc Osiris? Ou la politique sous le linceul de la religion (enquêtes dans les Textes des Pyramides, 3)," *ENiM* 3 (2010): 77–107; Nuzzolo, "Royal Architecture," 187–88; and Massimiliano Nuzzolo, "The Sun Temples of the Vth Dynasty: A Reassessment," *SAK* 36 (2007): 239–40. Shalomi-Hen's argument that Osiris was a foreign deity introduced to Egypt in the late Fifth Dynasty is controversial and less likely (Shalomi-Hen, "Dawn of Osiris," 456–69).

34. Hays, "Death of the Democratisation of the Afterlife," 118–30 and Harold M. Hays, "The Entextualization of the Pyramid Texts and the Religious History of the Old Kingdom," in Der Manuelian and Schneider, *Towards a New History*, 200–226. See also Hays, *Organization*.

35. A recent overview of the Sixth Dynasty, which follows the arguments of Kanawati that I describe throughout this chapter, is Naguib Kanawati and Joyce Swinton, *Egypt in the Sixth Dynasty: Challenges and Responses* (Wallasey, UK: Abercromby, 2018).

36. Hays, "Entextualization," 218.

37. Bárta, "Architectural Innovations," 121. See also Miroslav Bárta, "Filling the Chambers, Rising the Status: Sixth Dynasty Context for the Decline of the Old Kingdom," *CRIPEL* 28 (2009–2010): 145–56.

prominence of Osiris, the sun god remained an extremely important deity that was closely tied to kingship, and the cult of Re became centralized in Heliopolis.[38]

The central administration's interest in more peripheral areas only increased during the Sixth Dynasty. For example, kings began to construct and/or renovate gods' temples in the provinces and oases. They also constructed increasing numbers of royal *ka* chapels in or near these temples.[39] Kings began issuing exemption decrees for provincial temples as well, excluding them and their personnel from the collection of certain goods or corvée labor.[40] Following the reign of Unas, increasing numbers of high-ranking officials chose to be buried in the provincial governorates, or nomes, in which they were stationed rather than around the capital in Memphis.[41]

The first pharaoh of the Sixth Dynasty was Teti, who erected his pyramid in Saqqara, near the pyramids of Djoser, Userkaf, and Unas (fig. 1.3). It is possible that he chose this location to align himself directly with these ancestors.[42] It is unclear whether Teti was related to Unas, and he may have ascended the throne by marrying Unas's daughter Iput, who then gave birth to the future king Pepi I.[43] Based largely on archaeological evidence from the elite cemetery and tombs of the early Sixth Dynasty, Kanawati has suggested that there was some discord at the start of Teti's reign. Moreover, Teti seems to have taken unusual security precautions throughout his reign, and it is possible that he was ultimately assassinated.[44]

An ephemeral king named Userkare succeeded Teti, but this king left behind few traces.[45] According to Kanawati, Userkare, who probably did not belong to the main line of succession, might have been involved in Teti's assassination, or at least he took advantage of this situation and the young age of the rightful heir, Pepi I.[46] However, soon after, Pepi I claimed the throne, and with this king, the number of attested prisoner statues increased dramatically. Pepi I constructed his funerary monument in South Saqqara, and recent excavations in the necropolis surrounding his pyramid have demonstrated that this king wed a large number of women, possibly up to eight of them.[47] At the same time, the status of kings' wives who were not queen mothers seems to have increased, as is apparent from the practice of now burying these women under pyramids. Previously, only queen mothers had had pyramids. This was only one of a number of changes

---

38. Hana Vymazalová, "The Economic Connection between the Royal Cult in the Pyramid Temples and the Sun Temples in Abusir," in Strudwick and Strudwick, *Old Kingdom, New Perspectives*, 300–301. Concerning Heliopolis, see further Stephen Quirke, *The Cult of Ra: Sun-Worship in Ancient Egypt* (London: Thames & Hudson, 2001), 73–114.

39. Baud, "The Old Kingdom," 77; Papazian, "Perspectives," 77–79; Richards, "Kingship and Legitimation," 62–63; and Strudwick, *Texts*, 9.

40. Martin-Pardey, *Untersuchungen*, 127–31 and Warden, "Centralized Taxation," 482–88. Concerning Old Kingdom decrees, see also Hratch Papazian, *Domain of Pharaoh: The Structure and Components of the Economy of Old Kingdom Egypt*, HÄB 52 (Hildesheim: Gerstenberg, 2012), 101–18.

41. Bárta, "Kings," 172; Baud, "The Old Kingdom," 77; and Richards, "Kingship and Legitimation," 63. See also Juan Carlos Moreno García, "The 'Other' Administration: Patronage, Factions, and Informal Networks of Power in Ancient Egypt," in Moreno García, *Ancient Egyptian Administration*, 1034–35.

42. Kanawati, *Conspiracies*, 144.

43. Concerning Iput, see further Vivienne Gae Callender, *In Hathor's Image I: The Wives and Mothers of Egyptian Kings from Dynasties I–VI* (Prague: Charles University, 2011), 221–27. Teti's wife Khuit may have been a daughter of Unas as well (Callender, 217–21).

44. Kanawati, *Conspiracies*, 147–69.

45. See further Michel Baud and Vassil Dobrev, "De nouvelles annals de l'Ancien Empire égyptien. Une 'Pierre de Palerme' pour la VIe dynastie," *BIFAO* 95 (1995): 59–62.

46. Kanawati, *Conspiracies*, 157–71.

47. Audran Labrousse, "Huit épouses du roi Pepy Ier," in *Egyptian Culture and Society: Studies in Honour of Naguib Kanawati*, ed. Alexandra Woods, Ann McFarlane, and Susanne Binder (Cairo: Supreme Council of Antiquities, 2010), 297–314. Callender prefers to recognize seven wives (Callender, *In Hathor's Image*, 267 n. 48, see further 232–71).

that Pepi I introduced in regard to royal women. Additionally, queens' mortuary temples also became larger and more complex over time, and from the reign of Pepi I on, the titulary for queens became richer. Callender has argued that this latter trend may be associated with the large number of nonroyal women whom Pepi I married.[48]

Indeed, two of the most prominent Sixth Dynasty queens were sisters from an influential family from the southern city of Abydos in Middle Egypt.[49] Pepi I married both of them, and Ankhnespepi I gave birth to Pepi I's successor, Merenre, while Ankhnespepi II remarried Merenre following Pepi I's death, mothered the future king, Pepi II, and acted as his regent during the early years of his reign.[50] Their brother Djau was appointed vizier, one of the highest administrative positions, though it is unclear whether this occurred before or after the sisters' marriage.[51] Their father, Khui, was a high official, and their mother was named Nebet. Some scholars, including Naguib Kanawati, have identified this Khui and Nebet with other contemporaneous elite couples with the same names, including a Nebet with the title of vizier, who was also married to a Khui. However, it seems most likely that all of these individuals were distinct and that Nebet the vizier was not Nebet the mother of Ankhnespepi I, Ankhnespepi II, and Djau. Moreover, Callender has recently argued that the vizier's title that Nebet held was actually a religious epithet, which first appeared for royal and elite women at the end of the Sixth Dynasty, and not an administrative post, as was typical for this title.[52] Regardless, based on the frequent reoccurrence of these names and others, Christopher Eyre suggested that a single extended family may have dominated the government in southern Middle Egypt from the reign of Pepi I to the end of the Old Kingdom.[53]

The marriages between Pepi I and Ankhnespepi I and II would seem to have been political ones, signaling an attempt by Pepi I and the central administration to establish ties with an important elite, and possibly, provincial family.[54] This suggests that some contemporary officials were powerful and influential individuals, to whom the king felt he needed to align himself. It is possible that this was part of an attempt to modify the balance of power of provincial officials in order to prevent anyone from becoming too pow-

---

48. Callender, 326–32.

49. Concerning this family and their links with the Eighth Dynasty, see Papazian, "State of Egypt," 406–10. On the other hand, Kanawati and Swinton have argued that this family was related to the royal family and that intermarriage between royalty and private high officials was not occurring during the Old Kingdom (Naguib Kanawati, "The Vizier Nebet and the Royal Women of the Sixth Dynasty," in *Thebes and Beyond: Studies in Honour of Kent R. Weeks*, ed. Zahi Hawass and Salima Ikram [Cairo: Supreme Council of Antiquities, 2010], 115–25 and Kanawati and Swinton, *Egypt*, 82–87).

50. See further Callender, *In Hathor's Image*, 249–71; Audran Labrousse, "Une épouse du roi Mérenrê Ier: La reine Ânkhesenpépy II," in Bárta and Krejčí, *Abusir and Saqqara...2000*, 485–90; and Jean Leclant and Audran Labrousse, "Les reines Ankhnespépy II et III (fin de l'Ancien Empire): campagnes 1999 et 2000 de la MAFS," *CRAIBL* 145 (2001): 374–76. Regarding the sisters' name, see further Yannis Gourdon, "Le nom des épouses abydéniennes de Pépy Ier et la formule de serment à la fin de l'Ancien Empire," *BIFAO* 106 (2006): 89–104.

51. Papazian "State of Egypt," 407 n. 56.

52. Vivienne Gae Callender, "It's All in the Family: A 6th Dynasty Conundrum," in *Rich and Great: Studies in Honour of Anthony J. Spalinger on the Occasion of His 70th Feast of Thoth*, ed. Renata Landgráfová and Jana Mynářová (Prague: Charles University, 2016), 19–27. See also Baud, *Famille royale*, 2:629–31; Callender, *In Hathor's Image*, 254–55; Henry Fischer, *Varia*, Egyptian Studies 1 (New York: The Metropolitan Museum of Art, 1976), 74–75; Kanawati, *Conspiracies*, 174–75; Kanawati, *Governmental Reforms*, 31–33 and 62–64; Kanawati, "Vizier Nebet," 115–25; and Papazian, 408–9.

53. Eyre, "Weni's Career," 113.

54. Bárta, "Kings," 172. Kanawati argued that the family may have originally been established at the capital and only moved to Abydos after Nebet was appointed vizier (Kanawati, *Governmental Reforms*, 62–63 and Kanawati, *Conspiracies*, 173–76). But Papazian has expressed doubt about this (Papazian, "State of Egypt," 408–9). Moreover, as I discussed above, Kanawati's argument that Nebet the vizier was the mother of Ankhnespepi I and II is problematic.

erful.⁵⁵ Indeed, Pepi I's marriages do not necessarily indicate that the king's own power or influence had diminished, but this is a question that I return to in the final section of this chapter.⁵⁶

Another high official who served Pepi I further demonstrates the growing importance of and the central administration's interest in Abydos. Weni was a powerful high official who rose in rank during the reigns of Teti and Pepi I, eventually becoming a vizier and Overseer of Upper Egypt under Merenre. He recorded his upward journey and important events from his career in an autobiography, which he had inscribed in his tomb.⁵⁷ This text was typical of new categories of private autobiographies that appeared at the end of the Fifth Dynasty and became popular during the early Sixth Dynasty; these detailed the rise of the deceased through the ranks of the government and highlighted important activities that he had undertaken on behalf of the king that he had served.⁵⁸ Weni's text specifically makes reference to a harem conspiracy during the reign of Pepi I for which Weni heard testimony. Bárta has suggested that this event, along with the possible murder of Teti, demonstrates that the king was no longer considered by all of his subjects to be of a divine nature and thus untouchable.⁵⁹ Weni's autobiography also mentions several expeditions and military campaigns that Weni led on behalf of the king.⁶⁰ Through this inscription, both materially and textually, Weni emphasized his close relationship to the king and his role as an agent of the pharaoh in the provinces. Furthermore, Janet Richards has argued that Weni's tomb in Abydos was essentially a massive ideogram for the power of the central government; it conspicuously manifested the state's control on an important provincial landscape.⁶¹

Bárta has described a concentration of wealth and influence occurring across the country in the mid-Sixth Dynasty, with Pepi I probably being one of the last kings during whose reign large private tombs were still built in the capital.⁶² During the reign of Merenre, Pepi I's son and successor, there was instead an enormous increase in provincial burials, particularly with local governors, or nomarchs, constructing their tombs within their own nomes, where they presumably now resided as well.⁶³ This seems to signal the increasing prominence of the nomarchs and the further political and economic influence of the provinces. Merenre constructed his own pyramid complex in South Saqqara, and although this has yet to be fully excavated, presently no prisoner statues have been discovered there (fig. 1.3).

The final pharaoh to erect prisoner statues within his pyramid complex, which was also in South Saqqara, was Pepi II, the last king of the Sixth Dynasty (fig. 1.3). According to tradition, he reigned for over ninety years, but more recently, scholars have suggested that his reign was around sixty years.⁶⁴ Because of his long reign, Pepi II must have inherited the throne at a very young age. His mother, Ankhnespepi II,

---

55. Strudwick, *Texts*, 9.
56. In this regard, see further Martin-Pardey, *Untersuchungen*, 143–52.
57. For a translation of this inscription, see Simpson, *Literature*, 402–7. Concerning Weni's career and his inscription, see further Eyre, "Weni's Career" and Janet Richards, "Text and Context in Late Old Kingdom Egypt: The Archaeology and Historiography of Weni the Elder," *JARCE* 39 (2002): 75–102.
58. Kloth, *(Auto-) biographischen Inschriften*, 243–46 and 283–85; Richards, "Kingship and Legitimation," 68; and Strudwick, *Texts*, 46.
59. Miroslav Bárta, "Ancient Egyptian History as an Example of Punctuated Equilibrium: An Outline," in Der Manuelian and Schneider, *Towards a New History*, 10. Kanawati has argued that the harem conspiracy mentioned in Weni's biography occurred early in the reign of Pepi I, and later in his reign, this king faced another conspiracy that the vizier Rawer led (Kanawati, *Conspiracies*, 170–82).
60. I return to these in ch. 3.
61. Richards, "Text and Context."
62. Bárta, "Architectural Innovations," 117–18 and Bárta, "Egyptian Kingship," 269.
63. Bárta, "Kings," 172 and Kanawati, *Governmental Reforms*, 55.
64. Baud, "Ménès," 124 and 129.

acted as his regent during his early years as king, and this seems to have increased her prominence, as I discuss further below. Pepi II's paternity is less certain, and scholars have debated whether he was the son of this queen and Pepi I or Merenre.[65]

Throughout Pepi II's reign, the prominence and power of the nomarchs grew, in contrast to that of the high officials still residing in the capital.[66] Indeed, the simplicity and small size of the elite tombs in the capital, particularly in comparison to earlier private tombs constructed there, further reflects this trend.[67] Scholars have long debated the degree of control that the central government had in this regard and over the provinces in general during Pepi II's reign; I return to this question in the final section of this chapter.

Like Pepi I, Pepi II seems to have married a similar, large number of women, probably between six to eight.[68] Moreover, their funerary monuments reflect the continuing growth in status and prominence for Old Kingdom royal women, which climaxed under Pepi II.[69] The pyramid complex of Ankhnespepi II is the monument that most closely resembles a king's monument, with various architectural features, such as an *antichambre carrée* in her mortuary temple, which were typically reserved for kings' complexes.[70] Moreover, this queen would appear to be the first royal woman to have had Pyramid Texts inscribed on the walls of her funerary apartments. Until the late Sixth Dynasty, this had been a privilege solely for the king. Her status as regent to Pepi II likely was the reason for this innovation. However, four other wives of Pepi II were subsequently given this benefit as well, and they also have Pyramid Texts carved on the walls of their tombs.[71]

It is evident that over the course of the late Old Kingdom, prerogatives of the king gradually diminished and the influence and status of the elite high officials who surrounded him grew. The conception of king-

---

65. For example, see Callender, *In Hathor's Image*, 268–69; Vassil Dobrev, "The South Saqqara Stone and the Sarcophagus of Queen Mother Ankhesenpepy (JE 65908)," in Bárta and Krejčí, *Abusir and Saqqara...2000*, 392 n. 45; Leclant and Labrousse, "Reines Ankhnespépy II et III," 376; and Labrousse, "Épouse," 490.

66. Bárta, "Kings," 172–73 and Kanawati, *Governmental Reforms*, 88–103.

67. Bárta, "Architectural Innovations," 121–22 and Naguib Kanawati, *The Egyptian Administration in the Old Kingdom: Evidence on Its Economic Decline* (Warminster: Aris & Phillips, 1977), 35–37.

68. Callender, *In Hathor's Image*, 271–306 and 344 and Papazian, "State of Egypt," 411.

69. Callender, 287 and 328.

70. Callender, 327. However, an *antichambre carrée* first appeared in the mortuary temple of Djedkare's wife, Queen Setibhor (Mohamed Megahed and Hana Vymazalová, "Neues zum Pyramidenbezirk der Königin Setibhor, der Gemahlin des Djedkare-Isesi," trans. Christine Mende, *Sokar* 39 [2020]: 64–79; Mohamed Megahed and Hana Vymazalová, "Notes on the Newly Discovered Name of Djedkare's Queen," in *Guardian of Ancient Egypt: Studies in Honor of Zahi Hawass*, vol. 2, ed. Janice Kamrin et al. [Prague: Charles University, Faculty of Arts, 2020], 1023–41; Peter Jánosi, "Die Pyramidenanlage der "anonymen Königin" des Djedkare-Isesi," *MDAIK* 45 [1989]: 187–202; and Mohamed Megahed, "The Pyramid Complex of 'Djedkare's Queen' in South Saqqara: Preliminary Report 2010," in Bárta, Coppens, and Krejčí, *Abusir and Saqqara...2010*, 616–34). I discuss the *antichambre carrée* further in ch. 4.

71. This includes Neith, Iput II, Oudjebten, and Behenou (Catherine Berger-el Naggar and Marie-Noëlle Fraisse, "La paroi est de la chamber funéraire de la reine Béhénou," in Hein, Billing, and Meyer-Dietrich, *Pyramids*, 189). However, Pyramid Texts also could have been inscribed on perishable materials deposited in the tombs of royal women, as fragments of a wooden box that were inscribed with Pyramid Texts in the tomb of Meretites II demonstrate (Jean Leclant and Audran Labrousse, "Découvertes récentes de la Mission archéologique française à Saqqâra (campagnes 2001–2005)," *CRAIBL* 150 [2006]: 107–8). There is some debate as to whether Behenou, whose monument was recently discovered, was a wife of Pepi I or Pepi II. The MAFS team responsible for excavating her tomb identified her as the wife of Pepi I based on the location of her pyramid, but they noted that her Pyramid Texts shared more in common with those of Iput II and Oudjebten rather than Ankhnespepi II and thus were probably inscribed during the reign of Pepi II after those of Ankhnespepi II (Catherine Berger-el Naggar and Marie-Noëlle Fraisse, "Béhénou, 'aimée de Pépy,' une nouvelle reine d'Égypte," *BIFAO* 108 [2008]: 1–27). However, Callender and Papazian prefer to simply see her as a wife of Pepi II (Callender, *In Hathor's Image*, 297–99 and Papazian, "State of Egypt," 413).

ship would have shifted along with the role of the king in Egyptian society. The divide between the king and the rest of humanity, or at least the elite, shrank over the course of the Fifth and Sixth Dynasties, and the changing policies and practices of the pharaohs suggest an effort continually to adjust and renegotiate the nature of kingship while maintaining and upholding the institution of kingship itself.

2.2. The Prisoner Statues

2.2.1. Niuserre

The German Egyptologist Ludwig Borchardt began excavating Niuserre's pyramid complex in 1902, and he continued working there for three seasons.[72] During the 1903–1904 season, he discovered three prisoner statue fragments, which were transported to Berlin along with other finds and then unfortunately destroyed during the Second World War.[73] Borchardt identified two of the fragments—Berlin, ÄM 17912 (C.1.1), which was a head, and Berlin, ÄM 17913 (C.1.2), which was a fragment of a left shoulder and arm—as coming from a single statue, although the fragments themselves did not join (figs. 2.1 and 3.1).[74] Both of these fragments had remains of a large back pillar. Most of the pillar was the same width as the prisoner's body, and thus formed a flat surface from which the body projected in extremely high relief. Toward the top, the pillar narrowed so that it did not extend beyond either side of the prisoner's head. As a result of the pillar, the prisoner's arms were not actually pulled backwards, which would have been impossible with the pillar directly behind him. Rather, his preserved upper arm hung straight down and was held against his body. The bonds on his upper arm, which sat just below his biceps, confirmed his prisoner status. They consisted of four strands of rope that were intricately carved with a diagonal pattern meant to mimic twisted fibers.

The third fragment that Borchardt discovered, ÄM 17914 (C.1.3), was significantly smaller. It was a fragment of the left forearm and bonds, but it did not fit with the left shoulder fragment described

Figure 2.1. Prisoner statue fragment from the valley temple of Niuserre in Abusir; Fifth Dynasty. Berlin, ÄM 17913. Photograph courtesy of the Ägyptisches Museum und Papyrussammlung, Staatliche Museen zu Berlin – PK.

---

72. Ludwig Borchardt, *Das Grabdenkmal des Königs Ne-user-re*, Ausgrabungen der Deutschen Orient-Gesellschaft in Abusir 1902–1904 1; WVDOG 7 (Leipzig: Hinrich, 1907).

73. My thanks go to curators Olivia Zorn and Klaus Finneiser (Ägyptisches Museum und Papyrussammlung, Staatliche Museen zu Berlin) for passing along this information concerning the fragments' destruction.

74. Borchardt, *Grabdenkmal des Königs Ne-user-re*, 42. Borchardt realized that the head and torso fragment belonged to the same statue when preparing all of the finds for transport to Berlin (Ludwig Borchardt, Entry "Sonntag April 3, 1904," p. 239, Ludwig Borchardt's notebook for the DOG, funerary complex of Niuserre at Abusir, 1903–1904, Ägyptisches Museum und Papyrussammlung, Staatliche Museen zu Berlin – PK, Berlin, Germany). In the same place, he described the flattened head of the statue and questioned whether the hand of a king might have rested on top. Despite the fragments that he discovered being from the Fifth Dynasty, he noted that they were similar to a Nineteenth Dynasty figure from Medinet Habu in the Cairo Museum, presumably the colossal statue of Merenptah he referenced in later publications, which may be from Medinet Habu. I return to this idea below.

Figure 2.2. Statue of Ramses VI "smiting" a Libyan from the Karnak cachette; Twentieth Dynasty, New Kingdom. Gray granite; H. 104 cm, W. 22 cm, D. 35 cm. Luxor, Luxor Museum J.902. Photograph: Tara Prakash, courtesy of the Luxor Museum.

above, and thus, it must have belonged to a second prisoner statue. A very small portion from a back pillar remained attached to the back of the bent elbow, proving that this statue also had a back pillar. The position of the bonds on this fragment differed from that on the larger shoulder fragment, although the bonds themselves were depicted in the same fashion, with four strands of rope that were incised with a diagonal pattern. On the smaller fragment, the bonds were placed on top of the elbow crease, directly above the elbow, rather than higher on the upper arm.

Because of a smooth surface on the top of the head fragment, on which Borchardt suggested something must have originally rested, the excavator likened the Niuserre prisoner statues to New Kingdom smiting statues that depict the king grasping a bound foreigner in one hand and a weapon in the other (fig. 2.2).[75] Borchardt noted in particular a colossal statue of the Nineteenth Dynasty pharaoh Merenptah smiting a Libyan and proposed that royal statues must have similarly accompanied the Niuserre captives, with the king's hand originally placed on top of the captives' flat heads.[76] Although at the time Borchardt was working Alexandre Barsanti had already excavated prisoner statue fragments from the pyramid complex of Unas, these fragments remained poorly known for decades, as I describe in chapter 2.2.3 below, and it is quite possible that Borchardt himself was unaware of them. Instead, he looked for parallels in significantly later material. However, following the subsequent discovery of numerous prisoner statue fragments in the complexes of Niuserre's successors, it is clear that Borchardt's comparison is incorrect. Indeed, the foreigners within the later New Kingdom smiting statues, instead of having flat heads upon which the kings' fists rest, have heads that taper up and into the kings' fists, a three-dimensional variation of the kings' grasping of the hair that is seen in two-dimensional smiting scenes (compare figs. 1.5 and 2.2). Rather, the flattened head of ÄM 17912 (C.1.1) was directly in line with the top of the back pillar and was likely a result of this. Thus, there is nothing to support Borchardt's reconstruction of the fragments as belonging to a composition that included the king, and instead they belonged to the first known freestanding prisoner statues.

---

75. Ludwig Borchardt, "Ausgrabungen der Deutschen Orient-Gesellschaft bei Abusir im Winter 1903–4," *MDOG* 24 (1904): 13 and Borchardt, *Grabdenkmal des Königs Ne-user-re*, 42.

76. Cairo, Egyptian Museum CG 1240; regarding this statue, see Hall, *Pharaoh Smites His Enemy*, 40; Hölscher, *Hohe Tor*, 43 and Abb. 39; and PM 1:775.

2.2.2. Djedkare-Isesi

In 1945, Abdel Salam Hussein, assisted by Alexandre Varille, began excavating Djedkare's pyramid complex. It was during these excavations, which continued until 1949, that Hussein discovered at least four prisoner statue fragments.[77] Unfortunately, the results of this work were never published due to the untimely deaths of Hussein and Varille and the loss of much of their documentation.[78] Although other archaeologists resumed excavations at the Djedkare complex, including Ahmed Fakhry, Mahmoud Abel Razek, and Mohamed Megahed, who is currently working there, Hussein seems to have been the only one who found prisoner statue fragments.[79] However, their existence did not become more widely known until Fakhry's excavations in 1952.[80]

The four fragments that Hussein discovered probably belong to four different prisoner statues. Three of the fragments are quite large. One consists of the lower body of a prisoner, who wears a short kilt with a hem carved in relief and a belt that is tied in an elaborate knot with two tassels hanging down the front of either side of his lap (SCA no. 2232; C.2.1; fig. 2.3).[81] The second, and largest, fragment includes almost the full body of a prisoner statue (SCA no. 2244; C.2.2; fig. 2.4). This is the only fragment from the complex of Djedkare in which the bonds are preserved. Unlike the two statues from the complex of Niuserre, here only two plain strands of rope were carved, with no incised pattern on them. They were positioned slightly above the elbow crease and the elbow. This prisoner also wears a plain short kilt with an incised hem and a wide plain belt but with no tassels. Unfortunately, the front of the belt is no longer visible due to a large fissure that runs down the center of the fragment. The bottom of his long hairstyle was carved in high relief behind his shoulders on either side of a back pillar that runs the entire length of the fragment. Behind the hair, the end of a fillet that must have been tied around his head hangs down to the middle of

---

77. These fragments are now in SCA Saqqara Store Magazine 1. My thanks go to Mohamed Megahed for kindly passing along this information and the inventory numbers.

78. Varille did publish a very brief note describing their 1945–1946 season (Alexandre Varille, *À propos des pyramides de Snefrou* [Cairo: Imprimerie Schindler, 1947], 1 and 17). He did not explicitly mention the prisoner statues there, but he did refer to the beautiful pieces of sculpture in relief and in the round that they had already discovered. In a recently published report that Varille wrote to Drioton concerning the excavations, Varille did not mention the prisoner statues either (see Patrizia Piacentini, "Excavating the Egyptological Archives of the Università degli Studi di Milano: The Varille Documentation on the Pyramid Complex of Djedkare-Izezi at Saqqara," in *Abusir and Saqqara in the Year 2015*, ed. Miroslav Bárta, Filip Coppens, and Jaromír Krejčí [Prague: Faculty of the Arts, Charles University, 2017], 355–68).

79. Concerning the history of excavations at this complex, see Mohamed Megahed, "Neue Forschungen im Grabbezirk des Djedkare-Isesi," *Sokar* 22 (2011): 27–31 and Megahed, "Pyramid Complex," 616–19.

80. The first published reference to them would appear to be Jean Leclant, "Fouilles et travaux en Égypte, 1952–1953," *Orientalia* 23 (1954): 68. Here, Leclant, in mentioning Ahmed Fakhry's renewed exploration of this complex, noted that Hussein had previously found interesting architectural statue fragments, including djed-pillars, sphinxes, lions, rams, and prisoner statues. Fakhry himself only noted the existence of "statues of foreign prisoners" once in his publications without specifying who discovered them, but he implied that he had not (Ahmed Fakhry, *The Pyramids* [Chicago: University of Chicago Press, 1961], 181). Jean-Philippe Lauer and Leclant also mentioned that Fakhry had told them that an ample series of prisoner statues had been discovered during excavations of Djedkare's complex, but they did not name the excavator (Jean-Philippe Lauer and Jean Leclant, "Découverte de statues de prisonniers au temple de la pyramide de Pépi I," *RdE* 21 [1969]: 60 n. 2). To my knowledge, Fakhry's archive does not mention the prisoner statues at all, and no statues have been found at the Djedkare complex since Fakhry finished his work there in 1952. Maragioglio and Rinaldi also mentioned the prisoner statues in their description of the Djedkare complex but without naming the excavator (Vito Maragioglio and Celeste Ambrogio Rinaldi, *L'Architettura della Piramidi Menfite*, vol. 8, trans. Alfred Ernest Howell [Rapallo: Officine Grafiche Canessa, 1975], 82).

81. For an extended discussion of the costumes of the Djedkare prisoner statues, including parallels and the implications of the costumes, see ch. 3.3.

Figure 2.3. Prisoner statue fragment (SCA no. 2232) from the mortuary temple of Djedkare-Isesi in Saqqara; Fifth Dynasty. Photograph courtesy of the Egyptological Library and Archives, Università degli Studi di Milano.

Figure 2.4. Prisoner statue fragment (SCA no. 2244) from the mortuary temple of Djedkare-Isesi in Saqqara; Fifth Dynasty. Photograph: A. Amin, courtesy of Mohamed Megahed.

his upper back. The third large fragment is the bust of another prisoner statue (SCA no. 2233; C.2.3; fig. 3.2). Like SCA no. 2244 (C.2.2), the surface of SCA no. 2233 is very poorly preserved, and the statue was attached to a back pillar.

The back pillars of the prisoner statues from the complex of Djedkare are quite different from those that were used for the prisoner statues from the complex of Niuserre (compare figs. 2.1, 2.3, 2.4, and 3.1). Niuserre's back pillars were wide but not very deep. Thus the entire body of the statue projected from the front of the pillar and the upper arms were not pulled back but had to hang straight down against the torso. In contrast, Djedkare's back pillars are extremely deep but not nearly as wide. The arms of the prisoners are pulled back and were carved in relief on either side of the pillar, particularly those of SCA no. 2244 (C.2.2), whose arms are set further back than the arms of SCA no. 2232 (C.2.1). Unlike the prisoner statues from the complex of Niuserre, the elbows are only slightly bent, and the forearms hang down behind the prisoner's body, with the fists resting behind or toward the back of the buttocks. Related to the angle of the Djedkare prisoner statues' arms is the level of the elbows along the torsos; because the arms are pulled fairly far back, the elbows are quite high, namely, at the level of the ribcage.

The fourth fragment from the complex of Djedkare is only a small piece of the upper part of a head, consisting of primarily the eyes and forehead (C.2.4; fig. 3.3).[82] While it is possible that this belongs with the headless lower body fragment SCA no. 2232 (C.2.1), a reconstruction that Varille implied by placing a photograph of C.2.4 above one of SCA no. 2232 (C.2.1) on one of the notecards in his archive, the hairstyle that C.2.4 has does not seem to match with the kilt SCA no. 2232 (C.2.1) wears, as I will discuss in chapter

---

82. For the identification of this fragment as a prisoner statue, see ch. 3.1.2.

3.3.[83] Consequently, C.2.4 probably belongs to a fourth prisoner statue. The total height of the statues from this complex seems to have been around 90–100 cm, and both heads appear to have been close to 20 cm tall.[84]

2.2.3. Unas

The evidence for Unas's prisoner statues is especially problematic. The first excavations at this king's pyramid complex were those of Alexandre Barsanti, who worked there from 1899–1901 and in 1903.[85] In 1929, Cecil Firth, under the auspices of the Egyptian Antiquities Service, resumed work there.[86] However, neither of these men mentioned finding prisoner statue fragments at this complex in their publications. Then in 1937, Jean-Philippe Lauer returned to the complex and completed the excavation of the mortuary temple. In the final report, a photograph that Pierre Lacau had taken of a fragment of a prisoner statue's torso and bound right arm (C.3.1) was published (fig. 2.5).[87] Lacau had apparently taken a number of photographs during Barsanti's excavations, and he made these available to Lauer for the publication, although neither Barsanti nor Lacau had made any sort of inventory.[88] While one cannot rule out the possibility that Firth also discovered prisoner statues, it would seem that currently the evidence only supports Barsanti finding at least one fragment.[89] Lauer did not discover any additional prisoner statue fragments, and he never located the fragment captured in Lacau's photograph. Today the fragment remains lost, and the total number of fragments from this complex is still completely unknown.

Figure 2.5. Prisoner statue fragment from the mortuary temple of Unas in Saqqara, Fifth Dynasty. Photograph courtesy of the Institut français d'archéologie orientale.

Lacau's photograph depicts the torso of a prisoner statue. There are no measurements for this fragment, but based on the image alone, his body appears to be quite short and squat, particularly in comparison to Djedkare's prisoner statues. The torso seems to be fairly roughly modeled, with a deep incision marking the abdominal muscles and a large navel. The upper line of a kilt or belt may run across his torso, below

---

83. Inv. N. 3122, Box 48, Varille Collection, Egyptological Library and Archives, Università degli Studi di Milano, Milan, Italy.

84. This is based on my approximate measurements using scales in the photographs and Megahed's measurements (Mohamed Megahed, "Sculptures from the Pyramid Complex of Djedkare Isesi at South Saqqara: A Preliminary Report," *Prague Egyptological Studies* 17 [2016]: 26). See the catalogue (C.2.1–C.2.4) for the exact and approximate measurements: https://doi.org/10.5913/2022877.

85. Alexandre Barsanti, "Rapports de M. Alexandre Barsanti sur les déblaiements opérés autour de la pyramide d'Ounas pendant les années 1899–1901," *ASAE* 2 (1901): 244–57; Alexandre Barsanti and Gaston Maspero, "Fouilles autour de la pyramide d'Ounas," *ASAE* 1 (1901): 150–90; and Alexandre Barsanti and Gaston Maspero, "Fouilles autour de la Pyramide d'Ounas (1902–1903)," *ASAE* 5 (1904): 69–83.

86. Cecil Firth, "Report on the Excavations of the Department of Antiquities at Saqqara (November, 1929–April, 1930)," *ASAE* 30 (1930): 185–89.

87. Audran Labrousse, Jean-Philippe Lauer, and Jean Leclant, *Le temple haut de complexe funéraire du roi Ounas*, MAFS 2, BiEtud 73 (Cairo: Institut français d'archéologie orientale, 1977), 131 and pl. XL, doc. 133.

88. Labrousse, Lauer, and Leclant, 73 n. 4.

89. I found no record of whether or not Firth excavated prisoner statues fragments from the complex of Unas.

the navel. Only the right arm is visible in the photograph. His elbow is set much lower than the elbows of Djedkare's prisoner statues; it is at the level of his navel with his forearm connecting to the side of his right hip. This indicates that the arm was not pulled back as sharply, though there is some stone representing negative space between the body and arm. However, the bonds were executed in the same fashion (with two plain strands of rope) and in the same position (directly above the elbow and elbow crease) as the Djedkare prisoner statues. Unfortunately, it is impossible to know, based on the angle of the photograph, whether this statue had a back pillar.

2.2.4. Teti

In 1906, James Quibell began work at Teti's complex, and it was during his excavations there in 1908 that he discovered the fragmentary bust of a prisoner statue (Saqqara, Imhotep Museum JE 40047; C.4.1), though at the time he did not recognize it as a statue of a bound captive (fig. 2.6).[90] Most of the prisoner's left shoulder is missing, but the position of his right shoulder is unusual. Rather than being pulled back, as is typical for the prisoner statues, his right shoulder is held straight, and the very small remaining portion of the right arm is actually set slightly in front of the shoulder. Therefore, the elbow could not have been set behind his back, and likely not even straight against his side, but must have been slightly in front of his body.

The only known prisoner statues whose arms were not pulled behind them were those from the Niuserre complex. As I discussed above, their upper arms hung down straight along their sides because of the wide back pillars behind them (fig. 2.1). Yet the bonds around their arms made their restrained position clear. On the other hand, the Teti prisoner statues have no back pillars. Thus, there was no compositional reason to adjust the position of the arm. Unfortunately, not enough remains of the left shoulder to determine whether it was in the same position. Moreover, the other preserved prisoner statue fragment from the Teti complex, which I discuss in more detail below, includes a left elbow that is pulled behind the body (fig. 2.7). Therefore, the right shoulder and arm of JE 40047 may have been poorly executed or an artists' mistake that resulted in an awkward angle and position of the arm and elbow. However, it is also possible that this statue, which certainly still should be categorized as a prisoner statue based on his facial features and hairstyle, as I elaborate in chapter 3.1.3, was in a slightly different position, perhaps with his arms bound in front of his body.[91] Indeed, his shoulders and neck, which seem to be slightly rounded or hunched, may suggest a different uncomfortable or submissive position.

---

90. Saqqara, Imhotep Museum JE 40047. James Quibell, *Excavations at Saqqara, 1906–1907*, SAE (Cairo: Institut français d'archéologie orientale, 1908) and James Quibell, *Excavations at Saqqara, 1907–1908*, SAE (Cairo: Institut français d'archéologie orientale, 1909). For the identification of this fragment as a prisoner statue, see ch. 3.1.3. The archive of Quibell's work at Saqqara is largely complete at the Egyptological Library and Archives of the Università degli Studi di Milano; for more on this archive, see Christian Orsenigo, "Digging at Sakkara in Milan: The James E. Quibell Archive," *KMT* 27.4 (Winter 2016–2017): 32–44 and Christian Orsenigo, "James E. Quibell Records on Saqqara in the Archives of Alexandre Varille," in Bárta, Coppens, and Krejčí, *Abusir and Saqqara...2015*, 675–84. However, the only mention of the prisoner statue fragment is in a 1907–1910 notebook listing objects sent to the Egyptian Museum. This notebook page is also duplicated in Patrizia Piacentini, "The Preservation of Antiquities: Creation of Museums in Egypt during the Nineteenth Century," in *Egypt and the Pharaohs: Pharaonic Egypt in the Archives and Libraries of the Università degli Studi di Milano*, vol. 2, ed. Patrizia Piacentini (Milan: Università degli Studi di Milano, 2011), 34–35. Interestingly, the archive also contains a photograph of one of the prisoner statue fragments that Gustave Jéquier later excavated at the pyramid complex of Pepi II (see C.6.8).

91. Foreigners bound with their arms in front of their bodies can be seen in the reliefs from the pyramid complex of Sahure (see Berlin, ÄM 21782 and Ludwig Borchardt, *Das Grabdenkmal des Königs Sahu-re*, 2 vols., Ausgrabungen der Deutschen Orient-Gesellschaft in Abusir 1902–1908 6–7, WVDOG 14, 26 [Leipzig: Hinrichs, 1910–1913], 2:Bl. 5–7).

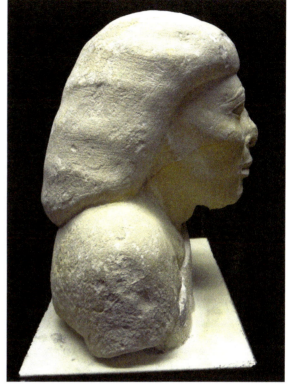

Figure 2.6. Prisoner statue bust from the mortuary temple of Teti in Saqqara, Sixth Dynasty. Saqqara, Imhotep Museum JE 40047. Photographs: Tara Prakash, courtesy of the Imhotep Museum.

Several decades later, the Mission archéologique française de Saqqâra (MAFS) began excavating Teti's pyramid complex.[92] In January of 1966, under the direction of Jean-Philippe Lauer and Jean Leclant, they uncovered a small fragment of a prisoner statue's left arm and torso (Bloc 64; C.4.2; fig. 2.7).[93] The left arm is clearly pulled back and held against the body, with the forearm running down the side of his hip. Like the Unas prisoner statue, the elbow of Bloc 64 is set at waist height. The right arm is no longer preserved. For this reason, it is possible that this fragment does belong with the bust Quibell discovered, which is missing its left arm. If this were the case, the arms of this prisoner statue might be in different positions, with the right arm (Quibell's fragment, JE 40047) slightly in front of the body and the left arm (Lauer and Leclant's fragment, Bloc 64) pulled back behind the body. Although there is a chance that a prisoner statue could have had arms in different positions, it is much more likely that Bloc 64 is actually part of a second prisoner statue from the Teti complex.

The bonds of Bloc 64 have been further simplified from those of the earlier prisoner statues and are now only plain bands on either arm, but their position has not changed, and they still run above the elbow crease and the elbow. For the first time, a restraint securing the prisoner's arms behind his back is visible. This is a plain bar that extends out from the arm bonds along the back between the elbows. While the Unas prisoner statue may have had something similar to this as well, one cannot be sure, in the same way that

---

92. The project is now the Mission archéologique franco-suisse de Saqqâra.
93. Jean-Philippe Lauer and Jean Leclant, *Le temple haut du complexe funéraire du roi Teti*, MAFS 1, BiEtud 51 (Cairo: Institut français d'archéologie orientale, 1972) 3, 84, and 98–99 and fig. 73. This is currently located in SCA Saqqara Store Magazine 1.

Figure 2.7. Drawing of a prisoner statue fragment (Bloc 64) from the mortuary temple of Teti in Saqqara; Sixth Dynasty. Courtesy of the MAFS.

one cannot know whether or not he had a back pillar, since the fragment is lost and Lacau's photograph only shows its front.

Between the excavations of Quibell and the MAFS, Cecil Firth also worked at Teti's pyramid complex from 1920 until 1924. Unfortunately, he never managed to fully publish his findings before his unexpected death in 1931.[94] His first archaeological report, which he wrote while his work around the Teti pyramid was still under way, included only four pages on the king's monument based on the research that he had conducted there up until 1922. In this, he made no mention of prisoner statue fragments, though he did note that he had found very few objects that dated to the original construction and use of the monument, repeating a comment that Quibell had also made before him.[95] However, Firth's archive at the Institut français d'archéologie orientale (IFAO) includes the unpublished manuscript of a final archaeological report that he wrote following his excavations in the Teti pyramid cemetery.[96] In chapter 1, Firth noted that he had found fragments of prisoner statues among debris filling a deep shaft to the north of Teti's mortuary temple (C.4.3).[97] These originally must have been erected inside the king's monument. In later publications, Lauer also briefly mentioned the discovery of other very mutilated prisoner statue fragments at the complex of Teti, but he did not include any reference to the excavator or the excavation date.[98] These very mutilated fragments to which Lauer referred are likely the same that Firth discovered in the early 1920s.

---

94. Lauer and Leclant, 4.

95. Cecil Firth and Battiscombe Gunn, *Teti Pyramid Cemeteries*, SAE (Cairo: Institut français d'archéologie orientale, 1926), 8 and Quibell, *Excavations…1907–1908*, 20. Firth repeats this on page 5 in ch. 1 of his unpublished manuscript ("Excavations at Saqqara: Teti Pyramid Cemeteries II, Archaeological Report" MS, Box 1, Cecil Firth fonds, Archives scientifiques, Institut français d'archéologie orientale, Cairo, Egypt).

96. Firth, "Excavations at Saqqara: Teti Pyramid Cemeteries II, Archaeological Report" MS, Box 1, Firth fonds.

97. The pages are unnumbered. This comment appears on page 5 of ch. 1, which is focused on the mortuary temple of Teti. Firth underlined "some pieces of statues of prisoners" and "debris filling the deep shaft," but the significance of the underlining is unclear. Battiscombe Gunn worked with Firth at the Teti pyramid complex, but Gunn's Archive at the Griffith Institute, University of Oxford does not include any references to or drawings of the prisoner statue fragments that Firth discovered.

98. Jean-Philippe Lauer, "Recherches et travaux à Saqqarah (campagnes 1967–1968 et 1968–1969)," *CRAIBL* 113 (1969): 477 and Jean-Philippe Lauer, "Travaux et découvertes à Saqqarah (campagne 1968–1969)," *BSFE* 56 (1969): 22.

Unfortunately, I have been unable to locate these fragments or any images of them. For this reason, it is currently impossible to estimate exactly how many prisoner statues originally decorated Teti's pyramid complex. Moreover, one cannot approximate the full height of Teti's prisoner statues either. However, the height of JE 40047 (C.4.1) is 19 cm, and its width is 20 cm; the height and width of the head alone is 14 cm and 15 cm, respectively.

2.2.5. Pepi I

The MAFS, originally under the direction of Lauer and Leclant and later under Labrousse, began excavating Pepi I's pyramid and mortuary temple in South Saqqara in the mid-1960s.[99] From 1968–1988, they discovered over seventy-nine prisoner statue fragments around this king's mortuary temple (C.5.1–C.5.71; figs. 2.8–2.21, 3.4–3.13, and 5.1).[100] These belong to at least sixteen and probably closer to twenty prisoner statues, making the number of concretely attested statues at Pepi I's complex significantly higher than that for any of his predecessors.[101] This sizeable number, which should be seen as a minimum since it remains possible that additional statues and fragments are no longer preserved, contrasts with the meager remains from the earlier pyramid complexes and strongly suggests that Pepi I originally commissioned more prisoner statues than his predecessors.

The Pepi I prisoner statues were carved from two different types of local limestone: a flaky, white limestone and a grayish limestone that is much heavier and denser (compare figs. 2.9 and 2.10).[102] The fragments

---

99. For the history of excavations at this complex, see Audran Labrousse, *Le temple funéraire du roi Pépy Ier: Le temps de la construction*, MAFS 6, MIFAO 137 (Cairo: Institut français d'archéologie orientale, 2019), 3–8. See also Audran Labrousse, "Les complexes funéraires du roi Pépi Ier et de trois reines," *Les dossiers d'archéologie* 146–147 (1990): 80–87 and Jean Leclant, *Recherches dans la pyramide et au temple haut du pharaon Pepi Ier, à Saqqarah* (Leiden: Nederland Instituut voor het Nabije Oosten, 1979), 17–23.

100. These fragments are mostly divided between the MAFS storeroom at Saqqara and SCA Saqqara Store Magazine 1, with two fragments likely now in the El-Arish National Museum (see C.5.3 and C.5.10). The number of fragments must remain approximate because connecting fragments were often reattached and assigned a single registration number, and the details of how fragments connected were often not fully recorded. However, the excavators assigned seventy-three registration numbers. The MAFS team assigned all prisoner statue fragments a PP (Pépy Prisonniers) number. Those fragments that were sent to the SCA storeroom were also registered with a FE (French Excavation) number. Throughout this book I refer to the PP numbers, but see the catalogue for the appropriate FE numbers: https://doi.org/10.5913/2022877. The MAFS still holds unpublished photographs, drawings, and brief notes for the excavated fragments. I am very thankful to Philippe Collombert, the current director of the MAFS, for making these available to me. The archive of Jean-Philippe Lauer at the IFAO does not include any additional material relating to the prisoner statues, and unfortunately, I was not able to learn any further information concerning his small archive at the Institut de France. The Jean Leclant archive at the College de France only includes material on the Pyramid Texts from his work in Saqqara, and his archive that will be going to the Institut de France was still in his widow's possession at the time of my research and writing.

101. Audran Labrousse recently calculated the number of prisoner statues at the Pepi I complex to be up to 584 based on the hypothesis that they stood side by side under every triumph scene in the mortuary temple (Labrousse, *Temple funéraire*, 57). He estimated the total length of such relief scenes, despite the fact that the excavators only discovered a relatively small number of scattered fragments from them, and multiplied this by the average width of the prisoner statues' bases. However, there is no reason to assume that prisoner statues were lined up directly next to each other underneath every triumph scene. Moreover, any reconstruction of the wall reliefs from this pyramid complex is highly tentative because so few fragments were discovered and none of the reliefs were still intact. The number of excavated prisoner statues fragments from this complex suggests that Labrousse's estimate is much too high. I discuss the triumph scenes from this complex and their relationship to the prisoner statues in detail in ch. 4.

102. There is some variation in the color of each limestone type. For example, some fragments of dense, gray limestone are darker than others. However, the primary and most clear differentiation is between the flaky, white and dense, gray limestones. Concerning the limestones used in Saqqara, see Dietrich Klemm and Rosemarie Klemm, *The Stones of the Pyra-*

Figure 2.8. Prisoner statues from the pyramid complex of Pepi I in Saqqara following the 1968–1969 excavation season. Lauer and Leclant, "Découverte," pl. 8 A.

carved from the gray limestone were often better polished and finished than those carved from the white limestone. Both types of limestone were plastered and painted, though in some cases, the paint may have been applied directly to the stone, without a layer of plaster.[103] Overall, the paint jobs are rather sloppy (e.g., there seems to have been no effort to paint the restraints a different color from the skin) and thus seem to have been done relatively quickly. Many of the bodies appear to have traces of a dark orangey-red paint (figs. 2.9 and 2.11). Several of the bodies may have also been covered with a darker or blackish layer of paint applied on top of the red (fig. 2.12). The skin color of these prisoner statues likely relates to their ethnicity, and I return to this idea in the following chapter. Additionally, the bottoms of at least some of the bases also may have been plastered and painted a reddish color similar to the dark orangey-red color found on the skin, although further analysis is necessary to prove that this is original pigment and not subsequent accumulations (fig. 2.13).[104] The color red could have apotropaic qualities in ancient Egypt, and

---

mids: Provenance of the Building Stones of the Old Kingdom Pyramids of Egypt (Berlin: de Gruyter, 2010), 136–37 and Ashley Cooke, *The Architecture of Mastaba Tombs in the Unas Cemetery*, The Munro Archive Project: Studies on the Unas Cemetery in Saqqara 1 (Leiden: Sidestone, 2020), 46–52.

103. Further study and technical analysis is necessary to determine whether all of the coloration remaining on the Pepi I prisoner statues is indeed from ancient pigment and to draw conclusions on what the pigments might have been and how the statues were originally painted. Thus my remarks regarding paint remain tentative.

104. For example, PP 39 (C.5.39) and PP 45 (C.5.45).

Figure 2.9. Prisoner statue fragment (PP 56) from the pyramid complex of Pepi I in Saqqara; Sixth Dynasty. Photograph: Tara Prakash, courtesy of the MAFS.

Figure 2.10. Prisoner statue fragment (PP 59) from the pyramid complex of Pepi I in Saqqara; Sixth Dynasty. Photograph: Tara Prakash, courtesy of the MAFS.

Figure 2.11. Prisoner statue fragment (PP 46) from the pyramid complex of Pepi I in Saqqara; Sixth Dynasty. Photograph: Tara Prakash, courtesy of the MAFS.

Figure 2.12. Prisoner statue fragment (PP 41) from the pyramid complex of Pepi I in Saqqara; Sixth Dynasty. Photograph: Tara Prakash, courtesy of the MAFS.

Figure 2.13. Prisoner statue fragment (PP 45) from the pyramid complex of Pepi I in Saqqara; Sixth Dynasty. Photograph: Tara Prakash, courtesy of the MAFS.

scholars have argued that it was used on areas of later coffins to protect the deceased within the coffin.[105] If the bottom of the prisoner statues had been painted red, it may have had a similar function—not to protect the statue but to protect and divide it from the consecrated temple ground on which it stood.[106]

---

105. John H. Taylor, "Patterns of Colouring on Ancient Egyptian Coffins from the New Kingdom to the Twenty-Sixth Dynasty: An Overview," in *Colour and Painting in Ancient Egypt*, ed. William Vivian Davies (London: British Museum Press, 2001), 176 and Anders Bettum, "Nesting: The Development and Significance of the 'Yellow Coffin' Ensemble," in *Proceedings First Vatican Coffin Conference 19–22 June 2013*, vol. 1, ed. Alessia Amenta and Hélème Guichard (Città del Vaticano: Edizioni Musei Vaticani, 2017), 78.

106. Kathlyn Cooney first suggested this idea to me, and I am grateful to her for discussing it with me.

The statues consistently have their arms pulled and bound behind their backs, although the exact position of the elbows and their level along the torso varies. For the first time, it is clear that *some* of the statues are also bending forward at the waist, though this is not the case for all of them. This seems to be an attempt to convey better the discomfort of their position and the sharp degree to which their arms have been pulled behind their backs, causing them to lean forward. The statues also tend to have fairly flat chests and backs with minimal modeling.[107]

The hands are always held in fists with the thumbs depicted. Almost all of the fists have a clear depression with a small, round peg-like object in their center. Similar peg-like objects are often found in the hands of Egyptian stone statues, and scholars have debated how to interpret them. It is quite possible that the object is an abstracted staff, or an emblematic indicator of status, as Marianne Eaton-Krauss has contended.[108] However, Henry Fischer argued against these explanations, noting that the peg-like objects are also sometimes found in the hands of women, children, and the prisoner statues. For a number of reasons, including their shape, color, and his belief that the Egyptians were not prone to symbolic abstraction in other cases, Fischer proposed that these elusive objects are actually bolts of cloth. In his opinion, cloth could lend itself to a variety of uses and therefore it was not surprising to find a piece of cloth occasionally in the hands of women, children, or prisoners, who would not ordinarily be expected to hold a staff or baton.[109]

But there are several important differences that Fischer overlooked between the peg-like objects that the prisoner statues hold and most of those that are found in the hands of other Egyptian statues. Perhaps most notable is their shape. Fischer noted that as a rule, the rounded peg-like object projects at both ends of the fist and cites only a handful of examples where the object projects only in the front or does not project at all.[110] On the other hand, the peg-like objects that the Pepi I prisoner statues hold never extend out the back of their fists and often barely project from the front of their fists.[111] Indeed, the carving of the peg-like objects among the Pepi I statues was not consistent. Some statues, namely, PP 24 (C.5.24) and PP 35 (C.5.35), did not have them, while others, particularly PP 4 (C.5.4), held a very clearly differentiated peg-like object (fig. 2.17).[112] Moreover, in regard to statues of Egyptians, Fischer observed that only in a few cases were the peg-like objects painted the same color as the hands that hold them. In most cases, they seem to have been painted white or left unpainted.[113] Yet, for the Pepi I prisoner statues, the peg-like objects seem to have been generally painted the same color as the hands that hold them.

Because of these differences, the peg-like object that the prisoner statues hold is likely not the same as the one that many male statues of Egyptians hold, and Fischer's proposal that all Egyptian statues are holding a bolt of cloth is problematic. To my knowledge, there are no typical associations between foreigners or prisoners and cloth, and there is no reason to think that this is what the prisoner statues hold. It is possible that the prisoner statues' peg-like objects are emblematic staffs or staves meant to reference their status as foreign leaders, as the different peg-like objects probably do for statues of Egyptian males. But

---

107. PP 66 (C.5.64), whose chest and back is rounded and nicely modeled, is an exception.

108. Marianne Eaton-Krauss, "The Location of Inscriptions on Statues of the Old Kingdom," in *Sitting beside Lepsius: Studies in Honour of Jaromir Malek at the Griffith Institute*, ed. Diana Magee, Janine Bourriau, and Stephen Quirke (Leuven: Peeters, 2009), 132 n. 20.

109. Henry Fischer, "An Elusive Shape within the Fisted Hands of Egyptian Statues," *MMJ* 10 (1975): 9–21.

110. Fischer, 11 and 11 n. 5.

111. The shape of the peg-like objects of two Pepi II statues is the same, as I discuss in the next section.

112. Interestingly, PP 24 and PP 35 are not very well carved or finished.

113. Fischer, "Elusive Shape," 12–13. However, Fischer did mention that the cases that he observed where the peg-like objects were not painted differently could be due to negligence on the part of the painter, which could also be the case for the prisoner statues.

Figure 2.14. Prisoner statue body (PP 1) from the pyramid complex of Pepi I in Saqqara; Sixth Dynasty. Photographs courtesy of the MAFS.

since the object does not extend on both sides of the prisoner statues' fists, in *any* example, and it was not consistently carved, it is more conceivable that what the prisoner statues hold is not an object at all, but rather the artists roughly carved this form, a form with which they were familiar, to fill the space within the fists. In this case, the peg-like object actually represents negative space.

The carving of the Pepi I prisoner statues' fingers and the position of their fists along their legs varies. Five of the fragments have fingers, while for those fragments without fingers, the fist was simply depicted as a plain ball with a long thumb (fig. 2.18).[114] The fists were most often placed on the side of the thighs or hips. The variant positions, with either the thumb or the entire fist on top of the lap, mostly occur for fragments with poor proportions and modeling, except for PP 4 (C.5.4; fig. 2.17). The higher the fist was set against the legs, the more the elbows of the prisoner were pulled back. In doing this, the artists appear to have been trying to emphasize the discomfort and pain of the prisoners. However, as the elbows were pulled further back, the stone representing negative space between the body and arms increased, and the overall impression was not necessarily more effective or evocative. PP 3 (C.5.3) is a good example in this regard (fig. 2.16).

---

114. PP 3 (C.5.3), PP 6 (C.5.6), PP 7 (C.5.7), PP 8 (C.5.8), and PP 10 (C.5.10) have fingers.

Figure 2.15. Prisoner statue body (PP 2) from the pyramid complex of Pepi I in Saqqara; Sixth Dynasty. Photograph: Mario Carrieri, Milan/The Menil Foundation.

Often the carving of the bonds was not fully executed, particularly along the front of the arm. Indeed, the bonds of the Pepi I statues are particularly interesting because of their variability. The arms of some statues are bound with strands of rope, others have a plain band serving as the bonds, and still others have a combination of rope and band bonds (compare figs. 2.14–2.17 and 2.19). In these latter instances, they give the impression that the artists simply ran out of time before they had finished carving all of the individual ropes. In the cases where the rope bonds were completed, the number of strands could vary between three and four, with four being more common. Generally, if the statue has band arm bonds, it has a plain bar representing a restraint along its back (fig. 2.16). On the other hand, if it has rope arm bonds, it has lashings, in which the horizontal strands of rope across the arms connect to vertical strands of rope along the back, as though the vertical rope is wrapped around a pole between the elbows (fig. 2.14). But once again there are exceptions, which gives the impression that the artists ran out of time before they were able to finish detailing the arm bonds and lashings. This variability in types and executions seems to indicate that these details did not matter as long as the overall impression of being bound was the same.

The knees are squared and geometric, and all of the feet are curled underneath. On three statues individual toes were carved splayed on the ground, visible from the side of the statue, and on two other statues, lines indicating toes were carved on the back of the feet (fig. 2.20).[115] Only PP 1 (C.5.1) had both types of toes carved, which created an extremely unnatural effect (fig. 2.14). Generally, toes are less common; most of the statues (seven) simply have plain feet that curl under.

The feet rest on roughly carved, uneven, rectangular bases. These bases generally extend on all sides of the statue, though the amount of extension varies greatly.[116] The bases of the Pepi I statues may be another new development; certainly the Djedkare statues and likely the Niuserre statues, which both have back pillars, did not have integral bases. Once again, it is impossible to know whether the Unas and Teti statues had bases, but if the presence of an integral base correlates with the lack of a back pillar, it is likely that the Teti statues had bases, since they do not have back pillars. There was no desire to make the Pepi I bases uniform, and they range in size. Height varies between 7 and 12 cm, width varies between 23 and 32 cm, and depth varies between 36 and 55 cm. Even the height, width, or depth of a single base could vary up to 5 cm from side to side. The size of the bases could be related to their original placement, but the variation

---

115. PP 1 (C.5.1), PP 2 (C.5.2), and PP 9 (C.5.9) had toes carved on the fronts of their feet, and PP 1 (C.5.1) and PP 8 (C.5.8) had toes carved on the backs of their feet.

116. The base of PP 35 (A.5.35) is the only example that does not fully extend, specifically in the back while the front and sides do extend, but this statue was very poorly executed.

Figure 2.16. Prisoner statue body and head (PP 3 and 23) from the pyramid complex of Pepi I in Saqqara; Sixth Dynasty. Photographs courtesy of the MAFS.

within the measurements of single bases also suggests that this was another detail that the artists, their overseers, and/or their patron felt they did not need to standardize.

The clothing of the Pepi I prisoner statues is more simplified and uniform than earlier statues, as all of the Pepi I statues wear the same type of plain short kilt. There is no pattern or elaboration on these, in contrast to the incised hem of the kilts of the Djedkare prisoner statues (see fig. 2.3). The vast majority of fragments have the bottom of the kilt depicted in relief (figs. 2.15, 2.16, and 2.18).[117] In other words, the kilt is raised above the level of the thighs. Three fragments only have a simple line incised along the bottom of the kilt (fig. 2.17).[118] Two other fragments have no indication on the legs that the kilt has ended, but the triangle of stone representing negative space between both thighs makes the kilt clear (fig. 2.14).[119] Six of the fragments have their legs spread apart, while most fragments have their legs together (compare figs. 2.14–2.18).[120] The length of the kilts varies from halfway down the thighs to just above the knee. Some fragments have belts, for others the kilt seamlessly transitions into the torso, and still others have a line marking the top of the kilt, rather than a full belt (compare figs. 2.14–2.18 and 2.21). However, these minor variations seem to be

---

117. Because of the location of the break, PP 10 (C.5.10) may have had his kilt indicated with relief.
118. This is PP 4 (C.5.4), PP 5 (C.5.5), and PP 39 (C.5.39).
119. See PP 1 (C.5.1) and PP 7 (C.5.7).
120. PP 1 (C.5.1), PP 3 (C.5.3), PP 7 (C.5.7), PP 38 (C.5.38), PP 59 (C.5.57), and PP 72 (C.5.70) have their legs spread.

Figure 2.17. Prisoner statue fragments (PP 4) from the pyramid complex of Pepi I in Saqqara; Sixth Dynasty. Photograph courtesy of the MAFS.

the result of either different hands or unsystematic workmanship that was less concerned with carving identical or fully finished statues, rather than being an explicit attempt to depict different types of clothing. Therefore, unlike the complicated and varying costumes that the Djedkare statues wear, the dress of the Pepi I prisoner statues is basic and consistent.

Clearly, there is a high degree of variability in the modeling, details, and polishing of the Pepi I prisoner statues, and overall, the fragments give the impression that the artists never finished carving the statues. The basic shape of the body parts was always carved, but the level of musculature and naturalism varies. For example, the back can be simply a flat surface, a straight line could be carved down the center of this flat surface to suggest that the arms are pulled back and that the back is constricted, or the trapezius muscles can be rounded. In regard to the proportions of the statues, the legs are usually too long for the size of the upper body, the lower legs are often too large for the thickness of the upper legs, the knees tend to be big, and the feet are always much too large in comparison to the rest of the body.

Certain fragments have details, such as nipples, fingers, and toes, incised, while others do not. In some cases, the less detailed fragments are nicely polished and finished, suggesting that the artists of these statues had a degree of choice and prioritized finishing their surface rather than adding details. It also demonstrates that identical details, as well as fully carved and polished statues, were apparently not necessary. Rather the overall position of the bodies was the primary concern, and the exact representation of the kilt or bonds or hands and feet did not matter.

The backs of the fragments were consistently less finished than the fronts. Regardless of how well finished the front of a statue might be, there are significantly more tool marks visible on the back. On the other hand, the back surfaces vary, with some being better finished than others, and this generally corresponds with the front surface (i.e., the better the front, the better the back). In many cases, the bases are also less finished than the rest of the statue, as was the stone representing negative space between the lower leg and the base. The upper bodies tend to be better finished than the lower bodies, and tool marks are almost always visible in crevices or areas that were harder to polish, such as between the arm and body or between the legs. The degree to which the surfaces of some of the larger fragments and joined fragments could vary from area to area is striking. For example, most of the legs and kilt of PP 9 (C.5.9) were well polished, as was the front half of the top of his base. But his back, feet, the back of his base, and the stone representing negative space are extremely rough. Similarly, the upper legs, buttocks, and top of the base of PP 8 (C.5.8) were well polished in contrast to the rear portion of the sides of his base, his feet, and his lower legs, which were only barely differentiated from the unpolished stone representing negative space below them (fig. 2.20).

Figure 2.18. Prisoner statue fragment (PP 6) from the pyramid complex of Pepi I in Saqqara; Sixth Dynasty. Photograph courtesy of the MAFS.

Figure 2.19. Prisoner statue fragment (PP 14) from the pyramid complex of Pepi I in Saqqara; Sixth Dynasty. Photograph courtesy of the MAFS.

Figure 2.20. Prisoner statue fragment (PP 8) from the pyramid complex of Pepi I in Saqqara; Sixth Dynasty. Photograph courtesy of the MAFS.

The bodies of PP 1 (C.5.1), PP 2 (C.5.2), and PP 3 (C.5.3) are largely complete because the excavators were able to join multiple fragments (figs. 2.14–2.16). The height of these bodies is around 60 cm.[121] The height of the best preserved heads is around 20–21 cm, while their width is around 18–19 cm and their depth is around 20–22 cm. Therefore, the total height of the complete statues may have been approximately 80 cm, plus or minus up to 10 cm. Overall, the measurements of the smaller fragments are consistent with this overall height.

Figure 2.21. Prisoner statue fragment (PP 29) from the pyramid complex of Pepi I in Saqqara; Sixth Dynasty. Photograph: Tara Prakash, courtesy of the MAFS.

2.2.6. Pepi II

The Swiss Egyptologist Gustave Jéquier began excavating the pyramid complex of Pepi II in 1925, and he worked there until 1936.[122] During his excavations, Jéquier discovered an extremely large number of prisoner statue fragments, and it seems almost certain that Pepi II had more prisoner statues in his pyramid complex than any of his predecessors (C.6.1 and C.6.4–15; figs. 2.22–2.24, 3.14–3.24, and 5.2).[123] Appendix 1 in the third volume of

---

121. The maximum width and depth for all of the statues is that of the base, the measurements of which were discussed above.

122. Gustave Jéquier, *Le monument funéraire de Pépi II*, 3 vols., FouillesSaqq (Cairo: Institut français d'archéologie orientale, 1936–1940).

123. I have only included those fragments for which I have photographs in the catalogue: https://doi.org/10.5913/2022877. Five fragments were transferred to the Egyptian Museum in Cairo and are now in different museums across Egypt (Cairo, GEM 1101 [C.6.1]; Cairo, Egyptian Museum JE 57202 [C.6.4]; Cairo, National Military Museum JE 51730 [C.6.5]; Cairo, National Military Museum JE 51731 [C.6.6]; and Suez, Suez National Museum JE 51729 [C.6.7]). The vast majority of fragments

Jéquier's final report was specifically dedicated to the prisoner statue fragments and was the only place in his three-volume report that Jéquier mentioned them. It consists of only two and a half pages of text and two illustrative plates.[124] In this, Jéquier estimated that he had found the remains of approximately thirty statues but suggested that this probably only represented a small part of the total number.[125] Jéquier also very briefly discussed the statues in one of his annual preliminary excavation reports and in two other publications, including a summary of his research at Saqqara, in which he described finding innumerable fragments and suggested that the original number of prisoner statues should have been at least one hundred.[126] Moreover, he tantalizingly commented that the Pepi II prisoner statues could constitute a new chapter in the history of Egyptian art, if they were not so damaged.[127]

Jéquier never made any inventory of his findings and did not comprehensively record or photograph the statues as he excavated them. While I have been unable to confirm Jéquier's numbers, the material from Pepi II's complex in museum collections and the photographs that I have discovered attest to at least thirteen or fourteen prisoner statues.[128] This does not include many of the fragments that remain in the Egyptian storeroom. Even if one is wary of Jéquier's suggestions for the total number of statues being close to one hundred, there is presently no evidence that contradicts his estimate of finding fragments from around thirty statues, and with this number, Pepi II might have had almost double the number of statues as Pepi I.

In general, the Pepi II prisoner statues seem to be very high-quality sculptures. The carving was fully executed, and the surfaces were regularly finished and polished, though tool marks are sometimes visible on small areas that would have been more difficult to reach. While there are slight variations between the bodies, they are extremely uniform. The prisoners are all in the same position, and for the first time among the prisoner statues, the artists have succeeded in conveying the discomfort of the upper body. The elbows are tightly bound behind the back, creating tension in the shoulders, chest, and back and a slight paunchiness to the stomach. The prisoners lean forward a little at the waist, but the chest is pulled upwards from the tight binding of the elbows. This position is particularly apparent for JE 45782 (C.6.3; fig. 2.24), JE 51729 (C.6.7; fig. 2.23), and GEM 1101 (C.6.1; fig. 2.22). Some of Pepi I's artists were clearly trying to convey the same pain and discomfort, but their attempts were not as successful. For example, as I mentioned above, the elbows of PP 3 (C.5.3) are pulled well behind his torso and his rib cage juts forward, but his torso ends up looking unnatural, particularly from the sides, where there is now too much stone representing

---

were kept in the storeroom Jéquier constructed adjacent to Pepi II's mortuary temple for many years following their excavation but are now in SCA Saqqara Store Magazine no. 1. Unfortunately, at least one of these fragments (C.6.10) may have recently found its way onto the art market, perhaps following the Egyptian Revolution in 2011, when Jéquier's storeroom was disturbed.

124. Jéquier, *Monument funéraire*, 3:27–29 and pls. 47 and 48.

125. Jéquier, 3:28. In an earlier description, published in 1931, he mentioned having found around a dozen heads by that point in his work (Gustave Jéquier, "Planche 22," in *Documents pour servir à l'étude de l'art égyptien*, vol. 2, by Jean Capart [Paris: Les Éditions du Pégase, 1931], 22).

126. Gustave Jéquier, *Douze ans de fouilles dans la nécropole memphite: 1924–1956* (Neuchâtel: Université de Neuchâtel, 1940), 64–65; Jéquier, "Planche 22," 21–23; and Gustave Jéquier, "Rapport préliminaire sur les fouilles exécutées en 1926–1927 dans la partie méridionale de la nécropole memphite," *ASAE* 27 (1927): 60.

127. Jéquier, "Rapport préliminaire…1926–1927," 60.

128. This estimate does not include two other Pepi II prisoner statue fragments (from two different statues) that are now in the Egyptian Museum in Cairo, namely, JE 45781 (C.6.2) and JE 45782 (C.6.3). These were found in 1916, prior to Jéquier's excavations, likely around the pyramid of Queen Oudjebten. There are also three unprovenanced, reconstructed prisoner statues (London, BM EA 75198 [C.7.2]; New York, MMA 47.2 [C.7.3]; and New York, MMA 64.260 [C.7.4]) that can be attributed to the Pepi II pyramid complex (see further A.1).

Figure 2.22. Reconstructed prisoner statue from the pyramid complex of Pepi II in Saqqara; Sixth Dynasty. Cairo, GEM 1101. Photographs: Tara Prakash, courtesy of the Grand Egyptian Museum.

negative space between his arms and body (fig. 2.16). Furthermore, from the rear view, where his back is a completely flat surface, there is little sense that his elbows have been tightly lashed. While the back of JE 45781 (C.6.2) does seem to be flat, the backs of GEM 1101 (C.6.1) and JE 51729 (C.6.7) are well rounded (figs. 2.22 and 2.23). Moreover, the artists of JE 45782 (C.6.3) even incised lines across the back to indicate the flexed trapezius muscles (fig. 2.24).

The treatment of the torsos and shoulders of JE 45781 (C.6.2), JE 45782 (C.6.3), JE 51729 (C.6.7), GEM 1101 (C.6.1), C.6.8, and C.6.10 is extremely similar, while the torso of C.6.9 appears to be the most different, with pectorals that are more emphasized and a narrower waist. All of the arm restraints for the available Pepi II statues consist of thick strands of rope that were carved completely around the arm. It seems quite likely that all of these statues have four strands.[129] The back restraints have lashings, which were fully carved on all three sides (upper, outer, lower) of the mass between the elbows. However, there is some

---

129. The bonds of C.6.10 might be different, but this is inconclusive. At least three strands are visible on the right arm,

Figure 2.23. Reconstructed prisoner statue from the pyramid complex of Pepi II in Saqqara; Sixth Dynasty. Suez, Suez National Museum JE 51729. Photographs: Tara Prakash, courtesy of the Suez National Museum.

variation in the direction of the rope itself: the strands of GEM 1101 (C.6.1)'s lashing are vertical and perpendicular to the arm bonds, while those of JE 45782 (C.6.3) and JE 51729 (C.6.7) are slightly slanted toward the left (figs. 2.23 and 2.24).

Unfortunately, the lower bodies of only two statues, GEM 1101 (C.6.1) and JE 51729 (C.6.7), are currently available (figs. 2.22 and 2.23). But they were both very well carved and are consistent with each other. The prisoners kneel on small, thick bases of an even size whose surface has been roughly polished. Both bases have a height of 10 cm. The width and depth of the base of GEM 1101 (C.6.1) is 26 cm and 43 cm, respectively, while that of JE 51729 (C.6.7) is 23 cm and 37 cm, respectively. They both wear plain short

---

while two or three seem to be on the left arm, although this is difficult to determine in the photographs, and both arms are also clearly damaged.

kilts, which were depicted in high relief on top of the legs; and belts, although the belt of GEM 1101 (C.6.1) is wider and comes up higher on either side of his stomach. Their fists are held on either side of their thighs. Inside the fists are round, peg-like objects like those of the Pepi I prisoner statues, and fingers were carved on the outside of the fists. The right thumb of GEM 1101 (C.6.1) is preserved and includes a carefully incised fingernail. Their feet, in stark contrast to the large blocks that the Pepi I prisoner statues have for feet, were rounded and modeled from both the side and the back. They clearly curve under, and the two or three outermost toes are splayed out on the base. The overall proportions of the statues, particularly the feet in comparison to the rest of the body, are much more accurate than those of the Pepi I statues. In fact, the feet and lower legs are a little bit too small for the size of the heavy hips and buttocks, in contrast to the extremely large Pepi I feet.

Figure 2.24. Prisoner statue fragment from the pyramid complex of Pepi II in Saqqara; Sixth Dynasty. Cairo, Egyptian Museum JE 45782. Photograph courtesy of the Egyptian Museum.

GEM 1101 (C.6.1) is 82.5 cm tall while the height of JE 51729 (C.6.7) is 85 cm. The height of the heads, including beards, seems to have been generally around 20 cm, though the height of JE 45781's (C.6.2) head is 26 cm, including his beard. Therefore, there was some variation in the original sizes. The measurements of the smaller fragments are consistent with these numbers.

2.3. Changes and Similarities among the Prisoner Statues

There are clearly certain variations among the prisoner statues from each complex and even among those statues from a single complex, particularly that of Pepi I. These can be both minor and major. For example, a relatively minor change is the depiction of the arm bonds. The earliest fragments from the complex of Niuserre had four intricately carved strands of rope. The remaining statues from the complexes of Djedkare and Unas only have two strands of rope, with no carved details on them. A fragment from the complex of Teti indicates that at least one statue from this complex does not have strands of rope carved at all, but rather the bonds were depicted as a plain band across the arm. The statues from the complex of Pepi I have both types of bonds, namely, plain bands and rope. Moreover, for those statues with rope bonds from this complex, the number of strands varies between three and four. The statues from the Pepi II complex do not have the same variation. Rather all of the preserved fragments have four strands of rope carved. Regardless of this fluctuation, all of the prisoner statues seem to have had some sort of bonds carved on the arms. Clearly this was most important, and it was likely left to the artists to choose how to depict the bonds.

The variability of the bonds at the Pepi I complex further supports this interpretation. At this complex in particular, it is possible to get a sense of the choices left to the artists. For example, on some statues the artists depicted toes and fingers, while on other statues they did not. Clearly these features were not considered necessary. While the differences in the Pepi I prisoner statues' execution and detailing that I described above could be the marks of different artistic hands that worked on the statues (i.e., Artist A preferred to carve fingers but Artists B and C did not), they could also be the result of experimentation or extra time that an artist had with a statue.[130] In other words, Artist A sometimes carved fingers and sometimes he did not depending on how much time he spent with the statue.

A more major change among all of the prisoner statues concerns the back pillar and, as a result of it, the overall carving of the statues' position, which becomes more complicated and expressive over time. The statues from the Niuserre complex did not have their arms pulled back because of the wide back pillar behind them. Djedkare's artists adjusted this pillar, making it deeper and thinner, which enabled the prisoners' arms to be depicted painfully pulled far behind the back on either side of the pillar. With this new type of back pillar the prisoners' arms were further back and their elbows were higher than they would be in later statues without back pillars, as it was then necessary to lower the arms and keep them alongside the body in order to reduce the negative space, thus producing a more compact form. Without photographs of the backs of the Unas statues or the fragments themselves, one cannot say with certainty whether or not these statues had back pillars, but perhaps the squatter, compact nature of the fragment in the one available photograph along with the lower level of this fragment's elbow very tentatively suggests that it had no back pillar (C.3.1; fig. 2.5). Nevertheless, with the way that Djedkare's artists manipulated the pillar to better express the desired position of the statues, it may not be surprising that soon artists decided to completely do away with the pillar; certainly by the reign of Teti, this is the case. All of the Sixth Dynasty statues were carved fully in the round, which made their bound position more conspicuous. While some of Pepi I's artists attempted to depict the tension and pain of the torso, shoulders, and back as a result of the arms' position, the artists of Pepi II were the most successful in this regard.

The prisoner statues with back pillars may recall in form predynastic figurines attached to poles and the Hierakonpolis door socket that I described in chapter 1, as well as Late period statues of prisoners bound to poles, but it is less clear whether the symbolism was the same or similar (fig. 1.7).[131] Certainly, it is possible that the Old Kingdom Egyptians conceived of the pillar as a "pole" that further restricted the prisoner statues. On the other hand, the pillar was practical; it provided stability to the statue and may have been linked to the statues' role in the decoration of the pyramid complex. The fact that the later prisoner statues do not have pillars only further complicates the pillars' interpretation. I return to the various symbolic and conceptual implications of the back pillars and their disappearance in chapter 5.

The setting of the statues on an integral base might have begun at the same time that the back pillar vanished. Those statues that definitely have back pillars, from the complexes of Niuserre and Djedkare, do not have bases. They could have been set on some other type of base or platform within the pyramid complex or more likely, as there is no direct evidence for an external base and no need for one as the large back pillar probably was a sufficient means of stability, they could have simply been set on the ground, probably near or against a wall because of their back pillars. Unfortunately, there are no available lower body fragments from the complexes of Unas and Teti, so one cannot be certain when exactly the integral bases appeared. However, the Pepi I and Pepi II statues undeniably have bases, which the artists might have started carving in lieu of the back pillars. The bases of Pepi I are less evenly shaped, vary more in

---

130. Scholars generally believe that ancient Egyptian artists were organized in workshops, which Rita Freed has defined as "a group of artisans working cooperatively in the same place over a period of time and observing a common model" (Rita E. Freed, "Stela Workshops of Early Dynasty 12," in *Studies in Honor of William Kelly Simpson*, vol. 1, ed. Peter Der Manuelian [Boston: Museum of Fine Arts, 1996], 297). However, much less is known about how each workshop was organized, and undoubtedly there was significant variation across time and place. Moreover practices likely fluctuated among contemporary or neighboring workshops as well. Different master artists may have preferred to organize things according to their own unique preferences. A detailed study on the organization of the sculptors who carved a group of seated statues of the Middle Kingdom pharaoh Senusret I is Dohrmann, "Arbeitsorganisation."

131. See my discussion in ch. 1.3 for references.

size, and were often poorly finished. Moreover, based on the available examples, they are also frequently deeper and wider than those from the Pepi II complex. In any case, a correlation between the presence of a base and the lack of a back pillar does seem logical as the base would have served to stabilize and support the statues that did not have back pillars to do this.

In contrast to the increasing expressiveness of the position, there seems to be a decline in the bodies' detailing and elaboration over time. The twisted fibers of the rope bonds on Niuserre's prisoner statues were fully carved. Djedkare's prisoner statues wear complicated kilts, belts, and sashes. Neither of these features are present on the statues of Pepi I and Pepi II. These later statues all wear identical, plain short kilts. The only variation is the way in which the kilts were carved and their length. If these statues have belts, and there are numerous examples from the complex of Pepi I that do not, they are plain, wide ones. This declining interest in elaborating the bodies does not seem to have affected the heads, whose facial features and hairstyles were intricately carved in both the Fifth and Sixth Dynasties. I highlight this in chapter 3.

The number of statues certainly seems to have increased over time.[132] The archaeological evidence suggests that there were only a handful of statues in the earliest complexes, but by the reign of Pepi I, the pharaoh was commissioning large numbers of statues to be set up inside his complex. Pepi I had at least sixteen to twenty statues, and Pepi II likely had many more. Because of the scant data from the complexes of Unas and Teti, it is difficult to determine whether this number steadily increased or whether there instead was a big jump during the reign of Pepi I. Perhaps the meager remains would suggest that the number of statues at the Unas and Teti complexes was not overly large and was more in line with the number from the Niuserre and Djedkare complexes, but this is a highly tentative proposition.

In many ways, the poor carving and finishing of the Pepi I statues stands apart from the other prisoner statues, which in general were well executed. Moreover, one cannot argue that the increased number of statues resulted in poorer quality final products because the more numerous Pepi II statues were higher quality. All of the known Pepi II statues are better finished and executed than even the best Pepi I ones. Four rope bonds were uniformly carved; the rope lashings on the backs could be naturalistically slanted; the position is more expressive; more details were consistently depicted, including fingers, thumbnails, and toes; the bases are evenly shaped and sized; and the statues were fully carved and polished. It is difficult to understand why the Pepi I statues are so much more haphazard. Fully carved and polished statues, with identical details, were apparently not necessary at this complex, as I argued above. Rather the overall position of the bodies was the primary concern, and the exact representation of the kilt or bonds or hands and feet did not matter. For this reason, it is possible that the artists were working quickly or carelessly and that this is the primary explanation for the variation that I described above; the artists may have run out of time for some statues, or they may have simply not cared whether or not the statues were uniform.[133] The king himself or his high officials ultimately must have found the statues acceptable given that they were still used within Pepi I's complex, and the statues' level of execution and finishing may partly relate to the way in which they were used, as I further explore in chapter 5.

---

132. I first introduced this idea in Tara Prakash, "Enemies of the State: The Old Kingdom Prisoner Statues and Three-Dimensional Representations of Foreigners," *Bulletin of the American Research Center in Egypt* 208 (2016): 56 and Tara Prakash, "The Prisoner Statue 'Fragments' in Milano," *Egyptian & Egyptological Documents, Archives, Libraries* 5 (2015/2016): 26–27.

133. Concerning the need for sculptors to optimize their time and some of their methods for doing so, see Slawomir Rzepka, "Methods of Optimizing Sculptor's Work during the Old Kingdom," in *Egyptology at the Dawn of the Twenty-First Century: Proceedings of the Eighth International Congress of Egyptologists Cairo, 2000*, vol. 2, ed. Zahi Hawass (Cairo: The American University in Cairo Press, 2003), 467–73.

The size of the statues also appears to have fluctuated from complex to complex. There are no preserved measurements for the destroyed Niuserre fragments. Therefore, the size of the first prisoner statues is unknown. Moreover, I was unable to find any measurements for fragments from the Unas complex. Based on the available evidence, the largest statues may have been those from the complex of Djedkare, which were approximately 90–100 cm tall. The Pepi I and Pepi II statues, which themselves must have been close to the same size, ranging in height between 80–90 cm, seem to have been slightly smaller. It is also possible that the Pepi II statues were minutely taller than the Pepi I ones. The heads from these three complexes, namely, Djedkare, Pepi I, and Pepi II, were of a similar size, with an average height of about 20 cm. For this reason, the statues from the complex of Teti, whose full height cannot be estimated because of the scant remains and data, *may* have been slightly smaller, since the preserved head from this complex, JE 40047 (C.4.1), is only 14 cm tall.

These conclusions are speculative as they are based on the measurements of only some statues and a portion of these measurements are estimated. Furthermore, one should not assume that all of the statues from a single complex were the exact same size. In the same way that the size of the bases could have varied because of placement and original location, the overall statue sizes could have differed for the same reason. For example, at the complex of Pepi II, where statues were placed in multiple parts of the king's monument, as I discuss in chapter 4, statues placed in one part of the complex may have all been the same size while those set in a different area could have been smaller or larger. However, presently this scenario is only a theoretical possibility, and none of the preserved data supports it. Instead, there is no marked variation between the sizes of the statues within a single complex. Rather all of the statues from the same complex seem to have been around the same size, and the variation, which is relatively minor, is only between complexes.

2.4. The Prisoner Statues as Symbols of Kingship

That the prisoner statues appeared during the reign of Niuserre is perhaps not particularly surprising, given the significant number of innovations and developments that occurred in many aspects of Egyptian society and material culture around this time. These included changes in the central and provincial administration and royal and nonroyal funerary architecture, as I have described above. Overall, these changes reflect evolving conceptions and expressions of kingship.[134] Indeed, Bárta has argued that Niuserre's reign was a turning point, which initiated a long, slow decline throughout the rest of the Old Kingdom. The central administration lost more and more power and influence to increasingly wealthy elite families, despite each king's various efforts to reestablish control and authority. By the end of the Sixth Dynasty, according to Bárta, the royal institution and the capital had effectively lost control of the provinces.[135] Many of the dramatic changes that occurred in the middle of the Fifth Dynasty do seem closely tied to Niuserre, and this king clearly had an important role in the subsequent development of the Old Kingdom. However, whether these changes actually marked a decline that ultimately led to the end of the Old Kingdom is more uncertain, and I will return to this question below.

---

134. See also here Bárta and Dulíková, "Divine and Terrestrial," 32–35.

135. For Bárta's arguments, which he has articulated in a number of places, see especially Bárta, "Ancient Egyptian History," 8–12; Bárta, "Architectural Innovations;" Bárta, "Kings," 167–75; Bárta, "Egyptian Kingship," 262–78; and Miroslav Bárta, "Temporary and Permanent: Status Race and the Mechanism of Change in a Complex Civilization: Ancient Egypt in between 2900 and 2120 BC," in *Crisis to Collapse: The Archaeology of Social Breakdown*, ed. Tim Cunningham and Jan Driessen (Louvain-la-Neuve: Presses universitaires de Louvain, 2017), 285–88.

Chapter 2: The Evolution of the Prisoner Statues during the Late Old Kingdom   57

The prisoner statues appear to be another innovation of Niuserre, emerging during a dynamic period of Egyptian history, and as chapter 4 will demonstrate, they fit with this king's experimentation in the decoration, particularly the three-dimensional decoration, of his pyramid complex. The architecture and decoration of the pyramid complex seemed to become increasingly symbolic and significant throughout the Fifth Dynasty, as the sheer size and monumentality of the complex became less important. Consequently, kings experimented with new motifs, forms, and structures that could better convey the evolving conceptions of kingship. The prisoner statues were one of these. Interestingly, this architectural and decorative experimentation was not only evident in royal funerary architecture, but also mid-Fifth Dynasty elite funerary architecture, as the tomb of Ptahshepses demonstrates. The reign of Niuserre marked an overall new interest in architectural creativity. I return to the other ways in which this manifested in Niuserre's pyramid complex in chapter 4.

Janet Richards recognized a major shift between the Fifth and Sixth Dynasties, more so than that which occurred from the Fourth to the Fifth Dynasty.[136] However, the prisoner statues are one of the features that link these periods. In many ways, they reflect the broader atmosphere of late Old Kingdom society. As large-scale depictions of defeated foreigners, they were powerful testaments to the king's supremacy and dominance. This is likely the primary reason why Niuserre's successors not only continued carving prisoner statues but also began to devote more and more resources to them. This becomes particularly apparent during the reign of Pepi I, who probably erected significantly more prisoner statues than any of his predecessors. With Pepi II, not only did the number of statues increase dramatically again, but their quality did as well.

By the Sixth Dynasty, the power dynamics of the central administration seemed to be shifting with the king realizing the influence and wealth of the high officials who surrounded him. Many of the policies and actions of these kings seem to reflect an effort to appease these men and their families while also trying to rein them in and control them. For example, Pepi I and Pepi II's practice of marrying elite women from influential private families clearly benefitted these families, increasing their prominence, but it also pulled the elite closer to the central administration. At the same time, the late Old Kingdom kings' efforts to consolidate power in the hands of fewer officials could be seen as an effort to lessen the number of wealthy men and families that surrounded him.

Yet whether or not this also reflected a gradual decentralization and decline of the central administration is less clear. Indeed, there has been a lot of debate concerning the kings' increasing interest in the provinces, high officials' move away from the capital to more distant areas, and the tendency of the central government to promote local elites to high offices. Bárta interpreted all of this as a loss of central authority, with the nomarchs and other high officials beginning to act on their own outside of the king's grasp.[137] Michel Baud suggested that the new interest in the provinces was not only economic but also political. He interpreted the provincial officials as loyal to the king and perhaps a counterweight to various incidents and troubles at the court, such as the harem conspiracy of Pepi I and the possible murder of Teti. Yet in the policy of promoting local elites to high office, Baud recognized the seeds of the dissolution of central power as these officials became increasingly autonomous.[138]

On the other hand, Moreno García, while noting a change in the balance of power at the beginning of the Sixth Dynasty, emphasized that these changes, which were likely the result of a tumultuous political environment in the capital, should not be overestimated; instead they can more accurately be interpreted

---

136. Richards, "Kingship and Legitimation," 64–81.
137. See references in n. 135 above.
138. Baud, "The Old Kingdom," 77–80.

as the result of a greater visibility of the state's local representatives, rather than the result of completely new policies. The changes were attempts to extend the king's authority.[139] Moreover, according to Moreno García, the king maintained control over the provinces until the end of the Old Kingdom, and nothing implies that the provinces became increasingly autonomous during the Sixth Dynasty; rather despite any growing wealth or influence, they still remained closely tied to the state.[140]

Eyre, Richards, and Strudwick have also made similar arguments as Moreno García, namely, that the prominence of the provinces may not indicate a move toward decentralization but instead an attempt to govern and exploit these regions more effectively. These provincial officials did not contribute to the decline of central authority, until perhaps the center itself became weak at the end of the Sixth Dynasty.[141] While Kanawati did see the central administration's turn to the provinces, especially during the reign of Merenre, as a decentralization, like Eyre, Richards, and Strudwick, he understood this to be a deliberate state policy aimed at better controlling production in the provinces, rather than the result of a weak central government and growing power of high officials.[142]

Ultimately, there is probably not a straightforward answer that would explain these changes in provincial policies and administration, and to some degree they could reflect both a gradual decline in central power and influence during the Sixth Dynasty even as the state maintained control and attempted to exploit provincial resources. Certainly it makes sense that the king would want to assert his authority in the provinces and would employ local agents to do so. Indeed, as Richards has argued, royal policies aimed at the provinces during the late Old Kingdom may have served ideological as well as administrative goals, intended to impress upon these areas the legitimacy of the king.[143] At the same time, in connecting himself to and bestowing his favors upon the provinces, the king was inevitably increasing the wealth and influence of his provincial agents and their families. Thus, the central administration and the king may have been very slowly losing control in some sense even as they were working to assert it.

Changes in religion during the late Old Kingdom reflect similar royal tendencies and concerns. As I described above, Hays has argued that the Pyramid Texts do not suggest different religious beliefs and conceptions of the afterlife for royalty and the elite but rather different expressions of and modes of decorum for these beliefs.[144] While they clearly imply a broader shift in religion, the use of the Pyramid Texts should also be seen as another effort on the part of the kings to distinguish themselves from the elite. Consequently, they also demonstrate a change in royal ideology. Callender has interpreted the increasing status and influence of Sixth Dynasty royal women in a similar way. By bestowing high-ranking titles, kingly elements of funerary architecture, and Pyramid Texts on his wives, including those who came from nonroyal backgrounds, Pepi II raised their status and thus enhanced his own position and majesty.[145]

John Baines has discussed how reliefs from Pepi II's mortuary temple depict a growing divide between the king and the elite, with Pepi II's reliefs having a higher proportion of divine representations than those

---

139. Moreno García, "Territorial Administration," 121–24.

140. Moreno García, 138. See also Juan Carlos Moreno García, "Building the Pharaonic State: Territory, Elite, and Power in Ancient Egypt in the 3rd Millennium," in Hill, Jones, and Morales, *Experiencing Power*, 185–217.

141. Eyre, "Weni's Career," 109–110 and 117–18; Richards, "Kingship and Legitimation," 63–81; Strudwick, *Administration*, 346; and Strudwick, *Texts*, 9–10.

142. Kanawati, *Governmental Reforms*, 55, 96, and 131.

143. Richards, "Kingship and Legitimation," 63 and 70–81.

144. See n. 34 above. See also Nuzzolo, "Royal Architecture," 190.

145. Callender, "It's All in the Family," 26 and Callender, *In Hathor's Image*, 271–306 and 327–40; in contrast to Labrousse, who interprets the rising prominence of queens as a threat to the king's authority (Labrousse, "Huit épouses"). If this were the case, the Sixth Dynasty kings may have been concerned with differentiating themselves from not only the elite but also the queens.

of the Fifth Dynasty king Sahure.[146] This contrasts the reality of late Old Kingdom politics and society; the king's status was actually diminishing. The reliefs illustrate an ideal, and they were part of the king's efforts to elevate himself and emphasize his divinity. Likewise, the popularity of the prisoner statues during the late Old Kingdom reflects contemporary changes in the conception of kingship. In this light, the Sixth Dynasty kings' growing use of prisoner statues was another way for them to assert their power and differentiate themselves. In their subject matter, the prisoner statues were royal symbols of authority, as I discussed in chapter 1.2. The increasing use of them may reflect the king's need and desire to reaffirm his dominance and distinction, as he was doing through other means, such as the Pyramid Texts, administrative policies, and royal women. The prisoner statues depicted a motif that only kings could use and were an expensive statue type that only kings could afford. By erecting larger and larger numbers, the king strongly distinguished himself from those who surrounded him. They were not propagandistic or any sort of explicit reference to troubled times and a decline in central authority, but their growing numbers reflect the king's attempt to set himself apart and perhaps partly indicate a degree of royal insecurity.

In discussing the history of the late Old Kingdom in this chapter, I have deliberately omitted one important aspect, namely, Egypt's relations with its foreign neighbors during this period. Indeed, by the Sixth Dynasty, these were increasing and growing more hostile, particularly with cultures living to the south. This development also corresponds to the greater number of prisoner statues during the reigns of Pepi I and Pepi II and may be another reason why the number of statues increased. However, the relationship between Egypt's foreign interactions and the prisoner statues is neither simple nor straightforward. In the next chapter, I examine this further while considering the heads of the prisoner statues.

---

146. Baines, "Kingship before Literature," 143–52. I discuss the reliefs from the late Old Kingdom pyramid complexes and their relationship to the prisoner statues in ch. 4.

Chapter 3
Expressiveness and Ethnicity: The Prisoner Statue Heads

In contrast to characterizations of the prisoner statues' bodies as repetitive and summary, over the years, scholars have routinely praised the prisoner statues' heads and interpreted them as unusually expressive and emotive.[1] Many have described the heads as extremely realistic, with some going so far as to suggest that they are portraits or that the artists might have modeled them after actual foreigners.[2] Indeed, the prisoner statue heads have been at the center of unresolved debates concerning their ethnicity partly because the statues were not inscribed with any names, titles, or ethnic designations.[3] While nearly all scholars have described the statues as depicting foreigners, it has been much more difficult for Egyptologists to agree on the type of foreigner that any given statue portrays. This is particularly true for the later prisoner statues, namely, those from the pyramid complexes of Pepi I and Pepi II.[4] Moreover, a few scholars have

---

1. Bothmer, "On Realism," 378–86; Marsha Hill, "173. Kneeling Captive," in Arnold, Grzymski, and Ziegler, *Egyptian Art*, 440; Marsha Hill, "174. Kneeling Captive," in Arnold, Grzymski, and Ziegler, *Egyptian Art*, 441; Jéquier, *Douze ans*, 64–65; Ambrose Lansing, "An Old Kingdom Captive," *BMMA* 5 (1947): 152; Lauer and Leclant, "Découverte," 58–60; and Leclant, *Recherches*, 8.

2. Bothmer, "On Realism," 378–86; William C. Hayes, *The Scepter of Egypt: A Background for the Study of the Egyptian Antiquities in The Metropolitan Museum of Art*, 2 vols. (New York: The Metropolitan Museum of Art, 1953–1978), 1:115; Jéquier, *Monument funéraire*, 3:28; Jéquier, "Planche 22," 22; Jéquier, "Rapport préliminaire...1926–1927," 60; Jean-Philippe Lauer, *Saqqara: The Royal Cemetery of Memphis* (New York: Scribner's Sons, 1976), 180; Jean-Philippe Lauer, "Travaux aux pyramids de Saqqarah et à leurs complexes monumentaux," *BIE* 60 and 61 (1978–1979, 1979–1980): 102; Lauer and Leclant, "Découverte," 58; and Vandier, *Manuel*, 3:138. On the other hand, Ritner argued that the statues do not represent individual enemies but serve as symbols of the traditional enemies of Egypt (Ritner, *Mechanics*, 116).

3. There is no evidence for inscriptions on any part of the prisoner statues, including the bodies, bases, or back pillars.

4. There have been numerous attempts by previous scholars to assign ethnicities to the Pepi I and Pepi II prisoner statues. Concerning the Pepi I statues, see *Cinquante années à Saqqarah de Jean-Philippe Lauer: Exposition organisée par le service des musées du Cairo au musée palais du Manial, 13 Avril 1980–15 Mars 1981* (Cairo: Organisme Général des Imprimeries Gouvernementales, 1983), 19; Jean-Philippe Lauer, "Cinquante années de recherches et travaux aux pyramides de Saqqarah," *CRAIBL* 124 (1980): 563; Jean-Philippe Lauer, "Rapport sur les travaux à Saqqarah (26 Novembre 1969–25 Mars 1970)," *ASAE* 62 (1977): pls. 3–5; Lauer, "Recherches...1967–1968 et 1968–1969," 472–76; Jean-Philippe Lauer, "Recherches et travaux à Saqqarah (campagnes 1972–1973)," *CRAIBL* 117 (1973): 328; Lauer, *Saqqara*, 180; Jean-Philippe Lauer, "Les statues de prisonniers du complexe funeraire de Pepi Ier," *BIE* 51 (1969–1970): 40–41; Lauer, "Travaux aux pyramids," 102; Lauer, "Travaux...1968–1969," 19–21; Lauer and Leclant, "Découverte," 58–60; Jean Leclant, "Fouilles et travaux en Égypte et au Soudan, 1972–1973," *Orientalia* 43 (1974): 184; and Jean Vercoutter, "The Iconography of the Black in Ancient Egypt: From the Beginnings to the 25th Dynasty," trans. William Granger Ryan, in *The Image of the Black in Western Art*, vol. 1, rev. ed., ed. David Bindman and Henry Louis Gates (Cambridge: Belknap Press of Harvard University Press, 2010), 46–47. For the Pepi II statues, see Jéquier, *Douze ans*, 64–65; Jéquier, *Monument funéraire*, 3:28; Jéquier, "Planche 22," 22–23; Lauer, "Recherches et travaux...1967–1968 et 1968–1969," 476; Lauer, "Statues de prisonniers," 41–42; W. S. Smith, *History of Egyptian Sculpture*, 84; and Vercoutter, "Iconography," 44–47.

questioned whether some of the statues might actually depict Egyptians since according to the Egyptian belief system, rebellious Egyptians were also enemies of the king and thus analogous to foreigners, as I mentioned in chapter 1.2.[5]

This chapter analyzes the prisoner statues' heads in order to examine why they look the way that they do and to reconsider their expressiveness, individuality, and ethnicity. The following section demonstrates that the features of the Fifth Dynasty heads are different from those of the Sixth Dynasty heads. Overall, the Fifth Dynasty prisoner statues do not show the expressiveness, individuality, and the same treatment of ethnicity as the Sixth Dynasty prisoner statues.

There are multiple reasons for this, and a number of factors influenced the artists of the Sixth Dynasty prisoner statues. A primary one, which I discuss in the second section of this chapter, was a change in artistic style that occurred during the late Old Kingdom. Statues carved in the new style, which Egyptologists variously refer to as the "Second Style" or the late Old Kingdom style, are significantly more expressive than statues carved in the traditional style of the earlier Old Kingdom.[6] Thus this new style accounts for the expressiveness of the Sixth Dynasty prisoner statue heads, and their expressiveness is not unique or unusual, as previous scholars have described it. Nor does it have anything to do with affect or emotion. Instead these prisoner statues offer some of the best-known examples of the late Old Kingdom style.

The Second Style also helps explain the impression of realism that the Sixth Dynasty prisoner statue heads have given to modern viewers since statuary carved in this style often looks more dynamic and realistic. But the prisoner statues are not naturalistic renderings of particular foreigners, as I discuss in the third section of this chapter, which is focused on the ethnicity of the prisoner statues. All of the prisoner statues represent generic foreigners, and none of them depict Egyptians. At the same time, during the Sixth Dynasty there was a change in the way that the artists depicted the prisoner statues' foreignness, and this resulted in the individuality of these heads. Unlike the artists of the earlier heads, who employed the stereotypical features that were used for foreigners during the late Old Kingdom, the artists responsible for the Pepi I and Pepi II prisoner statues mixed and matched facial features among the heads at each complex in order to create individualized, imaginary foreigners.

While the late Old Kingdom style, which itself was quite variable and flexible, may partly account for the change in the treatment of the prisoner statues' ethnicity, this change also coincided with a change in the nature of actual interactions between Egyptians and foreigners, and this is another factor that helps explain why the Sixth Dynasty prisoner statues look the way that they do. As I discuss in the fourth section of this chapter, there is evidence of more foreigners living in Egypt and more high officials frequently traveling abroad at that time. Egypt's presence in areas outside the Nile Valley was stronger, and Egyptian society appears to have been more multicultural, with increased knowledge of the outside world. The artists of the Pepi I and Pepi II prisoner statues seem to have been trying to visualize this new and broader world, and the change in the prisoner statues' ethnicity reflects a shifting conception of ethnic identity and the Egyptians' understanding of foreignness.

---

5. Laurel Bestock, *Violence and Power in Ancient Egypt: Image and Ideology before the New Kingdom*, Routledge Studies in Egyptology 5 (New York: Routledge, 2018), 125–27 and Borchardt, *Grabdenkmal des Königs Ne-user-re*, 42.

6. Both terms are misleading as they imply that there was only one style in the early Old Kingdom (a "first style") and one style in the late Old Kingdom (a "second style"). These terms also suggest that the later style replaced the earlier style and that neither coexisted. This was not the case. Throughout most, if not all, of the late Old Kingdom one finds examples of both styles, and artists could employ these styles to varying degrees. Additionally, these styles were prevalent in the Memphite region. Much less is known concerning the art of the provinces for most of the Old Kingdom, and there were undoubtedly local styles and trends that also coexisted. However, despite these issues, the terms have become conventional within Egyptology. For this reason, I continue to employ them here, and I use them interchangeably.

3.1. The Prisoner Statue Heads

In the following section, I briefly outline the corpus of prisoner statue heads from each pyramid complex; these observations form the basis for my arguments in the rest of this chapter.[7] Many previous discussions of the prisoner statues' ethnicity and expressiveness were founded on particular statues or groups of statues, but scholars have tended to assume conclusions were true of the prisoner statues in general. By considering all of the known heads comprehensively, it becomes clear that their features differed significantly over time, and therefore, one cannot speak of the heads as a uniform group that all show expressiveness or ethnicity in the same way across the late Old Kingdom.

Moreover, the facial features and hairstyles of the heads from the pyramid complexes of Pepi I and Pepi II can be subdivided according to their size, shape, and execution, and I break down and explicate the various types in this section using a series of tables. These demonstrate that the feature types at each complex were subtly varied and mixed and matched between the heads. Each head from the Pepi I and Pepi II pyramid complex was a compilation of different feature types, and there is no pattern to how the features were coordinated. The variation of feature types appears to have been random, and it ultimately gives the impression that the heads from these complexes are each unique and individualized. This relates to their ethnicity, to which I return in the third section of this chapter.

3.1.1. Niuserre

Borchardt only discovered a single prisoner statue head at the pyramid complex of Niuserre (ÄM 17912; C.1.1; fig. 3.1). His nose and mouth are badly damaged, but his face was clearly full and round with minimal modeling, and his small eyes were deeply incised with rounded eyeballs. Small remains of stone that would seem to have been along his throat were likely traces of a chin beard. He had a short, tiered hairstyle, which appears to have been fairly broad and heavy.[8] The flat top of his head, which I discussed in chapter 2.2.1, was a result of the large back pillar attached behind him. As I have mentioned, Borchardt determined that this fragment belonged to the same statue as ÄM 17913 (C.1.2), which had rope bonds on the left arm (fig. 2.1). Therefore, there can be no doubt that this head is from a prisoner statue.

Figure 3.1. Prisoner statue head from the valley temple of Niuserre in Abusir; Fifth Dynasty. Berlin, ÄM 17912. Photograph courtesy of the Ägyptisches Museum und Papyrussammlung, Staatliche Museen zu Berlin – PK.

---

7. For fuller descriptions of the heads and their features, see the catalog: https://doi.org/10.5913/2022877.

8. His hairstyle includes a sharp corner at the temple, where the upper portion of hair around the head connects to the lower portions of hair that fall on either side of his face. Nadine Cherpion identified this feature among private statuary with short, tiered wigs (Nadine Cherpion, "La statuaire privée d'Ancien Empire: indices de datation," in *Les critères de datation stylistiques à l'Ancien Empire*, ed. Nicolas Grimal, BiEtud 120 [Cairo: Institut français d'archéologie orientale, 1998], 104–5). This is common for many of the prisoner statues with tiered hairstyles until the reign of Pepi II when the transition at the temple of many of the tiered hairstyles seems to be more like Cherpion's other type, which is rounded.

3.1.2. Djedkare-Isesi

The face of the prisoner statue bust from the pyramid complex of Djedkare-Isesi (SCA no. 2233; C.2.3) is almost completely destroyed, but deep furrows underneath his eyes and radiating from the wings of his nose are still visible (fig. 3.2). He wears a long tripartite hairstyle that falls midway down his chest and upper back, where it is carved in high relief on either side of the back pillar. His large ears protrude in front of this, and a wide fillet crosses around his head, directly above his forehead. It is likely that his hairstyle was similar to that of SCA no. 2244 (C.2.2), who, despite missing his head, still has the remains of a long full hairstyle with the hanging ends of a ribbon carved on either side of his back pillar (fig. 2.4).

Figure 3.2. Prisoner statue bust (SCA no. 2233) from the mortuary temple of Djedkare-Isesi in Saqqara; Fifth Dynasty. Photograph: Mohamed Megahed.

Figure 3.3. Prisoner statue head fragment from the mortuary temple of Djedkare-Isesi in Saqqara; Fifth Dynasty. Photograph courtesy of the Egyptological Library and Archives, Università degli Studi di Milano.

The smallest prisoner statue fragment that Hussein discovered at the Djedkare complex, which can be identified as such by his facial features and hairstyle, consists of only the upper half of a head, including the eyes and forehead (C.2.4; fig. 3.3).[9] Although the very top of the head is missing, based on what remains, the hairstyle is the same type that SCA no. 2233 (C.2.3) wears, with sections flowing down on either side of his face and a wide fillet wrapping around, directly above his forehead. C.2.4's left ear is also preserved, protruding in front of the hair. His eyes are large and almond shaped, and his plastic upper eyelids and eyebrows were executed in rounded relief. The size and shape of his eyes and those of SCA no. 2233, including the plastic upper eyelids and the distance of the eyes from the hairline, is the same.

3.1.3. Teti

There is nothing overt that indicates that the bust that Quibell discovered in the early twentieth century at the pyramid complex of Teti was once part of a prisoner statue, as only a small portion of his shoulders remains (Saqqara, Imhotep Museum JE 40047; C.4.1; fig. 2.6).[10] Indeed, Quibell only described it as an Old Kingdom limestone statue and did not recognize that it depicted a foreigner or a prisoner, at least not in 1909 when his excavation report was published.[11] The fragment was not published as belonging to a pris-

---

9. I first made this argument in Prakash, "Prisoner Statue 'Fragments'," 20–21.
10. Regarding the position of his shoulders, see further ch. 2.2.4.
11. Quibell, *Excavations...1907–1908*, 113. It is possible that Quibell realized or had a suspicion that the bust he had discovered belonged to a prisoner statue prior to his death in 1935. Today, a photograph of an unpublished prisoner statue bust that Jéquier found at the pyramid complex of Pepi II (C.6.8) is in Quibell's archive at the Università degli Studi di Milano (Quibell Collection, Egyptological Library and Archives, Università degli Studi di Milano, Milan, Italy; concerning the

Chapter 3: Expressiveness and Ethnicity: The Prisoner Statue Heads 65

Figure 3.4. Prisoner statue head (PP 32) from the pyramid complex of Pepi I in Saqqara; Sixth Dynasty. Photograph courtesy of the Egyptological Library and Archives, Università degli Studi di Milano.

Figure 3.5. Prisoner statue head (PP 18) from the pyramid complex of Pepi I in Saqqara; Sixth Dynasty. Photograph courtesy of the Brooklyn Museum.

oner statue until following the excavations of Lauer and Leclant in the 1960s, after they had discovered a second fragment and realized that the bust that Quibell had found was also part of a prisoner statue.[12]

Comparison with the heads of the Djedkare and Pepi I prisoner statues confirms that this is certainly the head of a prisoner statue. The eyes of the head from the Teti complex, with their plastic eyebrows and upper eyelids executed in low relief, are almost identical to those of C.2.4 from the Djedkare complex and would likely be extremely similar to SCA no. 2233 (C.2.3) if this face were better preserved (figs. 3.2 and 3.3). The eyeballs themselves are large and convex. For the bottom half of the face, one must look to the statues from the complex of Pepi I as this part of the face does not remain on any of the Djedkare prisoner statues. The fleshy nasolabial folds, delicately carved nose, philtrum, and vermillion border that encircles the entire mouth are features that can all be found among the Pepi I prisoner statues (compare especially PP 32; C.5.32; fig. 3.4).

The hairstyle and beard of the bust from the Teti complex also firmly establish that this fragment is from a prisoner statue. The hairstyle is wavy and falls behind his shoulders, forming a U-shape along his back. The surface of the hairstyle is plain and was not incised; rather, the waves were depicted with horizontal undulations. Several of the statues from the pyramid complex of Pepi II seem to wear similar hairstyles (see especially C.6.8) as well as one of the unprovenanced prisoner statues in the Metropolitan Museum of Art, which can be attributed to the Pepi II complex (MMA 64.260; C.7.4; fig. 1.2).[13] Even the ears

---

Quibell collection in general, see further Orsenigo, "Digging at Sakkara" and Orsenigo, "James E. Quibell Records"). This bust has a hairstyle that is very similar to the one that the Teti bust wears. Quibell and Jéquier must have been communicating, as Jéquier almost certainly sent this photograph to Quibell. Indeed, a print of the same photograph also remains preserved in Jéquier's fonds in Neuchâtel, Switzerland (in 1JÉQUIER-6, fonds Jéquier, Archives de l'Etat de Neuchâtel, Neuchâtel, Switzerland; previous inventory number T1-4-79 in Binder 1531). Perhaps Quibell recognized its similarity to the bust that he had discovered years before, though unfortunately I have found no written documentation to confirm this suspicion.

12. Lauer and Leclant, *Temple haut*, 3, 84, 98–99 and pl. 32b. See also Lauer, "Recherches...1967–1968 et 1968–1969," 477; Lauer, "Statues de prisonniers," 42; Lauer, "Travaux...1968–1969," 22; and Lauer and Leclant, "Découverte," 60.

13. Concerning the prisoner statues in the Metropolitan Museum of Art, see further A.1 and Tara Prakash, "The Prisoner

of MMA 64.260 are done in the same fashion, as small knobs that project from the hair on either side of the face. One finds a similar treatment of the ears on PP 18 (C.5.18) from the pyramid complex of Pepi I (fig. 3.5).[14] Finally, despite damage to the chin of the Teti bust, the remains of a small beard are visible running along his throat and neck.

3.1.4. Pepi I

Between the 1960s and 1980s, Lauer, Leclant, Labrousse, and the MAFS discovered sixteen extremely detailed, well-carved prisoner statue head fragments from the pyramid complex of Pepi I (PP 16–23, 27, 28, 32, 55, 60, 61, 63, 65; C.5.16–C.5.23, C.5.27, C.5.28, C.5.32, C.5.53, C.5.58, C.5.59, C.5.61, C.5.63; figs. 2.16 and 3.4–3.13).[15] As I described in chapter 2.2.5, many of the bodies from this complex seem to have traces of pigment that suggest that they were originally covered with a dark orangey-red color (figs. 2.9 and 2.11). Several of the bodies may have also been covered with a darker or blackish layer of paint applied on top of the red (fig. 2.12). The Pepi I heads also show evidence of having been painted.[16] Traces of what seems to be a reddish pigment can still be seen on the faces and hairstyles of PP 17 (C.5.17), PP 19 (C.5.19), PP 20 (C.5.20), and PP 61 (C.5.59; figs. 3.7–3.9).[17] The surface of PP 21 (C.5.21) is not as well preserved, but in his notes on this head, Bothmer questioned whether it had been originally painted yellow (fig. 3.10).[18] If these prisoner statues were painted different colors, it almost certainly relates to their ethnicity; I return to this possibility in the third section of this chapter.

For three of the fragments, little can be said because of their poor documentation.[19] But the various features of the remaining thirteen heads can be subdivided according to their size, shape, and execution,

---

Statues in the Metropolitan Museum of Art and the British Museum: From the Late Old Kingdom to Today," *SAK* 49 (2020): 197–221.

14. While half-protruding ears were frequently represented on Old Kingdom scribal statues with the half-long wig, it was also used for foreigners. Regarding the half-protruding ear in Egyptian statuary, see further Dorothea Arnold, "Image and Identity: Egypt's Eastern Neighbours, East Delta People and the Hyksos," in *The Second Intermediate Period (Thirteenth–Seventeenth Dynasties): Current Research, Future Prospects,* ed. Marcel Marée, OLA 192 (Leuven: Peeters, 2010), 194.

15. All of these fragments are now in SCA Saqqara Store Magazine 1, which was sealed to scholars at the time of my research and writing. Therefore, my observations are based on photographs and notes in the archives of the MAFS in Paris, France; the archives of Bernard Bothmer in the Egyptological Library and Archives of the Università degli Studi di Milano, the Brooklyn Museum (Brooklyn, New York) and the Institute of Fine Arts, New York University (New York, New York); the SCA's Center of Documentation in Cairo, Egypt; and the Image of the Black at the Hutchins Center, Harvard University in Cambridge, Massachusetts.

16. Further study and technical analysis is necessary to prove that all of the coloration remaining on the Pepi I prisoner statues is indeed from ancient pigment and to draw conclusions on what the pigments might have been and how the statues were originally painted.

17. Lauer also observed traces of red pigment on PP 17 (C.5.17); Lauer, "Recherches…1967–1968 et 1968–1969," 476 and Lauer, "Statues de prisonniers," 41.

18. Box 16–17, Bothmer Collection, Milan. Bothmer also noted that PP 60 (C.5.58) might have originally been plastered and painted, though there are no visible paint traces in photographs of this head.

19. Based on the excavators' drawing in the MAFS archives, PP 55 (C.5.53) is a small, thin fragment depicting the back of a tiered hairstyle, but with no photographs, the details of the hairstyle are unclear. However, I have included PP 55 in table 1. PP 63 (C.5.61) is a fragment of a prisoner statue's right eye; I have only located a simple sketch of this in the MAFS archives, and therefore, I have omitted it from all of the below tables. Unfortunately, the excavators did not draw or photograph PP 65 (C.5.63) at all. According to their brief notes and a very poor photograph in the SCA registration book, the face of this head is entirely destroyed, but he may have been wearing a tiered hairstyle. Because I am not certain of his hairstyle, I have not included PP 65 (C.5.63) in the tables below.

Chapter 3: Expressiveness and Ethnicity: The Prisoner Statue Heads 67

Figure 3.6. Prisoner statue head and body fragment (PP 16) from the pyramid complex of Pepi I in Saqqara; Sixth Dynasty. Photograph courtesy of the MAFS.

Figure 3.7. Prisoner statue head (PP 17) from the pyramid complex of Pepi I in Saqqara; Sixth Dynasty. Photograph: Mario Carrieri, Milan/The Menil Foundation.

Figure 3.8. Prisoner statue head (PP 19) from the pyramid complex of Pepi I in Saqqara; Sixth Dynasty. Photograph courtesy of the Brooklyn Museum.

Figure 3.10. Prisoner statue head (PP 21) from the pyramid complex of Pepi I in Saqqara; Sixth Dynasty. Photograph: Mario Carrieri, Milan/The Menil Foundation.

Figure 3.11. Prisoner statue head (PP 22) from the pyramid complex of Pepi I in Saqqara; Sixth Dynasty. Photograph courtesy of the Egyptological Library and Archives, Università degli Studi di Milano.

Figure 3.9. Prisoner statue head (PP 20) from the pyramid complex of Pepi I in Saqqara; Sixth Dynasty. Photograph courtesy of the Egyptological Library and Archives, Università degli Studi di Milano.

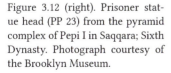

Figure 3.12 (right). Prisoner statue head (PP 23) from the pyramid complex of Pepi I in Saqqara; Sixth Dynasty. Photograph courtesy of the Brooklyn Museum.

Figure 3.13 (right). Prisoner statue head (PP 60) from the pyramid complex of Pepi I in Saqqara; Sixth Dynasty. Photograph courtesy of the Egyptological Library and Archives, Università degli Studi di Milano.

as tables 1–7 demonstrate.[20] While the feature categories are clearly recognizable, the artists subtly altered each rendering, so that even within a feature type there is a degree of variability.[21] Furthermore, the combination of these features on every statue differs. Overall, this created the impression that each head is unique.

The Pepi I heads can be categorized according to their type of hairstyle, which table 1 summarizes.

Table 1. Division of Pepi I prisoner statue head fragments based on their hairstyle.

Type 1 – Short and tiered	Type 2 – Short and plain	Type 3 – Plain with central part and fillet	Type 4 – Plain with central part
PP 16	PP 18	PP 20	PP 17
PP 19	PP 21	PP 23	
PP 27	PP 22	PP 61	
PP 28	PP 60		
PP 32			
PP 55			
6	4	3	1

Four different hairstyle types are clear. Within each type, the length, size, and shape of each hairstyle slightly differ. There are also other small variations. For example, on PP 27 (C.5.27), who has a short and tiered hairstyle (Type 1), there seems to be the remains of a wide horizontal band that must belong to a fillet crossing on top of one of his hair layers. None of the other heads with this type of hairstyle has a fillet. Additionally, PP 18 (C.5.18), who has a short and plain hairstyle (Type 2), has small tabs that must abstractly represent ear lobes or possibly earrings projecting out from the sides of his hair, next to his face (fig. 3.5). These are not present on any of the other heads with the short and plain hairstyle. The execution of all of the hairstyles is particularly varied, with some having visible tool marks and being much more roughly carved than others.[22] Indeed, in certain cases, such as PP 61 (C.5.59), the carving of the hair does not seem to have been fully finished.[23]

I have divided the faces of the Pepi I prisoner statues into three different categories based on their overall shape; this is listed in table 2.[24]

---

20. PP 27 (C.5.27) and PP 28 (C.5.28), which are fragments from the backs of heads, are only included in table 1.

21. I summarize the primary distinctions between each feature type here. For fuller descriptions of the various types and the minor variations within them for each head, see Tara Prakash, "Depictions of the Foreign 'Other': The Old Kingdom Prisoner Statues" (PhD diss., Institute of Fine Arts, New York University, 2017), 147–57.

22. The surface of PP 18 (C.5.18) is poorly preserved and weathered, and around the top of the head, there seems to be some type of encrustation in a roughly circular pattern. It is difficult to identify this material and its relationship to the limestone, but it looks as though it could be a build-up of plaster. In his notes, Bothmer also described it as a mortar on top of the tool marks (Box 16–17, Bothmer Collection, Milan). If it is indeed a mortar, it remains unclear when it was applied. Supposing that it was part of an original correction or addition to the head, it surely was not meant to only cover up the tool marks that remain visible in this area as the other fragments demonstrate that visible tool marks were acceptable and even common.

23. On PP 61, considerable tool marks are visible on the entire surface, and the bottom line of the fillet's right side does not appear to have been fully carved; the top line continues a little further back and then fades out as well.

24. PP 23 (C.5.23), PP 32 (C.5.32), and PP 61 (C.5.59) have suffered too much damage to accurately judge their face shape.

Table 2. Division of Pepi I prisoner statue head fragments based on their face shape.

Type 1 – **Round** (with broad foreheads and fleshy, full cheeks)	Type 2 – **Oval** (with broad, high foreheads and full cheeks)	Type 3 – **Tapered** (with high cheekbones and exaggerated nasolabial folds)
PP 16 PP 19 PP 22	PP 21 PP 60	PP 17 PP 18 PP 20
3	2	3

Pepi I's artists also employed three different types of brows for the heads (table 3).[25]

Table 3. Division of Pepi I prisoner statue head fragments based on their brows.

Type 1 – **Deeply carved with a sharp edge** (shape is fairly straight over the center of the eyes)	Type 2 – **Slightly modeled** (shape is more straight)	Type 3 – **Relief** (particularly toward the outer eye; shape is high and rounded)
PP 16 PP 17 PP 19 PP 32 PP 61	PP 21 PP 60	PP 20 PP 23
5	2	2

On the other hand, there are five different types of eyes among them (table 4).

Table 4. Division of Pepi I prisoner statue head fragments based on their eyes.

Type 1 – **Fully rimmed** (almond shaped with a delicate band of rounded relief that extends slightly at the corners)	Type 2 – **Partially rimmed** (almond shaped with band of relief only partially carved; canthi deeply incised and exaggerated)	Type 3 – **"Puffy" lower lid** (shape is smaller and narrower; upper outline deeply incised but lower lid rimmed with thick and uneven relief; outer canthus extends straight out and inner canthus deeply carved and extends diagonally down)	Type 4 – **Incised outline with small and narrow shape** (outer canthus is a sharp corner that sometimes extends; inner canthus deeply carved and always extends diagonally down)	Type 5 – **Incised outline with large and round shape**
PP 16	PP 17	PP 19 PP 20 PP 23 PP 61	PP 18 PP 22 PP 32 PP 60	PP 21
1	1	4	4	1

---

25. This area is too damaged to evaluate on PP 18 (C.5.18) and PP 22 (C.5.22).

Noses are particularly difficult to evaluate as nearly all of the statues have suffered at least some damage to this area of the face; I discuss the implications of this further in chapter 5. However, among six of the heads, I tentatively identified three different types of noses (table 5).[26]

Table 5. Division of Pepi I prisoner statue head fragments based on their noses.

Type 1 – **Broad and short** (wide, flat bridge that develops into a broad tip with deeply carved wings that flare out; subtle but fleshy nasolabial folds)	Type 2 – **Broad and long** (deeply carved and exaggerated nasolabial folds)	Type 3 – **Thin and long** (sharp bridge with deeply carved wings and nasolabial folds)
PP 19 PP 22 PP 32 PP 60	PP 23	PP 20
4	1	1

Furthermore, where preserved, all of the faces have clear philtrums that were delicately carved.[27]

The bottom portion of the faces of PP 16 (C.5.16), PP 18 (C.5.18), PP 23 (C.5.23), and PP 61 (C.5.59) is either damaged or missing. For the other seven heads, four different types of mouths are present (table 6).

Table 6. Division of Pepi I prisoner statue head fragments based on their mouths.

Type 1 – **Full lips with sharp vermillion borders**	Type 2 – **Full lips with ridge vermillion border on upper lip** (sharp vermillion border on lower lip; upper lip vermillion carved below the fleshy upper lip creating a ridge as the border)	Type 3 – **Thin lips with ridge vermillion borders** (vermillion carved below the fleshy lip creating a ridge as the borders; straight upper border)	Type 4 – **Very thin upper lip** (no accentuated vermillion borders)
PP 21	PP 22 PP 32	PP 17 PP 19 PP 20	PP 60
1	2	3	1

Finally, the faces of PP 18 (C.5.18), PP 23 (C.5.23), and PP 61 (C.5.59) are too damaged to determine whether or not they had beards. However, the remaining eight heads did have this feature, and they can be organized into three different types, as table 7 outlines.

---

26. The noses of PP 16 (C.5.16), PP 17 (C.5.17), PP 18 (C.5.18), PP 21 (C.5.21), and PP 61 (C.5.59) are too damaged to evaluate them.

27. This includes PP 17 (C.5.17), PP 19 (C.5.19), PP 20 (C.5.20), and PP 32 (C.5.32).

Table 7. Division of Pepi I prisoner statue head fragments based on their beards.

Type 1 – Small beard below chin only	Type 2 – Larger beard below chin and attached to throat and neck	Type 3 – Long conical chin beard with chinstrap
PP 21 PP 22 PP 60	PP 17 PP 19 PP 20 PP 32	PP 16
3	4	1

Table 8 demonstrates that all of these different feature types were mixed and matched among the Pepi I heads.[28]

Table 8. Types of facial features and hairstyles among the Pepi I prisoner statue heads.

	Hairstyle	Face shape	Brow	Eyes	Nose	Philtrum	Mouth	Beard
PP 16	1	1	1	1	N/A	N/A	N/A	3
PP 17	4	3	1	2	N/A	Yes	3	2
PP 18	2	3	N/A	4	N/A	N/A	N/A	N/A
PP 19	1	1	1	3	1	Yes	3	2
PP 20	3	3	3	3	3	Yes	3	2
PP 21	2	2	2	5	N/A	N/A	1	1
PP 22	2	1	N/A	4	1	N/A	2	1
PP 23	3	N/A	3	3	2	N/A	N/A	N/A
PP 32	1	N/A	1	4	1	Yes	2	2
PP 60	2	2	2	4	1	N/A	4	1
PP 61	3	N/A	1	3	N/A	N/A	N/A	N/A

* "N/A" indicates that I was unable to evaluate that particular part of the head, and numbers refer to the types designated in tables 1–7.

There is no obvious pattern for the way in which features were applied to them. For example, a particular type of face shape or eye type does not always correlate with a particular type of nose or mouth. Rather the different types of features were seemingly unsystematically employed and put together in contrasting ways for each head. Moreover, the actual rendering of each feature type differed slightly, as I mentioned above. Thus, even each representation of the "relief" brow type (Type 3) or the "incised outline with small and narrow shape" eye type (Type 4) was slightly dissimilar. This is particularly true for the types of hairstyles. The result is a series of heads that each look distinctly different from one another and give an impression of variety and individuality.

---

28. I have not included PP 27 (C.5.27), PP 28 (C.5.28), or PP 55 (C.5.53) in table 8. They all have tiered hairstyles, but I was not able to categorize any of their other features because of the angle of the MAFS photographs or because they were only hair fragments.

Figure 3.14. Prisoner statue head from the pyramid complex of Pepi II in Saqqara; Sixth Dynasty. Cairo, Egyptian Museum JE 45781. Photograph courtesy of the Egyptian Museum.

Figure 3.15. Prisoner statue head from the pyramid complex of Pepi II in Saqqara; Sixth Dynasty. Cairo, Egyptian Museum JE 57202. Photograph courtesy of the Egyptian Museum.

Figure 3.16. Prisoner statue head from the pyramid complex of Pepi II in Saqqara; Sixth Dynasty. Cairo, National Military Museum JE 51730. Photograph: Mario Carrieri, Milan/The Menil Foundation.

Figure 3.17. Prisoner statue head from the pyramid complex of Pepi II in Saqqara; Sixth Dynasty. Cairo, National Military Museum JE 51731. Photograph: Archives de l'Etat de Neuchâtel, fonds Jéquier (1852–1946), Temple de Pepi II, 1JEQUI-ER-6.

Figure 3.18. Prisoner statue bust from the pyramid complex of Pepi II in Saqqara; Sixth Dynasty. Photograph: Archives de l'Etat de Neuchâtel, fonds Jéquier (1852–1946), Temple funéraire de Pepi II, 1JEQUIER-10.

Figure 3.19. Prisoner statue bust from the pyramid complex of Pepi II in Saqqara; Sixth Dynasty. Photograph: Archives de l'Etat de Neuchâtel, fonds Jéquier (1852–1946), Temple funéraire de Pepi II, 1JEQUIER-10.

Chapter 3: Expressiveness and Ethnicity: The Prisoner Statue Heads 73

Figure 3.21. Prisoner statue head from the pyramid complex of Pepi II in Saqqara; Sixth Dynasty. Photograph: Archives de l'Etat de Neuchâtel, fonds Jéquier (1852–1946), Temple funéraire de Pepi II, 1JEQUIER-10.

Figure 3.22. Prisoner statue head from the pyramid complex of Pepi II in Saqqara; Sixth Dynasty. Photograph: Archives de l'Etat de Neuchâtel, fonds Jéquier (1852–1946), Temple funéraire de Pepi II, 1JEQUIER-10.

Figure 3.20. Prisoner statue bust from the pyramid complex of Pepi II in Saqqara; Sixth Dynasty. Photograph: Archives de l'Etat de Neuchâtel, fonds Jéquier (1852–1946), Temple funéraire de Pepi II, 1JEQUIER-10.

3.1.5. Pepi II

It remains unclear exactly how many prisoner statue head fragments Gustave Jéquier discovered during his work at the Pepi II pyramid complex.[29] However, the fourteen heads that I have studied can also be divided according to their features (Cairo, GEM 1101; Cairo, Egyptian Museum JE 45781 and JE 57202; Cairo, National Military Museum JE 51730 and JE 51731; Suez, Suez National Museum JE 51729; C.6.1, C.6.2, C.6.4–C.6.15; figs. 2.22, 2.23, 3.14–3.24, and 5.2).[30] Furthermore, the artists slightly varied their renderings and combined the types in different ways for each head, as Pepi I's artists had done.[31] On the other hand, while the execution of the features varies

Figure 3.23. Prisoner statue head from the pyramid complex of Pepi II in Saqqara; Sixth Dynasty. Photograph: Archives de l'Etat de Neuchâtel, fonds Jéquier (1852–1946), Saqqarah 1924 sqq, 1JÉQUIER-7 bis.

Figure 3.24. Prisoner statue head fragments from the pyramid complex of Pepi II in Saqqara; Sixth Dynasty. Photograph: Archives de l'Etat de Neuchâtel, fonds Jéquier (1852–1946), Temple funéraire de Pepi II, 1JEQUIER-10.

---

29. I discussed the issues surrounding the study of the Pepi II prisoner statue fragments and the material that Jéquier discovered at this complex in ch. 2.2.6.

30. I directly studied some of these heads while my comments for others are based on published and archival photographs.

31. As I did for the Pepi I heads, I summarize the primary distinctions between each feature type among the Pepi II prisoner statue heads here. For fuller descriptions of the various types and the minor variations within them, see Prakash, "Depictions of the Foreign 'Other'," 158–66.

among the heads, overall the Pepi II prisoner statue heads are more fully and better finished than the Pepi I heads. The same dichotomy in finishing is present between the bodies from each complex as well.[32]

The hairstyles of the Pepi II heads can be categorized into four different overall types, as table 9 demonstrates.

Table 9. Division of Pepi II prisoner statue fragments based on their hairstyle.

Type 1 – **Wavy** (full and heavy with horizontal undulations)	Type 2 – **Plain with a fillet**	Type 3 – **Plain** (no waves or fillet)	Type 4 – **Short and tiered**
JE 51731 JE 57202 C.6.8	C.6.13	C.6.9	GEM 1101 JE 45781 JE 51729 JE 51730 C.6.10 C.6.11 C.6.12 C.6.14 C.6.15
3	1	1	9

Most of the heads have the "short and tiered" hairstyle (Type 4), which also has three distinct subtypes, as table 10 shows.

Table 10. Subdivision of the "short and tiered" hairstyle (Type 4) for the Pepi II prisoner statue fragments.

Subtype 1 – **Multiple front layers above the forehead** (total number of layers in hairstyle varies between 6–8)	Subtype 2 – **Single front layer above the forehead and shorter layers below this**	Subtype 3 – **Uppermost and bottommost layers plain and without rectangular segments that signify curls** (possibly unfinished?)
GEM 1101 JE 51729 C.6.10 C.6.11 C.6.14	JE 51730 C.6.12 C.6.15	JE 45781
5	3	1

Table 11 outlines the four different face shapes that are present among the Pepi II prisoner statue heads, excluding C.6.13 whose right side is missing.[33]

---

32. For the prisoner statue bodies, see ch. 2. I return to this observation and discuss its implications in ch. 5.
33. However, it seems most likely that the face of C.6.13 was oval shaped (Type 2).

Table 11. Division of Pepi II prisoner statue fragments based on their face shape.

Type 1 – **Round** (with full cheeks and broad, short forehead)	Type 2 – **Oval** (with full cheeks and longer face)	Type 3 – **Square** (with full cheeks, broad forehead, and squared jawline)	Type 4 – **Tapered** (with narrow chin and prominent cheekbones)
JE 51729 C.6.10 C.6.11 C.6.12 C.6.14 C.6.15	GEM 1101 JE 57202 C.6.8	JE 45781 JE 51730 C.6.9	JE 51731
6	3	3	1

Concerning facial features, the faces of C.6.11, C.6.12, C.6.14, and C.6.15 are too badly destroyed to presently evaluate any of their facial features. Among the other ten heads, there are three different types of brows (table 12).

Table 12. Division of Pepi II prisoner statue fragments based on their brows.

Type 1 – **Subtle** (modeled with a mild arch toward the nose and a sharp curve toward the outer canthus)	Type 2 – **Sharp** (deeply carved line with a mild arch toward the nose and a sharp curve toward the outer canthus)	Type 3 – **Relief**
GEM 1101 JE 45781 JE 51729 C.6.13	JE 51730 C.6.9 C.6.10	JE 51731 JE 57202 C.6.8 (?)
4	3	3

The other facial features of C.6.10 are too badly damaged to categorize them based on Jéquier's photographs. Among the remaining nine heads, there are three different types of eyes (table 13).

Table 13. Division of Pepi II prisoner statue fragments based on their eyes.

Type 1 – **Large shape with incised outline** (very lightly carved bottom line and half circle for upper line; tilted slightly upwards; canthi extend out with a line)	Type 2 – **Narrow shape and upward tilt** (deeply carved inner canthus)	Type 3 – **Narrow shape with flat bottom** (upper line more deeply carved and deeply carved inner canthus that extends)
GEM 1101 JE 45781 JE 57202 C.6.13	JE 51729 JE 51731	JE 51730 C.6.8 C.6.9
4	2	3

However, one should note that the distinction between all of the Pepi II eye types is quite subtle; indeed, the various eye types are much more similar to one another than the eye types of the Pepi I prisoner statue heads (table 4). For example, all of the Pepi II eyes were outlined with incised lines; none were rimmed with a thin band of relief, as some of the Pepi I eyes were. The eyeballs are also much flatter than those from the Pepi I complex.

All of the noses of the Pepi II prisoner statues have suffered damage, and I return to this observation in chapter 5, but I have tentatively identified three different types (table 14).

Table 14. Division of Pepi II prisoner statue fragments based on their noses.

Type 1 – **Short** (broad and flaring wings that are deeply carved; prominent nasolabial folds that emerge out and down)	Type 2 – **No nasolabial folds** (broad and short shape)	Type 3 – **Long** (subtle nasolabial folds)
JE 51729 JE 51730 JE 57202 C.6.8 C.6.9 C.6.13	GEM 1101	JE 45781 JE 51731
6	1	2

At the same time, like with their eyes, the Pepi II noses seem to be more homogenous to each other than the noses of the Pepi I prisoner statues (table 5). The head of GEM 1101 (C.6.1) is broken down its center, and because of this, most of its mouth is destroyed. Among the other eight heads, there are three different mouth types (table 15).

Table 15. Division of Pepi II prisoner statue fragments based on their mouths.

Type 1 – **Sharp vermillion borders** (fairly straight shape; thin upper lip; lower lip swells slightly in center)	Type 2 – **Ridge vermillion borders** (lip vermillion carved below the fleshy lip creating a ridge as the borders; fuller lips and slight smile)	Type 3 – **Pouty lips** (lips puff in center and no exaggerated vermillion borders)
JE 51730 JE 51731 C.6.9	JE 51729 JE 57202 C.6.8 C.6.13	JE 45781
3	4	1

The cutaneous upper lip is only preserved, fully or partially, on six heads, and table 16 records whether or not these heads had philtrums.

Table 16. Presence of a philtrum for the Pepi II prisoner statue heads that have this area preserved.

Yes	Likely No	No
JE 51729 JE 57202	JE 51730 JE 51731 C.6.13	JE 45781
2	3	1

The lower portion of C.6.12 is too damaged to determine whether or not he had a beard, but based on what remains, this does seem most likely. JE 51730 (C.6.5), JE 51731 (C.6.6), C.6.11, C.6.13, C.6.14, and C.6.15 all had chin beards that were attached to their throats and necks, but the beards are too damaged to evaluate them further. However, one finds significant variation among the better-preserved beards, as table 17 shows, and I have identified five different beard types.

Table 17. Division of Pepi II prisoner statue fragments based on their beards.

Type 1 – Full (runs along jawline and extends into a triangular chin beard with a rounded point; differentiated from the stone representing negative space behind it, which connects to the throat and neck, with thin vertical lines indicating strands of hair)	Type 2 – Tapered (long, triangular chin beard that tapers to a rounded point and connects to the throat and neck)	Type 3 – Square and short (below chin)	Type 4 – Short flare (below chin)	Type 5 – Long flare (below chin)
JE 57202	JE 45781 C.6.9	C.6.8	GEM 1101 JE 51729	C.6.10
1	2	1	2	1

Table 18 illustrates that there was a similar treatment of the Pepi II prisoner statues as those of Pepi I, with different types of features swapped between the heads.

Table 18. Types of facial features and hairstyles among the Pepi II prisoner statue heads.

	Hairstyle	Face shape	Brow	Eyes	Nose	Philtrum	Mouth	Beard
GEM 1101	4: Subtype 1	2	1	1	2	N/A	N/A	4
JE 45781	4: Subtype 3	3	1	1	3	No	3	2
JE 51729	4: Subtype 1	1	1	2	1	Yes	2	4
JE 51730	4: Subtype 2	3	2	3	1	Likely no	1	Chin beard
JE 51731	1	4	3	2	3	Likely no	1	Chin beard
JE 57202	1	2	3	1	1	Yes	2	1
C.6.8	1	2	3 (?)	3	1	N/A	2	3
C.6.9	3	3	2	3	1	N/A	1	2
C.6.10	4: Subtype 1	1	2	N/A	N/A	N/A	N/A	5
C.6.11	4: Subtype 1	1	N/A	N/A	N/A	N/A	N/A	Chin beard
C.6.12	4: Subtype 2	1	N/A	N/A	N/A	N/A	N/A	N/A
C.6.13	2	N/A	1	1	1	Likely no	2	Chin beard
C.6.14	4: Subtype 1	1	N/A	N/A	N/A	N/A	N/A	Chin beard
C.6.15	4: Subtype 2	1	N/A	N/A	N/A	N/A	N/A	Chin beard

* "N/A" indicates that I was unable to evaluate that particular part of the head, and numbers refer to the types designated in tables 9–17.

Once again, no clear pattern is apparent, and the result is a diversified group of heads. On the other hand, the Pepi II statues are more similar to one another. The types of features show less variation. For example, the shapes of all of the eyes, noses, and mouths is much more similar among the Pepi II heads than it was among the Pepi I heads, despite there being subtle differences that can still be categorized into different types. In general, the Pepi II eyes are large and almond shaped, the noses are broad, and the lips are thick and full. I consider some possible reasons for why the Pepi II heads are more homogenous than the Pepi I heads in the next section.

The variation of and slight modifications to the facial features and hairstyles among the Pepi I and Pepi II prisoner statues resulted in a series of individualized heads. No two statues looked the same. This was a strategy that the artists intentionally employed to depict the statues' ethnicity, and it differed from the strategy of the Fifth Dynasty artists. However, before turning to the statues' ethnicity it is necessary to consider the style of the facial features more generally and the way that this developed over time.

3.2. The Expressiveness of the Prisoner Statues and the Late Old Kingdom Style

As I mentioned at the start of this chapter, the faces of the prisoner statues have been lauded for their expressiveness in contrast to most Old Kingdom statuary. This is particularly true in regard to statues from the pyramid complexes of Pepi I and Pepi II, which not only are more expressive, but also are better known and have been much better published since their respective discoveries.[34] Most notably, in the early 1980s, Bernard Bothmer conducted the only previous in-depth study of the prisoner statues' heads, reexamining all of the heads from the pyramid complex of Pepi I.[35] He repeatedly emphasized their expressiveness and considered it to be indicative of emotion. Moreover, based on their expressions and facial features, he identified the specific emotions that particular heads conveyed.[36] These included "glum stupor" (PP 22; C.5.22; fig. 3.11), "anguished despair" (PP 60; C.5.58; fig. 3.13), "tense resignation" (PP 23; C.5.23; fig. 3.12), "silent suffering" (PP 20; C.5.20; fig. 3.9), and "serenity" (PP 17; C.5.17; fig. 3.7).[37] Moreover, he interpreted the face of PP 19 (C.5.19), which he noted at first appears to be smiling or at least looks contented, as actually representing extreme pain: "To this day there are people who as a sign of great agony involuntarily look amused" (fig. 3.8).[38]

The eyes of the Pepi I prisoner statues especially impressed Bothmer: "In all instances they are well modeled, well finished, rather large and distinctly convex; that is to say, slightly popping."[39] He understood this to be unusual in comparison with most Old Kingdom statuary and argued that it must have something to do with their status as prisoners. One of his possible explanations was based on the position of the viewer, who would have stood above the kneeling statue and, when looking down, only been able to see

---

34. My discussion here remains focused on the excavated fragments, but three unprovenanced reconstructed statues (London, BM EA 75198; New York, MMA 47.2 and 64.260; C.7.2, C.7.3, and C.7.4), which undoubtedly came from the pyramid complex of Pepi II, have also been discussed in this regard at length. My arguments concerning the expressiveness and ethnicity of the Pepi II prisoner statues apply to these statues as well. For a complete analysis of them, see Prakash, "Prisoner Statues."

35. Bothmer, "On Realism," 378–86. The study was originally published in *Expedition* 24:2 (Winter 1982): 27–39. I briefly introduced Bothmer's research on the Pepi I prisoner statues in Prakash, "Prisoner Statue 'Fragments.'" 22–24.

36. Bothmer, "On Realism," 373, 379, and 385. I focus on the question of emotion and pain, in regard to the prisoner statues and representations of foreigners more generally, in Tara Prakash, "Bruised, Beaten, and Broken: Interpreting and Misinterpreting the Pain of Foreigners in Ancient Egyptian Art," in *Visualiser les émotions dans l'Égypte ancienne: Images et textes*, edited by Rania Merzeban et al., BiEtud (Cairo: Institute français d'archéologie orientale, forthcoming).

37. Bothmer, 385.
38. Bothmer, 386.
39. Bothmer, 383.

the hair and upper part of the face, particularly the protruding eyes. Bothmer's other suggestion, which he felt was more compelling, was that the bulging eyes were expressive and part of the artists' efforts to convey suffering.[40]

Bothmer was certainly right that the faces of the Pepi I prisoner statues are extremely expressive; with slight smiles, prominent nasolabial folds, and large eyes, most of the statues give this impression, and their variability and individuality, which I described above, only contributes to such a sense since each face looks different from the others. But Bothmer's interpretation of these features and the meanings that he attributed to the faces' overall expressiveness are incorrect. Pepi I's artists were not trying to represent the prisoners' emotions. Instead they were employing the prevailing stylistic attributes, which included slight smiles, prominent nasolabial folds, and large eyes. Most Sixth Dynasty statuary was more expressive than statuary of the early Old Kingdom.

Smooth, idealized faces characterize the statuary of the early Old Kingdom, but Sixth Dynasty royal and elite statuary usually looks significantly different. Edna Russmann was the first scholar to fully identify and characterize this late Old Kingdom style, which she referred to as a second style; it has since come to be known as the Second Style.[41] In regard to the faces of statues depicted in this style, Russmann described the following characteristics: (1) very large wide eyes; (2) little plastic modeling of the facial planes, except for prominent nasolabial folds; (3) the lower part of the face tapers sharply in a way that crowds, but also emphasizes the mouth; (4) the mouth was characteristically represented as a pair of thick lips, sometimes with a slight upturn; (5) the lips end abruptly at either side, leaving the corners open.[42] A sharp or ridged vermillion border, plastic eyebrows, globular eyes, and deeply carved and/or extended inner canthi are also primary features of this style. Overall, the facial features of the late Old Kingdom style are highly exaggerated, giving the face a more expressive, individualized, and realistic quality.

It is extremely difficult to precisely date when the new style appeared and to outline its development. Russmann, Harvey, and Ziegler traced its origins to Saqqara during the reign of Unas, but traits that seem to anticipate the style can already be found in statuary of the mid-Fifth Dynasty.[43] For most of the Sixth Dynasty, the Second Style seems to have coexisted with the earlier traditional style, and it was not until

---

40. Bothmer, 383–85.
41. Edna R. Russmann, "A Second Style in Egyptian Art of the Old Kingdom," *MDAIK* 51 (1995): 269–79. For subsequent discussions of the style and its features, see Julia C. Harvey, *Wooden Statues of the Old Kingdom: A Typological Study*, Egyptological Memoirs 2 (Leiden: Brill, 2001), 5; Karol Myśliwiec, "A Contribution to the Second Style in Old Kingdom Art," in *Servant of Mut: Studies in Honor of Richard A. Fazzini*, ed. Sue D'Auria (Leiden: Brill, 2008), 170–78; James F. Romano, "Sixth Dynasty Royal Sculpture," in Grimal, *Critères de datation stylistiques*, 235–304; Christiane Ziegler, "Nonroyal Statuary," in Arnold, Grzymski, and Ziegler, *Egyptian Art*, 66–70; Christiane Ziegler, "Nouveaux témoignages du 'Second Style' de l'Ancien Empire," in *Perspectives on Ancient Egypt: Studies in Honor of Edward Brovarski*, ed. Zahi Hawass, Peter Der Manuelian, and Ramadan B. Hussein, ASAE Suppl. 40 (Cairo: Supreme Council of Antiquities, 2010), 459–74; and Hourig Sourouzian, "Old Kingdom Sculpture," in Lloyd, *Companion to Ancient Egypt*, 868–69 and 877–80. I focus on the "Second Style" in statuary here, but it was also used for late Old Kingdom reliefs although it developed in statuary first: see Edward Brovarski, "A Second Style in Egyptian Relief of the Old Kingdom," in *Egypt and Beyond: Essays Presented to Leonard H. Lesko upon His Retirement from the Wilbour Chair of Egyptology at Brown University June 2005*, edited by Stephen E. Thompson and Peter Der Manuelian (Providence: Department of Egyptology and Ancient Western Asian Studies, Brown University, 2008), 49–89. Cyril Aldred and William Stevenson Smith had previously commented on certain traits of the late Old Kingdom style (Cyril Aldred, "Some Royal Portraits of the Middle Kingdom in Ancient Egypt," *MMJ* 3 [1970]: 29–35 and W. S. Smith, *History of Egyptian Sculpture*, 82–90).
42. Russmann, "Second Style," 270.
43. Russmann, 275–76; Harvey, *Wooden Statues*, 5; and Ziegler, "Nonroyal Statuary," 64–66.

Figure 3.25. Statue of the high official Demedji and his wife Henutsen, probably from Giza or Saqqara; Fifth Dynasty. Limestone; H. 83 cm, W. 50.8 cm, D. 51 cm. New York, MMA 51.37. Photograph: The Metropolitan Museum of Art, New York, Rogers Fund, 1951.

Figure 3.26. Kneeling statuette of Pepi I; Sixth Dynasty. Graywacke, alabaster, obsidian, copper; H. 15.2 cm, W. 4.6 cm, D. 9 cm. Brooklyn, Brooklyn Museum 39.121. Photograph: Brooklyn Museum, Charles Edwin Wilbour Fund, 39.121.

the end of this period that the new style appeared fully developed, with its features being more exaggerated and its use widespread.[44]

The heads of the prisoner statues fit into this timeline and help to illustrate the rise and coalescence of the late Old Kingdom style. With his plump full face, small eyes, and subtle brow ridge, the prisoner statue head from the complex of Niuserre (ÄM 17912; C.1.1) fits well into the highly idealizing style of the mid-Fifth Dynasty and the early Old Kingdom (fig. 3.1). There are three known statues of Niuserre himself, and according to these, the treatment of the prisoner statue's eyes and cheeks is similar to that of the king's own portrait.[45] Moreover, Niuserre's prisoner statue head closely resembled other examples

---

44. See Harvey, 5.

45. Cairo, Egyptian Museum JE 36707 and Rochester, Memorial Art Gallery 42.54 belong to a striding statue of the king; Cairo, Egyptian Museum JE 28466 is a seated statue of Niuserre; and Munich, Staatliche Sammlung Ägyptischer Kunst AS 6794 is a dyad. For all three statues, see Miroslav Verner, *The Statues of Raneferef and the Royal Sculpture of the Fifth Dynasty*, Abusir 28 (Prague: Charles University, 2017), 52–82 and pls. I.3.2.1–I.3.4.2. Two statue fragments have also been attributed to Niuserre (Beirut, Musée national libanais No. B. 7395 and Los Angeles, LACMA 51.15.6; see Verner, *Statues of Raneferef*, 83–85 and pls. I.3.5.1 and I.3.6.1).

of contemporary elite statuary, such as the head of the high official Demedji from his pair statue with his wife, Henutsen, which is now in the Metropolitan Museum of Art (fig. 3.25).[46] The eyes, brow, hairstyle/wig, and round face of Demedji and the Niuserre prisoner statue are comparable.

The significant damage to the two prisoner statue heads from the Djedkare complex (SCA no. 2233; C.2.3 and C.2.4) makes it more difficult to compare them fully to other Fifth Dynasty statuary (figs. 3.2 and 3.3). Furthermore, no faces or heads of Djedkare are known.[47] But the treatment of C.2.4's eyes, with their rimmed upper lids and plastic eyebrows, is similar to other Fifth Dynasty elite statues, including a standing statue of Snefru-nefer from the late Fifth Dynasty.[48] The small remains of the inner corner of SCA no. 2233's (C.2.3) left eye suggest that his eyes were treated the same. On the other hand, the sagginess beneath his eyes and the deep furrows that radiate from his nostrils may be more expressive features that anticipate the Second Style. They could also be artistic attempts to exaggerate the statues' non-Egyptianness by emphasizing nonidealizing features and essentially caricaturing them. This was a common practice for Egyptian representations of foreigners. These interpretations of SCA no. 2233 are not mutually exclusive; the artists could have been experimenting with new treatments of facial features, which would become common for the Second Style, on these particular statues specifically because they represented foreigners.

The prisoner statue bust from the pyramid complex of Teti (JE 40047; C.4.1) shares some features with the Djedkare prisoner statues, such as the plastic eyebrows and rimmed upper eyelid, while also seeming to foreshadow the Pepi I prisoner statues, including in the treatment of the vermillion border and the fleshy nasolabial folds (fig. 2.6). These latter features clearly reflect the emergence of the Second Style. Indeed, the prisoner statues from the complexes of Teti, Pepi I, and Pepi II consistently exhibit many of the features associated with this style, including large, dominant eyes with emphasized inner canthi; fleshy and/or deeply carved nasolabial folds; tapered lower faces; and pronounced vermillion borders.

James Romano first observed the Second Style among the Pepi I prisoner statue heads and specifically compared PP 19 (C.5.19) with a kneeling statuette of Pepi I himself (figs. 3.8 and 3.26).[49] This statuette of Pepi I has frequently been cited as one of the best examples of the late Old Kingdom style.[50] And to varying degrees, the Pepi I prisoner statues echo Pepi I's facial features. For example, the treatment of the king's mouth is most like that of PP 22 (C.5.22) and PP 32 (C.5.32), with full lips and a ridged vermillion border (figs. 3.4 and 3.11). His fleshy cheeks with subtle nasolabial folds resemble those of PP 21 (C.5.21; fig. 3.10) and PP 22 (C.5.22; fig. 3.11), while his large and delicately rimmed eyes recall those of PP 16 (C.5.16; fig. 3.6).

As I mentioned above, the Second Style traits gradually became more extreme during the reign of Pepi II.[51] This can be seen in some of the facial features of the Pepi II prisoner statues. For example, the Pepi II statues tend to have much larger eyes than the Pepi I statues. Most of their noses are short and broad.[52] The lips also tend to be thicker than those of the Pepi I prisoner statues. The philtrum was not

---

46. New York, MMA 51.37. See Catharine H. Roehrig, "125. Pair Statue of Demedji and Henutsen," in Arnold, Grzymski, and Ziegler, *Egyptian Art*, 365–67, cat. no. 125.

47. There are fragments from the lower portion of two seated statues of this king (Verner, *Statues of Raneferef*, 106–14 and pls. I.5.2.1–I.5.3.5).

48. Vienna, Kunsthistorisches Museum Ägyptisch-Orientalische Sammlung ÄS 7506. See Christiane Ziegler, "135. Snefru-nefer Standing," in Arnold, Grzymski, and Ziegler, *Egyptian Art*, 384–85, cat. no. 135.

49. Romano, "Sixth Dynasty Royal Sculpture," 269 n. 138.

50. Brooklyn, Brooklyn Museum 39.121. Marsha Hill, "170. Pepi I Kneeling," in Arnold, Grzymski, and Ziegler, *Egyptian Art*, 434–35, cat. no. 170; Romano, 242–43; and Russmann, "Second Style," 273.

51. Harvey, *Wooden Statues*, 5.

52. However, this nose type was also the most common among the Pepi I prisoner statues.

always carved for the Pepi II statues in contrast to the Pepi I statues, which could be related to an overall less consistent rendering of this feature during the end of the Old Kingdom. Indeed, Romano noted prominent philtrums on the statues of Pepi I, but none or barely perceptible ones on Pepi II's statues.[53] It seems most likely that the greater uniformity among the Pepi II prisoner statues that I described above, in contrast to the Pepi I prisoner statues, is partly a result of the increased dominance of the late Old Kingdom style at this time.

The increasing expressiveness of the prisoner statues' kneeling and bound position over the Sixth Dynasty, which I discussed in the last chapter, coincides with the rise of the Second Style and may partly be a result of it; I return to this idea in chapter 6. But in other ways, the new style is less apparent in the bodies of the Pepi I and Pepi II prisoner statues than it is in their faces. The bodies of statues depicted in the late Old Kingdom style tend to be elongated with wide shoulders and pinched waists. They also display a notable lack of musculature, and the artists frequently carved away material representing negative space. Heads can appear disproportionately large, and fingers and toes can be overly long.[54]

The heads of the Pepi II prisoner statues, where still attached or rejoined to torsos, do tend to be overly large for their respective bodies (figs. 2.22, 2.23, and 3.18–3.20). Moreover, the musculature of the Pepi I and Pepi II prisoner statues can be relatively stylized. However, musculature was rendered, and torsos are often fairly broad. Additionally, stone representing negative space was never carved away. Therefore, in general the bodies of the Sixth Dynasty prisoner statues show less Second Style influence than the heads, and it is unclear why.

The features of the Pepi I prisoner statue heads that struck Bothmer as unusual, including large, convex eyes and slight smiles, are all typical of the late Old Kingdom style, and the expressiveness that Bothmer described in regard to the heads is a result of this expressive style rather than an effort on the part of the Egyptian artists to convey the prisoners' emotions. The faces of the Pepi I prisoner statues do not depict suffering any more than the face of the kneeling statue of Pepi I does. Instead, the artists were following contemporary stylistic conventions, and the Sixth Dynasty prisoner statues need to be recognized as important examples of the late Old Kingdom style. Indeed, as statues of foreign enemies, they complicate arguments that the Second Style had a religious meaning and was tied to funerary beliefs.[55]

In addition to being expressive, Second Style facial features also appear more realistic than the idealized facial features that were conventional in the early Old Kingdom. As mentioned above, multiple scholars, including Bothmer, have commented on the supposed realism of the prisoner statues' heads. But once again, the Second Style helps to account for this impression, and the seemingly realistic features of the Sixth Dynasty prisoner statues are not unusual for their time period. The variability of the heads also contributes to this impression, since each head is different from the others. However, the faces are not life-like renderings of actual foreigners and their foreignness was generic.

3.3. The Ethnicity of the Prisoner Statues

Scholars have debated the ethnicity of the prisoner statues since their initial discovery in the twentieth century.[56] Egyptologists have regularly noted that many of the heads, particularly those from the pyramid

---

53. Romano, "Sixth Dynasty Royal Sculpture," 266.
54. See references in n. 41 above.
55. For such arguments, see Russmann, "Second Style," 278; Romano, "Sixth Dynasty Royal Sculpture," 270–71; Ziegler, "Nonroyal Statuary," 70; and Myśliwiec, "Contribution," 173.
56. See n. 4 above.

complexes of Pepi I and Pepi II, do not correspond with stereotypical representations of foreigners in Old Kingdom art. For this reason, they have questioned whether these heads might be more realistic depictions and possibly even portraits of foreigners. However, the individuality of the Pepi I and Pepi II prisoner statue heads was the result of mixing and matching different types of hairstyles and facial features, as I discussed above. Although each head looks unique, it is actually the amalgamation of set feature types. This gives the impression of many different people, whose features mark them as non-Egyptian. The ethnicity of the earlier prisoner statues was not treated in the same way. Instead, the Fifth Dynasty artists followed standard conventions and used the traditional Old Kingdom foreigner stereotypes for these prisoner statues. Therefore there was an important shift in the treatment of the prisoner statues' ethnicity in the Sixth Dynasty, but all of the known prisoner statues represent foreigners.

In chapter 1.2 I discussed the role of foreigners in the ancient Egyptian belief system. They were symbols of evil and negative forces, and one of the king's most fundamental duties was to destroy and contain them. Foreigners were regularly depicted in the bound captive motif, namely, the form of the prisoner statues, in order magically to ensure their defeat and the king's power and supremacy. But the pharaoh was responsible for eradicating anything and anyone who threatened the state, including those that came from inside Egypt. Egyptians who did not uphold Egyptian ideology or who jeopardized the established system, such as criminals or rebels, theoretically marked themselves as "bad," and "bad" Egyptians could be likened to foreigners and assigned a similar status and symbolism.[57] Indeed, Upper and Lower Egypt were frequently listed as places that the king had subjugated alongside foreign lands.[58] Similarly, Egyptians were sometimes represented in the bound captive motif or tied up and defeated.[59] However, such representations are much less common than representations of bound and defeated foreigners, and Ann Macy Roth has suggested that the Egyptians may have been somewhat uncomfortable with explicitly depicting Egyptians on the same level as foreigners in imagery despite the fact that they theoretically could be likened to each other.[60]

Despite the rarity of Egyptians depicted in the bound captive motif, a couple of scholars have questioned whether some of the prisoner statues, specifically ones that wear short, tiered hairstyles, might depict Egyptians. This hairstyle, which is typical for Nubians during the Old Kingdom, also resembles the short, tiered wigs that Egyptian high officials commonly wore in Old Kingdom relief and statuary (e.g., fig. 3.25). Consequently, Borchardt interpreted the prisoner statue head (ÄM 17912; C.1.1) with this hairstyle that he discovered from the pyramid complex of Niuserre as representing an Egyptian prisoner (fig. 3.1).[61] Recently, Laurel Bestock supported Borchardt's conclusion and extended it, arguing that some prisoner statues with short, tiered hairstyles from the pyramid complex of Pepi II also depict elite Egyptians.[62]

However, all of the known prisoner statues with intact chins, regardless of hairstyle, have beards; this indicates that none of the statues represent Egyptians. While elite Egyptian high officials often wore small chin beards in two-dimensional representations, such beards are rare in three-dimensional depictions,

---

57. Beaux, "Enemies étrangers," 40–53; Koenig, "Image of the Foreigner"; and O'Connor, "Egypt's Views of 'Others.'"
58. Eric Uphill, "The Nine Bows," *Jaarbericht van het Vooraziatisch-Egyptisch Genootschap Ex Oriente Lux* 19 (1965–1966): 393–420.
59. For example, in the tomb of Qenamun (TT 93), anthropomorphized toponyms include Egyptians (see New York, MMA 30.4.69 and Norman de Garis Davies, *The Tomb of Ken-Amun at Thebes*, MMAEE 5 [New York: The Metropolitan Museum of Art, 1930], pl. 11,A). For other examples of bound Egyptians, see Beaux, "Enemies étrangers," 40–53.
60. Roth, "Representing the Other," 239–40.
61. Borchardt, *Grabdenkmal des Königs Ne-user-re*, 42.
62. Bestock, *Violence*, 125–27.

particularly during the Old Kingdom.⁶³ Moreover, in the case of Egyptians, chin beards may have been associated with status; when they were represented it was usually on powerful high officials.⁶⁴ If certain prisoner statues with short, tiered hairstyles and beards did depict Egyptians they would both be quite unusual according to Old Kingdom artistic conventions and apparently represent very high status officials, essentially on par with or above those responsible for overseeing and carving the prisoner statues, and it seems extremely unlikely that the artists would have rendered their colleagues and superiors as anonymous rebels among other foreigners. Similarly there is nothing to indicate that the prisoner statues represent specific Egyptian high officials who fell out of favor. The image of such men would most likely have been eradicated, not preserved in stone.⁶⁵

Theoretically, it might be more likely that some prisoner statues represent lower status Egyptians, such as the herders found in relief scenes of daily life inside Old Kingdom private tombs, rather than elite Egyptians. Such men could be portrayed with facial hair and beards.⁶⁶ But they never wear elaborate hairstyles, like those that the prisoner statues wear. Instead they often appear to be bald or have receding hairlines. Moreover, as for elite Egyptian high officials, these beards primarily appear to be a feature of two-dimensional art. When Egyptian peasants and workers were portrayed in three-dimensional art, which occurred infrequently, the artists did not carve beards on them.⁶⁷

On the other hand, Old Kingdom artists usually represented foreigners, in both relief and statuary, with beards, and they were used for all types of ethnicities.⁶⁸ Beards were a symbol of foreignness, and they could mark the wearer as non-Egyptian. Therefore, in the case of the prisoner statues, the beard is a feature of their foreignness. Since all of the known prisoner statues have beards, they all depict foreigners.

Egyptian artists regularly represented foreigners in a stereotypical fashion, with distinct features, beards, hairstyles, clothing, and accessories. These attributes served to differentiate them from Egyptians. In cases where similar features were used for Egyptians, such as the small square chin beard and the short, tiered hairstyle that I mentioned above, additional attributes, the overall composition, and the larger context of the imagery indicates whether the artists were portraying foreigners or Egyptians. Multiple schol-

---

63. Harvey, *Wooden Statues*, 46; Marianne Eaton-Krauss, *The Representations of Statuary in Private Tombs of the Old Kingdom*, ÄgAbh 39 (Wiesbaden: Harrassowitz, 1984), 31; and Elisabeth Staehelin, *Untersuchungen zur ägyptischen Tracht im Alten Reich*, MÄS 8 (Berlin: Hessling, 1966), 92–93.

64. See examples in Eaton-Krauss, 31 n. 152 and Arnold, Grzymski, and Ziegler, *Egyptian Art*, 110–11, 245, 396, 408–14, 458, and 475.

65. Kanawati has argued that this was the case for a number of high officials who fell from favor during the late Old Kingdom (Kanawati, *Conspiracies*, 161–69).

66. Concerning such herders, see Andrés Diego Espinel, "'Unusual Herders': Iconographic Development, Diffusion and Meanings of Dwarves, Boys and Lame and Emaciated People as Drovers from the Old Kingdom to the Early Middle Kingdom," in *Old Kingdom Art and Archaeology 7: Proceedings of the International Conference; Università degli studi di Milano 3–7 July 2017*, ed. Patrizia Piacentini and Alessio Delli Castelli, *Egyptian & Egyptological Documents, Archives, Libraries* 6 (Milan: Pontremoli, 2019), 418–35, with further bibliography.

67. For serving statues, which depict these subjects, see Ann Macy Roth, "The Meaning of Menial Labor: 'Servant Statues' in the Old Kingdom Serdabs," *JARCE* 39 (2002): 103–21 and Marsha Hill in Arnold, Grzymski, and Ziegler, *Egyptian Art*, 386–95.

68. I discuss the stereotypical features of foreigners in relief, including their beards, below. Some of the wooden bound captive figurines from the pyramid complex of Raneferef also have beards; I discuss them further below as well. Other representations of three-dimensional foreigners with beards from the Old Kingdom include Alexandria, Alexandria National Museum JE 49613 (see Firth, "Preliminary Report," 99 and pl. 4b and Firth and Quibell, *The Step Pyramid*, 1:14, 66, 115, and pl. 57,1); Cairo, Egyptian Museum TR 18/2/26/5 A–B (see Firth and Quibell, 1:75 and 113 and pl. 57,2 and 3); Cairo, Egyptian Museum CG 396 (see Borchardt, *Statuen und Statuetten*, 2:14, cat. no. 396); Cairo, Egyptian Museum CG 1165/ JE 32013 (see Borchardt, 4:87, cat. no. 1196); Suez, Suez National Museum JE 40291; and London, Petrie Museum UC 14884.

ars have noted that the facial features of foreigners are often not idealizing and sometimes appear naturalistic.[69] This also may have visually marked foreigners off from Egyptians, who were typically idealized, but, as I discussed above in regard to the Second Style, the degree of idealization in Egyptian art varied across time periods and nonidealizing features are not necessarily more naturalistic or realistic even if they give this impression. In general, Egyptian artists were most concerned with visually expressing the foreignness of a figure rather than portraying the physical likeness of foreign ethnicities.

In reliefs from the late Old Kingdom royal pyramid complexes, three foreign types were represented: Nubians, Asiatics, and Libyans.[70] Interestingly, the number three signified plurality in ancient Egypt, and it seems possible that the Old Kingdom Egyptians deliberately chose to use three foreign stereotypes as a way to symbolize all foreigners. At the same time, the three foreign types were clearly differentiated from one another (fig. 3.27). Nubians, whom the Egyptians considered to be Southerners, wear the same short, tiered hairstyle and short, square chin beards that many Egyptian high officials were depicted wearing throughout the Old Kingdom. The Nubians' hair can be further embellished with fillets and/or braids, which were both non-Egyptian accoutrements. Their faces are round and full with fleshy nasolabial folds. Nubians also generally wear a collar or neckband; a short kilt, often with a wide belt that has a knot and bolt of cloth on the back and a sash around the hips; and sometimes

Figure 3.27. A stereotypical Nubian (left), Asiatic (middle), and Libyan (right) from a relief that decorated the bottom of the causeway of Sahure in Abusir; Fifth Dynasty. Modified from Borchardt, *Grabdenkmal des Königs Sahu-re*, 2:Bl. 6.

---

69. Sally-Ann Ashton and Donald Spanel, "Portraiture," in *The Oxford Encyclopedia of Ancient Egypt*, vol. 3, ed. Donald Redford (Oxford: Oxford University Press, 2001), 56–58; Dimitri Laboury, "Portrait versus Ideal Image," *UCLA Encyclopedia of Egyptology*, ed. Willeke Wendrich (Los Angeles: UCLA, 2010), http://digital2.library.ucla.edu/viewItem.do?ark=21198/zz0025jjv0, 2; and Claude Vandersleyen, "Porträt," *LÄ* 4:1076. Ann Macy Roth has argued that there was no differentiation in facial features between foreigners and Egyptians during the Old Kingdom and that those characteristics that are often called foreign, including wrinkles and facial creases, overly large noses, and angled eyes, are simply nonidealizing (Roth, "Representing the Other," 241–45). But the consistency of differentiation between the facial structure of Nubians in comparison to Libyans and Asiatics, in both Old Kingdom statuary and relief, strongly suggests that the Egyptians considered particular facial features as distinctive of ethnic stereotypes. At the same time, this does not preclude their use for Egyptians or contradict the interpretation of them as nonidealizing.

70. Concerning the identification of these types and the stereotypical representations of Nubians, Asiatics, and Libyans in the Old Kingdom, see Roth, "Representing the Other," 162–66 and Andrés Diego Espinel, *Etnicidad y territorio en el Egipto del Reino Antiguo*, AulÆg-Stud 6 (Bellaterra: Universitat Autònoma de Barcelona, 2006), 159–72. Good examples of foreigners in late Old Kingdom reliefs can be found in Borchardt, *Grabdenkmal des Königs Ne-user-re*, Abb. 31 and Bl. 8–12; Borchardt, *Grabdenkmal des Königs Sahu-re*, 2:Bl. 1 and 5–8; and Jéquier, *Monument funéraire*, 2:pl. 38 and 3:pls. 12–14.

a chevron-shaped upper armband.⁷¹ Undoubtedly, Old Kingdom Nubians are the most Egyptian-looking foreigners.

Asiatics and Libyans, whom the Egyptians categorized as Northerners, were more clearly differentiated from Egyptians and Nubians.⁷² While Asiatics and Libyans share several features, they were still visibly distinct from one another. Both wear conical or triangular beards that can have chinstraps or fully cover the lower portion of the face. Both also wear longer hairstyles, which fall past their shoulders. This hairstyle can be wavy, particularly for Libyans, who tend to have a front curl or lock as well. On the other hand, Asiatics usually wear a fillet. Asiatics' and Libyans' ears are often visible in front of their hair, while the Nubians' hairstyle usually covers their ears. Both Asiatics and Libyans were regularly shown with tapered faces, high cheekbones, and exaggerated or deeply carved nasolabial folds, although all of these traits were not necessarily used in every depiction. Additionally, Asiatics generally wear a simple kilt with a plain belt, while Libyans were depicted with penis sheaths, crisscrossing sashes over the torso, and a long tail.

The wooden bound captive figurines from the pyramid complex of Raneferef, which I discussed in chapter 1, illustrate some of the ways that these stereotypical features of Nubians, Libyans, and Asiatics that were common in Old Kingdom reliefs could be adapted for three-dimensional art (fig. 1.11).⁷³ The ethnicity of the Raneferef figurines is recognizable from their heads, and their facial features and attributes are relatively consistent with contemporary two-dimensional depictions of foreigners, with the exception of the Nubians being clean-shaven rather than having a beard. On the other hand, rather than carve the distinctive costumes that artists used in the reliefs, the artists of the Raneferef figurines carved all of the statuettes with plain, short kilts.⁷⁴ The artists may have felt that the heads adequately conveyed the foreignness and specific ethnicity of the figurines, so carving the costumes, which might have taken more time and energy, was unnecessary.

Like the Raneferef figurines, the Fifth Dynasty prisoner statues generally correspond with the foreigner stereotypes that one finds in Old Kingdom reliefs. With his short, tiered hairstyle and beard, the Niuserre prisoner statue head (ÄM 17912; C.1.1) represented a Nubian (fig. 3.1). Based on their hairstyle with a fillet, the two preserved heads from the complex of Djedkare (SCA no. 2233; C.2.3 and C.2.4) represent Asiatics (figs. 3.2 and 3.3). The deep furrows that extend from SCA no. 2233's nose further support this identification. They may be nonidealizing attributes meant to differentiate and mark him as Asiatic. However, given the time period of Djedkare's reign, namely, in the mid-Fifth Dynasty, it is possible that they are also tied to the very beginnings of the Second Style, as I suggested above.

One can also identify the ethnicity of the two preserved body fragments from Djedkare's pyramid complex (SCA no. 2232; C.2.1 and SCA no. 2244; C.2.2) based on their clothing and, in the case of SCA no. 2244, the remains of the hairstyle on his back. SCA no. 2232, a lower body fragment, depicts a Nubian.⁷⁵ This fragment wears a short kilt with a hem carved in relief and a belt that is tied in an elaborate knot

---

71. These men have occasionally been identified as Puntites (Borchardt, *Grabdenkmal des Königs Saḥu-re*, 2:15, 17, and 19–21 and Bestock, *Violence*, 90 and 147 n. 5), but this is very unlikely and not generally accepted (see further Roth, 242–45 and Torgny Säve-Söderbergh, *The Navy of the Eighteenth Egyptian Dynasty*, UUÅ 6 [Uppsala: Lundequistska Bokhandeln, 1946], 10–11 n. 3).

72. I discussed this briefly in chapter 1.2.

73. Concerning these figurines and their ethnicity, see further Prakash, "Reconsidering," 138–46.

74. The Libyan (Cairo, Egyptian Museum JE 98182(b)) also seems to have a plain belt.

75. Cf. Megahed, "Sculptures," 24–33, who identified all of the Djedkare prisoner statues as Asiatics. I briefly discussed this Nubian costume in regard to the Djedkare prisoner statues in Prakash, "Prisoner Statue 'Fragments,'" 18–20.

with two tassels hanging down the front of either side of his lap (fig. 2.3).⁷⁶ This is the belt and sash that Nubians often wear in reliefs. SCA no. 2244 depicts an Asiatic (fig. 2.4). He wears a plain short kilt with a bottom hem and a plain belt, and the remains of a long hairstyle and the ends of a fillet hang down his back on either side of the back pillar. Both his costume and hairstyle are consistent with the reliefs of Asiatics.

Based on comparison with the Raneferef figurines and the Fifth Dynasty reliefs, the head from the Teti complex (JE 40047; C.4.1) may depict a Libyan (fig. 2.6). His prominent high cheek bones and tapered face would suggest a Northerner, while his wavy hairstyle, that does not have any fillet or other type of accoutrement, is more indicative of a Libyan than an Asiatic. However, the treatment of the later prisoner statues' ethnicity changed dramatically, as I describe below, and this casts some doubt on the identification of the Teti statue's ethnicity. It is possible, though perhaps not likely, that this change in the treatment of ethnicity actually began with Teti's prisoner statues.⁷⁷

Previous scholars recognized that the Pepi I and Pepi II prisoner statue heads do not correspond with the stereotypical representations of Nubians, Libyans, and Asiatics from contemporary reliefs. As a result, they struggled to identify the ethnicity of the statues from these later complexes and questioned whether these statues might be more realistic.⁷⁸ For example, Lauer and Leclant tentatively identified various Pepi I prisoners as foreigners from the south, the north, or the surrounding deserts, but they noted the enormous diversity between the heads and the many inconsistencies between their individualized features and those of other foreigners in Old Kingdom art. Ultimately they concluded that the heads must be so precise in their ethnic characteristics, being portraits of different actual foreigners, that further study was needed for more definitive identifications and such a study would possibly help in determining the ethnic environment of Old Kingdom Egypt.⁷⁹ Similarly, in regard to the Pepi II heads, Jéquier noted their variability and that "on y constate un effort très marqué de rendre les types ethniques ou plutôt certains représentants déterminés des races avec lesquelles les égyptiens étaient en rapports"; he felt that if the heads were not portraits, then they were at least sculpted from models. But without the names of the depicted ethnicities on the statues, Jéquier recognized that the identification of the heads' ethnicities was rather difficult and could not be done precisely, beyond noting that certain features seemed to be indicative of Nubians, Libyans, and Asiatics.⁸⁰

The prisoner statues of Pepi I and Pepi II are not realistic depictions of foreigners and they are not portraits, a term that I define as a depiction of a specific individual that presents some unique and recognizable quality of that person, whether physical or not.⁸¹ Although the statues are in the form of individ-

---

76. See ch. 2.2.2 for full description of the Djedkare prisoner statues' clothing.

77. The change was probably tied to the increase in the number of prisoner statues, which most likely occurred during the reign of Pepi I. I discuss this idea further below, while I proposed the number of prisoner statues at each complex in ch. 2.

78. See n. 4 above, in addition to the sources I mention here.

79. Lauer and Leclant, "Découverte," 58–60 and Lauer, *Saqqara*, 180. See also Lauer, "Recherches...1967–1968 et 1968–1969," 470–76; Lauer, "Statues de prisonniers," 40–41; and Lauer, "Travaux...1968–1969," 19–21.

80. Jéquier, "Planche 22," 22–23. See also Jéquier, *Monument funéraire*, 3:28.

81. "Portraiture" continues to be an extremely contested term in the study of ancient Egyptian art, with some scholars preferring not to use it. However, the arguments against the existence of Egyptian portraiture largely stem from interpretations that evaluate Egyptian art according to modern western standards, which generally consider a portrait as necessarily realistic and representing the true physical appearance of the subject often with or following direct observation, rather than through the eyes of the ancient Egyptians. The Egyptians certainly intended the majority of their statuary as portraiture. Indeed, they took great care to record identity on many statues, but they primarily did this by including the subject's name, which they understood as containing the essence of identity, rather than fashioning the statue in the exact likeness of the subject. In these cases, the name expressed a unique and recognizable quality of the subject, making the statue a portrait, regardless of the degree to which the statue was realistic and conveyed the subject's actual physical appearance. Thus the

ual people, these people were generic. The artists of Pepi I and Pepi II essentially created ethnic hybrids, mixing and matching particular types of facial features and hairstyles that one would expect to find on foreigners in order to create more individualized faces. Tables 8 and 18 demonstrate how the artists did this. At first glance the heads look lifelike, but they are not. This technique could have been accomplished by moving artists who were responsible for particular aspects of the carving from statue to statue. As I discussed in the previous chapter, there were a number of variations in the execution and detailing of the Pepi I prisoner statues' bodies. For example, some statues had fingers and toes carved, while others did not. These variations could be the marks of different artistic hands that worked on the statues. Similarly, the different types of facial features and hairstyles among the Pepi I and Pepi II heads could also be the work of individual artists. But one should not assume that a single artist consistently rendered a particular feature or detail in the same fashion. Indeed, one artist certainly could have been responsible for carving multiple types of features and hairstyles.

Regardless of how this technique was accomplished, it gave the impression of many different types of people. All were foreign and recognizably non-Egyptian, yet none were depictions of specific ethnicities. Some statues were made to look more Southern or Northern than others, thus making them believable and vaguely recognizable, but they all portray imaginary foreign individuals. PP 16 (C.5.16) is one of the more obvious examples of this and the resulting contradictions between stereotypical ethnic features (fig. 3.6). He has a very round face with a short, tiered hairstyle, which would seemingly identify him as a Southerner, but he wears a Northern type of beard that is long and conical with a chinstrap. The ultimate impression or message from the prisoner statues of Pepi I and Pepi II is that the king has symbolically conquered and dominated all imaginable peoples, not only Nubians, Libyans, and Asiatics.[82]

Moreover, the Egyptians might have understood the variation itself to be symbolically non-Egyptian. Another example of this use of variation to distinguish Egyptians from non-Egyptians is found during the Middle Kingdom. A model from the tomb of the high official Mesehti depicts Nubian archers while a second model from the same tomb features Egyptian soldiers. The Egyptians are more uniform in height, while the height of the Nubians is more varied.[83] Similarly, the diverse facial features and hairstyles of the Pepi I and Pepi II prisoner statues may have not only served to differentiate them but also further signified their Otherness.

If the Pepi I prisoner statues were painted different colors this would have additionally reinforced their variability.[84] The coloration of foreigners during the Old Kingdom was not nearly as systematic as it became in later periods.[85] In the Old Kingdom, Nubians seem to have been mostly colored the same as Egyptian males, namely, a darkish red, though by the First Intermediate period, there are multiple exam-

---

term is quite applicable to Egyptian art. Further discussion and different definitions of the term can be found in Ashton and Spanel, "Portraiture"; Assmann, "Preservation and Presentation"; Laboury, "Portrait versus Ideal Image"; Spanel, *Through Ancient Eyes*; and Vandersleyen, "Porträt." See also Edna R. Russmann, *Eternal Egypt: Masterworks of Ancient Art from the British Museum* (Berkeley: University of California Press, 2001), 32–39.

82. Laurel Bestock previously questioned whether the artists intended the ethnicity of the prisoner statues to be ambiguous, thus allowing a multiplicity of identities to be grafted onto each statue (Bestock, *Violence*, 127).

83. Manfred Bietak, "Zu den nubischen Bogenschützen aus Assiut: Ein Beitrag zur Geschichte der Ersten Zwischenzeit," in *Mélanges Gamal eddin Mokhtar*, vol. 1, ed. Paule Posener-Kriéger, BiEtud 97 (Cairo: Institut français d'archéologie orientale, 1985), 87–97 and Roth, "Representing the Other," 244.

84. I discussed the evidence for this in ch. 3.1.4 above and ch. 2.2.5. Certainly this could have been the case for the Pepi II prisoner statues as well, and paint could have been used in conjunction with the stereotypical features of the Fifth Dynasty statues too, but at present I have only observed what appear to be paint traces on the statues of Pepi I.

85. Concerning the skin color, and other attributes, of foreigners in later periods, see further Roth, "Representing the Other," 165–71.

ples of Nubians depicted with darker skin colors than Egyptians and this may have occasionally been the practice already in the late Old Kingdom.[86] Old Kingdom Northerners, namely, Asiatics and Libyans, were sometimes painted with dark-yellow skin, which would correspond with later conventions and serve to distinguish them from Egyptians and Nubians, but not always. In general the coloration of foreigners in the Old Kingdom was relatively haphazard. For example, in a smiting scene from the mortuary temple of Niuserre, Ludwig Borchardt described the feet of a group of foreigners that the king is smiting as being painted yellow, red-brown, and brown.[87] Only the feet of the foreigners are preserved in this fragment so it is impossible to know how the coloration related to the foreigner stereotypes that were used in the late Old Kingdom reliefs. But Niuserre's artists seem to have employed different colored paint to increase the variability of the foreigners. Similarly, in the mortuary temple of Sahure, there is a reddish Asiatic standing between a Libyan who is the same reddish color as he and a more orangey or yellowish Asiatic.[88] Therefore, there clearly was an effort to show the pharaoh dominating different foreigners through the use of different skin colors, although particular colors were not systematically used for each foreigner stereotype. This haphazard way of painting foreigners seems to have been the practice, at least occasionally, throughout the late Old Kingdom. As such, it would not be surprising if the artists of the Pepi I prisoner statues had painted the statues different colors.

It is noteworthy that Pepi I and Pepi II's artists did not bother to carve clothing that might have been indicative of specific ethnic groups on these prisoner statues, as Djedkare's artists had done, and instead they employed plain short kilts for all of the statues. This is in contrast to the reliefs from these complexes where the artists continued to employ the traditional foreigner stereotypes and give the foreigners distinct costumes consistent with them.[89] As the Raneferef figurines show, the ethnic clothing was not necessary. On the one hand, the Pepi I and Pepi II prisoner statues' plain kilts further created the sense that they were generic foreigners, all identical and fully interchangeable enemies of the king. Yet at the same time, their varying heads served to emphasize their number and individuality.

Indeed, this new treatment of ethnicity is first readily apparent at the complex of Pepi I, and if this was the first complex where it was employed, which I think is most likely, the new treatment of ethnicity would correspond with the increased number of prisoner statues that this king had in comparison to his predecessors.[90] Moreover, the artists of Pepi I were probably responsible for innovating this new technique to visualize foreignness and difference. Artists would have been the ones who employed and executed the conventional stereotypes for foreigners. Therefore, it was most likely artists who devised a different treatment. Pepi I commissioned his artists to create a large group of different kneeling, bound foreigners.

---

86. Henry Fischer, "The Nubian Mercenaries of Gebelein during the First Intermediate Period," *Kush* 9 (1961): 56–63.

87. Borchardt, *Grabdenkmal des Königs Ne-user-re*, Abb. 64.

88. In his line drawings, Borchardt identified the skin color of the reddish Libyan and Asiatic as red-brown and that of the yellowish Asiatic as dark yellow (Borchardt, *Grabdenkmal des Königs Sahu-re*, 2:Bl. 5 and 7). Interestingly, he also depicted the reddish Asiatic as having a different beard, namely, a short, square chin beard, than the yellowish Asiatic, who has a pointed chin beard that covers the entire lower portion of his face. The hairstyles and kilts of both Asiatics is the same and correlates to those that Asiatics normally wear. Unfortunately, the beard of the reddish Asiatic is no longer preserved in the relief itself, which is now in Berlin, because of a break that runs through this foreigner's head (Berlin, ÄM 21782). If Borchardt's line drawing is correct, it is possible that these are two different types of Asiatics, that the artists varied the beards to create ethnic hybrids, or that the artists could have made a mistake.

89. Labrousse, *Temple funéraire*, 53–57 and 140 and pl. 8; Jéquier, *Monument funéraire*, 2:pl. 38 and 3:pl. 14. I consider why the stereotypes continued in the reliefs and not the statues at the end of this chapter.

90. There is a small possibility that the technique was used at the pyramid complex of Teti, as I questioned above, and perhaps even at that of Unas. There are no prisoner statue heads or bodies with distinct costumes or attributes that shed light on the treatment of ethnicity at the Unas complex.

Rather than employ the contemporary standard foreigner stereotypes, as was the usual practice, his artists decided to convey Otherness and the concept of multitude in a new way.

The artists of Pepi II employed the same technique to represent foreignness, though they executed it in a slightly more restrained fashion. There also seems to be fairly clear cases of artistic experimentation. Indeed, as the facial features became more standardized due to the late Old Kingdom style, the artists seem to have turned their attention to the beards and hairstyles, resulting in more diversity and creative details among the Pepi II heads than exists among the Pepi I ones. For example, JE 57202 (C.6.4) is the only head with a widow's peak (fig. 3.15). His beard, with incised individual strands of hair on the chin portion, is also unique. Both of these features could be the result of the artist trying something new, not always successfully as in the case of the widow's peak. But since these statues represented foreign prisoners and not important (and paying) Egyptians, such as the king or elite high officials, the artists may have felt more at ease or been more willing to experiment.

The Nubian, Libyan, and Asiatic stereotypes that the Egyptian artists employed during the Old Kingdom did not directly visualize the contemporary historical reality, which was far more complex. The same is true of the generic ethnicity of the Pepi I and Pepi II prisoner statues. Yet the imagery was not divorced from reality either. The dramatic change in the treatment of the prisoner statues' ethnicity occurred as Egypt's interactions with its neighbors shifted during the Sixth Dynasty. Toward the end of the Old Kingdom, a new multicultural climate seems to have arisen in Egypt, which would have particularly affected the elite, and the artists' treatment of the Pepi I and Pepi II prisoner statues' ethnicity is evidence of a corresponding change in their conception of ethnicity.

3.4. Egypt's Interactions with Foreigners during the Old Kingdom

The ancient Egyptians encountered foreigners in multiple ways and scenarios. The state frequently traded with neighboring kingdoms and cultural groups. The king authorized such activity, but elite Egyptians were responsible for administering it, and they often traveled to foreign lands and interacted with foreigners to carry it out. At times, particularly toward the end of the Old Kingdom, private merchants may have also been involved.

Similarly, the state organized mining expeditions in order to obtain raw materials and precious metals and stones. Indeed, the available evidence indicates that throughout the Old Kingdom, the Egyptian state's desire to obtain resources, raw materials, and luxury goods was the driving force behind their foreign policies. Like trade, mining seems to have been regarded as a type of military expedition, and both trade and mining parties regularly included military escorts.[91] These expeditions required Egyptian men to travel into the desert for extended periods of time. While spending time in the desert was certainly different from spending time inside a foreign city, the desert was not uninhabited and the men on mining expe-

---

91. Maksim Lebedev, "Exploiting the Southern Lands: Ancient Egyptian Quarrying, Mining, and Trade Missions to Nubia and Punt during the Old Kingdom," in *Nubian Archaeology in the XXIst Century: Proceedings of the Thirteenth International Conference for Nubian Studies, Neuchâtel, 1st–6th September 2014*, ed. Matthieu Honegger, OLA 273, Publications de la Mission archéologique suisse à Kerma 1 (Leuven: Peeters, 2018), 277 and Ian Shaw, "Exploiting the Desert Frontiers: The Logistics and Politics of Ancient Egyptian Mining Expeditions," in *Social Approaches to an Industrial Past: The Archaeology and Anthropology of Mining*, ed. Bernard Knapp, Vincent Pigott, and Eugenia Herbert (London: Routledge, 1998), 246–48 and 255–56. See further Ian Shaw, "Pharaonic Quarrying and Mining: Settlement and Procurement in Egypt's Marginal Regions," *Antiquity* 68 (1994): 108–19 and Eckhard Eichler, *Untersuchungen zum Expeditionswesen des ägyptischen Alten Reiches*, GOF 26 (Wiesbaden: Harrassowitz, 1993).

ditions would have encountered the vestiges of seminomadic peoples, if not the peoples themselves. The nature of this contact could be either hostile or peaceful. For example, rock inscriptions at Wadi Maghara in the Sinai document expeditions that Third Dynasty kings sent into this region and depict royal smiting scenes.[92] Whether these commemorated victories and/or served as warnings, they attest to engagement with foreign landscapes and populations. But not all encounters were aggressive or violent, if the smiting scenes do in fact reference actual hostile interactions, and local populations likely assisted and/or were recruited by Egyptian mining expeditions. Indeed titles and names indicate the types of individuals, including Egyptian interpreters and foreigners, who took part in such expeditions throughout the Old Kingdom.[93]

There were also armed conflicts and warfare between the Egyptians and foreign kingdoms or polities. Such militaristic interventions were also under the state's purview, and typically occurred in conjunction with Egypt's desire to control trade routes or access resources. But during the Old Kingdom, these always occurred outside of Egypt; at no point were Egypt's own borders threatened.

All of these various types of interactions, specific examples of which I provide below, exposed the ancient Egyptians, particularly royalty and the elite, to non-Egyptians, even if the intensity and nature of this exposure fluctuated with the type of interaction. The Egyptian men traveling beyond Egypt's borders into the desert, outlying territories, and foreign cities would have encountered different cultures and ethnicities and brought stories and tokens of them back to Egypt (fig. 3.28). Moreover, the Egyptian state forcibly settled foreigners and prisoners of war within its borders. Undoubtedly, immigration and emigration also

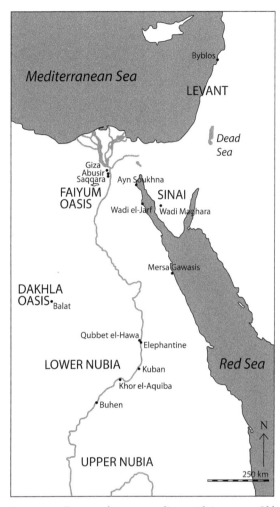

Figure 3.28. Egypt and its surroundings with important Old Kingdom sites.

---

92. Bestock, *Violence*, 180–85.

93. Lanny Bell, "Interpreters and Egyptianized Nubians in Ancient Egyptian Foreign Policy: Aspects of the History of Egypt and Nubia" (PhD diss., University of Pennsylvania, 1976); Andrés Diego Espinel, "Surveyors, Guides and Other Officials in the Egyptian and Nubian Deserts: Epigraphic and Historical Remarks on Some Old Kingdom Graffiti," *RdE* 65 (2014): 29–48; Henry Fischer, "A Scribe of the Army in a Saqqara Mastaba of the Early Fifth Dynasty," *JNES* 18 (1959): 233–72; Thomas Schneider, *Ausländer in Ägypten: Während des Mittleren Reiches und der Hyksoszeit*, 2 vols., ÄAT 42 (Wiesbaden: Harrassowitz, 1998), 1:22–23; Eichler, *Untersuchungen zum Expeditionswesen*, 168–234 and 256; and Sarah Parcak, "Egypt's Old Kingdom 'Empire'(?): A Case Study Focusing on South Sinai," in *Egypt, Israel, and the Ancient Mediterranean World: Studies in Honor of Donald B. Redford*, ed. Gary Knoppers and Antoine Hirsch, PAe 20 (Leiden: Brill, 2004), 51–57. I discuss the autobiographies and titularies of high officials who led foreign expeditions further below.

occurred in conjunction with trade, expeditions, and warfare. Therefore, even Egyptians who never left Egypt may have encountered foreigners.

While scholars often describe Egypt as having been more inward focused and isolated during the Old Kingdom in comparison to the Middle and New Kingdoms, new discoveries and studies have regularly called into question the idea that the Old Kingdom kings and state were detached from the broader ancient world and shown that the degree of Egypt's interactions with non-Egyptian places, cultures, and peoples was quite extensive throughout this period. Indeed, Thomas Schneider has recently observed that, "If there has been a constant in past reconstructions of Old Kingdom foreign relations, it is the fact that assumptions have been outstripped by new evidence and reassessments."[94]

At the same time, the available data also indicate that the relationship between Egyptians and foreigners, particularly those living to the south, was different during the Sixth Dynasty in comparison to the rest of the Old Kingdom. The nature of contact with foreign lands and peoples shifted at that time, becoming more decentralized, hostile, and complex. Similarly, the number of non-Egyptians living in Egypt increased. Overall, Sixth Dynasty Egypt was more multicultural, particularly for the elite. These changes coincided with the new treatment of ethnicity seen among the Pepi I and Pepi II prisoner statues. The artists of the statues, who were responsible for the new treatment as I argued above, were employees of the state and elite men themselves. They were also in contact with high-ranking officials, who oversaw their work. Because of this, the artists would be aware of the changing cultural climate around them, and the new treatment of the prisoner statues' ethnicity was a reaction to it.

3.4.1. The Third, Fourth, and Fifth Dynasties

During the Third, Fourth, and Fifth Dynasties, mining and trade expeditions accounted for the majority of opportunities through which the Egyptians would have been exposed to foreign places and people. The state was responsible for commissioning and overseeing them, and the activity appears to have been highly centralized. The products of such expeditions largely benefitted the king, particularly during the Third and Fourth Dynasties when the power of the king was at its height, as I discussed in chapter 1, and all expeditions likely occurred with his knowledge and authorization. The number of elite Egyptians who were interacting with foreigners, either at home or abroad, was less during these dynasties than during the Sixth Dynasty, and Egypt appears to have been fully in control of such interactions, facing few, if any, serious threats to their sovereignty. But this does not mean that Egypt was isolated or detached from the ancient world that surrounded it.

Prior to the Old Kingdom, Egypt seems to have been closely involved with its neighbors in all directions, and the traditional assessment of the early Old Kingdom has often been that these close interactions essentially ceased. According to this narrative, the early Old Kingdom pharaohs are thought to have enjoyed relative security that was the result of the First and Second Dynasty kings' aggressive policies toward surrounding regions, which ultimately led to the depopulation of the lands closest to Egypt. While the kings of the Third and Fourth Dynasties conducted trade and mining expeditions to acquire luxury products, their attention was primarily focused on internal matters, including pyramid building, and their contact with outsiders was significantly less than that of their predecessors.[95]

---

94. Thomas Schneider, "The Old Kingdom Abroad: An Epistemological Perspective; With Remarks on the Biography of Iny and the Kingdom of Dugurasu," in Der Manuelian and Schneider, *Towards a New History*, 438.

95. For example, see Baud, "The Old Kingdom," 71–80; Malek, *In the Shadow*, 98–100; and Ellen Morris, *Ancient Egyptian Imperialism* (Hoboken, NJ: Wiley-Blackwell, 2018), 39–40.

While the intensity of Egyptian interactions with foreign groups certainly varied throughout these periods, there are a number of issues with the conclusion that the Third and Fourth Dynasties were more isolated. Indeed, a scarcity of data for the early Old Kingdom may be largely to blame for this impression.[96] For example, scholars often describe Lower Nubia, the region directly to the south of Egypt, as having been largely uninhabited by indigenous populations throughout the early Old Kingdom.[97] The early First Dynasty kings adopted aggressive, expansionist policies into the region, which was home to the A-Group culture, perhaps in order to establish direct trade relations with groups living further to the south, and by the Second Dynasty, Lower Nubia appears to have been under Egypt's control. However, it seems increasingly unlikely that Lower Nubia was ever completely depopulated even though there is currently only a small amount of archaeological evidence that attests to this. While Reisner's identification of the B-Group culture has been dismissed and the B-Group is no longer accepted as an archaeological group, ceramic remains found at multiple sites in Lower Nubia, especially southern ones, suggest the presence of Nubians living in the region between the end of the A-Group in the Early Dynastic period and the appearance of the C-Group in the late Old Kingdom.[98]

There is no doubt that Egypt exploited Lower Nubia in the early Old Kingdom, and in doing so, they must have interacted with the peoples living there. Egyptian royal annals, namely, the Palermo Stone, records a raid in Lower Nubia dating to the reign of Sneferu that took seven thousand captives and two hundred thousand cattle as booty, and rock inscriptions at the site of Khor el-Aquiba in Lower Nubia, which may date to the Fourth Dynasty, mention the taking of seventeen thousand Nubians as prisoners and an Egyptian army of twenty thousand men.[99] The numbers in these texts may have been exaggerated, perhaps to enhance their significance and impact, since the current archaeological evidence from Lower Nubia does not support the presence of such a large population living there.[100] But it seems most likely that similar events did take place even if not to the magnitude of which the texts boast. Additionally, inscrip-

---

96. As Schneider has discussed in Schneider, "Old Kingdom Abroad," 429–38.

97. For overviews of Egyptian–Nubian interactions prior to and during the Old Kingdom, see further László Török, *Between Two Worlds: The Frontier Region between Ancient Nubia and Egypt 3700 BC–500 AD*, PAe 29 (Leiden: Brill, 2009), 23–73; Karola Zibelius-Chen, *Die ägyptische Expansion nach Nubien: Eine Darlegung der Grundfaktoren* (Wiesbaden: Reichert, 1988); and Harry S. Smith and Lisa L. Giddy, "Nubia and Dakhla Oasis in the Late Third Millennium B.C.: The Present Balance of Textual and Archaeological Evidence," in *Mélanges offerts à Jean Vercoutter*, ed. Francis Geus and Florence Thill (Paris: Éditions Recherche sur les Civilisations, 1985), 317–24.

98. See Brigitte Gratien, "La Basse Nubie à l'Ancien Empire: Egyptiens et autochtones," *JEA* 81 (1995): 43–56; Georg Meurer, *Nubier in Ägypten bis zum beginn des Neuen Reiches: Zur Bedeutung der Stele Berlin 14753* (Berlin: Achet, 1996), 60; and Stephan Seidlmayer, "Beispiele nubischer Keramik aus Kontexten des Hohen Alten Reiches aus Elephantine," in *Ägypten im afro-orientalischen Kontext – Gedenkschrift Peter Behrens*, ed. Daniela Mendel and Ulrike Claudi, Afrikanistische Arbeitspapiere Sondernummer (Cologne: Universität zu Köln, 1991), 337–50, all with further bibliography.

99. T. Wilkinson, *Royal Annals*, 141–43 PS r. VI.2; Heinrich Schäfer, *Ein Bruchstück altägyptischer Annalen* (Berlin: Verlag der Königl. Akademie der Wissenschaften, 1902), 30; Jesus Lopez, "Inscriptions de l'Ancien Empire à Khor el-Aquiba," *RdE* 19 (1967): 51–66; and Wolfgang Helck, "Die Bedeutung der Felsinschriften J. Lopez, Inscripciones rupestres Nr. 27 und 28," *SAK* 1 (1974): 215–25. Concerning the date of the Khor el-Aquiba inscriptions, Lopez originally dated them to the Sixth Dynasty, while Helck argued that they actually date to the Fourth Dynasty.

100. These numbers have troubled scholars as many think that they are impossibly large in comparison to the meager archaeological evidence that dates to the early Old Kingdom in Lower Nubia. For example, László Török and David O'Connor suggested that the booty actually came from Upper Nubia, which was home to the late Pre-Kerma or early *Kerma Ancien* culture (Török, *Between Two Worlds*, 55–56 and David O'Connor, *The Old Kingdom Town at Buhen*, MEES 106 [London: Egypt Exploration Society, 2014], 332–33; concerning the Pre-Kerma and *Kerma Ancien*, see recently Derek Welsby, "Kerma Ancien Cemeteries: From the Batn el-Hajar to the Fourth Cataract," in Honegger, *Nubian Archaeology*, 35–63, with further bibliography). While this is possible, there were Nubians living in Lower Nubia from the Second to the Sixth Dynasties and thus there is no reason to think that the textual records are completely wrong.

tions dating to the Fourth Dynasty indicate mining and quarrying activity in Lower Nubia at this time; this activity continued during the Fifth Dynasty.[101]

The Egyptians were also trading with the peoples living further to the south in Upper Nubia throughout the Old Kingdom. In order to facilitate access to mining and quarrying sites in Lower Nubia and to support the trade with Upper Nubia, the Egyptians established a settlement at the site of Buhen, likely during the reign of Khafre.[102] There, excavators discovered evidence for copper or gold production.[103] A smaller settlement at Kuban may have functioned as an intermediary point along the route from Egypt to Buhen.[104] The Egyptian border was at Elephantine, which played an important role in Egyptian interactions and involvement with its southern neighbors. The city seems to have been somewhat of a melting pot, with a heterogeneous Egyptian-Nubian population not only during the Old Kingdom but also for most periods of its existence.[105]

Trade expeditions to the legendary land of Punt, further to the south, for incense and other precious goods are first attested in the Fifth Dynasty, though the Egyptians may have been in contact with that region before this.[106] The location of Punt remains unknown and debated, perhaps lying somewhere near northern Eritrea and/or Ethiopia and/or the southern part of the Arabian peninsula, and Punt could be reached by both land and sea, but the maritime route may have been the most common during the Old Kingdom.[107] Harbor sites along the Red Sea coast, such as Wadi el-Jarf, Ayn Soukhna, and Mersa Gawasis, which were in use for other destinations, particularly in the Sinai, at various times throughout the Old Kingdom, could have served as embarkation points.[108] Recently discovered blocks from the causeway of

---

101. Eichler, *Untersuchungen zum Expeditionswesen*, 143–46; Diego Espinel, "Surveyors," 29–37; Lebedev, "Exploiting the Southern Lands," 278; and Gratien, "Basse Nubie," 46.

102. O'Connor, *Old Kingdom Town*. O'Connor preferred to identify much of the Nubian pottery, which accounted for approximately 6 percent of the ceramic sample, as A-Group and as belonging to an earlier Nubian settlement that predated the Egyptian one (O'Connor, *Old Kingdom Town*, 289–317), while Gratien suggested that the pottery belonged to Lower Nubians who were contemporary with the Egyptians living at Buhen (Gratien, "Basse Nubie," 49–56).

103. O'Connor, 337 and Shaw, "Exploiting the Desert Frontiers," 244. See also Lebedev, "Exploiting the Southern Lands," 277–78.

104. O'Connor, 336–37; Gratien, "Basse Nubie," 46–47; Smith and Giddy, "Nubia and Dakhla Oasis," 319; and Walter B. Emery and L. P. Kirwan, *The Excavations and Survey between Wadi es-Sebua and Adindan 1929–1931*, 2 vols., Mission archéologique de Nubie, 1929–1934 (Cairo: Service des antiquités de l'Égypte, 1935), 1:26 and 58.

105. Lebedev, "Exploiting the Southern Lands," 282; Seidlmayer, "Beispiele nubischer Keramik," 337–50; Dietrich Raue, "Centre and Periphery: Elephantine and Its Surroundings in the Third Millennium BC," in *The First Cataract of the Nile: One Region – Diverse Perspectives*, ed. Dietrich Raue, Stephen Seidlmayer, and Philipp Speiser, SDAIK 36 (Berlin: de Gruyter, 2013), 149–55; and Claudia Näser, "Structures and Realities of Egyptian–Nubian Interactions from the Late Old Kingdom to the Early New Kingdom," in Raue, Seidlmayer, and Speiser, 135–48. Concerning Elephantine during the Old Kingdom, see Stephan Seidlmayer, "Town and State in the Early Old Kingdom: A View from Elephantine," in *Aspects of Early Egypt*, ed. Jeffrey Spencer (London: British Museum Press, 1996), 108–27.

106. Edel and Diego Espinel have argued that trade between Egypt and Punt may be attested as early as the reign of Sneferu (Elmar Edel, "Studien zu den Relieffragmenten aus dem Taltempel des Königs Snofru," in Der Manuelian, *Studies*, 199–208; Andrés Diego Espinel, "The Scents of Punt (and Elsewhere): Trade and Functions of *sntr* and *ꜥntw* during the Old Kingdom," in *Flora Trade between Egypt and Africa in Antiquity: Proceedings of a Conference Held in Naples, Italy, 13 April 2015*, ed. Ilaria Incordino and Pearce Paul Creasman [Oxford: Oxbow, 2017], 24; and Andrés Diego Espinel, *Abriendo los caminos de Punt: Contactos entre Egipto y el ámbito afroárabe durante la Edad del Bronce (ca. 3000 a.C.–1065 a.C.)* [Barcelona: Bellaterra, 2011], 182–86).

107. Concerning the location of Punt and the ongoing debate surrounding it, see Cooper, *Toponymy*, 299–311; Kathryn Bard and Rodolfo Fattovich, *Seafaring Expeditions to Punt in the Middle Kingdom: Excavations at Mersa/Wadi Gawasis, Egypt*, CHANE 96 (Leiden: Brill, 2018), 156–75; and Diego Espinel, *Abriendo los caminos*, 59–120.

108. Lebedev, "Exploiting the Southern Lands," 279 and 284–85. Concerning these harbor sites and activity to and from

Sahure show the king receiving an expedition upon its return from Punt, and an entry on the Palermo Stone refers to the bringing of products from Punt toward the end of Sahure's reign.[109] Egypt continued trading with Punt for the rest of the Old Kingdom, and there are textual references to expeditions to Punt that occurred during the reign of Djedkare-Isesi and the late Sixth Dynasty.[110]

During the Third, Fourth, and Fifth Dynasties, trade to the north was focused on the city of Byblos and the coastal northern Levant, from which Egypt was particularly interested in procuring timber.[111] The Early Dynastic state appears to have established a direct trading network with this region via seaborne routes rather than employing the overland route through the southern Levant that had previously been dominant, and Karin Sowada has suggested that the Fourth Dynasty might have witnessed the zenith of the seaborne Old Kingdom timber trade to Byblos.[112]

---

the Red Sea coast, see Pierre Tallet and Gregory Marouard, "The Harbor Facilities of King Khufu on the Red Sea Shore: The Wadi al-Jarf/Tell Ras Budran System," *JARCE* 52 (2016): 135–77; Pierre Tallet and Gregory Marouard, "The Harbor of Khufu on the Red Sea Coast at Wadi al-Jarf, Egypt," *NEA* 77 (2014): 4–14; Pierre Tallet, "Ayn Sukhna and Wadi el-Jarf: Two Newly Discovered Pharaonic Harbours on the Suez Gulf," *BMSAES* 18 (2012): 147–68; Bard and Fattovich, 8–10; Kathryn Bard, Rodolfo Fattovich, and Andrea Manzo, "The Ancient Harbor at Mersa/Wadi Gawasis and How to Get There: New Evidence of Pharaonic Seafaring Expeditions in the Red Sea," in *Desert Road Archaeology in Ancient Egypt and Beyond*, ed. Frank Förster and Heiko Riemer, Africa praehistorica 27 (Cologne: Heinrich-Barth Institut, 2013), 533–56; and Gregory Mumford, "Ras Budran and the Old Kingdom Trade in Red Sea Shells and Other Exotica," *BMSAES* 18 (2012): 111–14.

109. Tarek El Awady, "King Sahura with the Precious Trees from Punt in a Unique Scene!" in Bárta, *Old Kingdom Art*, 37–44; Tarek El Awady, *Sahure – The Pyramid Causeway: History and Decoration Program in the Old Kingdom*, Abusir 16 (Prague: Charles University, 2009), 155–86 and pls. 5–8; T. Wilkinson, *Royal Annals*, 168–71 PS v.IV.1; and Schäfer, *Ein Bruchstück altägyptischer Annalen*, 38. See also Lebedev, 279–81 and Diego Espinel, *Abriendo los caminos*, 186–92.

110. *Urk.* 1:129–30 and 140–41 and Strudwick, *Texts*, 332–33 and 340. See also Lebedev, 281 and Diego Espinel, 191–200.

111. For overviews of the evidence for Egyptian-Levantine interactions during the Old Kingdom, see Donald B. Redford, "Egypt and Western Asia in the Old Kingdom," *JARCE* 23 (1986): 132–43 and Karin Sowada, *Egypt in the Eastern Mediterranean during the Old Kingdom: An Archaeological Perspective*, OBO 237 (Fribourg: Academic Press, 2009), with important additions in Andrés Diego Espinel, "Egypt and the Levant during the Old Kingdom," review of *Egypt in the Eastern Mediterranean during the Old Kingdom: An Archaeological Perspective*, by Karin Sowada, *Aula Orientalis* 30 (2012): 359–67 and Karin Sowada, "Never the Twain Shall Meet? Synchronising Egyptian and Levantine Chronologies in the 3rd Millennium BC," in *Egypt and the Southern Levant in the Early Bronze Age*, ed. Felix Höflmayer and Ricardo Eichmann, Orient-Archäologie 31 (Rahden: Leidorf, 2014), 293–313. Concerning Egyptian relations with the northern Levant during the Early Dynastic period, see E. Christiana Köhler and Jean-Paul Thalmann, "Synchronising Early Egyptian Chronologies and the Northern Levant," in Höflmayer and Eichmann, 181–206. Egypt's relationship with the southern Levant in the late Early Dynastic period and the Third Dynasty is more difficult to ascertain. While Adams has argued that Egypt had lost interest in the region by this point and interactions were minimal, Sowada and de Miroschedji have suggested that the change in trade routes, which I mention below, and Egypt's close engagement with the northern Levant did not put a complete end to Egypt's interactions with the south Levant; instead their involvement changed to one based on commodity exchange, product acquisition, and diplomacy with local elites (Matthew J. Adams, "Egypt and the Levant in the Early/Middle Bronze Age Transition," in *The Late Third Millennium in the Ancient Near East: Chronology, C14 and Climate Change*, ed. Felix Höflmayer, OIS 11 [Chicago: Oriental Institute of the University of Chicago, 2017], 495–97; Sowada, *Egypt*, 53 and 245–49; Sowada, "Never the Twain," 294 and 298; Pierre de Miroschedji, "The Socio-Political Dynamics of Egyptian-Canaanite Interaction in the Early Bronze Age," in *Egypt and the Levant: Interrelations from the 4th through the Early 3rd Millennium BCE*, ed. Edwin C. M. van den Brink and Thomas E. Levy [London: Leicester University Press, 2002], 45–48; and Pierre de Miroschedji, "Les Égyptiens au Sinaï du nord et en Palestine au Bronze Ancien," in *Le Sinaï durant l'antiquité et le Moyen Âge: 4000 ans d'histoire pour un desert*, ed. Dominique Valbelle and Charles Bonnet [Paris: Editions Errance, 1998], 28–29). Copper may have been a particularly important resource that Egypt obtained from this area, particularly the Wadi Feinan and major trade centers like Arad.

112. Sowada, *Egypt*, 249. Concerning the shift in trade routes through this region at the beginning of the Early Dynastic period, see further Sowada, 245–48; Amnon Ben-Tor, "The Early Bronze Age," in *The Archaeology of Ancient Israel*, ed. Amnon Ben-Tor, trans. R. Greenberg (New Haven: Yale University Press, 1992), 96–123; and Adams, 497. Moreover, Egyptian vessels inscribed with the names of Khafre and Pepi I that were discovered at Ebla testify to official trade networks connect-

Mining in the Sinai may have intensified and increased at the beginning of the Fourth Dynasty under Sneferu and Khufu, whose massive building projects in Egypt would have required considerable resources from abroad. There is evidence of predynastic and Early Dynastic Egyptian expeditions into the south Sinai, but it was not until the Third Dynasty that Egypt gained direct control of the region, and for the rest of the Old Kingdom, they sent regular mining expeditions to the Sinai, primarily for turquoise and copper.[113] Excavations at the site of Wadi el-Jarf on the Red Sea coast have revealed the early Fourth Dynasty harbor that was the starting point for expeditions to the southwest Sinai, particularly Wadi Maghara, and possibly beyond.[114]

Mining in the Western Desert also appears to have increased with the beginning of the Old Kingdom.[115] Inscriptions from the reigns of Khufu and Radjedef at the site of "Radjedef's Water-Mountain" (Chufu 01/1), which is about 60 km southwest of Dakhla, testify to expeditions to procure pigments.[116] Moreover, Olaf Kaper and Harco Willems identified a series of Fourth or Fifth Dynasty hilltop sites on the periphery of the Dakhla Oasis as watch posts that were used to control the access roads to the oasis.[117] Indeed, the Egyptians seem to have established small permanent settlements in Dakhla and may have already exercised some degree of administrative control and organization over the region in the Fourth Dynasty; they certainly did so by the Fifth Dynasty.[118] But evidence of the pharaonic occupation of Dakhla and the Western Desert throughout the Old Kingdom has been found alongside that of the local Sheikh Muftah culture, whom the Egyptians may have generically designated Tjemehu and Tjehenu Libyans. The Egyptians appear to have coexisted with these individuals, some of whom may have acted as local guides.[119]

---

ing Ebla and Egypt and might also suggest that Egypt was in direct contact with this city from as early as the Fourth Dynasty, though it is perhaps more likely that Byblos or another city, such as Ugarit, served as exchange centers that connected the two instead (Sowada, 249–50; Andrés Diego Espinel, "The Role of the Temple of Ba'alat Gebal as Intermediary between Egypt and Byblos during the Old Kingdom," *SAK* 30 [2002]: 111; and Gabriella Scandone Matthiae, "Les rapports entre Ebla et l'Égypte à l'Ancien et au Moyen Empire," in Hawass, *Egyptology*, 487–93).

113. Eichler, *Untersuchungen zum Expeditionswesen*, 128–30; Gregory Mumford, "Tell Ras Budran (Site 345): Defining Egypt's Eastern Frontier and Mining Operations in South Sinai during the Late Old Kingdom (Early EB IV/MB I)," *BASOR* 342 (2006): 52–55; Sowada, 248–54; and Parcak, "Egypt's Old Kingdom 'Empire,'" 51–55. For predynastic and Early Dynastic rock inscriptions in the south Sinai, see Bestock, *Violence*, 175–80; Moustafa Rezk Ibrahim and Pierre Tallet, "Trois bas-reliefs de l'époque thinite au Ouadi el-Humur: aux origins de l'exploitation du Sud-Sinaï par les Égyptiens," *RdE* 59 (2008): 155–80; and Pierre Tallet and Damien Laisney, "Iry-Hor et Narmer au Sud-Sinaï (Ouadi 'Ameyra): Un complément à la chronologie des expéditions minières égyptiennes," *BIFAO* 112 (2012): 381–98.

114. Tallet, "Ayn Sukhna"; Tallet and Marouard, "Harbor of Khufu"; and Tallet and Marouard, "Harbor Facilities."

115. Parcak, "Egypt's Old Kingdom 'Empire,'" 47.

116. Klaus Peter Kuhlmann, "Der 'Wasserberg des Djedefre' (Chufu 01/1): Ein Lagerplatz mit Expeditionsinschriften der 4. Dynastie im Raum der Oase Dachla," *MDAIK* 61 (2005): 244–89; Klaus Peter Kuhlmann, "The 'Oasis Bypath' or the Issue of Desert Trade in Pharaonic Times," in *Tides of the Desert – Gezeiten der Wüste: Contributions to the Archaeology and Environmental History of Africa in Honour of Rudolph Kuper*, ed. Jennerstrasse 8 (Cologne: Heinrich-Barth Institut, 2002), 133–37; and Frank Förster, "Beyond Dakhla: The Abu Ballas Trail in the Libyan Desert (SW Egypt)," in Förster and Riemer, *Desert Road Archaeology*, 300, with additional bibliography.

117. Olaf Kaper and Harco Willems, "Policing the Desert: Old Kingdom Activity around the Dakhleh Oasis," in *Egypt and Nubia: Gifts of the Desert*, ed. Renée Friedman (London: British Museum Press, 2002), 79–94. See also Förster, 299–300.

118. Laure Pantalacci, "Balat: A Frontier Town and Its Archive," in Moreno García, *Ancient Egyptian Administration*, 197–98; Heiko Riemer, "Lessons in Landscape Learning: The Dawn of Long-Distance Travel and Navigation in Egypt's Western Desert from Prehistoric to Old Kingdom Times," in Förster and Riemer, *Desert Road Archaeology*, 84; and Smith and Giddy, "Nubia and Dakhla Oasis," 330.

119. Morris, *Ancient Egyptian Imperialism*, 42–45; Riemer, 84–102; Stan Hendrickx, Frank Förster, and Merel Eyckerman, "The Pharaonic Pottery of the Abu Ballas Trail: 'Filling Stations' along a Desert Highway in Southwestern Egypt," in Förster and Riemer, *Desert Road Archaeology*, 341–42; Colin Hope, "Egypt and 'Libya' to the End of the Old Kingdom: A View from

Throughout the Third, Fourth, and Fifth Dynasties, Egyptian–foreigner interactions were highly centralized, with the state initiating and controlling them. They occurred outside Egypt, in foreign cities like Byblos, and in and around Egyptian settlements outside Egypt, such as Buhen and Dakhla. But there is little doubt that foreigners visited and lived in Egypt throughout the Old Kingdom as well.[120] That foreigners themselves were an important economic resource in which the Egyptians were interested throughout the Old Kingdom is evident from a variety of textual sources, including the Palermo Stone entry and the Khor el-Aquiba inscriptions that I referenced above.[121] Additionally, reliefs along the causeway of Unas, which may or may not be related to one another, show battles with people who seem to be from the north and ships returning to Egypt with northerners onboard.[122] Moreover, reliefs at the pyramid complex of Sahure may depict the arrival of Asiatic and Puntite foreigners, who might also have been understood to be human capital.[123] These reliefs may testify to the *type* of events that happened in the Fifth Dynasty and before, but they probably do not record unique occurrences and they cannot be used as evidence of specific historical events since the purpose of the reliefs in the royal pyramid complexes was not to chronicle affairs.[124] However, what does seem evident, based on both the textual and artistic material, is that foreigners were regularly brought back to Egypt, whether through trade or force. At the same time, the number of foreigners living in Egypt increased in the Sixth Dynasty. In the Third, Fourth, and Fifth Dynasties, there were no major threats to Egyptian state security and its territories. Trade seems to have been peaceful,

---

Dakhleh Oasis," in *The Archaeology and Art of Ancient Egypt: Essays in Honor of David B. O'Connor*, vol. 1, ed. Zahi Hawass and Janet Richards, CASAE 36 (Cairo: Supreme Council of Antiquities, 2007), 399–415; and Clara Jeuthe, "Initial Results: The Sheikh Muftah Occupation at Balat North/1 (Dakhla Oasis)," *Archéo-Nil* 24 (2014): 103–14.

120. Manfred Bietak, "The Early Bronze Age III Temple at Tell Ibrahim Awad and Its Relevance to the Egyptian Old Kingdom," in Hawass, Der Manuelian, and Hussein, *Perspectives on Ancient Egypt*, 65–77; Zibelius-Chen, *Ägyptische Expansion*, 115–25; Meurer, *Nubier in Ägypten*, 83–129; Fischer, "Nubian Mercenaries," 75–77; Dominique Valbelle, "L'égyptien en Nubie," in *Études nubiennes: Conférence de Genève, actes du VIIe Congrès internation d'études nubiennes 3–8 septembre 1990*, vol. 1, ed. Charles Bonnet (Geneva: Bonnet, 1992), 359–60; Seidlmayer, "Beispiele nubischer Keramik"; L. Bell, "Interpreters," 51–75; and Schneider, *Ausländer in Ägypten*, 12–26.

121. See also Hartwig Altenmüller, "Die 'Abgaben' aus dem 2. Jahr des Userkaf," in *Gedenkschrift für Winfried Barta*, ed. Dieter Kessler and Regine Schulz, MÄU 4 (Frankfurt am Main: Lang, 1995), 37–48; Michele Marcolin, "*Iny*, a Much-Traveled Official of the Sixth Dynasty: Unpublished Reliefs in Japan," in *Abusir and Saqqara in the Year 2005*, ed. Miroslav Bárta, Filips Coppens, and Jaromir Krejčí (Prague: Czech Institute of Egyptology, 2006), 301–3; Michele Marcolin and Andrés Diego Espinal, "The Sixth Dynasty Biographic Inscriptions of Iny: More Pieces to the Puzzle," in Bárta, Coppens, and Krejčí, *Abusir and Saqqara...2010*, 609–10; and Sowada, *Egypt*, 200–201.

122. Bestock, *Violence*, 111–15 and Audran Labrousse and Ahmed Moussa, *La chaussée du complexe funéraire du roi Ounas*, BiEtud 134 (Cairo: Institut français d'archéologie orientale, 2002), 21–23, 127–28, figs. 16–21 and 27, and pls. 1b and 2b. Another scene that has drawn significant debate concerning its possible historicity is that of the so-called Libyan family. It is first preserved in the mortuary temple of Sahure but was repeated frequently afterwards. While it may include historical references, it seems far more likely that the scene was falsely historicizing rather than historical (see further Tara Prakash, "Depictions of Defeated Foreigners in the Late Old Kingdom Pyramid Complex: A Mythological Interpretation," in Piacentini and Delli Castelli, *Old Kingdom Art*, 456–61). One needs to consistently question whether this might be the case for many, and perhaps all, of the reliefs featuring foreigners from the late Old Kingdom royal funerary complexes.

123. Borchardt, *Grabdenkmal des Königs Sahu-re*, 2:27–28, 87–88, and Bl. 12–13 and El Awady, *Sahure*, 155–60 and pl. 5. Lebedev has questioned whether the presence of foreigners aboard Egyptian ships returning from a voyage could be a kind of trope or cliché as well as evidence of foreign policies (Lebedev, "Exploiting the Southern Lands," 280). On the other hand, Bietak suggested that the Asiatics in the scenes from the complex of Sahure were carpenters who were brought to Egypt to build ships (Manfred Bietak, "Zur Marine des Alten Reiches," in *Pyramid Studies and Other Essays Presented to I. E. S. Edwards*, ed. John Baines et al., Occasional Publications 7 [London: Egypt Exploration Society, 1988], 35–40).

124. I return to this idea in ch. 4.3. See also Schneider, "Old Kingdom Abroad," 438, in regard to the historicity of Egyptian texts and reliefs for Egyptian–Levantine relations during the late Old Kingdom.

and Egypt appears to have initiated, directed, and benefitted from skirmishes with local populations living in the neighboring regions.

3.4.2. The Sixth Dynasty

With the Sixth Dynasty, the nature of Egyptian–foreign interactions changed. There were new groups living to the south of Egypt and an increasingly complicated political situation in Lower Nubia. Foreign interactions seem to have become more antagonistic in general. At the same time, Egypt expanded westward and effectively colonized the Dakhla Oasis. Through trade and military expeditions, Egyptian officials were engaging more closely, frequently, and directly with foreigners, and more foreigners, particularly Nubians, seem to have been living in Egypt. The change in the Pepi I and Pepi II prisoner statues' ethnicity occurred against this backdrop, and it reflected the more culturally complex world in which the Egyptians were living.

The amount of textual evidence testifying to Egyptian activity abroad and foreigners living in Egypt also increased significantly in the Sixth Dynasty, but this does not necessarily mean that the interactions themselves had increased. Much of this textual evidence comes from tomb inscriptions of elite high officials, and extremely lengthy titularies and private autobiographies, in which one finds these descriptions or references to foreign interactions, did not appear until the late Fifth Dynasty; they only became common in the Sixth Dynasty, coinciding with the rising status and influence of high officials that occurred throughout the late Old Kingdom.[125] Therefore, one might falsely get the impression that frequent interaction was a new phenomenon, when it almost certainly was not. Instead the *references* to Egyptian–foreign interactions—and the significance of these interactions for elite Egyptians—may have increased rather than the Egyptian–foreign interactions themselves.

The autobiographies indicate the increasing prominence of high officials in foreign affairs.[126] In these inscriptions, the officials boast of the successful expeditions that they have led to both northern and southern lands. They always acknowledge the supremacy of the pharaoh and present their missions abroad as directed by and of benefit to the king. But over the course of the Sixth Dynasty, provincial officials, particularly those living at Elephantine, oversaw more and more of these expeditions and appear to have started to take on more active or pronounced roles in their organization and execution.[127] Just as private officials

---

125. See further ch. 2.1. Claudia Näser also noted that the flourishing of funerary autobiographies in the Sixth Dynasty might explain the greater amount of information on foreign interactions at this time (Näser, "Structures and Realities," 136). Relevant autobiographies include those of Kaiemtjennet at Saqqara (*Urk.* 1:180–86 and Strudwick, *Texts*, 282–85); Weni at Abydos (*Urk.* 1:98–110 and Strudwick, 352–57); Meryrenefer Qar at Edfu (*Urk.* 1:251–55 and Strudwick, 342–44); Harkhuf at Qubbet el-Hawa (*Urk.* 1:120–31 and Strudwick, 328–33); Pepynakht-Heqaib at Qubbet el-Hawa (*Urk.* 1:131–35 and Strudwick, 333–35); Sabni and Mekhu II at Qubbet el-Hawa (*Urk.* 1:135–40 and Strudwick, 335–39); a second Sabni at Qubbet el-Hawa (Strudwick, 339–40); Khnumhotep in the tomb of Khui at Qubbet el-Hawa (*Urk.* 1:140–41 and Strudwick, 340); and Iny (Marcolin, "*Iny*" and Marcolin and Diego Espinel, "Sixth Dynasty Biographic Inscriptions"). For discussion of these inscriptions and relevant titles and epithets, see Schneider, 436; Andrés Diego Espinel, "Bringing Treasures and Placing Fears: Old Kingdom Epithets and Titles Related to Activities Abroad," *Isimu* 18–19 (2015–2016): 103–46; Roman Gundacker, "The Significance of Foreign Toponyms and Ethnonyms in Old Kingdom Text Sources," in Höflmayer, *Late Third Millennium*, 333–426; Kamil O. Kuraszkiewicz, "The Tomb of Ikhi/Mery in Saqqara and Royal Expeditions during the Sixth Dynasty," *Études et Travaux* 27 (2014): 202–16; Deborah Vischak, *Community and Identity in Ancient Egypt: The Old Kingdom Cemetery at Qubbet el-Hawa* (Cambridge: Cambridge University Press, 2015), 25–32; Eichler, *Untersuchungen zum Expeditionswesen*, 234–54; Smith and Giddy, "Nubia and Dakhla Oasis," 322–24; and Ivan V. Bogdanov, "New Relief Fragments from the Tomb of the Seafarer *jnj*," *CdE* 93:186 (2018): 227–47.

126. In this regard, see also Diego Espinel, "Bringing Treasures," 124

127. Török, *Between Two Worlds*, 71; Smith and Giddy, "Nubia and Dakhla Oasis," 330; Vischak, *Community and Identity*,

began to take on greater administrative responsibilities for the maintenance of the Egyptian government, they seem to have become increasingly in charge of foreign affairs even as the king remained the central authority. Moreover, Sowada has also noted a weakening of the state's control over the products of foreign missions as seen in the fact that foreign imports began to appear in nonelite contexts beyond the royal burial grounds of northern Egypt.[128] Indeed, significant numbers of Levantine ceramics imported from the area around Byblos have been found at Elephantine.[129] Private individuals seem to have become more involved with the activities taking place outside Egypt's borders, playing greater roles in and benefiting more directly from them.

By the Sixth Dynasty, Egypt had strong commercial ties to the northern Levant, and Byblos was still Egypt's main trading partner in the north. The pharaohs sent frequent expeditions there and may have donated prestigious objects and furnishings to the temple of Ba'alat Gebal.[130] This activity was undoubtedly state-sponsored, and following the reign of Pepi II, Egypt's direct contact with Byblos seems to have ceased. Even during the late Sixth Dynasty, such trade may have been slowing down or changing given the lack of imported Levantine ceramics at Elephantine toward the end of the reign of Pepi II.[131] As the capital became less involved with foreign affairs, ties with Byblos and the Levant may have broken.

Egypt's relationship with Nubia during the Sixth Dynasty was more complex. The Egyptian settlement at Buhen appears to have been abandoned sometime in the mid- to late Fifth Dynasty for unknown reasons.[132] Around the same time or shortly afterwards, the C-Group culture appeared in Lower Nubia. Textual evidence in Egypt testifies to three polities that likely occupied the region: Wawat, Irtjet, and Setju.[133] The Egyptians seem to have clashed with these groups at least occasionally and perhaps regularly. For example, the autobiography of Pepinakht-Heqaib, inscribed in his tomb at Qubbet el-Hawa, records violent encounters with Wawat and Irtjet as well as with Northerners during the reign of Pepi II.[134] As a

---

28; and Eichler, *Untersuchungen zum Expeditionswesen*, 258–73. Vischak considers more broadly how this and other factors may have influenced the identity of the Elephantine high officials.

128. Sowada, *Egypt*, 251; cf. Diego Espinel, "Egypt and the Levant," 363.

129. Irene Forstner-Müller and Dietrich Raue, "Contacts between Egypt and the Levant in the 3rd Millennium BC," in Höflmayer and Eichmann, *Egypt and the Southern Levant*, 57–67 and Irene Forstner-Müller and Dietrich Raue, "Elephantine and the Levant," in *Zeichen aus dem Sand: Streiflichter aus Ägyptens Geschichte zu Ehren von Günter Dreyer*, ed. Eva-Maria Engel, Vera Müller, and Ulrich Hartung, Menes 5 (Wiesbaden: Harrassowitz, 2008), 127–48.

130. Diego Espinel, "Role of the Temple," 103–19.

131. Forstner-Müller and Raue, "Contacts," 57–67.

132. O'Connor, *Old Kingdom Town*, 335–36.

133. There is little doubt that Wawat included at least part of Lower Nubia, but the locations of Irtjet and Setju have been the subject of some debate following David O'Connor's argument that they should be situated in Upper Nubia (David O'Connor, "The Locations of Yam and Kush and Their Historical Implications," *JARCE* 23 [1986]: 35–39). For further discussion and references, see n. 140.

134. *Urk.* 1:133–35 and Strudwick, *Texts*, 334–35. See also Juan Carlos Moreno García, "War in Old Kingdom Egypt (2686–2125 BCE)," in *Studies on War in the Ancient Near East: Collected Essays on Military History*, ed. Jordi Vidal, AOAT 372 (Münster: Ugarit-Verlag, 2010), 32–33 and Török, *Between Two Worlds*, 66–68. Scholars have pointed toward this and other autobiographies, such as that of Weni (*Urk.* 1:101–5 and Strudwick, 354–55), and reliefs, including siege scenes in the Fifth Dynasty private tombs of Inti at Deshasha and Kaiemheset in Saqqara (Naguib Kanawati and Ann McFarlane, *Deshasha: The Tombs of Inti, Shedu and Others*, RACE 5 [Sydney: The Australian Centre for Egyptology, 1993], 24–25 and pls. 2 and 26–27 and Ann McFarlane, *Mastabas at Saqqara: Kaiemhest, Kaipunesut, Kaiemsenu, Sehetepu and Others*, RACE 20 [Oxford: Aris & Phillips, 2003], 33–34 and pls. 2a, 10–11, and 48; recent discussions of these scenes include Bestock, *Violence*, 225–30 and Anna-Latifa Mourad, "Siege Scenes of the Old Kingdom," *BACE* 22 [2011]: 135–58, both with further references) as well as the battle scene from the causeway of Unas that I described above, in support of increasing Egyptian aggression toward the southern Levant in the late Old Kingdom (for a recent discussion of Weni's autobiography in this regard, with numerous references to earlier analyses, see Gundacker, "Significance of Foreign Toponyms"). Several scholars have also suggested

result of these political and cultural changes in Lower Nubia during the Sixth Dynasty, Egyptian relations with the region fundamentally changed, and direct exploitation of Nubian natural resources significantly declined.¹³⁵

At the same time, occupation of the Dakhla Oasis intensified. An Egyptian settlement in Balat was founded by at least the early Sixth Dynasty, and over the course of this dynasty, it grew in size and prominence.¹³⁶ The nomarchs residing there were extremely influential and powerful individuals, as the *ka*-chapels of the last four nomarchs, who were in office during the reign of Pepi II, demonstrate. These men oversaw and controlled the Dakhla region and the desert roads leading in and out of the oasis.¹³⁷ They seem to have played leading roles in diplomacy and the trade and expeditions that passed through and were conducted within the Western Desert and exercised a good deal of independence from the king and central government. They further testify to the growing prominence of provincial high officials that occurred in the late Sixth Dynasty within Egypt overall and specifically in matters related to foreign affairs.

The increased Egyptian presence and interest in Dakhla appears to have been closely linked to the appearance of the C-Group, who may have interfered with or complicated Egyptian access to Upper Nubia and important trade partners in the south who had previously been reached primarily via Nile trade routes.¹³⁸ Because of this, the Egyptians needed to control the desert trade routes better. Indeed, the au-

---

that these conflicts may have taken place in the Sinai rather than the southern Levant, and the new absolute chronology for the latter region may lend support to this identification (Mumford, "Tell Ras Budran," 13–67; Parcak, "Egypt's Old Kingdom 'Empire,'" 54–55; and Gundacker, "Significance of Foreign Toponyms," but one should note Tallet and Marouard's redating of Tell Ras Budran to the early Fourth Dynasty in Tallet and Marouard, "Harbor Facilities," 168–77; concerning the new Early Bronze Age absolute chronology of the southern Levant, see Johanna Regev et al., "Chronology of the Early Bronze Age in the Southern Levant: New Analysis for a High Chronology," *Radiocarbon* 54 [2012]: 525–66 and Raphael Greenberg, "No Collapse: Transmutations of Early Bronze Age Urbanism in the Southern Levant," in Höflmayer, *Late Third Millennium*, 31–58, both with additional bibliography). However, in regard to Weni's autobiography, Felix Höflmayer has argued that presently it is not possible to localize the foreign lands to which Weni traveled and that we should also not assume the text's historicity (Felix Höflmayer, "Egypt and the Southern Levant in the Late Early Bronze Age," in Höflmayer and Eichmann, *Egypt and the Southern Levant*, 139). Mumford ("Tell Ras Budran," 56) also suggested that Weni's claim to have slain many tens of thousands during his first campaign was exaggerated. It is certainly possible that Egypt's relationship with foreigners living to the north, in the southern Levant and/or the Sinai, had become more antagonistic and hostile by the Sixth Dynasty, but it is difficult to point to strong evidence that proves this conclusion.

135. Lebedev, "Exploiting the Southern Lands," 277–79.

136. For Balat and its nomarchs, see further Lisa Giddy, *Egyptian Oases* (Warminster: Aris & Phillips, 1987), 174–205; Georges Soukiassian, Michel Wuttmann, and Laure Pantalacci, *Le palais des gouverneurs de l'époque de Pépy II: Les sanctuaires de ka et leurs dépendances*, Balat 6, FIFAO 46 (Cairo: Institut français d'archéologie orientale, 2002); Kaper and Willems, "Policing the Desert," 79–81; and Pantalacci, "Balat." Ellen Morris has argued that Egypt's relationship with Dakhla during this period should be classified as colonial (Morris, *Ancient Egyptian Imperialism*, 40–65).

137. Kaper and Willems have argued that the Egyptians may have felt that this region was safer or that they were exposed to fewer threats within it by the mid- to late Sixth Dynasty because a protective wall was not constructed during the expansion of 'Ain Asil in Balat that occurred around this time (phase III) while the earlier settlement had been confined largely to the area within the city walls (Kaper and Willems, 80–81). If correct, this would have implications in regard to the Egyptians' relationship with the local population, who continued to live in the area until the end of the Old Kingdom (see my discussion in the previous subsection).

138. For possible evidence of Egyptians in Upper Nubia, see Valbelle, "L'égyptien en Nubie." Morris has suggested that Egypt's settlement of Dakhla might also have been related to widespread aridification that occurred toward the end of the third millennium and Egypt's consequent need to provide agricultural security to its people while preemptively securing the oasis from seminomadic Libyans who might have been looking for such resources at the same time (Morris, *Ancient Egyptian Imperialism*, 49–52).

tobiography of the high official Harkhuf seems to testify to this situation.¹³⁹ It suggests that the political changes in Lower Nubia had made travel through this region less desirable, and on his third expedition to the polity of Yam, which the pharaoh Merenre had ordered, Harkhuf preferred to take the "oasis road." The exact location of Yam remains uncertain; while most scholars place it in Upper Nubia, some prefer to situate it further to the south and/or west.¹⁴⁰ Regardless of this debate, Yam was undoubtedly an important trading partner from whom Egypt obtained southern goods and raw materials, and the "oasis road" that Harkhuf took most likely left from Dakhla.

The Abu Ballas Trail also demonstrates the increasing importance of desert routes during this time.¹⁴¹ Based on the archaeological and textual evidence, it was heavily used for trade at the end of the Sixth Dynasty and during the First Intermediate period, and it seems to have connected Egypt with a number of distant regions, perhaps the most important of which was Yam.¹⁴² The fact that this trade was still flourishing in the First Intermediate period, unlike trade with Byblos, indicates that the state was less involved, and already in the late Sixth Dynasty control of it may have been primarily in the hands of the provincial elite, especially those living in Dakhla.

But not all Nubians in Lower Nubia and the surrounding deserts were enemies. The use of mercenaries increased during the Sixth Dynasty with the Egyptians conscripting Nubians as soldiers and for Egyptian expeditions. In his autobiography, Weni, who served under the pharaohs Teti, Pepi I, and Merenre, described the many Nubian soldiers in his army.¹⁴³ This practice continued into the First Intermediate period when there is significant evidence of Nubian mercenaries living within Egypt.¹⁴⁴ Overall the presence and significance of foreigners in Egypt may have risen during the Sixth Dynasty.¹⁴⁵

It is possible that execration figurines and texts were partly a response to this and the more antagonistic relationships that Egypt now had with many Nubians. These magical objects were akin to voodoo dolls, and names of the targeted people and places were written on them.¹⁴⁶ They may have first appeared in the Sixth Dynasty, and most examples date to the reign of Pepi II.¹⁴⁷ Most have also been discovered in the

---

139. *Urk.* 1:124–27 and Strudwick, *Texts*, 330–31. See also Kuhlmann, "'Oasis Bypath,'" 139–44 and Claude Obsomer, "Les expeditions d'Herkhouf (VIe dynastie) et la localization de Iam," in *Pharaons noirs: Sur la piste des quarante jours*, ed. Marie-Cécile Bruwier (Mariemont: Musée Royal de Mariemont, 2007), 39–52, with additional references.

140. Recent discussions of the location of Yam, with references to earlier arguments, can be found in Julien Cooper, "Reconsidering the Location of Yam," *JARCE* 48 (2012): 1–21; Obsomer, "Expeditions d'Herkhouf"; and Frank Förster, *Der Abu Ballas-Weg: Eine pharaonische Karawanenroute durch die Libysche Wüste*, Africa praehistorica 28 (Cologne: Heinrich-Barth Institut, 2015), 474–87.

141. Concerning the Abu Ballas Trail during the Old Kingdom and First Intermediate period, see further Kuhlmann, "'Oasis Bypath,'" 140–58; Förster, "Beyond Dakhla," 297–321; Hendrickx, Förster, and Eyckerman, "Pharaonic Pottery," 344–51; Frank Förster, "With Donkeys, Jars and Water Bags into the Libyan Desert: The Abu Ballas Trail in the Late Old Kingdom/First Intermediate Period," *BMSAES* 7 (2007): 1–36; and Förster, *Abu Ballas-Weg*.

142. Laure Pantalacci, "Broadening Horizons: Distant Places and Travels in Dakhla and the Western Desert at the End of the 3rd Millennium," in Förster and Riemer, *Desert Road Archaeology*, 283–96 and Joseph Clayton, Aloisia de Trafford, and Mark Borda, "A Hieroglyphic Inscription Found at Jebel Uweinat Mentioning Yam and Tekhebet," *Sahara* 19 (2008): 129–34.

143. *Urk.* 1:101 and Strudwick, *Texts*, 354. The army also included Tjemehu Libyans.

144. Lebedev, "Exploiting the Southern Lands," 286; Moreno García, "War," 26–30; Raue, "Centre and Periphery"; Török, *Between Two Worlds*, 71–72; and Fischer, "Nubian Mercenaries."

145. Lebedev, "Exploiting the Southern Lands," 286.

146. I introduced these figurines in ch. 1 and discuss them in greater detail in ch. 5.

147. Excavated examples from the Old Kingdom have been discovered at Balat (Nicolas Grimal, "Les 'noyés' de Balat," in Geus and Thill, *Melanges*, 111–21); Giza (Hermann Junker, *Giza VIII: Der Ostabschnitt des Westfriedhofs*, AAWWien 81 [Vienna: Akademie der Wissenschaften, 1947], 30–38 and Tf. 6b and 7; Abdel Moneim Abu Bakr and Jürgen Osing, "Ächtungstexte aus dem Alten Reich," *MDAIK* 29 [1973]: 97–133; and Jürgen Osing, "Ächtungstexte aus dem Alten Reich (II)," *MDAIK* 32 [1976]: 133–85; Saqqara (Joachim Friedrich Quack, "Some Old Kingdom Execration Figurines from the Teti

Memphite necropoli and seem to have been products of the state or central authorities, but as I discussed in the previous chapter, by the end of the Old Kingdom state matters were increasingly in the hands of private high officials rather than the king. Nearly all, if not all, of the foreigners named on the Old Kingdom execration figurines that remain readable were Nubians.[148] These testify to the increasingly complicated, unstable, and often hostile world within which the Egyptians found themselves, particularly in regard to their relationships with foreigners from the south.

The nature of Egypt's relationship with its neighbors shifted during the Sixth Dynasty. To the Egyptians, the world may have felt both smaller, with more foreigners residing in Egypt, and larger, as the Egyptian elite regularly spent time outside the country and lived away from the capital. The political and social developments that were occurring within the country seem to have influenced the role and standing that high officials had in foreign policy and trade; the state's control over this activity appears to have declined while provincial high officials became more and more involved. The autobiographies also suggest a growing sense of hostility and insecurity, and they describe an increasingly complex world. Political and societal changes were occurring, particularly to the south, that forced Egypt to devise other ways to acquire the resources that the elite had become accustomed to having.

This would have had an impact on the overall cultural climate of Sixth Dynasty Egypt, and the new treatment of ethnicity that one sees among the Sixth Dynasty prisoner statues seems to be a reaction to this more multicultural world in which the Egyptians, particularly the elite, were living. The change in the prisoner statues' ethnicity reflects a new conception of ethnicity itself, one that is more nuanced. The artists of the later prisoner statues were trying to depict a breadth of foreigners and ethnic diversity because of the increasingly diversified world that they inhabited.

3.5. The Prisoner Statues' Style and Ethnicity in the Context of the Late Old Kingdom

There are notable differences between the Fifth and Sixth Dynasty prisoner statues. This includes the degree of expressiveness and individuality in their facial features. The expressiveness is a repercussion of the late Old Kingdom style, which is first apparent among the prisoner statues at the pyramid complex of Teti. This style's influence continued among the Pepi I prisoner statues' heads. By the reign of Pepi II, the

---

Cemetery," *BACE* 13 [2002]: 149–60 and Teodozja Rzeuska, "Execration Again? Remarks on an Old Kingdom Ritual," *Polish Archaeology in the Mediterranean* 22 [2013]: 627–34); and Elephantine (Stephan Seidlmayer, "Execration Texts," in Redford, *Oxford Encyclopedia*, 487). Several unprovenanced examples have been dated to the Old Kingdom (Stefan Wimmer, "Neue Ächtungstexte aus dem Alten Reich," *BN* 67 [1993]: 87–100 and Andrés Diego Espinel, "A Newly Identified Old Kingdom Execration Text," in *Decorum and Experience: Essays in Ancient Culture for John Baines* [Oxford: Griffith Institute, 2013], 26–33). I discuss these in greater detail in ch. 5.3.

148. Wimmer restored the northern toponyms ꜥ3mw and stt on the Munich figurine. Mourad has followed his reading, but Diego Espinel refuted it (Anna-Latifa Mourad, "The Asiatic stt and sttyw from the Early Dynastic Period to the Middle Kingdom," in *The Cultural Manifestations of Religious Experience: Studies in Honour of Boyo G. Ockinga*, ed. Camilla Di Biase-Dyson and Leonie Donovan, ÄAT 85 [Münster: Ugarit-Verlag, 2017], 300–301 and Diego Espinel, 28 and 31). Posener also proposed a Semitic etymology for one of the names on a figurine that Junker discovered (Georges Posener, "Les empreintes magiques de Gizeh et les morts dangereux," *MDAIK* 16 [1958]: 252 n. 2). It is important to note that Egyptians are also named on the Old Kingdom execration texts.

style had become prevalent across Egypt, and the prisoner statues heads from this complex display a more uniform deployment of late Old Kingdom style attributes.

At the Pepi I pyramid complex, the facial features and hairstyles of the prisoner statues were mixed and matched among the heads, creating a variety of imaginary, individualized foreigners. This novel treatment of ethnicity may have been partly inspired by the late Old Kingdom style, which the artists were likely still developing and solidifying during the early Sixth Dynasty. This innovative new style may have prompted innovative representations of ethnicity. However, the new treatment of ethnicity primarily seems to reflect a new conception of ethnicity that arose as the nature of Egyptian interactions with foreigners shifted.

The artists were most likely responsible for the creative treatment of ethnicity seen among the Pepi I prisoner statues. They were the ones who chose how to depict foreigners, and thus they were the ones who chose not to use the foreigner stereotypes for the Pepi I prisoner statues and to develop an alternative. The artists of the Pepi II prisoner statues followed them and also chose to depict individualized foreigners rather than ethnic stereotypes. As members of the elite class, living and working in the capital, and in contact with the central government and high-ranking officials, who were largely running the government at this time, the royal artists responsible for the prisoner statues would have been aware of the changes in Egyptian–foreigner interactions that were contemporaneously occurring. They might have known that their superiors were more concerned about new cultural groups to the south who were impacting established Egyptian trade routes or that expeditions to the south were more frequently being sent through the desert to avoid armed conflicts with Nubians. They also might have heard about the Egyptian colony in the Dakhla Oasis, which had become quite large and well established in order for the Egyptians to better secure the Western Desert. Similarly, they might have encountered the Nubian mercenaries who were living in Egypt in increasingly large numbers, or at least heard stories about them. All of this would have influenced their understanding of foreignness and prompted the artists to try a new technique to depict it.

In many ways, the prisoner statues were a reasonable place to do this. The individuality and variability of the Pepi I and Pepi II prisoner statues enhanced their multiplicity, which was inherent in the large number of statues and was clearly important. The statues were also representations of foreigners, not images of important Egyptians. Certainly the king or his high officials must have approved the statues, and their ambiguous foreign ethnicity, but the prisoner statues' negative status was apparent and manifest in their position. For the king, it was the position of the statues that was most paramount to their purpose in his funerary monument since it referenced and reinforced his power and supremacy. Their exact ethnicity, or how it was portrayed, was less important in this regard. Therefore, the artists may have had more flexibility and opportunity to experiment with the heads.

The Egyptian sense of ethnic and cultural identity may have been changing, and the prisoner statues seem to encapsulate the artists' interest in and desire to explore and convey this. The change in ethnicity is both a reflection of and a reaction to the increasingly complex world in which the Egyptians, particularly the elite, lived. The heads of the Sixth Dynasty prisoner statues demonstrate one way that artistic change could manifest social and political change and show how complex this translation could be. In this way, the prisoner statues give insight into how broad historical changes could affect the people living through them.

The ethnic ambiguity of the Pepi I and Pepi II prisoner statues markedly contrasts with the stereotypical representation of foreigners found among the Fifth Dynasty prisoner statues and the late Old Kingdom triumph scenes. Yet none of these depictions mimetically reflect the reality of Egyptian interactions with foreigners. The stereotypical Nubians, Libyans, and Asiatics do not directly reproduce the actual foreigners with which the Egyptians interacted anymore than the generic imaginary foreigners of the Pepi I and Pepi II prisoner statues. Both the stereotypes and the later prisoner statues were essentially symbols of Otherness and the broad world that extended in all directions but theoretically was always under the king's authority. The three stereotypes may have signified multiplicity, since the number three traditionally represented plurality, just as the late prisoner statues did the same through individuality and variability. In this way, these representations more directly inform us about the Egyptians, including their beliefs and attitudes, than about actual foreign groups or individuals that the Egyptians encountered.

As I argued in the last chapter, the increase in the number of statues at the complex of Pepi I and again at that of Pepi II coincided with the decreasing power of the king. They were one of numerous efforts on the part of the pharaoh to differentiate himself from the increasingly influential high officials that comprised the Sixth Dynasty government. The prisoner statues were symbols of royal authority so the king commissioned more and more of them. Yet the carving of them was the job of his artists, and, as I showed in this chapter, the style, features, and execution of the heads primarily reflect the interests, concerns, and trends that were affecting the artists.

In this regard, it is notable that the Sixth Dynasty royal sculptors changed how they represented foreigners while the royal relief carvers did not. Throughout the Sixth Dynasty, even as the artists of Pepi I and Pepi II's prisoner statues represented the king's enemies in an inventive and unusual fashion, the reliefs of these kings continue to feature the same stereotypical Nubians, Libyans, and Asiatics. There are likely multiple reasons for this, including the possibility of distinct artistic practices for artists who worked in different media. But it also reflects the more traditional nature of relief decoration during the late Old Kingdom. Sculptors who worked in three-dimensions seem to have been more inclined to experiment and try new techniques or approaches than the artists who were responsible for two-dimensional art. The fact that attributes of the late Old Kingdom style first appeared among statuary before spreading to relief further reinforces this observation.[149] Indeed, this tendency of late Old Kingdom artists to experiment with statuary was the primary reason that the prisoner statues first appeared, as I show in the next chapter, which explores the relationship between the three-dimensional and two-dimensional decoration of the late Old Kingdom pyramid complex more fully.

---

149. Brovarksi, "Second Style," 49–89.

Chapter 4
The Prisoner Statues and the Pyramid Complex

A prisoner statue fragment has yet to be discovered in situ. As a result, the statues' original placement within each pyramid complex, and the way in which they corresponded to the architecture and the rest of the decorative program, is still a central question.[1] Chapter 4 considers this issue of location and original context. The available evidence, which I present here, demonstrates that there was not a single part of the pyramid complex that always contained a king's prisoner statues. Rather the location of the prisoner statues varied over time. Moreover, the statues were closely related to reliefs of triumph and domination, and they appeared during a period of experimentation in the mid-Fifth Dynasty when traditional two-dimensional motifs were transferred into three-dimensional statues. In many cases, the prisoner statues seem to have been set near similarly themed reliefs in order to compliment them. But the statues could also substitute for such reliefs. Overall, the developments in the decorative program of the late Old Kingdom pyramid complex that I discuss here, along with the architectural changes that I also outline, indicate how dynamic these monuments were. While scholars often describe them as standardized and repetitive, each king's funerary monument differed from those of his successors, and the designers, architects, and artists of the late Old Kingdom pyramid complexes consistently showed a significant degree of ingenuity, creativity, and flexibility.

Throughout this chapter, my analysis and commentary is centered on the parts of the pyramid complex that were decorated with reliefs and statuary, including prisoner statues; these consist of the valley temple, causeway, and mortuary temple.[2] The following section briefly introduces the late Old Kingdom pyramid complex and its overall plan, focusing on the monument of King Sahure. Scholars often describe this complex as a prototype that all subsequent Old Kingdom kings followed with only minor deviations; the remainder of this chapter shows why this interpretation is problematic. In the second section, I explicate the deviations in plan for the pyramid complexes of subsequent kings that had prisoner statues while also presenting the archaeological evidence for these statues' findspots. This demonstrates that the part of the complex (i.e., valley temple, causeway, or mortuary temple) that held prisoner statues changed over time, and there is no single part of the complex that can be identified as *the* place that always held prisoner statues. The third section of this chapter considers the two-dimensional decorative program of the Fifth and Sixth Dynasty pyramid complex, centering on the placement of reliefs with similar themes as the prisoner statues, namely, those that featured depictions of the king, or an agent of his, dominating enemies and

---

1. As I mentioned in ch. 1.1, to refer to the reliefs and statuary associated with the complex as merely decoration is misleading. On the one hand, they did serve to embellish and further beautify the architectural structures. However, they also did much more than this. The reliefs and statuary, replete with their own symbolisms and functions, added to the overall efficacy of the complex itself.

2. Concerning the architecture of the late Old Kingdom pyramid and funerary apartments, see further Audran Labrousse, *L'architecture des pyramides à textes*, 2 vols., MAFS 3, BiEtud 114 and 131 (Cairo: Institut français d'archéologique orientale, 1996–2000).

other analogous beings, in order to evaluate where in the temples and causeway such subject matter was appropriate. Then, in the following section, I focus on the overall sculptural program of the Old Kingdom pyramid complex and how this changed over time.

As I elaborate in the fifth section, the prisoner statues were closely related to reliefs of triumph and domination. The Egyptians seem to have conceived of them as three-dimensional variations of two-dimensional iconography since they appeared at a time when the sculptural program of the pyramid complex was expanding and new types of statues, that corresponded with the relief program and were inspired by it, were being used in the monuments. Throughout the rest of the Old Kingdom, the statues continued to function together with the relief program, and their location in each pyramid complex varied in accordance with the mutable placement of similarly themed reliefs. In the final section of this chapter, I discuss the implications of these developments of the late Old Kingdom pyramid complex's decorative program in light of the architectural changes that contemporaneously occurred. In doing so, namely, by considering the monuments' architecture and decoration together, it becomes clear that the late Old Kingdom pyramid complex was much less standardized and creatively stagnant than Egyptologists have previously assumed.

4.1. The Late Old Kingdom Pyramid Complex

Many scholars have described the pyramid complex of Sahure as an ideal prototype to which the later Old Kingdom kings continuously looked back and which they tried to emulate; according to these interpretations, the resulting standardization caused a decline in creativity and the overall quality of the architecture and wall reliefs of the later monuments.[3] Sahure's pyramid complex is one of the best-preserved monuments from the late Old Kingdom, and the remains testify to how striking its plan and architecture originally were. However, the subsequent kings of the Fifth and Sixth Dynasties were not simply copying Sahure. There was a continuous interest in redesigning each king's pyramid complex; the royal engineers, architects, and artists looked to the past, including to the pyramid complex of Sahure, and drew inspiration from it, but they also developed, refined, and adjusted each monument better to suit the needs and desires of the king whom they served. Modern scholars' impression of the later monuments as static and less innovative is partly the result of these monuments' poorer state of preservation in comparison to the state of Sahure's pyramid complex.

While the pyramid complex changed significantly throughout the Old Kingdom, by the Fifth Dynasty, it had four basic elements that were typically aligned along an east–west axis: the pyramid itself in the west marking the king's tomb; the mortuary temple, which was directly adjacent to the pyramid; the valley temple in the east and at the edge of cultivation; and the covered causeway, which connected the temples and led from the cultivation toward the pyramid in the desert (fig. 4.1).[4] Unlike during the Fourth Dynasty, when the size of the pyramid itself was the priority, the later kings devoted their resources to the temples,

---

3. For example, see Di. Arnold, "Royal Cult Complexes," 63; El Awady, *Sahure*, 50; Peter Jánosi, "Die Entwicklung und Deutung des Totenopferraumes in den Pyramidentempeln des Alten Reiches," in *Ägyptische Tempel: Struktur, Funktion und Programm (Akten der Ägyptologischen Tempeltagungen in Gosen 1990 und in Mainz 1992)*, ed. Rolf Gundlach and Matthias Rochholz, HÄB 37 (Hildesheim: Gerstenberg, 1994), 144; Peter Jánosi, "Die Pyramiden der Könige der 5. Dynastie," in *Die Pyramiden Ägyptens: Monumente der Ewigkeit*, ed. Christian Hölzl et al. (Vienna: Brandstätter, 2004), 87; Rainer Stadelmann, *Die ägyptischen Pyramiden: Vom Ziegelbau zum Weltwunder*, 3rd ed., KAW 30 (Mainz: von Zabern, 1997), 164–204; Dagmar Stockfisch, *Untersuchungen zum Totenkult des ägyptischen Königs im Alten Reich: Die Dekoration der königlichen Totenkultanlagen* (Hamburg: Kovač, 2003), 369; Verner, *Abusir*, 77; Bestock, *Violence*, 115–24; and Labrousse, *Temple funéraire*, 9–13.

4. In the scholarly literature the mortuary temple is variously referred to as the mortuary, funerary, upper, or pyramid temple. Concise overviews of each pyramid complex can be found in Lehner, *Complete Pyramids*; Stadelmann, *Ägyptischen*

which became larger and increasingly elaborate. These later pyramids were significantly smaller, and by the Sixth Dynasty, their size had become standardized. In addition to these four basic elements, a small satellite pyramid, which may have been associated with the king's *ka*, was also included within the complex enclosure wall, and monuments for the king's consorts were usually adjacent.[5]

Each king's pyramid complex was the primary location for his mortuary cult, and it functioned in this capacity following the king's death and burial.[6] At the same time, the complexes seem to have been cult places for particular divinities and many kinds of daily and special rituals that the king performed during his lifetime as well.[7] Additionally, statues of the king were the focus of cult and rituals, which may have taken place both during and after his lifetime, and this would have benefited not only the owner of the respective complex in which the cult took place but also the royal *ka* and kingship itself. Indeed, some scholars have questioned whether the statue cult that took place inside the mortuary temple was the foremost purpose of this part of the complex rather than the mortuary cult.[8]

Certainly, the interpretation of the pyramid complex, including the functions and symbolisms of its various elements, has been and continues to be the subject of significant debate. In the mid-twentieth century, Herbert Ricke and Siegfried Schott proposed that the temples and the causeway were largely

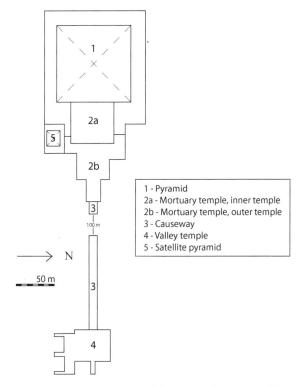

Figure 4.1. Schematic plan of the pyramid complex of Sahure in Abusir; Fifth Dynasty. Modified from Lehner, *Complete Pyramids*, 143.

Pyramiden; and Verner, *Pyramids*. Concerning causeways, see further El Awady, *Sahure*, 86–120. My descriptions of the architecture in this chapter draw from these sources and the original excavation reports, which I reference below.

5. Concerning the *ka* and the royal *ka*, see ch. 1.1. Regarding the satellite pyramid, see Di. Arnold, "Royal Cult Complexes," 70 and for the queens' pyramids, see further Peter Jánosi, *Die Pyramidenanlagen der Königinnen: Untersuchungen zu einem Grabtyp des Alten und Mittleren Reiches*, DÖAWW 13, Untersuchungen der Zweigstelle Kairo des Österreichischen Archäologischen Institutes 13 (Vienna: Verlag der Österreichischen Akademie der Wissenschaften, 1996).

6. Concerning the administration of complex construction and the funerary cult, see Hana Vymazalová, "The Administration of the Royal Funerary Complexes," in Moreno García, *Ancient Egyptian Administration*, 177–95.

7. Nuzzolo, "Sun Temples," 217 n. 6 and Nuzzolo, *Fifth Dynasty Sun Temples*, 23–24. The Abusir papyri have significantly contributed to scholars' understanding of the purpose and functioning of the pyramid complexes (see Paule Posener-Kriéger, *Les archives du temple funéraire de Néferirkarê-Kakai (Les Papyrus d'Abousir)*, BiEtud 65 [Cairo: Institut français d'archéologie orientale, 1976]; Paule Posener-Kriéger and Jean Louis de Cenival, *The Abu Sir Papyri* [London: Trustees of the British Museum, 1968]; Posener-Kriéger, Verner, and Vymazalová, *Pyramid Complex of Raneferef*; and Miroslav Verner, *The Pyramid Complex of Khentkaus*, Abusir 3 [Prague: Charles University, 1995]).

8. Dieter Arnold, *The Encyclopedia of Ancient Egyptian Architecture*, trans. Sabine H. Gardiner and Helen Strudwick, ed. Nigel Strudwick and Helen Strudwick (Princeton: Princeton University Press, 2003), 187–88; Labrousse, *Temple funéraire*, 14; and Barry Kemp, "Old Kingdom, Middle Kingdom, and Second Intermediate Period c. 2686–1552 BC," in *Ancient Egypt: A Social History* (Cambridge: Cambridge University Press, 1983), 85.

for the funeral rituals associated with the burial of the deceased king.⁹ Then in 1977, Dieter Arnold persuasively argued against this interpretation, contending that the pyramid complex was not arranged in order to accommodate funeral rituals and, in fact, that much of it did not directly relate to ritual activity at all, but rather the complex was an eternal residence for the king and its features primarily related to this aspect. While Arnold questioned whether the rooms and doorways would have been large enough to accommodate the funeral, he also emphasized the need to take the relief program, which had little to do with funerary rituals, into consideration when formulating theories on the complex in general.¹⁰

Following Arnold's seminal article, multiple scholars have attempted to do this and have put forth additional interpretations of the complex based on both the architectural and relief program.¹¹ For example, Matthias Rochholz suggested that the pyramid complex was intended to enable the king to continuously enact the *sed* festival and other renewal rituals, while David O'Connor argued that the temples and the causeway also had a cosmographic layer of meaning and that the basic structuring factor of the entire complex was the desire to have it represent the key cosmic processes, namely, cosmogony, cosmic renewal, and cosmic governance.¹² Moreover, just as scholars continue to debate the meaning of the overall pyramid complex, there are multiple interpretations regarding the symbolism and function of the relief program alone.¹³ Recently, Ćwiek suggested that the reliefs referenced the path that the revived deceased king took as he moved through his complex.¹⁴ El Awady argued against this idea and instead proposed that the scenes were intended both to ensure that the king accomplished his divine duties and to depict the deities' support of him. He emphasized that the relief program must be understood separately from the architecture.¹⁵ But while El Awady is right to caution against assuming a direct correlation between the reliefs and the architecture, it is equally problematic to assume that there is none. Overall the reliefs and the architecture must have functioned together coherently, and Arnold's argument that modern interpretations need to take both elements into account remains compelling.¹⁶

Ricke and Schott's proposal that the complex was the stage for the royal funeral is no longer generally accepted, but there remains a great deal of uncertainty concerning how to understand the functions and purposes of the complex and its various parts during the late Old Kingdom. This is complicated by the fact that the ancient Egyptians undoubtedly recognized and consciously constructed multiple layers of meanings and symbolisms within each monument, and these could change over time. I return to this idea and the rituals that took place within the late Old Kingdom pyramid complex, particularly as they relate to the

---

9. Herbert Ricke, "Bemerkungen zur ägyptischen Baukunst des Alten Reiches 2," in *Beiträge zur ägyptischen Bauforschung und Altertumskunde*, vol. 5, ed. Herbert Ricke (Cairo: Schweizerisches Institut für ägyptische Bauforschung und Altertumsunde, 1950), 1–128 and Siegfried Schott, "Bermerkungen zum ägyptischen Pyramidenkult," in Ricke, 131–252.

10. Di. Arnold, "Rituale und Pyramidentempel."

11. In addition to the discussions directly referenced here, see also Jürgen Brinks, *Die Entwicklung der königlichen Grabanlagen des Alten Reiches: Eine strukturelle und historische Analyse altägyptischer Architektur*, HÄB 10 (Hildesheim: Gerstenberg, 1979) and Stadelmann, *Ägyptischen Pyramiden*, 205–14.

12. Matthias Rochholz, "Sedfest, Sonnenheiligtum, und Pyramidenbezirk: Zur Deutung der Grabanlagen der Könige der 5. und 6. Dynastie," in Gundlach and Rochholz, *Ägyptische Tempel*, 255–80 and David O'Connor, "The Interpretation of the Old Kingdom Pyramid Complex" in *Stationen: Beiträge zur Kulturgeschichte Ägypten, Rainer Stadelmann gedwidmet*, ed. Heike Guksch and Daniel Polz (Mainz: von Zabern, 1998), 135–44. I further discuss the *sed* festival in ch. 5.4.2.

13. In addition to the ideas discussed below, see also Baines, "Kingship before Literature," 143–52 and Stockfisch, *Untersuchungen zum Totenkult*, 390–400.

14. Andrzej Ćwiek, "Relief Decoration in the Royal Funerary Complexes of the Old Kingdom: Studies in the Development, Scene Content and Iconography" (PhD diss., Warsaw University, 2003), 330–49.

15. El Awady, *Sahure*, 50–82.

16. See n. 10 for this argument.

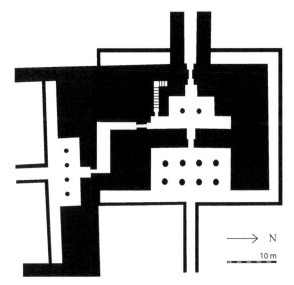

Figure 4.2. Valley temple of Sahure in Abusir; Fifth Dynasty. Modified from Borchardt, *Grabdenkmal des Königs Sahu-re*, 1:Bl. 16.

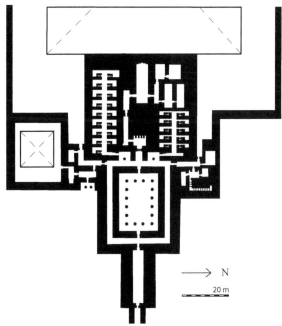

Figure 4.3. Mortuary temple of Sahure in Abusir; Fifth Dynasty. Modified from Borchardt, *Grabdenkmal des Königs Sahu-re*, 1:Bl. 16.

prisoner statues, in the following chapter, but it is clear that the ritual activity accomplished numerous things and served to benefit different beings and aspects of the king and kingship.

Sahure's monument, which Ludwig Borchardt excavated in the early 1900s, had the pyramid, mortuary temple, causeway, and valley temple arranged in a symmetrical fashion along the east–west axis (fig. 4.1).[17] His valley temple had two entrances, each with a landing ramp, which would have connected to the lake in front of the temple, and columned portico (fig. 4.2). The main entrance, to the east along the complex's axis, had two rows of four pink granite palmiform columns while the south entrance had a single row of four columns.[18] Both entrances led, via passages, to a T-shaped central hall with two additional columns. This room had a stairway leading to the roof, and it exited into the beginning of the causeway.

The causeway was 235 meters long and led straight to the mortuary temple's *pr-wrw*, or long entrance hall (fig. 4.3).[19] This connected to an open court, which was lined with sixteen pink granite palmiform columns and had a further corridor running around it.[20] In the court's northwest corner, Borchardt discovered remains of a decorated alabaster altar.[21] Both the entrance hall and the open court formed the mortuary

---

17. Borchardt, *Grabdenkmal des Königs Sahu-re*.
18. Concerning the columns in Old Kingdom monuments, see further Miroslav Verner, "The Columns of Abusir," in Bárta, *Old Kingdom Art*, 343–55.
19. Paule Posener-Kriéger first identified the entrance hall as the Egyptian *pr-wrw* (Posener-Kriéger, *Archives du temple funéraire*, 429–39 and 496–99). See also Di. Arnold, "Rituale und Pyramidentempel," 6–7.
20. For an interpretation of the open court, see Verner, *Abusir*, 87–88. Posener-Kriéger identified the open court as the Egyptian *wsḫt* (Posener-Kriéger, 429–39 and 499–501).
21. Regarding the alabaster altars in late Old Kingdom pyramid complexes, see further Mohamed Megahed, "The Altar of Djedkare's Funerary Temple from South Saqqara," in *Cult and Belief in Ancient Egypt: Proceedings of the Fourth International Congress for Young Egyptologists*, ed. Teodor Lekov and Emil Buzov (Sofia: East West, 2014), 56–62.

temple's outer temple, and a transverse corridor divided this from the inner temple, which included the rear central rooms. In the middle of the west wall of the transverse corridor, there was a low stairway that had deep niches on either side, each containing a column imitating bundled papyrus. The north and south walls of the niches had entrances to a series of storage magazines that sat on either side of the inner temple. These presumably held equipment and other materials that were used in the cultic and ritual activities of the temple. On both sides, the magazines were arranged symmetrically along a central corridor, but the south corridor was longer than the north, and thus this side had more magazines.

The stairway in the transverse corridor led to the inner temple, in which one first encountered a room with five statue niches that originally held cult statues presumably of the king in different guises.[22] Behind the five-niche chapel was the offering hall. This was accessed via a series of small rooms that ran to the south of the five-niche chapel and the offering hall. The west wall of the offering hall was adjacent to the east side of the pyramid, and a granite false door, which enabled the deceased king to move between his tomb below the pyramid and his temple, had originally been carved there.[23] To the north, the offering hall connected to a series of adjoining rooms that likely were also used for ritual and cultic purposes. Indeed, some of these rooms had libation basins and drainage systems, like the offering hall.

The inner walls of the valley temple, causeway, and mortuary temple were all decorated with high-quality painted, raised relief, and pavement and dados of black basalt, alabaster, and red granite were employed throughout. The widespread use of expensive, colorful stones and relief decoration throughout the pyramid complexes was common for the rest of the Old Kingdom.

Clearly, the pyramid complex of Sahure is very well preserved, and most of it has been excavated. This is not the case with the later Old Kingdom monuments. As a result, the monument of Sahure looms large in the Egyptological literature, and it has been easy for scholars to overlook the variations and developments in the plan and architecture of the pyramid complexes of Sahure's successors.

4.2. Architectural Developments and the Findspots of the Prisoner Statues

The plans and architectural features of the pyramid complexes that belong to the Old Kingdom kings who followed Sahure show some similarities to his complex, but there are also important deviations and developments. There seem to have been necessary elements and traditions that the kings and their architects followed, but there was also a great deal of flexibility and innovation. The following section focuses on the architectural changes and developments that occurred in the pyramid complexes that contained prisoner statues. Indeed, the prisoner statues themselves were a major addition to the late Old Kingdom pyramid complex, and they relate to other changes in the monuments' relief and sculpture program.

Moreover, the available archaeological evidence that I present here indicates that the location of the prisoner statues within each pyramid complex changed over time. Many scholars have proposed the causeway, the mortuary temple's entrance hall, and/or its open court as the probable parts of the pyramid complex that originally contained the prisoner statues.[24] These arguments generally assume that

---

22. I discuss these statues further in ch. 4.4.

23. Concerning the offering hall and late Old Kingdom false doors in general, see further Jánosi, "Entwicklung und Deutung."

24. Di. Arnold, "Old Kingdom Statues," 42; Di. Arnold, "Rituale und Pyramidentempel," 7; Di. Arnold, "Royal Cult Complexes," 73; Brinks, *Entwicklung der königlichen Grabanlagen*, 160; Marc Étienne, *Heka: Magie et envoûtement dans l'Égypte ancienne* (Paris: Éditions de la réunion des musées nationaux, 2000), 40; Hayes, *Scepter of Egypt*, 1:116; Hill, "173. Kneeling Captive," 440–41, cat. no. 173; Mark Janzen, "The Iconography of Humiliation: The Depiction and Treatment of the Bound

the statues' placement was the same in all of the pyramid complexes in which they were employed; the suggested locations apply to all prisoner statues, regardless of the pyramid complex. However, while the prisoner statues clearly form a coherent genre of statuary, distinguished by their material and subject matter, the group developed over time in significant ways, including their placement in the pyramid complex.[25] In the earliest complex to have prisoner statues, namely, that of Niuserre, these statues were set in this king's valley temple. Following Niuserre, prisoner statues were placed in mortuary temples. Finally, in the pyramid complex of Pepi II, who was the last king to commission prisoner statues and also the king with the most statues, prisoner statues were erected in both the valley and mortuary temples, and possibly even along parts of this king's causeway.

4.2.1. Niuserre

In the early 1900s, Ludwig Borchardt cleared the entirety of Niuserre's valley temple and mortuary temple, though he was unable to excavate the whole causeway.[26] As I mentioned in chapter 2, Niuserre's valley temple and causeway had originally been intended for his father, Neferirkare, but this king died well before his pyramid complex was complete. While Niuserre completed his father's mortuary temple, although with mudbrick rather than stone, he took over Neferirkare's valley temple and causeway as his own.

Niuserre's valley temple, which was more complex than Sahure's, also had two entrances, but the location of the secondary entrance differed from that in Sahure's valley temple (fig. 4.4).[27] The primary entrance, to the east and behind the harbor ramp, consisted of a portico with two rows of pink granite columns, which were shaped like papyrus bundles. This led to a central room with three statue niches of which the middle niche was the largest. To the south of the central room, two smaller rooms led to a staircase to the temple's roof and to the second entrance portico, which enabled access from the west and had only one row of four columns. Immediately to the north of the central niched room was another similarly sized room, which connected directly to the causeway. Because the causeway had originally been designed to connect to Neferirkare's mortuary temple, it was not straight but diverted to Niuserre's mortuary temple with a sharp bend in its upper end.

In the preliminary report, Borchardt indicated that he had found the three prisoner statue fragments (Berlin, ÄM 17912–17914; C.1.1–C.1.3), which he wrongly considered as part of royal smiting statues, as I discussed in chapter 2.2.1, in the valley temple's central room with the three statue niches, and thus he

---

Foreigner in New Kingdom Egypt" (PhD diss, University of Memphis, 2013), 58–59; Lansing, "An Old Kingdom Captive," 152; Lauer, "Recherches...1967–1968 et 1968–1969," 478; Lauer, *Saqqara*, 180; Lauer, "Statues de prisonniers," 42–43; Lauer, "Travaux...1968–1969," 23; Lauer and Leclant, "Découverte," 61; Megahed, "Altar," 59; Megahed, "Sculptures," 27; Ian Shaw, "Egypt and the Outside World," in *The Oxford History of Ancient Egypt*, ed. Ian Shaw (Oxford: Oxford University Press, 2000), 310; Stadelmann, *Ägyptischen Pyramiden*, 209; Stockfisch, *Untersuchungen zum Totenkult*, 374–75; and Verner, *Abusir*, 88.

25. I briefly discussed this change in the prisoner statues' original location and proposed the arguments included here in Prakash, "Depictions of the Foreign 'Other'," 461–62 and Prakash, "Prisoner Statue 'Fragments,'" 23–27.

26. Borchardt, *Grabdenkmal des Königs Ne-user-re*. Preliminary reports include Ludwig Borchardt, "Ausgrabungen der Deutschen Orient-Gesellschaft bei Abusir im Winter 1901-2," *MDOG* 14 (1902): 1–50; Ludwig Borchardt, "Ausgrabungen der Deutschen Orient-Gesellschaft bei Abusir im Winter 1902-3," *MDOG* 18 (1903): 1–33; and Borchardt, "Ausgrabungen...1903–4." Much more recently, the Czech Archaeological Mission opened trenches in order to further investigate Niuserre's causeway and valley temple (see Krejčí, "Nyuserra Revisted").

27. Although, Krejčí proposed that in having a second entrance Niuserre might have been imitating the plan of Sahure's valley temple (Krejčí, 521).

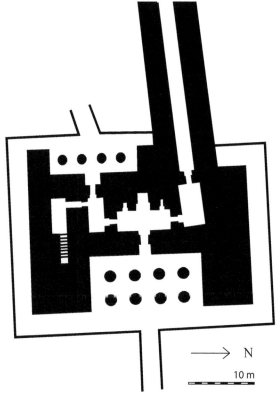

Figure 4.4. Valley temple of Niuserre in Abusir; Fifth Dynasty. Modified from Borchardt, *Grabdenkmal des Königs Ne-user-re*, Bl. 1.

suggested that the statue groups might have stood inside the niches.[28] However, it seems far more likely that statues of the king alone stood in these niches.[29] The prisoner statues were likely erected a little to the northeast of where Borchardt discovered them, close to the exit or at the exit to the causeway nearby reliefs featuring the triumphant pharaoh, as I discuss below. Indeed, Mark Lehner and Rainer Stadelmann also proposed this placement.[30]

Niuserre's mortuary temple also featured a number of important innovations and deviations from that of Sahure (fig. 4.5). Rather than being T-shaped and symmetrical along a central east–west axis, its layout resembled the shape of an L. This adaptation seems to have been necessitated by the location of Niuserre's complex, near the north wall of Neferirkare's mortuary temple. While placing his complex here enabled Niuserre to capitalize on Neferirkare's valley temple and causeway, and also possibly to symbolically align himself with his father by being near the earlier king's monument, it forced Niuserre's architects to contend with previous constructions and topographical features. This seems to have resulted in the particular shape of Niuserre's mortuary temple, with the outer temple south of the central axis of the inner temple.

The temple maintains the same primary features found in Sahure's. The slanted causeway led to the long entrance hall and the open court. But Niuserre's entrance hall may have had passages either in the center or western end of the north and south walls that led to five storage magazines and/or corridors that ran along the north and south sides of the open court.[31] If such doorways existed, the plan of Niuserre's entrance hall would differ from Sahure's. The storage magazines of the outer temple could also be accessed from the transverse corridor, whose east wall had doorways to the corridors that ran along the north and south sides of the open court to the magazines. The north end of the transverse corridor led to another temple entrance in the L-shaped temple's inner corner, and sixteen columns in the form of papyrus bundles supported the ambulatory of the open court.

There was extensive damage to areas of the inner temple, and thus it is difficult to reconstruct the exact placement of the five-niche chapel, assuming that Niuserre did in fact have this room in his mortuary temple. If he did, it may have been the first room of the inner temple, namely, the wide room on the central axis of the outer temple that was accessed via a low stairway from the transverse corridor. To the north of

---

28. Borchardt, "Ausgrabungen...1903–4," 13 and Borchardt, *Grabdenkmal des Königs Ne-user-re*, 42 and Abb. 24.

29. Bárta and Dulíková, "Divine and Terrestrial," 33; Krejčí, "Nyuserra Revisted," 521–22; and Verner, *Pyramids*, 319.

30. Lehner, *Complete Pyramids*, 149 and Stadelmann, *Ägyptischen Pyramiden*, 176.

31. The walls of the entrance hall were completely destroyed so such doors remain theoretical (compare Borchardt, *Grabdenkmal des Königs Ne-user-re*, 19–21 and Ricke, "Bemerkungen," 82). I chose not to draw either option in fig. 4.5 and left the walls of the entrance hall solid.

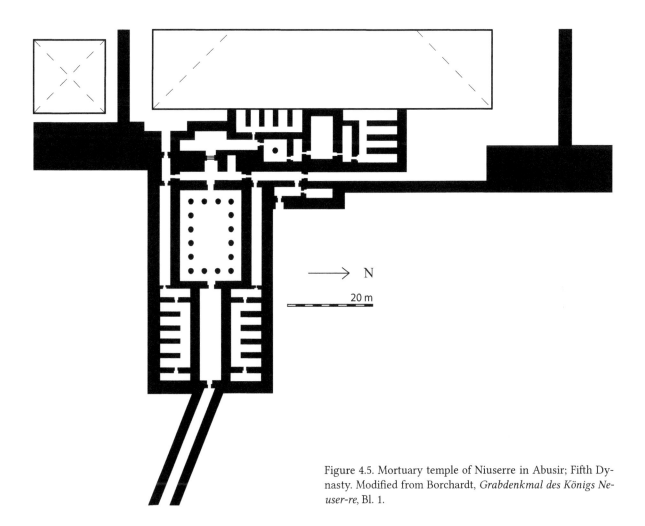

Figure 4.5. Mortuary temple of Niuserre in Abusir; Fifth Dynasty. Modified from Borchardt, *Grabdenkmal des Königs Neuser-re*, Bl. 1.

the low stairway, there was a deep niche that had originally contained a colossal, pink granite statue of a lion; I return to this statue in the fourth section of this chapter. Another innovation in Niuserre's mortuary temple is a square room with a single central column that led to the offering hall. This room, known today as the *antichambre carrée*, became standard in subsequent mortuary temples. While its exact meaning and purpose remains unclear, it was closely aligned with the offering hall and associated with deities and the *sed* festival, a renewal festival that centered on the king and kingship; in this way, it was one of the most sacred parts of the mortuary temple.[32] The five-niche chapel (?), *antichambre carrée*, and offering hall, which is still positioned against the center of the pyramid's east side, were arranged along a north–south axis, rather than positioned with the five-niche chapel directly in front of, or east, of the offering hall. Finally, an additional major innovation in the architecture of Niuserre's complex is two massive structures

---

32. Regarding this room, see further Mohamed Megahed, "The *Antichambre Carrée* in the Old Kingdom. Decoration and Function," in Landgráfová and Mynářová, *Rich and Great*, 239–58.

in the northeast and southeast corners of the enclosure wall. Borchardt designated these "*Eckbauten*" and suggested that they might be a type of precursor of the pylons that were common for later temples.[33]

4.2.2. Djedkare-Isesi

Although Hussein and Fakhry briefly explored Djedkare's valley temple, it has never been fully excavated nor has most of this king's causeway, which did not run precisely east–west but deviated slightly to the south.[34] For the first time at Djedkare's complex, there are remains of a small chapel at the entrance, or north side, of the pyramid, though this feature may have first appeared earlier.[35] Djedkare's mortuary temple, which is arranged along an east–west central axis, had massive square structures to either side of the outer temple along its east façade, similar to Niuserre's "*Eckbauten*" (fig. 4.6). However, Mohamed Megahed and Peter Jánosi have argued that these were not related to later pylons because of their square shape, perpendicular sides, and differences between the north and south structures. For example, the northern one is slightly smaller and more poorly preserved. They likened the southern structure to an enormous substructure or pedestal on which something might have originally been set. There was a small court to the east of it, to which the northern structure had no counterpart, and the deep wear marks on the pavement of the court and

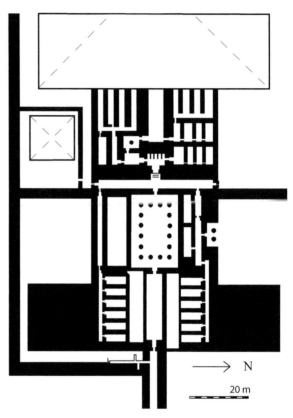

Figure 4.6. Mortuary temple of Djedkare-Isesi in Saqqara; Fifth Dynasty. After Megahed, Jánosi, and Vymazalová, "Neues," Abb. 2.

---

33. Borchardt, *Grabdenkmal des Königs Ne-user-re*, 22–23. See also Hourig Sourouzian, "L'apparition du pylône," *BIFAO* 81 (1981): 143.

34. Concerning the history of excavations at this complex and the problematic documentation, see ch. 2.2.2. A final excavation report has yet to be published. Preliminary reports include Ahmed Fakhry, *The Bent Pyramid*, The Monuments of Sneferu at Dahshur 1 (Cairo: Antiquities Department, 1959), 10, 13, 25, and 30–31; Peter Jánosi and Mohamed Megahed, "Eine fast vergessene Pyramidenanlage," *Antike Welt* 46.2 (2015): 51–60; Megahed, "Neue Forschungen"; Megahed, "Pyramid Complex"; Megahed, "Sculptures"; Mohamed Megahed, "Die Wiederentdeckung des Pyramindenbezirks des Djedkare-Isesi in Sakkara-Sud," *Sokar* 15 (2014): 6–19; Mohamed Megahed and Peter Jánosi, "The Pyramid Complex of Djedkare at Saqqara-South: Recent Results and Future Prospects," in Bárta, Coppens, and Krejčí, *Abusir and Saqqara...2015*, 237–56; Mohamed Megahed, Peter Jánosi, and Hana Vymazalová, "Neues von der Pyramidenanlage des Djedkare-Isesi: Grabungs- und Forschungsergebnisse 2015–2016," *Sokar* 34.1 (2017): 36–63; Mohamed Moursi, "Die Ausgrabungen in der Gegend um die Pyramide des *ḏd-kȝ-rʿ 'issj'* bei Saqqara," *ASAE* 71 (1987): 185–86; and Varille, À *propos des pyramides*, 17. See also Piacentini, "Excavating the Egyptological Archives," 355–68.

35. Concerning north chapels, see further Peter Jánosi, "Bemerkungen zu den Nordkapellen des Alten Reiches," *SAK* 22 (1995): 145–68.

on the ramp leading directly from the causeway into this court indicate that this area had been intensely used.[36]

Storage magazines surrounded the entrance hall of the mortuary temple (these were accessed from the transverse corridor), and the open court had sixteen pink granite palmiform columns. A doorway on the north end of the east wall of the transverse corridor provided access to a corridor that led to two rooms with an unclear function, the north magazines, and a portico with two columns of an uncertain form and material. This secondary entrance, which was in a similar position as the secondary entrance of Niuserre's mortuary temple, provided direct access, via a court, to a smaller pyramid complex with "kingly" features, including an *antichambre carrée*. This originally belonged to Djedkare's wife, Queen Setibhor.[37]

The arrangement of the primary rooms in Djedkare's inner temple would be followed by his successors: a door and low staircase in the middle of the west wall of the transverse corridor led into the five-niche chapel, which was placed directly in front of the offering hall along the central axis. However, the offering hall was accessed from the south via a vestibule and the *antichambre carrée*. The western wall of the offering hall, which originally contained the false door, was incorporated directly into the masonry of the pyramid. The rest of the inner temple, on either side of the central rooms, consisted of a large number of storage magazines.

Hussein was the only archaeologist who discovered prisoner statue fragments in Djedkare's pyramid complex, and the details and results of his excavations were never published.[38] However, photographs that Varille took during these excavations, which are preserved in Varille's archive at the Egyptology Library and Archives of the Università degli Studi di Milano in Italy, reveal that Hussein's work was restricted to the inner temple.[39] Moreover, in one photograph, a large fragment of the body of a prisoner statue (SCA no. 2244; C.2.2) is visible lying next to the remains of the in situ palmiform column in the center of Djedkare's *antichambre carrée* (fig. 4.7).[40] Other object photographs that Varille took are affixed to notecards, one of which records the findspot for a different prisoner statue fragment (SCA no. 2232; C.2.1) as "accidentelle."[41] For the other prisoner statue fragments, the notecards have no comments, and there is no associated written documentation that mentions the prisoner statues in the archive. However, Fakhry, in his brief reference to the Djedkare statues, confirmed that the fragments were not discovered in situ, and Varille's photographs emphasize the highly disturbed nature of the mortuary temple.[42] Therefore,

---

36. Jánosi and Megahed, "Eine fast vergessene Pyramidenanlage," 59–60; see also Megahed, Jánosi, and Vymazalová, "Neues," 42–44; cf. Sourouzian, "L'apparition du pylône," 143–44.

37. Setibhor's name was discovered very recently, and previously the owner of the complex was unknown. See further Megahed and Vymazalová, "Neues zum Pyramidenbezirk"; Megahed and Vymazalová, "Notes"; Jánosi, "Pyramidenanlage"; and Megahed, "Pyramid Complex."

38. While some of Hussein's finds, which remain in modern archaeological storerooms, are marked with the date of discovery, no information on their exact findspots remains for the objects other than that the material came from Djedkare's mortuary temple (Moursi, "Ausgrabungen," 185–86).

39. Concerning this material, see Piacentini, "Excavating the Egyptological Archives," 355–68 and Prakash, "Prisoner Statue 'Fragments.'" To my knowledge, there is no Hussein archive; indeed, Fakhry was unable to locate any of Hussein's journals or papers (Fakhry, *The Bent Pyramid*, 25 and Moursi, 185). Fakhry did describe finding the negatives of the photographs taken during the season of 1946–1949 in the photographic section of Saqqara, but I was not able to relocate these (Fakhry, 25). It is possible that these negatives were those of Varille's photographs that are now in the Università degli Studi di Milano.

40. Inv. N. 3180, Box 52, Varille Collection.

41. Inv. N. 3122, Box 48, Varille Collection. Neither "accidentelle" nor the lack of comments was unusual among these notecards.

42. Fakhry, *The Pyramids*, 181. Mohamed Megahed described the fragments as having been found "scattered in the temple" (Megahed, "Sculptures," 26).

Figure 4.7. Photograph of Hussein's excavations in the mortuary temple of Djedkare-Isesi showing a prisoner statue fragment near the in situ palmiform column of the square antechamber. While the statue is difficult to make out here, another excavation photograph, taken closer and from a different angle, confirms that this is a prisoner statue. Modified from Inv. N. 3180, Box 52, Varille Collection, Egyptological Library and Archives, Università degli Studi di Milano, Milan, Italy.

although the statues were not in their original position, Hussein discovered at least one of them in the *antichambre carrée*, while he found the others somewhere within the inner portion of the mortuary temple.

The excavation of the prisoner statues from the inner temple strongly suggests that they had originally been located inside the mortuary temple. Thus Djedkare seems to have relocated his prisoner statues from his valley temple to his mortuary temple. However, because his valley temple has never been excavated, one cannot know whether the plan of the valley temple changed or be certain that it did not also contain prisoner statues.

4.2.3. Unas

The evidence for Unas's prisoner statues is especially problematic, as I have mentioned in previous chapters. The earliest reference to prisoner statues from the pyramid complex of Unas was in the 1930s. In several publications of his findings at the pyramid complex of Pepi II, where he discovered large numbers of prisoner statue fragments, Jéquier noted that similar statues had previously been found in the mortuary temple of Unas but were of too little importance to be published.⁴³ He did not cite the excavator responsible for this discovery.

Barsanti discovered at least one small prisoner statue fragment (C.3.1) while excavating this king's pyramid complex. In the final report following Lauer's excavations of Unas's mortuary temple, a photograph of this fragment, which had been taken by Lacau during Barsanti's work, was published and described as possibly coming from the decoration of Unas's mortuary temple as well (fig. 2.5).⁴⁴ Indeed, Barsanti's work at the complex was primarily around this area.⁴⁵ The authors of the final report also seem to suggest this original location for Barsanti's fragment because of Jéquier's earlier references to prisoner statue fragments specifically from this part of the complex.⁴⁶ Other scholars, presumably following Jéquier, have also referred to multiple prisoner statue fragments from the mortuary temple of Unas as well.⁴⁷ Although it remains unclear to what fragments Jéquier was actually referring, the area said to be where any fragments were found has consistently been the mortuary temple. Indeed, despite extensive excavation of Unas's causeway and valley temple over the course of the twentieth century, there has been no mention of prisoner statue fragments in any of the ensuing publications.⁴⁸ Thus it seems most likely that Unas only had prisoner statues in his mortuary temple.

The plan of Unas's mortuary temple resembles that of Djedkare (fig. 4.8). However, Unas did not have any distinct massive structures at the front of his temple to its north and south. Rather this feature may have been somewhat incorporated into the east façade itself, as this wall in both corners is particularly thick and large, though still much thinner than the structures of Djedkare. The successors of Unas also continued to construct a similarly thick eastern façade.⁴⁹ Unas's open court had eighteen pink granite palmiform columns, two more than his predecessors had. The outer temple had an increasing number of storerooms, which were arranged somewhat irregularly with twice as many to the north of the entrance hall and open court as to the south. These did not have an upper level, and they were accessed from the transverse

---

43. Jéquier, *Douze ans*, 64; Jéquier, *Monument funéraire*, 3:28; and Jéquier, "Planche 22," 23. Several years later, William C. Hayes also referenced fragments of prisoner statues that came from the mortuary temple of Unas but with no citation to his source for this information (Hayes, *Scepter of Egypt*, 1:115).

44. Labrousse, Lauer, and Leclant, *Temple haut*, 131 and pl. 40, doc. 133. The preliminary reports include Étienne Drioton and Jean-Philippe Lauer, "Une inscription de Khamouas sur la face sud de la pyramide d'Ounas à Saqqarah," *ASAE* 37 (1937): 201–11; Jean-Philippe Lauer "Fouilles du Service des Antiquites à Saqqarah," *ASAE* 39 (1939): 447–67; and Jean-Philippe Lauer, "Note sur divers travaux effectues à Saqqarah en 1936 et 1937," *ASAE* 37 (1937): 103–15. However, they make no mention of prisoner statue fragments.

45. Barsanti, "Rapports"; Barsanti and Maspero, "Fouilles"; and Barsanti and Maspero, "Fouilles…1902–1903."

46. In other publications, Lauer and Leclant directly referenced Jéquier when mentioning prisoner statues from the mortuary temple of Unas (see Lauer and Leclant, "Découverte," 60 n. 3 and Jean Leclant, "Fouilles et travaux en Égypte et au Soudan, 1968–1969," *Orientalia* 39 [1970]: 333 n. 1). Lauer also made reference to very mutilated fragments from the mortuary temple of Unas elsewhere, with no citation or further information (see Lauer, "Recherches…1967–1968 et 1968–1969," 477; Lauer, "Statues de prisonniers," 42; and Lauer, "Travaux…1968–1969," 22).

47. For example, Manfred Bietak, "Saqqara," *AfO* 23 (1970): 208; F. W. von Bissing, *Ägyptische Kunstgeschichte: Von den ältesten Zeiten bis auf die Eroberung durch die Araber*, 3 vols. (Berlin: Aegyptologischer Verlag Miron Goldstein, 1934–1938), 2:57 n. 1; and Hayes, *Scepter of Egypt*, 1:115.

48. The final reports are Labrousse and Moussa, *Chaussée* and Audran Labrousse and Ahmed Moussa, *Le temple d'accueil du complexe funéraire du roi Ounas*, BiEtud 111 (Cairo: Institut français d'archéologie orientale, 1996). Preliminary reports include Selim Hassan, "The Causeway of Wnis at Sakkara," *ZÄS* 80 (1955): 136–39; Selim Hassan, "Excavations at Saqqara 1937–1938," *ASAE* 38 (1938): 518–21; and Abd-el-Salam Mohamed Hussein, "Fouilles sur la chaussee d'Ounas (1941–1943)," *ASAE* 43 (1943): 439–42. See also Louis Keimer, "Notes de lecture," *BIFAO* 56 (1957): 97–120 and Mohamed Awad M. Raslan, "The Causeway of Ounas Pyramid," *ASAE* 61 (1973): 151–69.

49. Sourouzian considers all of these structures and thick east façades, from Niuserre to Pepi II, related and early types of pylons (Sourouzian, "L'apparition du pylône," 143–45).

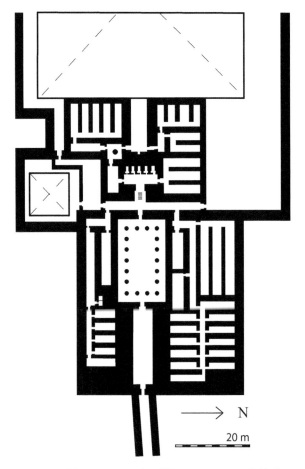

Figure 4.8. Mortuary temple of Unas in Saqqara; Fifth Dynasty. Modified from Labrousse, Lauer, and Leclant, *Temple haut*, fig. 3.

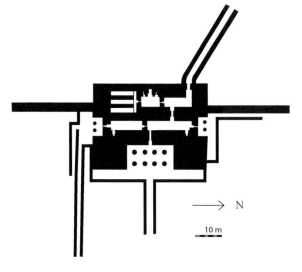

Figure 4.9. Valley temple of Unas in Saqqara; Fifth Dynasty. After Labrousse and Moussa, *Temple d'accueil*, fig. 5.

corridor. Magazines, at least some of which did seem to have an upper level, also surrounded the offering hall and five-niche chapel, again with more on the north side. Inside the *antichambre carrée*, there was likely a palmiform quartzite column.

Unas's causeway was extremely long, around 720 meters, and it was not straight but made three turns. Its roof had an open central slit to illuminate the passageway, and its walls were completely decorated. These are some of the best-preserved examples of relief scenes from a causeway, and I return to them in the following section.[50]

The plan of Unas's valley temple is quite different from the valley temples of Niuserre and Sahure and is larger than they are (fig. 4.9). It had three entrances. The primary entrance, to the east and along the temple's central axis, was approached from the harbor ramp and included a portico with two rows of four granite palmiform columns. The temple could also be accessed from the north and south, where smaller porticos with a single row of two similar columns stood. Two long, central rooms, running north–south, connected these three entrances inside the temple. From here, a single passage led to the rear of the temple where another long room led to the causeway. The excavators hypothesized that to the south of this room,

---

50. To the south of the upper part of the causeway, excavators discovered a limestone structure in the form of two large boats. These probably originally contained a pair of wooden boats. Concerning Old Kingdom boat burials, see recently Tarek El Awady, "Boat Graves in the Old Kingdom Royal Funerary Complexes," in *The Realm of the Pharaohs: Essays in Honor of Tohfa Handoussa*, ed. Zahi Hawass, Khaled Daoud, and Sawsan Abd El-Fattah, CASAE 37 (Cairo: Supreme Counsel of Antiquities, 2008), 177–200.

there may have been a room with three statue niches, based on the three-niche room in Niuserre's valley temple, and three magazines, but this area of the temple was completely destroyed.[51]

4.2.4. Teti

Teti's valley temple and causeway have yet to be excavated. Indeed, his valley temple has never been located, and his causeway, which must have been very long or very steep because of the location of his pyramid on relatively high ground, is no longer visible except for a small portion at its west end. The overall plan of Teti's mortuary temple was similar to that of Djedkare and Unas, but once again there was a significant increase in the number of storerooms both in the inner and outer temples (fig. 4.10).[52] Although these were not perfectly symmetrical, they were more symmetrically organized than those of Unas. The magazines of the outer temple were entered via the transverse corridor, while those of the inner temple seem to have been accessed from the five-niche chapel, the rear vestibule, and the offering hall. Another difference in Teti's mortuary temple was the access to the causeway, which itself may have been shifted to the south to accommodate earlier constructions. Rather than connect directly to the entrance hall, a long, narrow undecorated court ran along the south part of the temple's east façade and probably connected the entrance hall to the top of the causeway, which is destroyed. Additionally, Teti and the other Sixth Dynasty kings favored the use of square pillars instead of the elaborate columns that the Fifth Dynasty kings had employed.[53] Eighteen pink granite pillars supported the colonnade of Teti's open court, and the *antichambre carrée* contained a quartzite pillar.

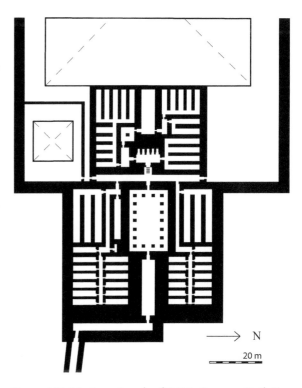

Figure 4.10. Mortuary temple of Teti in Saqqara; Sixth Dynasty. Modified from Lauer and Leclant, *Temple haut*, pl. 35.

---

51. Labrousse and Moussa, *Temple d'accueil*, 59–65. I included Labrousse and Moussa's hypothetical reconstruction of this area in fig. 4.9.

52. One should note that Lauer and Leclant depended heavily on the plan of Pepi II's mortuary temple to reconstruct parts of Teti's mortuary temple that were very badly or totally destroyed, including the rear vestibule, the *antichambre carrée*, and the magazines of the inner temple (Lauer and Leclant, *Temple haut*, 30–36). My fig. 4.10 is largely based on Lauer and Leclant's plan (Lauer and Leclant, pl. 35) and includes their reconstructions.

53. Labrousse interpreted this change as part of a trend toward archaism (Audran Labrousse, "The Pyramids of the Sixth Dynasty," in *The Treasures of the Pyramids*, ed. Zahi Hawass [Cairo: The American University in Cairo Press, 2003], 265), while Verner tied it to the decrease in the prominence of the sun god, which occurred at the end of the Fifth Dynasty and into the Sixth Dynasty and was most overt in the appearance of the Pyramid Texts inside the pyramid of Unas (Verner, "The Columns of Abusir," 355).

Because Teti's valley temple has never been located, it is impossible to know whether he had prisoner statues there, but he certainly had prisoner statues in his mortuary temple. James Quibell discovered the bust of a prisoner statue (Saqqara, Imhotep Museum JE 40047; C.4.1), which he did not recognize as such, during his excavations of Teti's mortuary temple.[54] Unfortunately, he did not provide a more precise location for the fragment, but his excavations were concentrated on the southern half of the inner temple. Quibell only succeeded in clearing about a quarter of the temple during his two seasons of work there, and it was not until 1920 that this work was resumed under the direction of Cecil Firth.[55] Firth found fragments of prisoner statues among debris filling a deep shaft to the north of the mortuary temple (C.4.3). These fragments should be seen as originating somewhere within the mortuary temple itself. Finally, the small prisoner statue fragment (Bloc 64; C.4.2) that Lauer and Leclant discovered also came from Teti's mortuary temple.[56]

Furthermore, Lauer and Leclant uncovered three large rectangular blocks of Tura limestone in the open court that they identified as statue bases from Teti's mortuary temple.[57] These were all the same height (about 50 cm) and the same length (about 1 m), but their width varied. One was narrower (53.5 cm) while the other two were thicker (61.5 cm and 62.5 cm). Their upper faces had rectangular depressions that were set about 10–15 cm from the block sides, except on one short end where the depression opened onto the side face. The depth of the depressions varied for each block, but they all inclined deeper toward the enclosed short end.[58]

Lauer and Leclant tentatively proposed that these bases had either been for statues of the king in the five-niche chapel or for prisoner statues, but at the same time they noted issues with both reconstructions. Regarding the five-niche chapel, the variation in the size of the blocks, with one more narrow than the others, seems to contrast with the niches themselves, which are usually the same size except for the central, *larger* one. Thus, the excavators concluded that it was doubtful that the bases fit into the niches.

Yet, based on their measurements and material, the blocks were not used as bases for the prisoner statues either. Lauer and Leclant did note that if the Teti prisoner statues had had similar dimensions as the Pepi I statues, whose bases were between 25–32 cm wide and 45–52 cm long, the depressions on the blocks would have been too large for the prisoner statues, particularly in length. However, it seems more likely that the Teti prisoner statues had actually been smaller than the Pepi I ones. If they had integral bases and these were also proportionately smaller, the depressions on the blocks would have been relatively even

---

54. His published reports include Quibell, *Excavations...1906–1907* and Quibell, *Excavations...1907–1908*. Lauer and Leclant were the first to recognize that the bust that Quibell had discovered belonged to a prisoner statue (Lauer, "Recherches...1967–1968 et 1968–1969," 477; Lauer and Leclant, "Découverte," 60; and Lauer and Leclant, *Temple haut*, 3, 84, 98–99 and pl. 32b).

55. Firth and Gunn, *Teti Pyramid Cemeteries*.

56. The excavations of the MAFS at the mortuary temple of Teti were undertaken primarily from 1965–1966. The final report is Lauer and Leclant, *Temple haut*. Preliminary reports include Jean-Philippe Lauer, "Travaux dans la necropole de Saqqarah (campagne 1965–1966)," *BSFE* 47 (1966): 20–35; Jean-Philippe Lauer, "Travaux d'anastylose et nouvelles recherches sur les pyramides et leurs complexes à Saqqarah," *CRAIBL* 110 (1966): 461–67; Jean Leclant, "Récentes recherches à la pyramide de Téti à Saqqarah," *BSFE* 46 (1966): 9–16; and Jean Leclant, "Récentes recherches à la pyramide de Téti, à Saqqarah," *BIE* 47 (1969): 53–63. Unfortunately, Lauer and Leclant did not publish any detailed information on the findspot of the fragment, beyond indicating that they found it somewhere within the mortuary temple (Lauer and Leclant, "Découverte," 60 n. 4 and Lauer and Leclant, *Temple haut*, 84 and 98–99). They also noted that little remained of the temple's decoration as the structure was largely leveled and the area was so disturbed (Lauer and Leclant, *Temple haut*, 59).

57. See here Lauer and Leclant, *Temple haut*, 101–2 and fig. 90.

58. The dimensions of the narrow block's depression are: L. 70.5 cm, W. 33 cm, D. 7.2–8.5 cm; for the second block (of width 61.5 cm): L. 79.5 cm, W. 40.5 cm, D. 6.5–9 cm; for the third block (of width 62.5 cm): L. 79.5 cm, W. 40.5 cm, D. 8–10.5 cm (Lauer and Leclant, 101–2).

larger than what Lauer and Leclant had supposed, and consequently the depressions are much too large for the Teti prisoner statues. Moreover, these blocks are Tura limestone, while the Teti prisoner statues are a lower-quality flaky, white limestone, and it seems highly unlikely that the statues would have been set into bases made from a higher-quality stone than the statues themselves.

4.2.5. Pepi I

Pepi I's valley temple and the vast majority of his causeway have never been excavated. However, during their complete excavation of the mortuary temple, from 1967–1988, the MAFS did clear the upper end of this king's causeway.[59] About fifteen meters from the temple façade, they discovered a granite door that provided access into the upper part of the causeway and the mortuary temple.[60] A similar feature was also present along Pepi II's causeway.

Once again, Pepi I's mortuary temple had a similar plan as those of his immediate predecessors but with some deviations (fig. 4.11). Pepi I's causeway approached the central axis of his mortuary temple, but rather than connect directly to the entrance hall, there may have been a small, perpendicular room between the causeway and entrance hall with lateral doorways, on its north and south walls, leading to smaller rooms that Labrousse identified as stations for guards to control access to the temple.[61] The open court included eighteen pink granite pillars, while a granite octagonal column had stood inside Pepi I's *antichambre carrée*.[62] The arrangement of the storerooms in his mortuary temple was slightly different from that of Teti's storerooms, but they were accessed in the same fashion and had a comparable amount of ground space dedicated to them. On the other hand, most of the magazines clearly had two stories, unlike at Teti's mortuary temple where the excavators were unable to determine this with any certainty because of the monument's poor state of preservation; I discuss the magazines of Pepi I in further detail below.

Figure 4.11 plots the findspots of the prisoner statue fragments that the MAFS team discovered during their work.[63] Most of these came to light over the course of two seasons, from 1968–1970. The 1968–1969 season was the first season of widespread excavations within the mortuary temple.[64] These were focused on the rear inner temple. To the south of the offering hall, five storage magazines, whose length ran east-

---

59. The final report for the MAFS excavations in the mortuary temple is Labrousse, *Temple funéraire*. Lauer and Leclant, who were the directors of these excavations until 1973 when Labrousse took over, also regularly published many preliminary reports in the following journals: *ASAE, CRAIBL, Orientalia, BIE*, and *BSFE*. See also Labrousse, "Complexes funéraires" and Leclant, *Recherches*, 17–23.

60. Jean Leclant, "Fouilles et travaux en Égypte et au Soudan, 1982–1983," *Orientalia* 53 (1984): 366–67.

61. Labrousse, *Temple funéraire*, 26. Excavators discovered fragments of the northern door, but no remains of the rooms, which are present at the pyramid complex of Pepi II. I followed Labrousse, fig. 10 and Rémi Legros, ed., *Cinquante ans d'éternité: jubilé de la Mission archéologique française de Saqqâra*, MAFS 5, BiEtud 162 (Cairo: Institut français d'archéologie orientale, 2015), fig. 3 in including both doors and rooms in fig. 4.11. Remains of similar doors at the top of the causeway have also been found at pyramid complexes from the Fourth and Fifth Dynasties (Labrousse, 26 n. 8).

62. For the column, see Jean Leclant, "Fouilles et travaux en Égypte et au Soudan, 1969–1970," *Orientalia* 40 (1971): 233.

63. For more detailed information on the findspots, see the catalogue (https://doi.org/10.5913/2022877). Other general discussions of the Pepi I prisoner statues, in addition to those cited below, include *Cinquante années*, 19; Lauer, "Cinquante années," 563; Jean-Philippe Lauer, *Le mystere de pyramides* (Paris: Presses de la Cité, 1988), pls. 35 and 36; and Lauer, *Saqqara*, 179–80.

64. See further Lauer, "Recherches...1967–1968 et 1968–1969," 466–79; Lauer, "Travaux aux pyramids," 101–2; Lauer, "Travaux...1968–1969," 16–24; Lauer and Leclant, "Découverte"; Leclant, "Fouilles...1968–1969," 332–33; and Leclant, *Recherches*, 8.

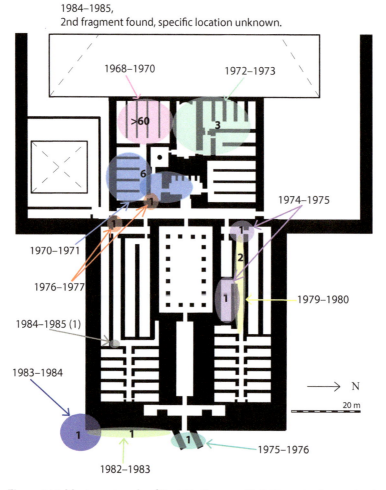

Figure 4.11. Mortuary temple of Pepi I in Saqqara; Sixth Dynasty. Approximate findspots of the prisoner statue fragments are highlighted with the number of fragments and excavation season indicated. For further information on findspots, see the catalogue. Adapted from Legros, *Cinquante ans d'éternité*, fig. 3.

west, were discovered.[65] The second level of the magazines was still present, a feature that was unusually well preserved in Pepi I's temple. This high level of preservation contrasted with the rest of the inner temple, which was almost completely razed.[66] The upper level of the northernmost magazine had been converted into a limekiln, with calcined walls and a thick layer of lime still remaining in situ. Nearby, in

---

65. In addition to the sources in the previous footnote, see also Labrousse, *Temple funéraire*, 116.

66. Labrousse concluded that the magazines had been burned sometime during the First Intermediate period or even at the end of the Old Kingdom, which made the stone useless to later stone robbers and available for the later lime burners to build kilns, as I mention below (Labrousse, 5). Lauer and Leclant also emphasized that Pepi I's mortuary temple, including its foundations, was severely disturbed and virtually destroyed in most areas, with the exception of the limekilns, whose architecture had inadvertently been preserved as the calcined stone could not be reused (for example, see Lauer, "Travaux aux pyramids," 101–4; Jean Leclant, "Fouilles et travaux en Égypte et au Soudan, 1976–1977," *Orientalia* 47 [1978]: 280; and Leclant, *Recherches*, 8). Concerning limekilns, the state of preservation, and later activity, at both the Pepi I complex and others, see further ch. 5.

converted into a limekiln, with calcined walls and a thick layer of lime still remaining in situ. Nearby, in the debris around these magazines, Lauer and Leclant unearthed over thirty prisoner statue fragments, including eight fragmented heads and the remains of approximately fifteen bodies (PP 1–24; C.5.1–C.5.24; fig. 2.8).[67] They concluded that the statues had been broken, collected, and left in preparation for the limekiln, though the kiln operations seemed to have stopped suddenly as the statue fragments had not yet been thrown in and a layer of lime still remained on the kiln's floor.[68]

Excavations during the following season, from 1969–1970, continued in the same area, namely, the magazines directly south of the offering hall and the corridor linking them.[69] In the clearing of the debris within this corridor, Lauer and Leclant discovered a similarly large number of prisoner statues fragments that also seemed to have been destined for the limekiln (PP 10, 25–31, 33–51; C.5.10, C.5.25–C.5.31, C.5.33–C.5.51).[70] In addition, another damaged head was found within the lower level of one of the two-storied magazines (PP 32; C.5.32). During the remainder of the MAFS work in Pepi I's mortuary temple, from 1970–1988, excavators sporadically discovered nineteen more prisoner statue fragments, the findspots of which I have noted on figure 4.11.[71]

Regarding the original placement of the prisoner statues, Lauer and Leclant suggested that all of the statues had once lined the length of the causeway.[72] However, all of the prisoner statues from Pepi I's pyramid complex were discovered within and around the mortuary temple. This implies that they were originally erected there, rather than in the causeway. Most of the fragments came from the area directly around the rear limekiln. The lime burners generally broke the statues in half at the waist, and, in a couple of cases, into smaller pieces. The pieces would still have been extremely heavy, but they were probably manageable to drag and carry twenty or thirty meters across the mortuary temple. On the other hand, if the statues had originally been set along the causeway, the lime burners would have had to drag the fragments a substantial distance, possibly up to hundreds of meters. If the lime burners knew that they had to carry the statues such a great distance, why did they not break all of the statues, not just a few, into smaller pieces? Moreover, relief fragments from Pepi I's mortuary temple were found with the prisoner statues in the debris surrounding the rear limekiln, presumably also waiting to be thrown into the kiln, and the dismantling of the mortuary temple seems to have occurred around the same time as this kiln was in use.[73] While the causeway cannot be completely dismissed, especially as it has never been excavated, based on

---

67. 20--50, Center of Documentation, Supreme Council of Antiquities, Ministry of Tourism and Antiquities, Cairo, Egypt. 20-50 in the Center of Documentation (distinct from 20--50) also includes a similar photograph of the central fragments that must have been taken at the same time. The fragments that were discovered in the 1968–1969 season were primarily published in an eight-page article, with several figures and plates (Lauer and Leclant, "Découverte," 56–62); this is the main publication usually cited for the Pepi I prisoner statues.

68. Lauer and Leclant, 62 and pl. 8A.

69. See further Lauer, "Rapport," 203–5; Jean-Philippe Lauer, "Recherches et travaux à Saqqarah (campagne 1969–1970)," *CRAIBL* 114 (1970): 489–503; Jean-Philippe Lauer, "Travaux et découvertes à Saqqarah (1970–1971)," *BSFE* 62 (1971): 41–46; Leclant, "Fouilles…1969–1970," 233; and Leclant, *Recherches*, 9.

70. Following the discovery of the first two groups of prisoner statues in this complex, see Lauer, "Statues de prisonniers."

71. The excavators originally identified two additional fragments (PP 53 and PP 54), which were found during the 1970–1971 season, as having come from prisoner statues, but this identification is incorrect.

72. Lauer, "Recherches…1967–1968 et 1968–1969," 478; Lauer, *Saqqara*, 180; Lauer, "Statues de prisonniers," 42–43; Lauer, "Travaux…1968–1969," 23; and Lauer and Leclant, "Découverte," 61. They proposed this original location not only for the Pepi I complex but for all of the complexes that had contained prisoner statues.

73. Lauer, "Recherches…1967–1968 et 1968–1969," 468; Lauer, "Statues de prisonniers," 38; and Leclant, "Fouilles… 1969–1970," 233.

the current evidence, it is far more likely that the Pepi I prisoner statues were originally set somewhere within this king's mortuary temple.

4.2.6. Pepi II

Gustave Jéquier began excavating the pyramid complex of Pepi II in 1925.[74] Over the course of eleven years, Jéquier cleared the valley temple, the east and west ends of the causeway, and the mortuary temple. Jéquier also uncovered a large rectangular terrace that could be reached by a harbor ramp on its northern and southern ends immediately in front and to the east of the valley temple. Since Jéquier, no major work has been undertaken at Pepi II's complex.

Figure 4.12. Valley temple of Pepi II in Saqqara; Sixth Dynasty. Modified from Jéquier, *Monument funéraire*, 3:pl. 2.

Once again, the plan of Pepi II's valley temple was different from his predecessors (fig. 4.12). It only had a single entrance, in the middle of the terrace's west wall, without a portico. This led into a rectangular room that had two rows of four limestone pillars. In its southeast corner, there seems to have been a doorway to four storage magazines. Behind the pillared room, a vestibule led to an additional five storage magazines in the southwest part of the valley temple. Indeed, Pepi II's valley temple had many more magazines than earlier preserved valley temples. The vestibule also connected to a staircase to the roof and a corridor that granted access to three additional magazines in the northwest portion of the temple, a second room with similar dimensions as the vestibule, and the causeway. The causeway took two turns and angled to the northeast. At the upper turn, there was a small room on the south side that may have been for a guard and that granted access to the upper causeway. A similar structure seems to have also been placed a few meters lower on the north side of the causeway. The plan of Pepi II's mortuary temple was similar to that of Pepi I's, including in the layout of the magazines (fig. 4.13). Eighteen quartzite pillars surrounded the open court, and an octagonal quartzite pillar was set inside the *antichambre carrée*.

Jéquier regularly described finding the prisoner statue fragments simply scattered in all corners of the monument and provided no further details.[75] He even questioned whether the dispersal was intentional, an idea that I will return to below.[76] He was clearly uncertain where the statues had originally been erected, but he favored the idea that they had been arranged in rows along the walls of the larger rooms in the mortuary temple, including the transverse corridor, the open court, or the entrance hall.[77] Following Jéquier's work, Rainer Stadelmann, Dagmar Stockfisch, and Andrzej Ćwiek also proposed that the statues had been set up in the open court.[78]

---

74. The final reports are Jéquier, *Monument funéraire*. Jéquier also published preliminary reports regularly in *ASAE*. In addition, see Jéquier, *Douze ans*.
75. Jéquier, *Douze ans*, 64; Jéquier, *Monument funéraire*, 3:27; and Jéquier, "Rapport préliminaire...1926–1927," 60.
76. Jéquier, "Planche 22," 22.
77. Jéquier, *Douze ans*, 65; Jéquier, *Monument funéraire*, 3:28; and Jéquier, "Planche 22," 22.
78. Stadelmann, *Ägyptischen Pyramiden*, 198; Stockfisch, *Untersuchungen zum Totenkult*, 80; and Ćwiek, "Relief Decoration," 142.

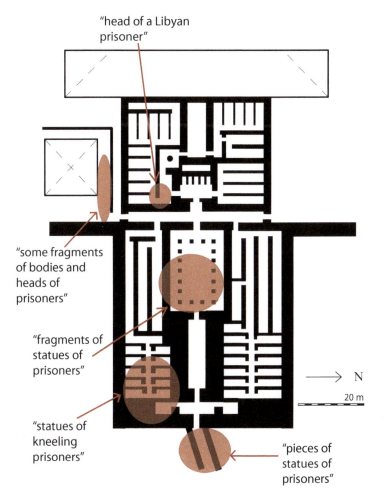

Figure 4.13. Mortuary temple of Pepi II in Saqqara; Sixth Dynasty. Approximate findspots of prisoner statue fragments are highlighted with the words of Jéquier from his notebooks included. Jéquier discovered all of these fragments during the 1926–1927 excavation season. Adapted from Jéquier, *Monument funéraire*, 3:pl. 29.

Unlike Jéquier's published accounts, which omit any information regarding the exact findspots of the statues, his excavation journals include more detail.[79] Using these, in conjunction with the published reports, I have traced and mapped his exposure of the statues (figs. 4.13 and 4.14). These maps make it clear that Jéquier did in fact find the fragments everywhere within the complex and even outside of the Pepi II enclosure itself. For example, he found one fragment of a head along the north face of the nearby mastaba of Shepseskaf, or the Mastabat Faraon, which he was also excavating at this time (fig. 4.14). He also found

---

79. These are now located in the Office des Archives de l'État and on deposit at the Musée d'ethnographie in Neuchâtel, Switzerland. The journals cover the full twelve years of Jéquier's research in South Saqqara and are organized by regular dated entries.

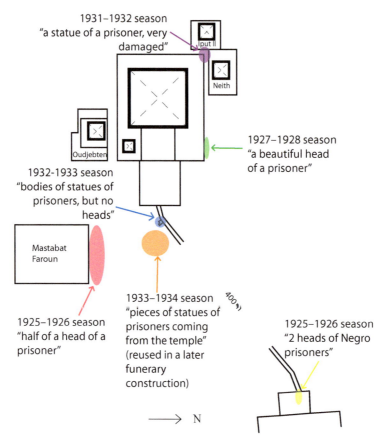

Figure 4.14. Schematic plan of the pyramid complex of Pepi II and environs (not drawn to scale) with approximate findspots of prisoner statue fragments highlighted. Excavation season and words of Jéquier from his notebooks are indicated. Adapted from Jéquier, *Monument funéraire*, 3:pl. 1 and Lepsius, *Denkmäler*, 1:Bl. 34.

fragments that had been reused in a private funerary construction, which may date to the First Intermediate period, located to the south of Pepi II's causeway.[80]

In the northwest corner of the Pepi II pyramid enclosure, at the corners of the pyramids of the queens Iput II and Neith, Jéquier found a very badly damaged statue. He also uncovered one head just outside the enclosure wall, by the courtyard to the north of the mortuary temple. In the small construction attached to the top of the south side of the causeway, he noted that he found bodies but not heads. Fragments of

---

80. Jéquier described finding this brick funerary construction in entries 116–118 for March 22–24, 1934 in his excavation journal for the 1933–1934 season (IV 12, Jéquier fonds). Here he noted that the reuse of the prisoner statue fragments demonstrated a date of a little bit later for this tomb and the others like it that were nearby but not much later considering the style of the offering table that was encased in a corner. He did not explicitly mention this specific tomb with the reused prisoner statues in his final report, but he may have described this group of tombs: small edifices of a funerary nature, probably dating to the First Intermediate period, with very irregular walls of brick or mud and uninscribed offering tables (Jéquier, *Monument funéraire*, 3:76). *If* he was referring to this group of tombs, then the prisoner statue fragments would have been reused in the First Intermediate period; I return to this possibility and its implications regarding the condition and treatment of the Pepi II prisoner statues in ch. 5.2.5.

two heads were also excavated near the rear exit of the valley temple. Yet, the largest number of prisoner statue fragments clearly came from the mortuary temple itself (fig. 4.13). Moreover, most of these seem to have been concentrated toward the front half of the temple: scattered about the open court, the southern magazines, and the upper portion of the causeway.

Although they contain much more detail than his published reports, Jéquier's journal entries are still quite vague. Regarding the prisoner statues, he usually mentioned finding either one head or "some" fragments. Moreover, it is clear that over time, he largely stopped recording the prisoner statue fragments that he was finding altogether because the number of fragments mentioned in the notebooks is certainly less than the hundreds of fragments he described in the published reports. Following the 1925–1926 and 1926–1927 seasons, when he referred to the prisoner statue fragments frequently, Jéquier seems to have only made note of them when they were discovered in more remote locations, outside the enclosure wall, or exceptionally well preserved examples. Overall, his later journal entries were more sporadic and generalized. While it is quite likely that he did find an especially large number from 1926–1927, when he excavated the southern half of the mortuary temple, it is also likely that as he realized the quantity of the fragments and they became a routine discovery, he stopped bothering to record most of them. This is probably why the plotted findspots are focused in the southern portion of the mortuary temple (see fig. 4.13). By the 1927–1928 season, when Jéquier cleared the northern side of the temple, the prisoner statue fragments had become commonplace.

Regardless of these issues, figures 4.13 and 4.14 clearly illustrate the highly scattered nature of the Pepi II prisoner statue fragments. As I noted above, Jéquier tentatively proposed that because the fragments were so widely distributed, they might have been intentionally scattered at some point after they were broken. However, there is presently no evidence that supports this idea. Instead, Jéquier's journal entries repeatedly refer to evidence for intrusive burials, reoccupation, and looting, and this later activity is most likely responsible for the fragments' dispersal.[81]

Pepi II had the largest number of prisoner statues, and this, together with the wide distribution of the fragments, indicates that the original statues were erected in multiple areas throughout the complex, rather than in a single room or part. Given that Jéquier discovered the largest number of fragments in the mortuary temple, like the kings before him, Pepi II must have placed prisoner statues somewhere in his mortuary temple. One cannot completely dismiss the possibility that the fragments that Jéquier discovered in the construction at the top of the causeway originally came from prisoner statues erected in the upper portion of the causeway (see fig. 4.14). Logistically, the causeway was a conceivable location. Jéquier determined the causeway was 2.4 m wide.[82] The depth of the bases of two reconstructed statues from this complex, which are now in the Suez National Museum and the Grand Egyptian Museum (C.6.7 and C.6.1 respectively), is around 40 cm (figs. 2.22 and 2.23).[83] Thus, two statues could have been set near either wall with sufficient room to easily pass through the corridor. However, it is equally likely that the fragments that Jéquier found in the construction had been displaced from the mortuary temple. The same cannot be said for the two prisoner statue heads that Jéquier discovered around the exit of Pepi II's valley temple (see fig. 4.14). These must have come from statues erected in the valley temple or the beginning of the causeway.

---

81. As I discuss in the following chapter, the statues were already in a fragmentary state during or soon after the reign of Pepi II, and this would have facilitated their inadvertent movement.

82. Jéquier, *Douze ans*, 72.

83. The depth of Suez, Suez National Museum JE 51729 is 38 cm, and the depth of Cairo, GEM 1101 (previously Cairo, Egyptian Museum JE 53670) is 43 cm.

Therefore, the archaeological evidence indicates that Pepi II had prisoner statues in his mortuary temple; in, or right near the exit of, his valley temple; and possibly in parts of his causeway. Based on the available data, the only other king who had prisoner statues in his valley temple was Niuserre. Following this king, the prisoner statues seem to have instead been used in mortuary temples until Pepi II placed them in both temples. Like the plans and architectural features of the late Old Kingdom pyramid complexes, the location of the prisoner statues within the complexes varied and was not uniform. But where in the temples were each king's prisoner statues set? In order to answer this question, it is necessary to turn to the relief program. As three-dimensional representations of the bound captive motif, the prisoner statues were closely related to reliefs of the triumphant pharaoh smiting and trampling his enemies.

4.3. The Relief Decoration

As I have already mentioned, the inner walls of the Fifth and Sixth Dynasty mortuary temples were regularly decorated with painted reliefs, and just as the late Old Kingdom kings and royal architects varied and adapted the plans and architecture of the pyramid complexes while following established traditions and protocols, as I outlined above, the royal patrons and their artists modified the relief program from complex to complex.[84] Certain types of reliefs were generally appropriate for particular parts of the complex, but the composition and placement of these reliefs within each part varied, and there were important innovations that occurred over time.

The location of two-dimensional scenes that featured depictions of conquered enemies indicates which parts of the temples and causeway would have been suitable for the prisoner statues. As I show here, such reliefs were carved in the valley temple around the entrances and the exit and in the causeway, particularly at the end closest to the valley temple. Within the mortuary temple, depictions of the triumphant king were common in and around the open court, but they were also placed in more transitional areas, including the transverse corridor and the rear vestibule. On the other hand, this subject matter was never set in the most sacred areas of the temple, namely, the *antichambre carrée*, the offering hall, and the core of the five-niche chapel. The location of these types of reliefs must be considered together with the archaeological evidence for the prisoner statues in order to determine where the statues stood in each pyramid complex. I do this and propose the placement of each king's prisoner statues in the fifth section of this chapter, while I focus on the relief program here.

Gay Robins identified four primary themes that were present in the late Old Kingdom pyramid complex relief program. These included inscriptions with the king's titles and names; the king as establisher of order; the legitimation and renewal of kingship, including the king's interaction with deities; and provisioning the deceased king.[85] Each theme could be represented with a variety of scene types, which often simultaneously conveyed more than a single theme. While these themes were consistent, the reliefs did not have to be, and each complex combined and reinterpreted the program in new and different ways.

The prisoner statues, as depictions of Egypt's defeated enemies, were certainly part of Robin's theme of the king as establisher of order. Indeed, they were three-dimensional variations of it. Similar two-dimensional subject matter included images of the king in the form of a sphinx or griffin trampling foreigners,

---

84. Useful summaries of the reliefs, including their locations in each complex, and their themes can be found in Ćwiek, "Relief Decoration" and Stockfisch, *Untersuchungen zum Totenkult*.

85. Gay Robins, *The Art of Ancient Egypt* (Cambridge: Harvard University Press, 1997), 58. See also Dorothea Arnold, "Royal Reliefs," in Arnold, Grzymski, and Ziegler, *Egyptian Art*, 83–101.

Figure 4.15. Relief fragments depicting the king smiting a Libyan, booty, and the Libyan "family" motif from the open court of the mortuary temple of Sahure in Abusir; Fifth Dynasty. After Borchardt, *Grabdenkmal des Königs Sahu-re*, 2:Bl. 1.

smiting scenes, and depictions of captives (figs. 4.15–4.18).[86] Hunting scenes should also be placed in this category, as foreigners could be likened to wild animals and the Egyptians clearly paralleled scenes of the king hunting animals with scenes of the king "hunting" foreigners.[87]

The pyramid complex of Sahure offers the best example of a complete relief program.[88] His complex demonstrates the frequency with which subject matter referring to the supreme power of the king and his ability to maintain order could be employed. For example, the smaller portico on the south side of the valley temple featured a hunt in the marshes.[89] In the valley temple's rear room, which led to the causeway, the king in the form of a griffin trampled foreign enemies.[90] Borchardt also discovered relief fragments featuring bound prisoners somewhere in the valley temple.[91] This theme continued on the walls at the bottom of the causeway, where gods led rows of bound prisoners (fig. 3.27).[92] While the entirety of Sahure's causeway was decorated, scenes of the king dominating enemies were limited to the causeway's lower end.[93]

In the mortuary temple, a desert-hunting scene decorated the outer wall on the south side of the corridor surrounding Sahure's open court, while fishing and fowling scenes decorated the corresponding outer wall on the north side.[94] The inside walls of the court featured multiple smiting scenes.[95] These incorporated images of accompanying booty and captives. There was also an enigmatic representation of a Libyan woman and two male children who are all identified by name (fig. 4.15). They have traditionally been interpreted as the family of a Libyan chief, who is also identified by name and whom the pharaoh smites in the accompanying scene that is largely destroyed. This motif made its first known appearance here, in Sahure's open court, but it was frequently repeated in later Old Kingdom pyramid complexes.[96]

Other pyramid complexes with more poorly preserved reliefs follow some similar patterns but also demonstrate that there was no set program and the exact placement of particular types of reliefs could

---

86. Concerning reliefs with this theme, see further Prakash, "Depictions of Defeated Foreigners," 454–65. The triumph scenes of trampling and smiting regularly included subscenes of bound captives, adoring foreigners, and booty. In this way, the triumph scenes also depicted the dominance of the Egyptian pharaoh and Egypt through the appropriation of foreign labor and resources. One can propose a similar interpretation for scenes of foreigners returning to Egypt on Egyptian boats; in these both foreigners and Egyptians alike stand together with their arms raised in adoration of the king. As these scenes lack the violence inherent in triumph scenes and prisoner statues, I do not discuss them here, but fragments of them have been found in Sahure's mortuary temple and the causeways of both Sahure and Unas (Borchardt, *Grabdenkmal des Königs Sahu-re*, 2:Bl. 11–13; El Awady, *Sahure*, 155–60 and pl. 5; and Labrousse and Moussa, *Chaussée*, 27–28 and fig. 27). See also Do. Arnold, "Royal Reliefs," 100 n. 76 and Bietak, "Zur Marine," 35–40.

87. However, hunting scenes were complex representations that also had other meanings. For a detailed study of the significance of hunting to royal and elite culture, see John Baines, *High Culture and Experience in Ancient Egypt*, Studies in Egyptology and the Ancient Near East (Bristol: Equinox, 2013), 187–234. For Old Kingdom hunting scenes, see Baines, "Kingship before Literature," 143–52.

88. As a result of this, scholars often describe Sahure's relief program as a prototype that the later Old Kingdom kings simply copied; I discussed this problematic tendency in regard to the pyramid complex of Sahure above and return to it again at the end of this chapter. For an interpretation of Sahure's relief program, see Do. Arnold, "Royal Reliefs," 94–98.

89. Borchardt, *Grabdenkmal des Königs Sahu-re*, 2:Bl. 15.

90. Borchardt, Bl. 8.

91. Borchardt, Bl. 3.

92. Borchardt, Bl. 5–7.

93. For the reliefs along Sahure's causeway, see also El Awady, *Sahure* and Zahi Hawass and Miroslav Verner, "Newly Discovered Blocks from the Causeway of Sahure (Archaeological Report)," *MDAIK* 52 (1996): 177–86.

94. Borchardt, *Grabdenkmal des Königs Sahu-re*, 2:Bl. 16 and 17.

95. Borchardt, Bl. 1–4.

96. Moreover, hundreds of years later, it reappeared on the pylon of Taharqa's temple at Kawa. For further discussion on the Libyan "family" motif, including citations to earlier interpretations, see Prakash, "Depictions of Defeated Foreigners," 456–57.

Figure 4.16. Relief fragments from a trampling scene at the end of the causeway of Niuserre in Abusir; Fifth Dynasty. After Borchardt, *Grabdenkmal des Königs Ne-user-re*, Bl. 10.

vary from complex to complex. As I argued above in regard to the plan and architecture, the later Old Kingdom kings did not simply follow Sahure's pyramid complex. For example, Niuserre's valley temple also featured a hunt in the marshes, but the trampling royal animals were moved to the bottom of the causeway, where scenes of them crushing foreign enemies were repeated on both the north and south walls (fig. 4.16).[97] Additionally, Borchardt discovered fragments from at least two smiting scenes in Niuserre's mortuary temple, but it was uncertain where these had originally been set.[98] Similarly, excavators discovered fragments from at least two smiting scenes that originally were somewhere in the mortuary temple of Unas. Other related fragments from Unas's mortuary temple depicted rows of bound captives.[99] The bottom of this king's causeway, at least on the north wall, seems to have been decorated similarly to Sahure's; one small fragment appears to show a line of deities with bound prisoners and another has three registers with kneeling, bound captives and captured animals.[100] A battle scene against Asiatics appeared in the middle of the causeway, but the king was not depicted in this.[101]

There were smiting scenes and bound captives in multiple parts of Pepi I's mortuary temple. A smiting scene, which featured the smiting of both a Libyan and a Nubian before the Libyan "family," seems to have been set on a wall in the open court, the entrance hall, or possibly the perpendicular room between the causeway and the entrance hall, and the transverse corridor featured at least two smiting scenes. Other fragments from smiting scenes were discovered in the rear of the mortuary temple, and they may have come from smiting scenes in rooms within the inner temple, such as the rear vestibule. Moreover, fragments of hunting scenes were found near the transverse corridor and the rear vestibule, as well as somewhere in the outer temple.[102] From these Audran Labrousse reconstructed a hippopotamus hunting scene and a fowling scene in the entrance hall and another hunting scene in the rear vestibule, but his reconstructions are based on the relief program from the pyramid complex of Pepi II, and, as I argue in this

---

97. Borchardt, *Grabdenkmal des Königs Ne-user-re*, 37–38, 45–49, Abb. 15 and 16, and Bl. 8–12.
98. Borchardt, 86–88 and Abb. 63–66.
99. Labrousse, Lauer, and Leclant, *Temple haut*, 89–94 and pls. 32 and 33.
100. Labrousse and Moussa, *Temple d'accueil*, 95–99 and pl. 15 and Labrousse and Moussa, *Chaussée*, 19–20 and figs. 14 and 15. The excavators also suggested that the Libyan "family" appeared as part of these triumph scenes based on the captured animals, which are placed above the Libyan "family" in Sahure's mortuary temple, but there are no other preserved fragments that support this. Neither the "family" nor fragments depicting a trampling or smiting scene are preserved.
101. Labrousse and Moussa, *Chaussée*, 21–23 and figs. 16–21.
102. Labrousse, *Temple funéraire*; Lauer, "Cinquante années," 563; Lauer, *Saqqara*, 83; Lauer, "Travaux aux pyramids," 102–3; Jean-Philippe Lauer, "Travaux et recherches à Saqqarah (15 Décembre 1974–28 Mars 1975)," *ASAE* 63 (1979): 141; Jean Leclant, "La 'famille libyenne' au temple haut de Pépi Ier," in *Livre du centenaire: 1880–1980*, ed. Jean Vercoutter, MIFAO 104 (Cairo: Institut français d'archéologie orientale, 1980), 49–54; Jean Leclant, "Fouilles et travaux en Égypte et au Soudan, 1974–1975," *Orientalia* 45 (1976): 285; Leclant, "Fouilles…1976–1977," 280; and Jean Leclant and Gisèle Clerc "Fouilles et travaux en Égypte et au Soudan, 1984–1985," *Orientalia* 55 (1986): 258. Labrousse reconstructs Pepi I's relief program largely based on that of Pepi II, which is problematic as I mention below (Labrousse, 51–142).

chapter, there were changes in the decorative program over time; thus scholars must be wary of assuming that the placement of reliefs in one complex was exactly the same as that in a different complex.[103]

Pepi II's pyramid complex was also fully decorated with very high-quality painted reliefs, which were better preserved than those of Pepi I, Teti, Unas, and Niuserre. Using the many fragments that he found and the lower courses of walls that remained in situ, Jéquier was able to roughly reconstruct much of this program. In the valley temple, Jéquier discovered very small nonconnecting fragments, which he suggested probably adorned the front columned hall. He identified some of the fragments as having come from a smiting scene and a scene of hunting in the marsh.[104] At the base of the causeway, both walls featured human and animal booty and deities leading processions of captives toward an alternating series of sphinxes and griffins, which were likely trampling foreign enemies.[105]

In the transversal chambers that one first encounters inside the mortuary temple, before reaching the entrance hall, there was a scene of the king smiting two Nubians. This seems to have been opposite another smiting scene.[106] The entrance hall was completely decorated, and the north wall included an image of the king hunting a hippopotamus.[107] On the other hand, there was no evidence to indicate that the walls of the open court had been decorated, unlike in the Fifth Dynasty mortuary temples.[108] However, the pillars themselves were decorated, based on the one that Jéquier recovered. While earlier columns and pillars bore the king's titulary and sometimes the names and representations of the goddesses Nekhbet or Wadjet, two adjoining faces of Pepi II's pillar featured images of a deity embracing the king; the other two faces were left blank. Jéquier assumed that the decorated sides faced into the court and thus concluded that this pillar was from the northwest corner of the court, where he reerected it.[109]

Toward the rear of Pepi II's mortuary temple, the transverse corridor was decorated with the king and deities, scenes from the *sed* festival, as well as a scene from the festival of the god Min, but also a scene of the king smiting a Libyan in front of the Libyan "family" motif (fig. 4.17).[110] Jéquier discovered a few fragments from a smiting scene involving Nubians in the five-niche chapel and speculated that two smiting scenes could have been on its east wall, framing the doorway from the transverse corridor.[111] The rear vestibule, connecting the five-niche chapel with the *antichambre carrée*, featured a large smiting scene on the south wall (fig. 4.18). Opposite, on the north wall, there was a hunting scene. Jéquier also discov-

---

103. Labrousse, 66–75 and 137–40.

104. Jéquier, *Monument funéraire*, 3:4 and pls. 4–9 and Gustave Jéquier, "Rapport préliminaire sur les fouilles exécutées en 1929–1930 dans la partie méridionale de la nécropole memphite," *ASAE* 30 (1930): 115–16.

105. Jéquier, *Monument funéraire*, 3:10–12 and pls. 12–18.

106. Jéquier, 21–22 and pls. 36–39.

107. Jéquier, 19–21 and pls. 32–35.

108. It is less clear whether or not the open courts of Teti and Pepi I were originally decorated, and presently it seems most prudent *not* to assume that Pepi II's undecorated open court represents the standard convention for all Sixth Dynasty open courts (cf. Labrousse, *Temple funéraire*, 78 and 266–83, who argues that this was the case; moreover, he proposes that Merenre decorated the court of Pepi I as a way to legitimize himself). The condition of Teti's relief program is extremely poor and prevents any conclusions in this regard, one way or another. Relief fragments were discovered in and near Pepi I's open court, including that of the smiting scene that I discussed above. However, Lauer and Leclant had different opinions as to whether these had come from the walls of the open court (compare Lauer, "Travaux…15 Décembre 1974–28 Mars 1975," 141, who concludes that these did come from the open court, with Leclant, "Fouilles…1974–1975," 285 and Leclant, "'Famille libyenne,'" 53, who is less certain). Labrousse situated this scene in the transversal room between the causeway and the mortuary temple's entrance hall (Labrousse, 51–57).

109. Jéquier, *Monument funéraire*, 3:22–24 and pl. 45. For a critical review of Jéquier's reconstruction, see Ćwiek, "Relief Decoration," 283–85.

110. Jéquier, 2:13–23 and pls. 8–29.

111. Jéquier, 24–25 and pl. 35.

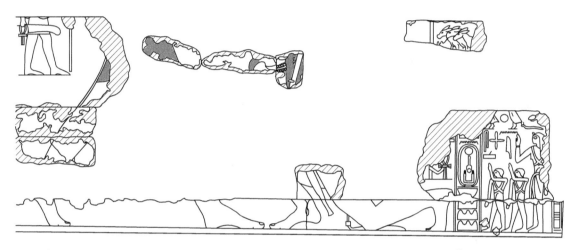

Figure 4.17. Relief fragments from a scene of the king smiting a Libyan in front of the Libyan "family" motif from the transverse corridor of the mortuary temple of Pepi II in Saqqara; Sixth Dynasty. After Jéquier, *Monument funéraire*, 2:pl. 8.

ered fragments depicting birds in this room and suggested they could have been part of another hunting scene.[112] The remainder of the temple, namely, the *antichambre carrée* and the offering hall, did not reference foreigners or hunting in any way but instead included scenes of butchering, offerings, and deities.[113]

There were clearly certain parts of the late Old Kingdom pyramid complex that regularly featured depictions of conquered enemies. These included the valley temple and the causeway, particularly at the end closest to the valley temple. In fact, the decoration of this portion of the causeway consistently included bound prisoners and/or trampling royal animals in all of the complexes where this area has been excavated, namely, those belonging to Sahure, Niuserre, Unas, and Pepi II. Labrousse and Moussa have suggested that the decoration of the bottom of the causeway was codified, though they noted that themes along the rest of the causeway seem to have been employed more freely.[114] Within the mortuary temple, depictions of the king hunting animals or defeating enemies seem to have been frequent and were *not* limited to the outer portions of the temple, unlike later New Kingdom conventions.[115] While this subject matter appears to have been common in and around the entrance hall and open court, it was also placed in more transi-

---

112. Jéquier, 26–33 and pls. 36–43.
113. Jéquier, 34–65.
114. Labrousse and Moussa, *Chaussée*, 15.
115. See further Robins, *Art of Ancient Egypt*, 131 and 170–72.

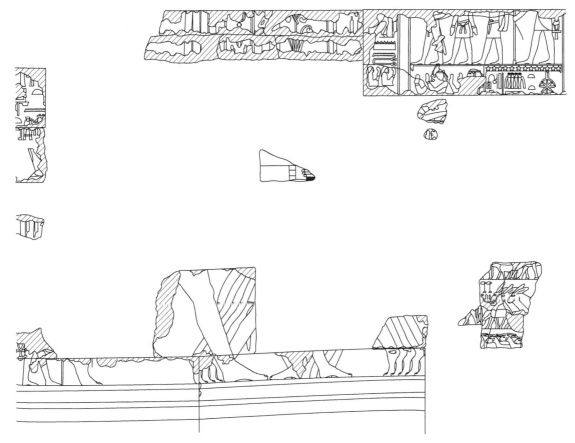

Figure 4.18. Relief fragments from a smiting scene with booty and bound captives from the rear vestibule of the mortuary temple of Pepi II in Saqqara; Sixth Dynasty. After Jéquier, *Monument funéraire*, 2:pl. 36.

tional areas, including the transverse corridor and the rear vestibule, which, in subject matter, shape, and its role as an entrance, seemed to parallel the entrance hall, but on a smaller scale. The variability is also notable. The composition, layout, and arrangement of different types of scenes featuring the king defeating nature and foreigners differed. However, this subject matter was never set in the offering hall and the *antichambre carrée*, which was closely aligned with the offering hall. In a few cases, including the pyramid complexes of Pepi I and Pepi II, smiting scenes might have been depicted in the five-niche chamber, but if so, they seem to have been placed by the doorway of this room and not in the heart of it. Thus the late Old Kingdom Egyptians appear to have considered images of enemies, who, even when being dominated by the king, were still inherently malevolent and dangerous entities, as inappropriate decoration for the most sacred parts of the mortuary temple, in which cult was performed; such imagery did not fit the functions of those rooms.

4.4. The Sculptural Decoration

A primary issue with many of the previous analyses of the late Old Kingdom pyramid complex's decorative program is their failure to take into consideration the three-dimensional decoration. Instead, scholars have almost entirely focused on the two-dimensional reliefs.¹¹⁶ Certainly, the lack of preserved remains severely complicates interpretations of the statuary program. For example, the five-niche chapel was likely included in all of the late Old Kingdom pyramid complexes, but there is very little evidence for what the statues that stood inside the niches looked like. While these statues certainly would have been the focus of cult, they also would have served to embellish the monument. For the mortuary temple of Neferirkare, papyri may indicate that the central statue represented the king as Osiris, while the two outermost ones depicted him as king of Upper and Lower Egypt; it is unclear what types of statues the other niches held.¹¹⁷ Although scholars have tended to assume that the form of these statues and their arrangement in the five niches was consistent throughout the late Old Kingdom, there is no evidence of this. It seems likely that each niche did contain a statue of the king, probably in different forms or regalia, thus illustrating the various aspects of kingship, but exactly what all of these statues looked like and whether they were the same for every king is unknown. Consequently, there are obvious issues with attempting to fully reconstruct any complex's three-dimensional program.

At the same time, the available evidence for the relief program is also extremely fragmentary. Yet, there is still a proclivity to analyze and offer interpretations of this, with the statuary program being entirely or almost entirely overlooked and dismissed as incomplete and problematic. However, when one considers what is available regarding the statuary program, it becomes clear that it was also originally an important part of the overall embellishment, and Egyptologists need to consider both the three-dimensional and two-dimensional decoration when trying to interpret the pyramid complex. Like the architecture and relief program, the statuary program changed over time and was varied from complex to complex. Particularly important in regard to the prisoner statues is a new interest in three-dimensional decoration during the Fifth Dynasty. At this time, different types of beings, which had previously been primarily depicted in the complexes' reliefs, began to be carved in three dimensions and placed throughout the pyramid complexes. These included bound captives, that is, the prisoner statues, and animals associated with the king, such as lions and griffons. In this way, the prisoner statues were part of a larger development in the decorative program of the late Old Kingdom pyramid complex.

The primary and most important statuary associated with any pyramid complex was that which depicted the king, and each complex had multiple royal statues within it. The five-niche chapel in the center of the mortuary temple most clearly illustrates this. The statues within the niches were certainly the focus of cult.¹¹⁸ Yet, the pyramid complex could contain other royal and divine statues as well, which probably also received cult while simultaneously adding to the complex's decoration. Indeed, statue cult was an important aspect of the rituals that occurred within each pyramid complex.

The tradition of adorning the complex with multiple statues of the king flourished during the reigns of the Fourth Dynasty kings Khafre and Menkaure. For example, Khafre's valley temple included twenty-three life-size, seated statues as well as many smaller figures. Menkaure's valley temple was also in-

---

116. For example, Stockfisch, *Untersuchungen zum Totenkult*, 390–400; El Awady, *Sahure*, 50–82; Ćwiek, "Relief Decoration," 330–49; and Baines, "Kingship before Literature," 125–74.

117. Posener-Kriéger, *Archives du temple funéraire*, 502 and 544–45. For further discussion, with references to earlier arguments, see Verner, *Statues of Raneferef*, 235–36; Di. Arnold, "Rituale und Pyramidentempel," 9–10; Rochholz, "Sedfest, Sonnenheiligtum, und Pyramidenbezirk," 265–66; and Stockfisch, 392–93.

118. For additional discussion on Old Kingdom cult statues, see Di. Arnold, "Old Kingdom Statues," 41–49; Filip Coppens and Hana Vymazalová, "Long Live the King! Notes on the Renewal of Divine Kingship in the Temple," in *Egypt in Transition: Social and Religious Development of Egypt in the First Millennium BCE*, ed. Ladislav Bareš, Filip Coppens, and Květa Smoláriková (Prague: Czech Institute of Egyptology, 2010), 89–90; and Hana Vymazalová and Filip Coppens, "Statues and Rituals for Khentkaus II: A Reconsideration of Some Papyrus Fragments from the Queen's Funerary Complex," in Bárta, Coppens, and Krejčí, *Abusir and Saqqara...2010*, 785–99. See also Kemp, "Old Kingdom," 85.

tended to hold a large number of his statues.¹¹⁹ The number of royal statues seems to have decreased significantly by the late Old Kingdom, though enough remains to indicate that this practice did not cease. For example, some fragments of a seated statue of Sahure wearing the white crown, similar to ones found in Khafre's complex, were discovered in the former's mortuary temple.¹²⁰ Alabaster fragments from a seated statue of Djedkare were discovered in this king's mortuary temple.¹²¹ An uninscribed red granite statue that Quibell discovered near the mortuary temple of Teti most likely depicts Teti himself and originally came from this temple.¹²² Jéquier uncovered only a single remaining statue of Pepi II at his complex. This small alabaster statue depicted him as a squatting, nude child with his finger to his mouth.¹²³ However, the poor state of preservation of these monuments must be kept in mind, as they likely originally contained much more than has been discovered.

There is also reason to believe that the statuary program at each complex could be varied and adapted when necessary. In this regard, the mortuary temple of Raneferef is particularly telling. This king had a relatively short reign, and at the time of his death, only a small portion of his mortuary temple had been completed. His successor Niuserre oversaw the construction of most of Raneferef's temple. As a result, it differed in multiple ways from other Fifth Dynasty mortuary temples, including that of Niuserre. One important way was in the amount of royal statuary that it originally contained: possibly up to fourteen statues in a variety of materials, including diorite, basalt, travertine, and wood, and ranging in height from approximately 35 cm to life-size.¹²⁴ Many of these seem to have been used in the *pr-twt*, "house of the statue," which the excavators identified as the hypostyle hall in the rear, south wing of Raneferef's temple.¹²⁵ While some statues, including one life-size image, may have stayed in this room permanently, the excavators suggested that some of the other smaller images would have been stored inside the adjacent magazines and brought into the *pr-twt* when needed.¹²⁶

The number of attested royal statues in Raneferef's mortuary temple is significantly more than those attested at other late Old Kingdom temples. This is likely tied to the unique circumstances under which

---

119. Di. Arnold, 41–42.

120. Borchardt, *Grabdenkmal des Königs Sahu-re*, 1:111 and Abb. 142 and W. S. Smith, *History of Egyptian Sculpture*, 46. Borchardt also discovered other fragments that might belong to additional royal statues.

121. Megahed, "Sculptures," 31–32.

122. Cairo, Egyptian Museum JE 39103. See W. S. Smith, *History of Egyptian Sculpture*, 82; Lauer and Leclant, *Temple haut*, 98, and Quibell, *Excavations...1906–1907*, 77 and pl. 31. Others have argued that this statue could depict Menkauhor, but archaeologically and stylistically, the attribution to Teti seems much more likely (see further Verner, *Statues of Raneferef*, 96–98 and pl. I.4.3.1; Vandier, *Manuel*, 3:33–34 and pl. 7,5; Jocelyne Berlandini, "La pyramide 'ruinée' de Sakkara-nord et le roi Ikaouhor-Menkaouhor," *RdE* 31 [1979]: 27; Edna R. Russmann, *Egyptian Sculpture: Cairo and Luxor* [Austin: University of Texas Press, 1989], 41–43 no. 15; and Romano, "Sixth Dynasty Royal Sculpture," 274–75).

123. Jéquier, *Douze ans*, 63 and fig. 19 and Jéquier, *Monument funéraire* 3:30–31 and pl. 49.

124. For these statues, see Verner, *Statues of Raneferef*.

125. Raneferef's hypostyle hall is the only known example of a hypostyle hall within an Old Kingdom pyramid complex (Miroslav Verner, "*Pr-twt*: The Cult Place of Raneferef's Statues," in Landgráfová and Mynářová, *Rich and Great*, 325 and Verner, *Pyramid Complex of Raneferef*, 151–52); for the origins and early evolution of the hypostyle hall, see Hosam Refai, *Untersuchungen zum Bildprogramm der großen Säulensäle in den thebanischen Tempeln des Neuen Reiches*, BeitrÄg 18 (Vienna: Afro-Pub, 2000), 25–29 and Dieter Arnold, "Hypostyle Halls of the Old and Middle Kingdom?" in Der Manuelian, *Studies*, 39–54.

126. Verner, *Statues of Raneferef*, 233–38; Benešovská, "Statues," 430–37; Posener-Kriéger, Verner, and Vymazalová, *Pyramid Complex of Raneferef*, 344–46; Verner, *Abusir*, 127–31; Verner, "*Pr-twt*," 325–30; and Verner, *Pyramid Complex of Raneferef*, 51–59 and 146–51. Statue fragments were found in other areas of the temple as well, many of which joined with fragments found near the hypostyle hall. A lot of those found elsewhere were in areas that seemed to function as dumps, and they may have originally stood in the hypostyle hall. But it is also possible that some of these royal statues were placed elsewhere in the temple.

Raneferef's temple was constructed. Indeed, it did not have a five-niche chapel, and the *pr-twt* may have functioned in lieu of this.[127] However, at the same time, the large amount of statuary may be a repercussion of a period of three-dimensional experimentation in royal mortuary decoration during the mid-Fifth Dynasty.[128]

The royal workshops would have also sculpted the prisoner statues, although they represent a different emphasis and focus. Yet, they also seem to have developed as part of this period of experimentation in the statuary of the pyramid complex. For example, as I mentioned above, Borchardt discovered within Niuserre's mortuary temple a colossal red granite statue of a lion or lioness that had been set in its own deep niche to the north of the entrance to the five-niche chapel. This was an innovation that was unique to Niuserre's complex. Moreover, at this complex Borchardt also found the head of a basalt lion that had served as a waterspout.[129]

The three-dimensional depiction of leonine animals—which were closely associated with kingship, as the trampling reliefs that I described above illustrate—within the royal pyramid complex can be traced back to the Fourth Dynasty and most notably the Great Sphinx at Giza. In the mortuary temple of the first king of the Fifth Dynasty, Userkaf, Cecil Firth discovered claws of a sphinx or lion made from gray stone.[130] Userkaf's successor, Sahure, had several sphinx or lion statues in his mortuary temple, including an elaborate libation table with lions.[131] With Sahure and Niuserre, the scale and number of leonine statues seems to have intensified. This trend continued during the reign of Djedkare. Along with the prisoner statue fragments, Hussein discovered limestone statues of a recumbent lion and a recumbent lion, sphinx, or griffin; one upright lion seated on his rear legs; one recumbent bovine; the head of another bovine; and an uncertain body fragment that could belong to an upright bovine.[132] As he did for the prisoner statue fragments, he recorded the findspots of some of these animal statue fragments as "accidentelle," while others had no notes. Thus, once again, little can be said beyond the fact that they came from the mortuary temple. Lauer discovered only two limestone fragments of standing animal paws at the mortuary temple of Unas.[133] However, at the turn of the twenty-first century, the SCA found the remains of four or five sphinx statues from Unas's valley temple; Zahi Hawass has suggested that these formed part of a processional avenue.[134] Hawass also referenced unpublished fragments of sphinx statues that were found at the

---

127. Verner, *Statues of Raneferef*, 233–36; Landgráfová, *Faience Inlays*, 11–12; Verner, "*Pr-twt*," 325–30; and Verner, *Pyramid Complex of Raneferef*, 150.

128. Interestingly, around the same time, one finds an increasing number of statues within private tombs as well (Bárta, "Architectural Innovations," 112).

129. Borchardt, *Grabdenkmal des Königs Ne-user-re*, 16–17, 64–65, 69–70 and Abb. 7, 44, and 47.

130. Firth noted this discovery in his excavation notebook, but the current location of the fragments is unknown (see Audran Labrousse and Jean-Philippe Lauer, *Les complexes funéraires d'Ouserkaf et de Néferhétepès*, BiEtud 130 [Cairo: Institut français d'archéologie orientale, 2000], 66–68).

131. Borchardt, *Grabdenkmal des Königs Sahu-re*, 1:111–13 and Abb. 142–45.

132. Inv. No. 3115–3120, 3127 and 3128, Box 48, Inv. No. 674, 689, 691–693, 695, 696, 3184, 3185, Box 52, Varille Collection. See also Megahed, "Sculptures," 27–31 and figs. 8–11 and Piacentini, "Excavating the Egyptological Archives," 361 and figs. 11–13. Photographs show that some of these fragments had unusual features, such as a flattened, sloping back of the upright lion and a protruding block on the back of the recumbent lion. It is possible that some of these statues served as ritual equipment, such as the libation table of Sahure, but direct study of the fragments is necessary to determine this. Varille noted similarities, particularly in the break patterns, between the upright lion statue from the Djedkare complex and the colossal lion statue that Borchardt had discovered at the complex of Niuserre.

133. Labrousse, Lauer, and Leclant, *Temple haut*, 129 and pl. 40, doc. 129–31.

134. Zahi Hawass, "Five Old Kingdom Sphinxes Found at Saqqara," in *Millions of Jubilees: Studies in Honor of David P. Silverman*, ed. Zahi Hawass and Jennifer Houser Wegner, CASAE 39 (Cairo: Supreme Council of Antiquities, 2010), 205–25. Hawass argued that these date to the reign of Unas though others (he does not mention who) dated them to the Late period.

pyramid complex of Teti.¹³⁵ On the other hand, no fragments of similar statues seem to have been found at the mortuary monument of any subsequent Sixth Dynasty king.¹³⁶

These animal statues, as well as the prisoner statues, represent a period of experimentation and innovation in the three-dimensional decoration of the pyramid complex. While the use of multiple animal statues began with the reign of Sahure, or possibly Userkaf, it was not until the reign of Niuserre that prisoner statues appeared. It would seem that the animal statues then reached their peak during the reign of Djedkare. Indeed, Hussein also uncovered fragments from four architectural pillars in the form of *djed*-signs at this mortuary temple.¹³⁷ Only two adjacent sides of each pillar were sculpted. Thus, the pillars originally seem to have been set into the corners of a room. Interestingly, similar pillars were also used at the complex of Unas, but these were carved with incised relief, unlike those of Djedkare, which were sculpted in high relief.¹³⁸ This further demonstrates Djedkare and his artists' interest in three-dimensional decoration. By the late Fifth or early Sixth Dynasty, the animal statues appear to have gradually fallen out of fashion. At the same time, the prisoner statues became increasingly popular, with larger and larger numbers of them being carved and new changes and developments occurring in their form, as I discussed in the previous chapters, and treatment, which I turn to in the next chapter.

4.5. The Original Placement of the Prisoner Statues and the Decorative Program

Statuary formed an important part of the decorative program of the late Old Kingdom pyramid complexes, and during the Fifth Dynasty there was an increased interest in statues that depicted subjects other than the king. These included foreign prisoners and different animals, particularly leonine ones. Yet, both the prisoner and animal statues still referenced the king. The king was solely responsible for the defeat and destruction of Egypt's enemies and the position of the prisoner statues implied his presence, even if he was not included in the composition. Similarly, lions, sphinxes, and griffons were closely associated with the pharaoh and considered to be manifestations of him. The bovine statues from the complex of Djedkare could be representations of a cow goddess, such as Hathor or Bat, both of whom were protectors of the king and affiliated with kingship.¹³⁹

The prisoner statues are three-dimensional representations of a motif, namely, the bound captive, that had been and continued to be popular in reliefs that covered the walls of the late Old Kingdom pyramid complex. Niuserre's artists transferred this from two-dimensions into freestanding statuary, at a time when there seemed to have been significant interest in three-dimensional art and notable sculptural activity, as the many statues of Raneferef and the increasing number of animal statues demonstrate. The early prisoner statues' back pillars only reinforce their monumentality and connection to the relief program.

---

135. Hawass, 223.

136. Although a fragmentary base for a sphinx statue of Pepi I was found in Haret el-Roum in El-Ghoureya, Cairo in 1891, and there would seem to be an unprovenanced sphinx of Pepi I in a private collection (Borchardt, *Statuen und Statuetten*, 2:90 no. 541 and Bl. 90 no. 541; Biri Fay, *The Louvre Sphinx and Royal Sculpture from the Reign of Amenemhat II* [Mainz: von Zabern, 1996]; and Megahed, "Sculptures," 31). There are also two known sphinx statuettes inscribed for Merenre: Edinburgh, NMS 1984.405 and Moscow, Pushkin Museum 4951 (Fay, 64 and pl. 84a–b, d).

137. Photographs and drawings in Box 48 and 52, Varille Collection. See also Megahed, "Sculptures," 26 and figs. 2 and 3 and Piacentini, "Excavating the Egyptological Archives," 361 and fig. 15.

138. Megahed, "Sculptures," 26 and Labrousse, Lauer, and Leclant, *Temple haut*, 130 and pl. 40, doc. 132.

139. Richard Wilkinson, *The Complete Gods and Goddesses of Ancient Egypt* (London: Thames & Hudson, 2003), 140–41 and 172.

One could perhaps understand the back pillar as akin to a wall itself, from which the prisoner projects in high relief.

There was a close relationship between the prisoner statues and reliefs of the triumphant pharaoh, and in many cases the prisoner statues were likely set nearby or under such reliefs. Unfortunately, the original placement of the prisoner statues in each pyramid complex must remain hypothetical because none of the prisoner statues were discovered in situ and no evidence of their emplacements have been found within the relevant pyramid complexes. However, by considering their findspots along with the location of similarly themed reliefs, which indicate which parts of the pyramid complex would have been appropriate places to erect prisoner statues, it is possible to suggest the most likely placements of each king's prisoner statues.

Based on their findspots, the statues from the complex of Niuserre were likely erected somewhere within his valley temple, probably close to or at the exit to the causeway. This was also an area that typically featured reliefs of the victorious king, with bound captives and leonine creatures trampling foreign enemies. Niuserre's prisoner statues would have reinforced this theme in three dimensions.

Djedkare-Isesi seems to have relocated his prisoner statues to his mortuary temple. Less is known of the Unas and Teti prisoner statues, but their excavation from the mortuary temple indicates that they were also placed somewhere inside this structure. Moreover, the importance of other forms of statuary appears to have started to diminish around this time, as there is no evidence that the Sixth Dynasty kings after Teti erected animal or sphinx statues. Rather their focus appears to have moved to the prisoner statues. Therefore, it is possible that, during this transitional period, Unas and Teti commissioned a greater number of prisoner statues than Niuserre and Djedkare, who only seem to have had a handful of prisoner statues, but the fragments are too poorly documented to draw this conclusion and the limited remains, as well as the fact that Unas and Teti still had sphinx statues, could themselves suggest otherwise.[140] But the number of prisoner statues certainly increased during the reign of Pepi I, and the statues also continued to be placed somewhere inside the mortuary temple.

Inside the mortuary temple, reliefs of the triumphant pharaoh, smiting or hunting, were typically placed near and in the entrance hall, the open court, the transverse corridor, and the rear vestibule. Therefore these are the most likely places that prisoner statues would have been set.[141] Dieter Arnold, Mark Lehner, Rainer Stadelmann, Audran Labrousse, and others have all proposed that the prisoner statues might have stood under scenes of the triumphant king in the mortuary temple in order to stress their message.[142] But it is very likely that the exact arrangement or location of the prisoner statues of Djedkare, Unas, Teti, and Pepi I was different at each complex given the overall variability of the plan and decorative program of the late Old Kingdom pyramid complex that I described above.

Excavators discovered some or all of the prisoner statue fragments from the complexes of Djedkare, Teti, and Pepi I in the inner temple (excluding the Pepi I fragments that were destined for the limekiln,

---

140. I discussed the original number of prisoner statues in each pyramid complex in ch. 2.

141. Fragments demonstrate that the theme of the king as establisher of order was realized in two-dimensions inside the mortuary temples of Djedkare, Unas, Teti, and Pepi I, even if the location of these reliefs is uncertain. For Unas and Pepi I, see discussion in the third section of this chapter. For Teti: Labrousse, Lauer, and Leclant, *Temple haut*, 64 and 94–95; Quibell, *Excavations...1907–1908*, 112 and pl. 54,6; and W. S. Smith, *History of Egyptian Sculpture*, 202. For Djedkare: Maragioglio and Rinaldi, *Architettura della Piramidi Menfite*, 82.

142. Di. Arnold, "Rituale und Pyramidentempel," 7; Di. Arnold, "Royal Cult Complexes," 73; Lehner, *Complete Pyramids*, 158; Stadelmann, *Ägyptischen Pyramiden*, 194; and Labrousse, *Temple funéraire*, 57. See also Megahed, "Sculptures," 27; Jean Revez, "Le traitement iconographique des prisonniers étrangers dans l'art pharaonique à travers une pièce de la collection Diniacopoulos," in *Life and Death in Ancient Egypt: The Diniacopoulos Collection*, ed. Jane E. Francis and George W. M. Harrison (Montreal: Concordia University, 2011), 43–44; and Schoske, "Erschlagen der Feinde," 460.

which the lime burners could have moved from anywhere inside the mortuary temple); these could have belonged to statues that were erected inside the rear vestibule. The backs of the Teti and Pepi I statues were fully executed, though in a rough fashion, in contrast to those of Djedkare. This could indicate that they were visible, though not the focus of attention, or that their positioning inside the mortuary temple had shifted. Additionally, as the number of statues increased, it is tempting to imagine the statues lined up. At the complex of Pepi I, there were certainly enough statues to have lined a large room in the temple, such as the open court or entrance hall, in addition to a few being placed in the rear vestibule. Indeed, Bernard Bothmer argued that the Pepi I statues had been placed in the open court, Miroslav Verner specified both the open court and perhaps also the entrance hall, Rainer Stadelmann preferred the entryway to the temple and the entrance hall, and Audran Labrousse identified particular statues that he believed had been set under smiting scenes in the entryway.[143]

While the prisoner statues often seem to have complemented reliefs of the triumphant king, as I have argued above, they also could have been used in lieu of such reliefs inside rooms where this subject matter was appropriate and typical. The pyramid complex of Pepi II offers a possible example of this. In this king's undecorated open court the prisoner statues could have substituted for the missing triumphal reliefs. Dorothea Arnold has contrasted the open court of Sahure, with its numerous triumph scenes, with that of Pepi II. She argued that the open court of Sahure was a stage for the king's enactment of his role as guarantor of order and prosperity, but "the designers of the Pepi II complex no longer regarded the pyramid temple courtyard as a place where kingship triumphant was made manifest." This signaled to her a changed concept of kingship and the religious ideas surrounding it: unlike Sahure, who was "regarded as a hero who performed deeds to ensure stability and abundance ... Pepi II is primarily a performer of rituals and a companion of the gods."[144]

Arnold rightly described a change in conceptions of kingship by the reign of Pepi II. However, with remains of at least seven smiting scenes and four trampling scenes in his valley temple, causeway, and mortuary temple, Pepi II actually had more reliefs of the triumphant pharaoh throughout his complex than any of his predecessors.[145] He also had more prisoner statues than any of his predecessors, and, based on their findspots—mostly scattered around the outer temple, including inside the open court—it seems quite likely that at least some of Pepi II's prisoner statues had originally been erected in his open court. Pepi II was still clearly very much concerned with expressing his role as guarantor of order. While Arnold's interpretation of these courts is possible, it is perhaps more likely that only the method of decorating the open court changed and that Pepi II and his artists replaced the open court triumph reliefs with prisoner statues.

Pepi II had prisoner statues in multiple parts of his pyramid complex, and statues set in other rooms of his mortuary temple might have complemented two-dimensional triumph scenes. This was also probably the case for the prisoner statues that Jéquier discovered in Pepi II's valley temple. Like the prisoner statues of Niuserre, it seems likely that Pepi II had prisoner statues around the exit of his valley temple; these would have reinforced the meaning and potency of the nearby trampling scenes.

The variability in the original placement of the prisoner statues is consistent with the variability in the architecture and decoration of the late Old Kingdom pyramid complex. They were another way that

---

143. Bothmer, "On Realism," 383; Verner, *Pyramids*, 355; Stadelmann, 194; and Labrousse, 57. Andrzej Ćwiek may follow most of these scholars in noting that it has been suggested that the Pepi I prisoner statues were deposited along the causeway or in the mortuary temple, below representations of the king, but he does not reference who suggested this (Ćwiek, "Relief Decoration," 136).

144. Do. Arnold, "Royal Reliefs," 97.

145. There may be other changes in the triumph scenes of Pepi II, including the regular inclusion of his *ka* behind him while he is smiting (see, e.g., figs. 4.17 and 4.18).

each king and the designers of his funerary monument could modify and refashion the pyramid complex. While the data from these structures are fragmentary and incomplete, what does remain demonstrates the diversity of the pyramid complexes, and scholars need to be wary of describing them as standardized.

4.6. The Embellishment of the Late Old Kingdom Pyramid Complex

The prisoner statues illustrate the need to consider both the two-dimensional and three-dimensional elements of the late Old Kingdom pyramid complex's decorative program in order to understand better the monument's overall meanings. At the same time, it is also necessary to consider its architecture and how this related to the decorative program. When one examines the complexes comprehensively, it becomes clear that they were not nearly as standardized as scholars have often assumed.

Presently, there is nothing to suggest that the plan of the valley temple was standardized at all beyond a basic rectangular shape, a front columned entrance or room approached from the harbor, and a rear exit to the causeway. Although the lack of excavated examples complicates any definitive conclusions in this regard, the valley temples of Sahure, Niuserre, Unas, and Pepi II all differ from each other, sometimes in significant ways. Certainly, particular features may show the influence of earlier temples. For example, the two entrances in Sahure's temple may have influenced Niuserre.[146] But there were other architectural innovations in Niuserre's temple, such as the three-niche room. Kings may have had more flexibility in designing their valley temples than they did for their mortuary temples. This could perhaps be related to the fact that a valley temple was not absolutely necessary, as the complexes of Raneferef and Neferirkare demonstrate, while a mortuary temple was. In this regard, it is interesting that the prisoner statues first appeared in a valley temple, where artistic and architectural experimentation may have been more possible.

The plans of the Sixth Dynasty mortuary temples were undoubtedly more consistent than those of the Fifth Dynasty. Yet, there were still architectural differences, particularly in the arrangement or sizes of magazines and the entries into the temples. The architects of all of the mortuary temples show a remarkable ability to adapt the plan when necessary. It is clear that the location of the complex was often prioritized over the need to construct an exact plan, particularly during the Fifth Dynasty and in the reign of Teti.[147] Certainly the suitability of the location seems to have played a part in its choice; the king and his architects did not choose a location that would have rendered construction extremely difficult. But the plan of the mortuary temple, as well as the layout of the causeway, was adaptable and could be modified to accommodate earlier constructions or topographical features. Moreover, these changes may have impacted future temples. For example, Teti may have needed to reposition his causeway because of previous constructions, and a narrow, undecorated court along the south side of his mortuary temple's east façade may have linked his causeway to the temples' entrance hall.[148] Pepi I's causeway led directly to the temple's central axis, yet there may have been a perpendicular front room or rooms prior to the entrance hall,

---

146. Jánosi, "Pyramiden," 98.
147. Brinks, *Entwicklung der königlichen Grabanlagen*, 153–56.
148. This space could have referred back to or had some relationship with the area, which Megahed and Jánosi interpreted as having had a cultic purpose, between the south massive and the enclosure wall at Djedkare's pyramid complex (see ch. 4.2.2).

in the same place as Teti's narrow court.¹⁴⁹ These rooms were certainly present in Pepi II's temple, where they were decorated.

At the same time, the Sixth Dynasty Egyptians may have largely turned their attention away from the monument's architecture and instead creativity primarily manifested in its decoration. Indeed, the variability of imagery and motifs also speaks against interpretations of the Sixth Dynasty pyramid complex as having been strictly standardized. For example, Pepi II seems to have redesigned the decoration of his open court. Staying within the boundaries of architectural and artistic decorum and still incorporating the necessary themes and iconography, he chose to reimagine the way in which these were presented, depicting himself interacting with deities on his pillars and referencing his maintenance of order with prisoner statues.

Scholars often focus on the repetitive nature of the themes in the decoration of the late Old Kingdom pyramid complex, implying that the repeated use of overall scene types indicates a lack of creativity. While the evidence is extremely incomplete, there is enough to see that the exact placement and details of the scenes could vary from complex to complex. For example, it is true that smiting scenes were a standard feature of the relief program and, like other triumph scenes, they tended to occur in similar areas of the complex. But this does not mean that every king put smiting scenes in the same rooms or on the same walls of his complex. Rather, they had a degree of choice. Moreover, a king could be represented smiting a single foreigner, two foreigners, or a large group of foreigners. There were also a variety of subscenes that could accompany this main scene, including that of the Libyan "family," but there was no set arrangement for these subscenes, and they could be employed and reimagined in different ways.¹⁵⁰ The same was true for the other themes of the decorative program.

While these variances in details, composition, and location may appear minor and inconsequential in comparison to major architectural developments, such as the change from a stepped pyramid to a true pyramid, they should not be discredited or dismissed as less meaningful. The lack of evidence may obscure the full degree of creativity and innovation of the late Old Kingdom, and it is also nearly certain that we do not fully understand what these "minor" changes signaled to the Egyptians. Regardless of their conspicuousness, they reflect the agency of the king, his architects, and/or his artists.

Consequently, scholars should be wary of assuming late Old Kingdom kings were simply following the decorative, as well as the architectural, choices that their predecessors made and exercise extreme caution when using the reliefs and plans from one complex to fill in blanks at other complexes. Indeed, the pyramid complex of Sahure might appear today as a prototype because its plan and relief program is the best preserved of the Old Kingdom. This is not to discredit the import of this complex. Certainly, it does represent a turning point in Old Kingdom royal mortuary architecture, introducing elements that would be repeated for the rest of this period and into the Middle Kingdom. But the degree to which the later Fifth and Sixth Dynasty kings were specifically turning back to Sahure's complex for inspiration and in order to emulate it, in contrast to being influenced by the complexes of other predecessors, is less clear.

The prisoner statues are a good example of the types of innovation in the Old Kingdom royal funerary monuments that may no longer be fully visible. That the prisoner statues would appear during the reign of Niuserre is consistent with the contemporary changes and developments in society, administration, and funerary architecture, including both royal and elite, that I described in chapter 2. Indeed, the mid-Fifth Dynasty was a period of three-dimensional experimentation within the royal funerary monuments; both

---

149. As I mentioned in ch. 4.2.5, this room/rooms is problematic. If it did not exist, the connection may be less direct, but in form and placement Pepi II's perpendicular entryway would still recall Teti's narrow court.

150. See further Prakash, "Depictions of Defeated Foreigners," 454–57.

the prisoner statues and the animal statues exemplify this. Dorothea Arnold has described striking changes that occurred in the relief program during the reign of Niuserre and continued through the end of the Old Kingdom. Following the reign of Sahure, there was a decline in the amount of mortuary temple wall space that may have featured reliefs and thus, less two-dimensional decoration. Furthermore, the format of reliefs seems to have changed, with a new focus on uniformity and large-figure compositions, rather than scenes featuring a large focal figure with rows of smaller figures performing innovative and complicated activities.[151] However, rather than signaling a decline in creativity during the late Old Kingdom, attention turned away from the relief program toward new forms of decoration, namely, the prisoner and animal statues. These, like the large-figure reliefs, reflect an interest in monumentality and scale.

At the same time, the statuary remained closely tied to the reliefs, and the prisoner statues should be understood as a new type of architectural decoration that developed during the reign of Niuserre. This helps explain why their placement changed over time. Like the reliefs, their location in the complex was somewhat mutable.

The flexibility of the prisoner statues is also reflected by the other changes that they underwent throughout the Sixth Dynasty, including the change in the treatment of their ethnicity during the reign of Pepi I, as I discussed in the last chapter, and their treatment in the reigns of Pepi I and Pepi II, as I consider in the next chapter. Indeed, it may be notable that the increase in the number of prisoner statues and the change in their treatment occurred alongside the growth in the number of storage magazines within the valley and mortuary temples. Miroslav Bárta has argued that the escalating amount of magazines indicates an increase in the importance of the cultic activities and the symbolism of rituals occurring inside the temples.[152] The changing treatment of the prisoner statues in the Sixth Dynasty may also reflect a similar trend toward ritualism, and it demonstrates the ways that the ritualization of the monuments varied over time, just as their architecture and decorative program did; the next chapter explores the ritualization of the pyramid complex further.

---

151. Do. Arnold, "Royal Reliefs," 90–98. Note that her calculations of wall space are necessarily rough and tentative due to the complicated data.

152. Bárta, "Architectural Innovations," 112 n. 22 and Bárta, "Egyptian Kingship," 266 and fig. 8.2.

Chapter 5
The Treatment of the Prisoner Statues and the Question of Ritualized Destruction

A complete prisoner statue has never been discovered, and over the last century or so, Egyptologists have debated the reasons for the statues' fragmentary condition. While archaeologists frequently find ancient statues in pieces, the consistency of the prisoner statues' broken state in combination with their subject matter has led many scholars to question whether they were intentionally damaged. Other imagery of bound captives, as symbols of evil and negative forces that the king needed to contain, were sometimes ritualistically destroyed.[1] Thus the issue is a complicated one: were the prisoner statues intentionally broken and if so, why, how, by whom, and at what point in their long life did this occur? And did it occur as part of a ritual?

This chapter reexamines the treatment of the prisoner statues in the late Old Kingdom pyramid complex using the material remains and archaeological evidence from each individual complex as the basis for all conclusions. After outlining the previous arguments concerning the condition of the prisoner statues below, I present the data itself in the second section. In doing this, I demonstrate that the treatment of the prisoner statues changed over time. Only the prisoner statues of Pepi I and Pepi II show evidence of having been intentionally damaged as part of their original function in each king's pyramid complex. The prisoner statues of Pepi I were methodically decapitated. The king's artists were responsible for this, and the decapitation may have been the final step in the statues' creation. On the other hand, the prisoner statues of Pepi II were violently smashed apart likely during or soon after the reign of Pepi II. However, there is nothing to suggest that the earlier prisoner statues were intentionally damaged in antiquity. Rather they appear to have been carved with the intention that they would permanently stand, intact, in each complex.

The differing treatment of the Pepi I and Pepi II statues indicates that the symbolic meaning of their destruction also varied. The prisoner statues of both kings were part of a ritualized context that served to benefit the pharaoh, but the significance and ritualization of the destructive action developed along with the change in the nature of the action itself; the remainder of this chapter considers how and why. In the third section, I discuss the evidence for execration figurines, which I introduced in chapter 1, during the Old Kingdom. These schematic figurines of bound captives could be broken in destruction rituals, and as such, the prisoner statues have frequently been compared to them. However, the ritualized context of the Pepi I and Pepi II prisoner statues was not the same as that of execration figurines, as I articulate in the fourth section of this chapter. Instead, the decapitated Pepi I prisoner statues were visualizations of the annihilated enemies of the deceased king, which were described in contemporary funerary literature. The statues, like these enemies, were treated as animals, butchered and ritually offered to the king to help sus-

---

1. See my discussion of the execration figurines in the third section of this chapter. For a much later example, see Kockelmann, "Fremdvölkerlisten."

tain him in the afterlife. On the other hand, the Pepi II prisoner statues were subjected to something akin to a royal smiting ritual, during which the king and/or his agents violently struck the statues.

The prisoner statues demonstrate some of the issues that arise when one attempts to reconstruct and categorize the rituals that occurred in the late Old Kingdom pyramid complexes, and I further explore two of these issues at the end of this chapter. First, the Pepi I and Pepi II prisoner statues illustrate the difficulties with trying to distinguish rituals of kingship that would have benefited the living king and the royal *ka* from mortuary rituals intended for the deceased ruler.[2] Rather rituals involving the prisoner statues simultaneously benefited both aspects of the king. Consequently, parts of the pyramid complex cannot be clearly categorized as places for the cult of only one aspect of the king either. Second, the developments in the treatment of the prisoner statues indicate that the ritual life of the late Old Kingdom pyramid complex was itself dynamic. Rather than trying to identify a system of rituals that broadly took place within these monuments, it would be more productive for scholars to consider the ritualization of each individual complex. Just as the decoration and architecture of the late Old Kingdom pyramid complex varied from monument to monument, as I showed in the last chapter, this chapter demonstrates that the rituals themselves were not fully standardized but could shift and change to accommodate the needs and desires of the monument's owner.

5.1. Previous Arguments concerning the Condition of the Prisoner Statues

For nearly a century, scholars have debated the reasons for the prisoner statues' consistently fragmentary state. In doing so, evidence from one complex has regularly been used to develop arguments that are then applied to the prisoner statues in general. This is problematic, and as a result of this tendency, Egyptologists have overlooked the differences in the treatment of the statues over time.

The first Egyptologist to propose that the prisoner statues may have been damaged intentionally in antiquity was Gustave Jéquier.[3] Following his excavation of the Pepi II prisoner statues, he described this material as, "sans exception," being broken at the neck and at the waist, after which the pieces were further divided in different ways with the most destructive actions being especially carried out on the heads and upper bodies.[4] Jéquier proposed that the funerary priests of Pepi II may have carried out the mutilation, either at a single time or during different occasions, as part of a triumph ritual or festival and suggested that the statues may have served as replacements for living foreign enemies. Indeed, he compared the Pepi II prisoner statues to Middle Kingdom execration figurines that had recently been discovered.[5] Some of these magical figurines were found in fragments, and Jéquier argued that the execration figurines had developed from the Old Kingdom prisoner statues. Although he noted that the Pepi II prisoner statues lacked the execration formula found on the execration figurines, he argued that the prisoner statues were still magical images with a ritualistic nature and, like the execration figurines, their destruction enforced the power of

---

2. On the royal *ka*, see further ch. 1.1.

3. For the following paragraph, see Jéquier, *Douze ans*, 65 n. 1; Jéquier, *Monument funéraire*, 3:28–29; and Jéquier, "Planche 22," 22. As I discussed in ch. 4.2.6, Jéquier also tentatively questioned whether the fragments had been deliberately disbursed at some point following the breakage, but there is nothing to support this idea (Jéquier, "Planche 22," 22).

4. Jéquier, *Monument funéraire*, 3:28.

5. Jéquier referenced Georges Posener, "Nouvelles listes de proscription (Ächtungstexte) datant du Moyen Empire," *CdE* 14:27 (1939): 39–46. As I described in ch. 1.2, execration figurines are rough human representations that can range in crudeness from a highly abstracted form to a fairly well executed statuette. What demarcates the genre is cursing formulas usually written upon the bodies. I discuss execration figurines in greater detail in ch. 5.3 below.

the king over his enemies. Subsequent scholars supported Jéquier's arguments, but they applied them to all of the known prisoner statues, not just those of Pepi II.⁶ Thus, the prisoner statues in general came to be described as ritual objects that functioned as substitutes for living enemies.

In 1969, Lauer and Leclant began uncovering the Pepi I prisoner statue fragments, and their excavations at this complex provided new data regarding the question of intentional damage. Lauer and Leclant discovered most of these fragments in the vicinity of limekilns. With this in mind, Lauer and Leclant dismissed Jéquier's theories, arguing that the fragments from the Pepi I complex provided concrete proof that the statues had not been part of any destruction ritual. Rather, their findspots next to limekilns, along with other debris and pieces of limestone from the temple, indicated that the limekilns were the reason for their systematic destruction and that the lime burners had broken all of the statues in order to more easily carry and deposit the pieces of stone into the kilns. Indeed, Lauer maintained that the extreme care seen in the execution of the statues' torsos and heads would hardly be justified if the statues were intended to be immediately sacrificed.⁷

Lauer and Leclant also noted that the lime production at the Pepi I mortuary temple seemed to have stopped suddenly as a layer of lime was left on the floor of one of the magazines that had served as a kiln and because limestone fragments, including the prisoner statues, had not yet been thrown into the kiln. Regarding the scattered prisoner statue fragments at the complex of Pepi II, they suggested that the situation could have been similar, namely, that the material was broken down, but lime production ceased before the material had been collected and brought to the kiln.⁸ Lauer and Leclant concluded: "Dans ces conditions, nous écartons, quant à nous, l'hypothèse d'une destruction rituelle des statues de prisonniers à laquelle Jéquier semblait pour sa part avoir plutôt acquiescé."⁹

Henry Fischer proposed a third possibility, namely, that the damage to all of the prisoner statues was the result of frightened individuals of a later period who had felt the need to "slay" the statues. He believed that Old Kingdom execration figurines supported this argument since they were not broken even though they were clay and could have been destroyed easily.¹⁰ According to Fischer, because the Old Kingdom Egyptians did not break apart all of the execration figurines, they likely did not break apart the prisoner statues.¹¹

No Egyptologists have supported Fischer's arguments. Instead, some scholars have accepted Lauer and Leclant's interpretations, while many others have refuted them, preferring to maintain that the statues were ritually executed as Jéquier had originally proposed.¹² However, the discussion has consistently been

---

6. I. E. S. Edwards, *The Pyramids of Egypt* (London: Penguin, 1947), 160 and Hayes, *Scepter of Egypt*, 1:116.

7. Lauer, "Recherches...1967–1968 et 1968–1969," 477–78; Lauer, "Statues de prisonniers," 42–43; Lauer, "Travaux...1968–1969," 22–23; and Lauer and Leclant, "Découverte," 61–62.

8. It is useful to note here that Jéquier did not report finding any limekilns within the Pepi II complex, neither in his final publication of the complex nor in his excavation journals, which are now in the Office des Archives de l'État and on deposit at the Musée d'ethnographie in Neuchâtel, Switzerland, although he did frequently record that parts of the structures were demolished and that there were many piles of stone waste and debris from looting and exploitation.

9. Lauer and Leclant, "Découverte," 62.

10. However, some Old Kingdom execration figurines were intentionally broken. I discuss these in greater detail in the third section of this chapter.

11. Henry Fischer, "Egyptian Art," *BMMA* 24 (1965): 53 and Henry Fischer, *Ancient Egyptian Representations of Turtles* (New York: The Metropolitan Museum of Art, 1968), 18.

12. Ritner, *Mechanics*, 116–17; Di. Arnold, "Rituale und Pyramidentempel," 7; Di. Arnold, "Old Kingdom Statues," 42; Essam M. Abd el-Razek, "A Note on the Difference between Execration Statues and Prisoners Statues," *GM* 147 (1995): 7; Verner, "Statuettes de prisonniers," 148; Hill, "173. Kneeling Captive," 440–41, cat. no. 173; Revez, "Traitement iconographique," 43–44; Janzen, "Iconography of Humiliation," 59; Schoske, "Erschlagen der Feinde," 461; and Marie Vanden-

framed in terms of all or nothing. In other words, scholars debate whether or not the prisoner statues, as a whole, were intentionally broken for ritualistic reasons without considering whether the answer to this question might have shifted over time or from complex to complex. My reexamination of the statues in the next section demonstrates that this approach is faulty and that the statues cannot be discussed as though they were a uniform group in this regard because their treatment did develop over the course of the late Old Kingdom. Moreover, previous scholars have assumed that all of the damage to the prisoner statues within a single pyramid complex occurred at the same time, but multiple phases of damage are equally possible.[13] This is definitely the case with the prisoner statues of Pepi I, as I discuss below.

5.2. The Condition of the Prisoner Statues

In this section I briefly survey the prisoner statue fragments from each complex, considering whether they exhibit any signs of human intervention, including tool or weapon marks, and attempting to identify breakage patterns. My findings are summarized in table 19.

While most scholars have pointed toward the consistent fragmentation of the prisoner statues as evidence of deliberate destruction, this alone should not automatically be taken as a sign of intentional damage or ritual manipulation. Indeed, Kasia Szpakowska and Richard Johnston have argued that details that might intuitively be thought to indicate ritual breakage of statuary, such as clean or even consistent breaks, might occur through accidental breakage as well.[14] While their comments were in regard to small, solid clay figurines of rearing cobras, and therefore, they do not necessarily apply to the nearly life-size, limestone prisoner statues, their experiments emphasize the need to approach fragmentary material cautiously.[15] In the following discussion, I base my arguments on multiple factors (i.e., not simply clean or consistent breaks). These factors include the presence of tool marks around the breaks and breakage patterns, as I mentioned, as well as the form and location of breaks.

I also take into consideration the archaeological data from each complex, which is important when examining who might have damaged the statues and when that damage might have occurred. I highlight any specific archaeological features, such as limekilns, that could be connected to the prisoner statues' fragmentary condition. However, one must keep in mind the numerous occupations of these pyramid complexes during later periods and acknowledge that all observations remain tentative as a result.[16] These

---

beusch, "Statue of a Prisoner," in *Pharaoh: King of Ancient Egypt*, ed. Marie Vandenbeusch, Aude Semat, and Margaret Maitland (Cleveland, The Cleveland Museum of Art, 2016), 123.

13. Regarding multiple phases of intentional damage to statuary, see Simon Connor, "Killing or 'De-Activating' Egyptian Statues: Who Mutilated Them, When, and Why?" in *Statues in Context: Production, Meaning and (Re)uses*, ed. Aurélia Masson-Berghoff, BMPES 12 (Leuven: Peeters, 2020), 295–98.

14. Kasia Szpakowska and Richard Johnston, "Snake Busters: Experiments in Fracture Patterns of Ritual Figurines," in *Mummies, Magic and Medicine in Ancient Egypt: Multidisciplinary Essays for Rosalie David*, ed. Campbell Price et al. (Manchester: Manchester University Press, 2016), 469. My thanks go to Kasia Szpakowska for discussing her experiments and sharing her results with me.

15. Similar experiments, which would include the making and subsequent breaking, in several different ways that re-enacted possible methods of accidental and intentional damage, of modern replicas, could be extremely enlightening and productive for the prisoner statues. However, they would also be far more laborious, time-consuming, and costly because of the prisoner statues' material and size.

16. For example, during the Twelfth Dynasty the mortuary cult of Pepi I, which had been abandoned during the First Intermediate period, seems to have restarted. The mortuary temple was partly renovated and restored, and the excavators found a large number of Middle Kingdom block statues and evidence that Middle Kingdom priests were living there. The cult was then permanently abandoned at the beginning of the Second Intermediate period. By the Rameside period, the temple

Table 19. Summary of the evidence and conclusions for intentional damage to the prisoner statues.

	Niuserre	Djedkare-Isesi	Unas	Teti	Pepi I	Pepi II
Back pillars	X	X	?			
Tool marks around breaks				? (possibly on JE 40047; C.4.1)	X (clear marks at body breaks)	
Evidence of blows around breaks						X
Clear breakage patterns					X (directly at the neck and around the torso to break the body into smaller pieces)	X (roughly in half and often around the shoulders and neck)
Clean breaks					X (neck only)	
Erasure or mutilation of facial features					X (some beards and noses)	X (some eyes and noses)
Limekilns recorded at the complex			X		X	
Intentionally damaged as part of original function	No	No	?	?	Yes	Yes
Intentionally damaged after the Old Kingdom	Unlikely	Unlikely	?	?	Yes	?

was partly destroyed and was being primarily used as a burial ground. Lauer and Leclant estimated that at least by Dynasty 22, a lime industry had developed, which systematically used the temple as a source for limestone to burn down into lime, while during the Ptolemaic and Coptic periods, the exploitation of stone was no longer focused on the temple but moved to the pyramid itself. See Audran Labrousse, "Le temple funéraire de Pépi I au Nouvel Empire," in *Memphis et ses nécropoles au Nouvel Empire: Novelles données, nouvelles questions,* ed. Alain-Pierre Zivie (Paris: Éditions du Centre National de la Recherche Scientifique, 1988), 67–68; Lauer, "Cinquante années," 563–64; Lauer, "Rapport," 205; Lauer, "Recherches...1969–1970," 492–93; Lauer, *Saqqara,* 90–93; Lauer, "Travaux...1970–1971," 41; Jean-Philippe Lauer, "Travaux effectués à Saqqarah de fin Novembre 1975 au 20 Mars 1976," *ASAE* 64 (1981): 152; Lauer, "Travaux aux pyramids," 102–3; Jean-Philippe Lauer, "Travaux à Saqqarah (campagne 1976–1977)," *ASAE* 65 (1983): 81; Leclant, "Fouilles...1969–1970," 233; Leclant, "Fouilles...1972–1973," 182; Jean Leclant, "Fouilles et travaux en Égypte et au Soudan, 1973–1974," *Orientalia* 44 (1975): 207; Jean Leclant, "Fouilles et travaux en Égypte et au Soudan, 1975–1976," *Orientalia* 46 (1977): 243; Leclant, "Fouilles...1976–1977," 280–81; Jean Leclant, "Fouilles et travaux en Égypte et au Soudan, 1977–1978," *Orientalia* 48 (1979): 362–63; Jean Leclant, "Fouilles et travaux en Égypte et au Soudan, 1979–1980," *Orientalia* 51 (1982): 67; Jean Leclant, "Fouilles et travaux en Égypte et au Soudan, 1981–1982," *Orientalia* 52 (1983): 483; Leclant, "Fouilles...1982–1983," 366–67; Jean Leclant, "Travaux de la Mission archéologique française de Saqqarah (campagne 1980)," *ASAE* 68 (1982): 58; Jean Leclant and Gisèle Clerc, "Fouilles et travaux en Égypte et au Soudan, 1983–1984," *Orientalia* 54 (1985): 356; Leclant and Clerc, "Fouilles...1984–1985," 258; Jean Leclant and Gisèle

monuments are very poorly preserved. While some are in worse condition than others, with the remains being more absent or fragmentary, excavators working at all six complexes often remarked upon the difficult archaeology, the lack or scattered nature of finds dating to the original occupation, or the massive amount of looting.[17]

5.2.1. Niuserre and Djedkare-Isesi

A particularly remarkable feature of both the Niuserre and Djedkare prisoner statues is the large back pillars, which I described in detail in chapter 2 (2.2.1 and 2.2.2).[18] By the late Fifth Dynasty, the royal artists certainly could have executed these large-scale kneeling statues without a back support if that had been desired or necessary. Indeed, Early Dynastic statues did not have back pillars, and there are limestone and granite examples, which vary in size, in kneeling and squatting positions.[19] Moreover, Old Kingdom achievements in statuary, such as the complicated positions of "serving statues" and a high-quality kneeling statue of the high official Kaemked, despite being on a smaller scale than the prisoner statues, were significant and underscore the considerable abilities of Fifth Dynasty artists.[20] Rather, the substantial size of these prisoner statues' back pillars indicates that their presence was intentional, or at least not considered problematic or inconsistent with the statues' original purpose and context.

While the back pillar had multiple roles, it essentially provided stability to a statue.[21] Consequently, the artists of Niuserre and Djedkare must have carved these prisoner statues with the intention that they

---

Clerc, "Fouilles et travaux en Égypte et au Soudan, 1985–1986," *Orientalia* 56 (1987): 317–18; Michel Wuttmann, "La restauration des appartements funéraires de la pyramide de Pépy Ier à Saqqâra," in *Études sur l'Ancien Empire et la nécropole de Saqqâra dédiées à Jean-Philippe Lauer*, ed. Catherine Berger and Bernard Mathieu, OrMonsp 9 (Montpellier: Université Paul Valéry, 1997), 449–60; and Rémi Legros, "Inhumations privées dans la nécropole de Pépy Ier," in Bárta, Coppens, and Krejčí, *Abusir and Saqqara...2015*, 211–18. Similar evidence for reoccupation and later activity has also been discovered at the other pyramid complexes that had prisoner statue fragments; see Borchardt, *Grabdenkmal des Königs Ne-user-re*, 157–62; Drioton and Lauer, "Inscription de Khamouas," 201–11; Firth, "Report on the Excavations," 188–89; Firth and Gunn, *Teti Pyramid Cemeteries*, 8; Jéquier, *Monument funéraire*, 3:30–49; Antonio J. Morales, "Traces of Official and Popular Veneration to Nyuserra Iny at Abusir, Late Fifth Dynasty to the Middle Kingdom," in Bárta, Coppens, and Krejčí, *Abusir and Saqqara...2005*, 311–41; Megahed, "Pyramid Complex, 618 and 627; and Quibell, *Excavations...1907–1908*, 19–22.

17. Firth and Gunn, 8; Labrousse, Lauer, and Leclant, *Temple haut*, 73; Labrousse and Moussa, *Temple d'accueil*, 67; Lauer, "Rapport," 205; Lauer, "Recherches...1969–1970," 498; Jean-Philippe Lauer, "Recherches et travaux à Saqqarah: campagnes 1970–1971 et 1971–1972," *CRAIBL* 116 (1972): 584–85; Lauer, *Saqqara*, 56; Lauer, "Statues de prisonniers," 38; Lauer, "Travaux aux pyramids," 101; Lauer and Leclant, *Temple haut*, 59; Leclant, "Fouilles...1969–1970," 233; Leclant, "Fouilles...1972–1973," 182–83; Leclant, "Fouilles...1981–1982," 483; Leclant, "Fouilles...1982–1983," 366; and Varille, *À propos des pyramides*, 1.

18. I briefly discussed the implications of these back pillars in Prakash, "Prisoner Statue 'Fragments,'" 17–27.

19. Notably, the kneeling statue of Hetepdief from Mit Rahina (Cairo, Egyptian Museum CG 1; see Marianne Eaton-Krauss, "Non-Royal Pre-Canonical Statuary," in Grimal, *Critères de datation stylistiques*, 212–13 and Edward L. B. Terrace and Henry G. Fischer, *Treasures of Egyptian Art from the Cairo Museum* [London: Thames & Hudson, 1970], 25–28) and the nearly life-size, limestone pair of squatting statues from Hierakonpolis (Quibell, *Hierakonpolis*, 6 and pl. 2 and Quibell and Green, *Hierakonpolis*, 13, 35 and pl. 1). The more complete of these squatting statues is in the Egyptian Museum in Cario (JE 32159). It had previously been described as a foreigner, but this argument is no longer tenable (Hourig Sourouzian, "Concordances et écarts: Entre statuaire et représentations à deux dimensions des particuliers de l'époque archaïque," in Grimal, *Critères de datation stylistiques*, 309–19 and Marsha Hill, *Royal Bronze Statuary from Ancient Egypt: With Special Attention to the Kneeling Pose*, Egyptological Memoirs 3 [Leiden: Brill, 2004], 241–42 n. 1). For all of these examples, and others, see Hill, 241–43.

20. Concerning the "serving statues," see further Roth, "Meaning of Menial Labor." For the statue of Kaemked: Cairo, Egyptian Museum CG 119; see Russmann, *Egyptian Sculpture*, 32–36. See also Hill, 243.

21. Baudouin van de Walle, "Rückenpfeiler," *LÄ* 5:315–18 and Eaton-Krauss, "Location of Inscriptions," 131–36. Addi-

would stand and endure in their full, unbroken form because carving such a large pillar conflicts with the idea of sculpting statues that were meant to be broken. Rather, the back pillars indicate that these earliest prisoner statues were not made with any destructive treatment in mind. They were expected to stand permanently in each king's funerary complex, and there is no evidence at the complexes of Niuserre and Djedkare that these prisoner statues were intentionally damaged as part of their original function.

Whether their current fragmentary state is the result of subsequent intentional damage that specifically targeted the statues or the inadvertent repercussion of later activity and the progressive decay and deterioration of the pyramid complex is presently more difficult to ascertain. While intruders certainly could have broken the statues to burn into lime or to reuse the stone, there is nothing concrete to support this.[22] For example, there seem to be no overt, visible signs of intentional damage on the fragments, such as chisel or pick marks.[23] There is also no conclusive evidence to support the argument that these prisoner statues were intentionally defaced in later periods because of their subject matter, as Fischer proposed. If they had been, one would expect the faces, heads, and necks to have been specifically targeted since these areas were often the focus of mutilation during the pharaonic period and late antiquity.[24]

Certainly the faces of the Niuserre and Djedkare prisoner statues are in poor condition, with certain features, like noses, missing (see figs. 3.1 and 3.2). Some or all of this damage could have been deliberate, but there are no visible marks that would enable this conclusion. While one cannot completely dismiss the possibility that post-Old Kingdom individuals targeted the prisoner statues of Niuserre and Djedkare, it is more likely that their condition is accidental, namely, the unintended result of the gradual degeneration of the monuments.

5.2.2. Unas

The scanty evidence for the prisoner statues from the mortuary temple of Unas makes it nearly impossible to propose even tentative conclusions regarding their original or subsequent treatment. As I described in chapter 2.2.4, the single attested fragment (C.3.1), for which only a poor quality photograph is currently available, is a torso, but without comparative examples from this complex, one cannot identify breakage patterns (fig. 2.5). Furthermore, there are no pronounced tool marks visible on the fragment.

---

tionally, the back pillar reinforced the impression of frontality, a quality that the majority of ancient Egyptian statues share (see Robins, *Art of Ancient Egypt*, 19–21).

22. In his description of the later occupation and destruction of the Niuserre complex, Borchardt did not mention limekilns (Borchardt, *Grabdenkmal des Königs Ne-user-re*, 157–62) and according to Mohamed Megahed, there is no evidence for limekilns in the immediate vicinity of Djedkare's mortuary temple (pers. comm.).

23. This is based on my study of photographs of these fragments.

24. Connor, "Killing," 281–302; Simon Connor, "Mutiler, tuer, désactiver les images en Égypte pharaonique," *Perspective* 2 (2018): 147–66; and David Frankfurter, "The Vitality of Egyptian Images in Late Antiquity: Christian Memory and Response," in *The Sculptural Environment of the Roman Near East: Reflections on Culture, Ideology, and Power*, ed. Yaron Z. Eliav, Elise A. Friedland, and Sharon Herbert, Interdisciplinary Studies in Ancient Culture and Religion 9 (Leuven: Peeters, 2008), 674–78. See also Peter Stewart, "The Destruction of Statues in Late Antiquity," in *Constructing Identities in Late Antiquity*, ed. Richard Miles (London: Routledge, 1999), 172–89. On iconoclasm in ancient Egypt, see Betsy Bryan, "Episodes of Iconoclasm in the Egyptian New Kingdom," in *Iconoclasm and Text Destruction in the Ancient Near East and Beyond*, ed. Natalie Naomi May, OIS 8 (Chicago: Oriental Institute of the University of Chicago, 2012), 363–94; Robert Ritner, "Killing the Image, Killing the Essence: The Destruction of Text and Figures in Ancient Egyptian Thought, Ritual, and 'Ritualized History,'" in May, *Iconoclasm and Text Destruction*, 395–405; and Edward Bleiburg and Stephanie Weissberg, *Striking Power: Iconoclasm in Ancient Egypt* (Brooklyn: Brooklyn Museum, 2019).

It is also unclear whether or not this prisoner statue had a back pillar because of the angle of the photograph. Its presence would have significant implications and suggest that the Unas prisoner statues were not intentionally broken immediately following their manufacture or as part of their original function, like the Niuserre and Djedkare prisoner statues. However, without evidence for this feature, little can be said in this regard and all possibilities should be considered realistic options.[25]

5.2.3. Teti

It is also difficult to draw conclusions regarding the treatment of the Teti prisoner statues. The small fragment that Lauer and Leclant discovered consists of the left arm, lower torso, and upper buttocks of a statue (Bloc 64; C.4.2; fig. 2.7). The excavators did not describe any marks of intentional damage on this fragment or hypothesize the reasons for its breakage, and with only a basic drawing known today, it is impossible to evaluate the breaks beyond noting their location.

The prisoner statue bust that Quibell discovered at this complex (Saqqara, Imhotep Museum JE 40047; C.4.1) is broken diagonally from left to right, with the entire right shoulder remaining (fig. 2.6). There is some damage on the front of the right shoulder at the break that could perhaps suggest that the statue was deliberately hacked apart from here.[26] On the other hand, the damage to the statue's face is minor and haphazard, and there are no marks that indicate that it was intentional.

This fragment does not have a back pillar; consequently, it seems most likely that none of the Teti prisoner statues had this feature since all of the prisoner statues from a single complex are generally consistent with one another. This change, which may have first occurred at the Unas complex, was likely a result of multiple factors. The disappearance of the pillar could reflect a new position of the statues within the mortuary temple, as I suggested in chapter 4.5.[27] Perhaps the back of the statues was now more visible, and thus, there was a desire to carve the statues fully in the round. At the same time, the late Old Kingdom style clearly influenced the facial features of the Teti prisoner statues, as I argued in chapter 3.2. The emergent style also might help explain the new concern for the back of the prisoner statues. The later statues, without back pillars, are much more expressive than the early examples with back pillars; their bound, kneeling position is more recognizable and suggestive. This is consistent with the overall increased interest in expressiveness that characterized the late Old Kingdom style. Therefore, the disappearance of the back pillar is probably tied to the changing styles.

While this development could reflect a new understanding of the statues and their role in the pyramid complex, with so little material from the Teti complex, it is difficult to interpret exactly what this was. Moreover, although the presence of a back pillar on a prisoner statue indicates that the statue was not originally intended to be broken, its absence does not necessarily mean the opposite, and the lack of back pillars on the Teti prisoner statues does not imply that Teti, his high officials, or his artists intentionally damaged or broke these statues despite their current fragmentary condition. The only possible evidence of intentional destruction for the preserved Teti statues is the damage to JE 40047 (C.4.1)'s right shoulder, and my interpretation of this as deliberate is highly tentative. Moreover, even if it was deliberate, there are no indications as to when it occurred. It is equally likely that the culprits were later inhabitants or

---

25. Regarding the relevant archaeological context, Barsanti did record finding a limekiln along the south wall of Unas's mortuary temple (Labrousse, Lauer, and Leclant, *Temple haut*, fig. 2).

26. The fragment, which is currently exhibited at the Imhotep Museum in Saqqara, has been set on a plaster base to keep it upright, making it impossible to examine the break face.

27. Concerning the original location of the Teti prisoner statues, see further chs. 4.2.4 and 4.5.

stone looters, from any ancient, medieval, or modern period, rather than the contemporaries of Teti or the king himself.[28]

5.2.4. Pepi I

As I described above, Lauer and Leclant discovered most of the Pepi I prisoner statue fragments in the vicinity of limekilns, and consequently they argued that the lime burners were responsible for the fragmentary condition of the statues. They believed that the lime burners had broken apart all of the statues in order to carry and deposit the pieces of stone into the kilns. They noted that the statues were regularly broken at the waist and neck. In their opinion, the break at the waist was to be expected as it permitted the division of the statue into two roughly equal parts that could more easily be transported, and the neck was naturally the most fragile point, and thus the head became separated from the body in the course of the various operations. Lauer and Leclant emphatically denied the idea that any of the prisoner statues had been intentionally damaged as part of their original function or display.[29]

However, the Pepi I fragments themselves actually reveal two separate phases of damage. First, the statues were carefully decapitated, likely as part of their original function and under the direction of Pepi I or his officials. Then, at a significantly later date, the lime burners arrived and further broke the statues into more manageable pieces to be burned down in their kilns.

Unlike the statues from any of the other pyramid complexes, every single prisoner statue from the Pepi I complex is broken at the neck. While the neck is inherently the most vulnerable area of most statuary, as Lauer and Leclant indicated, and over the millennia, the heads of many ancient Egyptian statues have broken off of their bodies, the consistency of this break among the Pepi I prisoner statues is unusual and abnormal. The breaks are invariably the same scalloped shape, running from the inside of each shoulder, immediately below the base of the neck. None of the body fragments have any portion of the neck still attached to the torso. Rather, the neck remains more or less attached to the head. Furthermore, the cleanness and precision of the neck breaks is impressive and equally uniform. For particular fragments, such as PP 14 (C.5.14) and PP 70 (C.5.68), it exactly follows the collarbone, resulting in a rather sharp, explicit line (fig. 2.19). Shorter hairstyles remain fully on the head fragments and not at all on the body fragments. On the other hand, the neck break often runs through longer hairstyles, leaving a portion still attached to the back (e.g., C.5.3 and C.5.68; fig. 2.16).

Only one statue has an intact nose, namely, PP 19 (C.5.19; fig. 3.8). On some heads, the noses appear to have been chiseled off and fully removed (figs. 3.5–3.7 and fig. 3.10).[30] In other cases, only part of the nose is missing; this damage may have been intentional and directed specifically at the nose or inadvertently caused while the head was being removed (figs. 3.4, 3.9, and 3.11–3.13).[31] The noses of ancient Egyptian statues are frequently broken or damaged, and Simon Connor has discussed how, in instances where this was deliberate, it was a means of deactivating or killing the statues.[32] This may be the case for the Pepi I prisoner statues.

---

28. One should note that Lauer and Leclant made no mention of a limekiln around Teti's mortuary temple in any of their publications.

29. Lauer, "Recherches...1967–1968 et 1968–1969," 477–78; Lauer, "Statues de prisonniers," 42–43; Lauer, "Travaux...1968–1969," 22–23; and Lauer and Leclant, "Découverte," 61–62.

30. PP 16 (C.5.16), PP 17 (C.5.17), PP 18 (C.5.18), PP 21 (C.5.21), and PP 61 (C.5.59).

31. PP 20 (C.5.20), PP 22 (C.5.22), PP 23 (C.5.23), PP 32 (C.5.32), and PP 60 (C.5.58).

32. Connor, "Killing," 288 and Connor, "Mutiler, tuer, désactiver" 161.

For some of the statues, including PP 3 (C.5.3) and PP 13 (C.5.13), the bottom of their beards remains on the front of their chests, below the neck break (fig. 2.16). However, for other statues, the beards appear to have been carefully chipped off of the chests, possibly with a point chisel.[33] This is most clear for PP 1 (C.5.1; fig. 2.14) and PP 2 (C.5.2; fig. 2.15).[34] On these statues, the outline of the beards is still visible, but the beard itself has been completely chiseled away. A similar attempt may have been started, though not completed, for PP 57 (C.5.55). The damage on the front of PP 46 (C.5.46) is also likely the result of the deliberate removal of a beard (fig. 2.11).

The consistency of the neck break, its cleanness and precision, and, perhaps most importantly, the removal of certain beards all indicate that the heads did not accidently fall off while the lime burners were dismantling and moving the statues, as Lauer and Leclant previously implied. Someone intentionally removed them. Moreover, most of the noses likely were erased and damaged as part of this action. The evidence further indicates that it was not the lime burners who did this, primarily because the consistency and level of care shown along the neck break is not present at any of the other break sites. Rather the haphazard and obvious other breaks suggest that these occurred at a different time, and I agree with Lauer and Leclant that the lime burners were responsible for them.

The other breaks vary in their position. While many of the statues were broken in half through the waist, as Lauer and Leclant described, this was not the case for all of them. For example, the bodies of PP 4 (C.5.4), PP 10 (C.5.10), and PP 11 (C.5.11) seem to have been broken into thirds (fig. 2.17). Even when broken through the waist, the break is not always in the exact same position. Moreover, the breaks themselves are usually jagged, and there was no effort to minimize or conceal the pick or chisel marks (see PP 59; C.5.57). As a result, smaller pieces, such as hands, have frequently fallen off. These breaks simply do not show the same care.

Overall, it would seem that the purpose of all the other breaks, besides that at the neck, was to fracture the statues into smaller, more manageable fragments that could be dragged more easily to the limekilns, as Lauer and Leclant had suggested. Many of the fragments were left in halves or thirds. However, sometimes marks show that the lime burners broke the statues into smaller pieces. For example, PP 72 (C.5.70) is a fragment of the front portion of the knees and base of a prisoner statue. On its right edge, there are clear square marks, possibly from a wedge, where the lime burners broke this piece off.[35] Arms were also broken off at the shoulder, as PP 66 (C.5.64), a fragment of the upper right part of a prisoner statues' torso, demonstrates (fig. 5.1). The large square marks on these break surfaces and the jagged breaks themselves are quite different from the clean, precise breaks at the neck. Another relatively frequent break is down the middle of the torso. On PP 66, there is also visible damage to the front of his chest with further square marks at the front of the inner break face, thus indicating that the fragment was fractured through the

---

33. Simon Connor has noted that when royal and divine statuary was intentionally damaged, the beard was often targeted because of its divine associations and protective ability (Connor, "Killing," 298 and Connor, "Mutiler," 161). However, this was a very different type of beard than the beard of the prisoner statues, which was a mark of their foreignness, as I argued in ch. 3.3. Therefore Connor's interpretation does not apply to the damaged beards of the prisoner statues.

34. Anna Serotta (associate conservator, Metropolitan Museum of Art) first suggested to me that a point chisel might have been used here (pers. comm.). My thanks go to her for discussing this material and the possible process of damage with me.

35. Serotta first advised me that the square marks, which are visible on certain fragments, such as PP 72 (C.5.70) and PP 66 (C.5.64), might be from a wedge (pers. comm.). The use of this tool, which was used to split stone while quarrying beginning in the Ptolemaic period, would be consistent with the lime burners' desire to break apart the stone indiscriminately and could help date the activity of the lime burners (concerning the use of the wedge, see Dieter Arnold, *Building in Egypt: Pharaonic Stone Masonry* [Oxford: Oxford University Press, 1991], 33 and 280–81). However, Lauer and Leclant estimated that the lime industry had begun at Pepi I's mortuary temple already by the Third Intermediate period (see n. 16 above).

Figure 5.1. Prisoner statue fragment (PP 66) from the pyramid complex of Pepi I in Saqqara; Sixth Dynasty. Top image is a view of the front of the fragment, showing the right side of the prisoner statues' chest and right pectoral. Center image is a view of the outer break surface, with tool marks, where the arm has been detached. Bottom image is a view of the prisoner statues' back and the inner break surface, with tool marks, through his chest. Photograph: Tara Prakash, courtesy of the MAFS.

chest from the front (fig. 5.1 top and bottom). These types of breaks only seem likely if the head had no longer been attached. Moreover, rope marks may still be visible on PP 2 (C.5.2; fig. 2.15). These could have occurred when the lime burners were dragging this fragment across the mortuary temple toward the kiln.

If the lime burners had only been interested in detaching the heads in order to create smaller fragments, they would not have put so much effort into carefully breaking them off. Indeed, the heads could have been more easily removed with a solid blow to their side. Nor would the lime burners have bothered to remove beards, which created the impression of decapitated men, since a beard clearly does not remain on a living man's chest after his head is cut off. Similarly, later individuals frightened of the prisoner statues, like those that Fischer proposed, would not have taken the time to remove the heads and beards cleanly. The care and consistency along the neck break of the Pepi I prisoner statues instead suggests that these statues were meant to be seen in this fashion, with distinct heads and bodies.

Indeed, the upper break surface of many of the chest fragments is smoother than the other break surfaces (see, e.g., PP 40, PP 46, PP 51, PP 66; C.5.40, C.5.46, C.5.51, C.5.64; figs. 2.11 and 5.1). This could be because the heads were removed significantly before the other damage occurred and the upper break surface is more weathered, since it was exposed for a longer period of time.[36] The difference could also be a coincidence of preservation. However, it perhaps is more probable that the upper break surface was hastily smoothed down or polished in order to remove all traces of the neck.

This is likely why Lauer and Leclant were unable to join more heads and upper torsos. Lauer and Leclant discovered sixteen head fragments. These seem to belong to sixteen dif-

---

36. Lauer and Leclant estimated that the lime industry had begun at Pepi I's mortuary temple at least by the Third Intermediate period (see n. 16 above).

ferent heads.³⁷ They also discovered sixteen different torso fragments that include at least part of the neck break.³⁸ Yet, they were only able to join the head and torso of one statue, namely, PP 16 (C.5.16; fig. 3.6). They also noted that a connection between PP 23 (C.5.23) and PP 3 (C.5.3) was possible, but that it was not clean (fig. 2.16).³⁹ Given that the overall number of fragments suggests that the total number of prisoner statues at the Pepi I complex had been between at least sixteen and twenty statues, it is remarkable that Lauer and Leclant were not able to match more of the heads and bodies.⁴⁰

Therefore, the heads of the Pepi I prisoner statues were not simply broken off from the bodies at the neck, but these statues were decapitated. This likely took place long before the lime burners arrived, at some point when the cult of Pepi I was ongoing and the statues were still fulfilling their original function inside the pyramid complex.

5.2.5. Pepi II

The prisoner statue fragments from the Pepi II pyramid complex are more battered than those from any other complex.⁴¹ However, the Pepi II prisoner statues were not systematically broken at the neck even though Jéquier described them this way.⁴² Although most of the available examples were broken around the bottom of the neck, the heads of at least four statues remain attached to their torsos (Suez, Suez National Museum JE 51729 (C.6.7), C.6.8, C.6.9, and C.6.10; figs. 2.23 and 3.18–3.20). Moreover, a portion of Cairo, Egyptian Museum JE 57202 (C.6.4)'s chest and back remains attached on the right side of his neck (fig. 3.15). Similarly, the torso fragment Cairo, Egyptian Museum JE 45782 (C.6.3) indicates that its accompanying, detached head may have had more of the chest and back attached to the left side of the neck (fig. 2.24). Even more of Cairo, Egyptian Museum JE 45781 (C.6.2)'s torso remains attached to his head, but this is still predominantly a head fragment (fig. 3.14). Therefore, the heads were not systematically removed from the bodies of the Pepi II prisoner statues, and for those statues that were broken around the neck, this break was not consistently in the same location.

---

37. Twelve of the heads are largely complete. PP 27 (C.5.27) is a fragment of a tiered hairstyle, PP 28 (C.5.28) is the lower portion of a head with a tiered hairstyle, PP 55 (C.5.53) is a small fragment of a tiered hairstyle, and PP 63 (C.5.61) consists of a right eye. PP 27, PP 28, and PP 55 definitely belong to different statues because their hairstyles differ from one another. While PP 63 could be from the same head as PP 27, PP 28, or PP 55, this seems unlikely based on the excavators' drawing, which includes a plain hairstyle rather than a tiered one (MAFS archives, MAFS, Paris, France).

38. PP 67 (C.5.65) is also a torso fragment and could be a seventeenth fragment with part of or the entire neck break preserved, but with no drawing or photographs of it, I am unsure what part of the torso it includes.

39. Notes for PP 3, MAFS archives.

40. The fact that the fragments were discovered over an extended period of time and divided between the MAFS storeroom and the SCA storeroom certainly complicated any attempts to join heads and bodies. However, as I outlined in ch. 4.2.5, Lauer and Leclant discovered the majority of the fragments, including most of the heads and upper torso fragments, during a single season (see fig. 2.8). While a more comprehensive examination, which would compare all of the currently known Pepi I prisoner statue fragments, might be more successful in joining heads and bodies, it seems highly likely that most of the heads would remain unpaired to bodies.

41. As I outlined in ch. 2.2.6, I was not able to directly examine or find photographs of the majority of the Pepi II prisoner statue fragments. Therefore, my observations on their condition and my conclusions on their treatment remain tentative. I first proposed some of these arguments in Prakash, "Prisoner Statues," 211–14.

42. Jéquier, *Monument funéraire*, 3:28. Despite writing this, the images Jéquier included show three fragments with heads still connected to torsos (Jéquier, pls. 47 and 48; on pl. 48, the bust in the right and left images of the center row is the same: see further C.6.8.), but scholars have continued to reiterate Jéquier's statement. For example, Lehner, *Complete Pyramids*, 163.

All of the available body fragments show that the statues were broken roughly in half. Jéquier described them as uniformly broken at the waist, but the breaks are not always exactly at the waist and instead most range somewhere between right above the navel and immediately below the belt.[43] All of these breaks are jagged, and portions of the arms seem to have fallen off as a result of the trauma that caused the breaks. The body fragments regularly have missing parts or areas of damage. Furthermore, there are no visible tool or chisel marks

Given the condition of the fragments and Jéquier's own conclusions, it seems most likely that blows, possibly from a mace, hammer, or another large, heavy object, caused the breaks and damage to the Pepi II prisoner statues. If the statues fell over while being hit, or were intentionally pushed over, further breaks could have occurred. The location of the breaks suggests that blows were often aimed at the midsections of the statues and their shoulders and heads. Indeed, some of the faces could also have been assaulted and disfigured as part of the same destructive actions.

The prisoner statue heads from the Pepi II pyramid complex are in much worse condition than those from any other complex, and Jéquier believed that the heads had been specifically targeted.[44] Indeed, he lamented that if they had not been so mutilated, the heads would have constituted a new chapter of Egyptian art history.[45] Every single face has at least some damage. For most of the heads, the entire face is quite battered. Moreover, the face of C.6.11 may show chisel marks (fig. 3.21). In other cases, such as Cairo, National Military Museum JE 51730 (C.6.5) and JE 51729 (C.6.7), the noses look like they might have been singled out and attacked (figs. 2.23 and 3.16). This may also be the case for the nose of Cairo, GEM 1101 (C.6.1), but the break through the head could very possibly have been the cause of the damage to the nose (fig. 2.22). On the other hand, JE 57202 (C.6.4), Cairo, National Military Museum JE 51731 (C.6.6), C.6.14, and C.6.15 only have damage to the tips of their noses and the bridges remain preserved (figs. 3.15, 3.17, and 3.24). The eyes of some of the heads might have been targeted as well. This is most clear for C.6.12, whose eyes look as though they were gouged out (fig. 3.22). The same might have occurred on C.6.14 (fig. 3.24). Some or all of this focused damage may have been intended to deactivate the statues, as I suggested for the ruined noses of the Pepi I prisoner statues. However, in other cases the heads may have just been subjected to additional blows while the statues were being broken.

The reconstructed statues from the Pepi II pyramid complex further support my argument that this king's prisoner statues were intentionally destroyed with a heavy object. On JE 51729 (C.6.7), one break runs through the center of his torso and another break line runs down between his legs and through the base (fig. 5.2). The missing middle part of his right arm may indicate that trauma to this area caused the two break lines to fracture up and down, rather than straight across through the middle of his body, where most of the Pepi II prisoner statues broke. Additionally, the right shoulder of GEM 1101 (C.6.1) is entirely modern restoration, and it seems quite possible that damage to this area caused his head to fall off and split in two down the middle (fig. 5.2). Similarly, when one sets aside the areas of modern plaster in the two reconstructed prisoner statues in the Metropolitan Museum of Art and the reconstructed prisoner statue in the British Museum, which can be attributed to the pyramid complex of Pepi II, one discovers that similar parts of these statues were destroyed, including all of their left shoulders, as well as the left arms of BM EA 75198 (C.7.2) and MMA 64.260 (C.7.4) and the left side of the head of BM EA 75198 (figs. 1.2, 1.4, and A.1).[46] Perhaps a blow, or series of blows, to this area of these statues by an individual swinging an instrument

---

43. Jéquier, 28.
44. Jéquier, 28 and Jéquier, *Douze ans*, 64.
45. Jéquier, "Rapport préliminaire...1926–1927," 60.
46. For these statues, see A.1. I discussed the restoration of these statues in detail in Prakash, "Prisoner Statues," 195–202.

Figure 5.2. Cairo, GEM 1101 (left) and Suez, Suez National Museum JE 51729 (right) from the pyramid complex of Pepi II at an earlier stage of reconstruction. This photograph may have been taken relatively soon after their transport to the Egyptian Museum in Cairo, where they both were originally displayed. Photograph: Archives de l'Etat de Neuchâtel, fonds Jéquier (1852–1946), Temple funéraire de Pepi II, 1JEQUIER-10.

caused the damage and the dislocation of the heads. Indeed, given the size and position of these statues, this area seems like a natural place for a right-handed person, standing in front of the statues and wanting to "injure" and cause significant damage to them, to aim. The same blows, additional blows, or the falling over of the statues could have resulted in the breaks around the waists.

There is little archaeological evidence to indicate when this destruction happened or who was responsible. Jéquier did not record any limekilns at the Pepi II complex, neither in his final publications nor in his excavation journals. Certainly, there might have been kilns in the area that were no longer preserved or that Jéquier did not record, and the statues still could have been broken by lime burners or other individuals who wanted the stone. However, as Jéquier himself noted, if they broke the statues for this reason, it is strange that they then left the fragments lying all around the complex.⁴⁷ Later inhabitants or individuals passing through the complex could have broken the statues in fear of the subject matter or as an act against threatening material, as Fischer suggested. But there is nothing that specifically supports this either.

Instead, given the evidence of intentional damage and original intervention from the complex of Pepi I, it is more probable that the statues were broken during or shortly after the reign of Pepi II and the current condition of the statues largely dates to this time period.⁴⁸ Indeed, Jéquier discovered some prisoner statue fragments reused in a private funerary construction to the south of Pepi II's causeway (fig. 4.14). As I suggested in chapter 4.2.6, based on comparison between Jéquier's excavation journal and final report, this funerary construction may be one of several that Jéquier provisionally dated to the First Intermediate period, which would mean that it had been erected relatively soon after the death of Pepi II. One cannot preclude the possibility that the builders of this structure broke apart some prisoner statues themselves in order to reuse the fragments, but it may be more conceivable that the fragments had already been lying around the complex and thus were readily available building material. If the First Intermediate period date is correct, this would further support my argument that the statues were intentionally broken during or right after the reign of Pepi II.

5.2.6. From Accidental to Intentional

The treatment, function, and significance of the prisoner statues changed over time. There was no intention to damage or break the earliest statues, namely, those from the complexes of Niuserre and Djedkare-Isesi, at the time of their original carving and erection. Instead, the back pillars further support the argument that I first proposed in chapter 4, namely, that these early prisoner statues were new and innovative forms of architectural decoration. They presented existing themes and subject matter, which formed a central aspect of the decorative program of the pyramid complex, in a different, three-dimensional format, and they were charged with symbolic meaning in the same way that two-dimensional depictions of bound captives were. In this way, the prisoner statues initially developed from artistic models: earlier and contemporary two- and three-dimensional depictions of foreign prisoners. They did not evolve from actual rituals, and the earliest prisoner statues were not ritually damaged.

The reigns of Unas and Teti, at the end of the Fifth Dynasty and the beginning of the Sixth Dynasty, seem to represent an important transitional phase for the prisoner statues. Because there are so few available prisoner statue fragments from these complexes, it is extremely difficult to draw even tentative conclusions on their treatment, but there is currently no conclusive evidence to support arguments that they were intentionally damaged.

While the Teti statues do not have back pillars, it is presently impossible to know whether or not the artists included this feature on the Unas statues. The discontinuation of the back pillar seems to be a step away from the permanent, earlier prisoner statues toward the later ones that were actively destroyed, and it could reflect a new understanding of the function and meaning of the prisoner statues already at the Teti and perhaps the Unas complex. The Egyptians may have begun to conceive of these prisoner statues as more than architectural decoration. However, it is equally possible that the artists stopped carving back pillars purely for aesthetic reasons, including those I outlined above. In this case, the understanding and role of the statues might not have changed until the reign of Pepi I. With so little evidence from this crucial period, it is difficult to comprehend the full significance of the Unas and Teti prisoner statues.

---

47. Jéquier, *Monument funéraire*, 3:29.
48. Though it remains possible that the fragments were further damaged at a later time.

On the other hand, by the reign of Pepi I, the active manipulation of the statues had become part of their function and significance as these prisoner statues were intentionally decapitated. This is the only complex where there is evidence for the systematic removal of the heads. The good condition of many of the heads, the precision and possible smoothing down of the neck break, and the chiseling of the beard from the chest indicate a slow and deliberate decapitation rather than a quick and violent one. Indeed, it would have required a degree of expertise in stoneworking and knowledge of the limestone's properties. For this reason, the artists themselves must have been the agents. They went around to each statue and carefully removed the heads from the bodies. According to Anna Serotta, they might have first carved a line around the neck, where they wanted the head to break off, and then used a point chisel to detach it. Any resulting marks could have been cursorily erased.[49]

This decapitation might have been the final step of the artistic process, and it may partly account for the poor execution of the Pepi I prisoner statues. As I outlined in chapter 2, many of the bodies of the Pepi I statues were roughly carved. Nearly all of them still have visible tool marks, and a large portion of them have areas that the artists did not seem to have finished. Some of the hairstyles are also covered with tool marks, which I described in chapter 3.1.4. However, the faces were all well carved and finished. One does not see this overt dichotomy in execution among the prisoner statues from any other pyramid complex.

It seems possible that the artists did not bother to finish the carving of all of the Pepi I prisoner statues, leaving some with roughly carved features or without particular details and a final polishing, because they expected another step in the artistic process that was going to further alter the appearance of the statues. The intact, and fully carved, statues might not have been understood as the final products, and therefore, the artists and possibly their overseers and patron, Pepi I, might not have felt the need to finish the steps of carving and polishing before moving to the last step of the artistic process, namely, the decapitation. This could also partly account for the extra attention given to these statues' faces and heads in contrast to their bodies; the significance of the faces and heads might have been heightened because of the impending decapitation, and thus the artists made sure to detail, vary, and fully finish them. In this way, the Pepi I prisoner statues could have been completed through their decapitation; the destructive action would have been positive and a necessary part of their production.

Interestingly, Bryan Just has made a similar argument in regard to three-dimensional statues of captives from the ancient Maya city of Toniná.[50] Maya statues were potently enlivened objects and imbued with the vital essences of those whom they depicted. In this way, they recall Egyptian statues, sharing a similar power and function. A number of headless captive statues have been discovered in Toniná, and Just has argued that these statues were decapitated with a blow to the base of the neck from a hafted, stone axe. Similar to the Pepi I prisoner statues, the Toniná captive statues were fully carved and then actively mutilated. Moreover, Just contended that "their subsequent 'destruction' would have been the essential impetus for their 'creation.'"[51] In this way, the destructive act was also positive since it was through this that the statues were made complete.

The nature of the destruction shifted at the pyramid complex of Pepi II, thus signifying a further development of the prisoner statues and their role in the monument. These prisoner statues were not systematically decapitated but instead were subjected to violent blows and haphazard defacement. The statues' archaeological context, in addition to the treatment of the prisoner statues at the complex of Pepi I, sug-

---

49. Pers. comm.

50. Bryan R. Just, "Modifications of Ancient Maya Sculpture," *RES: Anthropology and Aesthetics* 48 (2005): 75–78. My thanks go to Caitlin Earley for bringing this article to my attention.

51. Just, "Modifications," 77.

gests that this destruction occurred as part of the statues' original function in Pepi II's funerary monument, during or shortly after the reign of Pepi II. No expertise would have been necessary to enact it, and I consider who the agents might have been in the fourth section of this chapter.

5.3. Execration Figurines during the Old Kingdom

The prisoner statues of Pepi I and Pepi II were not the only three-dimensional representations of bound foreigners that were intentionally broken during the Old Kingdom. In this regard, it is necessary to compare their treatment to that of contemporary execration figurines. There are significant differences in the treatment of the execration figurines, as I describe here. For example, Old Kingdom execration figurines were largely found in private cemeteries, and they were consistently buried. These variations make it clear that the Pepi I and Pepi II prisoner statues were not treated as large-scale execration figurines and the destructive actions that they underwent were not the same as execration rituals, as previous scholars have implied, but it is quite possible that their damage had an apotropaic and execrative purpose in part.

Execration figurines are examples of *heka*, or magic.[52] All images in ancient Egypt were extremely powerful. The image of the bound captive alone had magical power; the depiction of the desired effect or event guaranteed its reality.[53] By depicting the enemies of the king, and thus the enemies of Egypt, bound and helpless, as the prisoner statues do, the Egyptians ensured that all evil forces, in all realms of the cosmos, would remain powerless and contained. The execration figurines take this further; the proscription formula that usually covers or is associated with them explicitly connects named threats, both foreign and domestic, with the generic captive form. Moreover, the active, ritualized manipulation of these figurines sets them apart from passive images of bound captives. While the exact content of the rituals remains unclear, they do seem to have changed over time and been somewhat variable, with elements not always appearing or being executed in different combinations. These elements could include breaking, binding, incineration, striking, and burial, all of which served to further damn and destroy the targeted individuals, places, and things that were mentioned on the figurines themselves.[54]

In many previous discussions of the prisoner statues, there has been a regular tendency to link the statues with or discuss them in relation to execration figurines. Indeed, in his introduction to Georges Posener's publication of execration figurines in the Brussels' Musées Royaux d'Art et d'Histoire, Jean Capart referred to the prisoner statues from the pyramid complex of Pepi II, which Jéquier had recently discovered.[55] Decades later, both Donald Redford and Yvan Koenig listed the prisoner statues as examples of execration texts and rituals without introducing alternate interpretations for the prisoner statues or emphasizing the differences between the prisoner statues and the execration figurines.[56] This lingering

---

52. Concerning *heka*, see further Étienne, *Heka*; Yvan Koenig, *Magie et magiciens dans l'Égypte ancienne* (Paris: Pygmalion, 1994); Geraldine Pinch, *Magic in Ancient Egypt* (London: British Museum Press, 1994); Jacco Dieleman, "Egypt," in *Guide to the Study of Ancient Magic*, ed. David Frankfurter, RGRW 189 (Leiden: Brill, 2019), 87–114; and Ritner, *Mechanics*.

53. Étienne, 18–19 and Ritner, 113–36.

54. For execration rituals, see further Étienne, 44–51; Pinch, *Magic in Ancient Egypt*, 93–94; Ritner, 136–80; Dieleman, "Egypt," 103–12; and Theis, "Ächtungstexte."

55. Jean Capart and Georges Posener, "Figurines égyptiennes d'envoûtement," *CRAIBL* 83 (1939): 66. Capart repeats this in his introduction to Georges Posener, *Princes et pays d'Asie et de Nubie: Textes hiératiques sur des figurines d'envoûtement du Moyen Empire* (Brussels: Fondation égyptologique reine Élisabeth, 1940), 5.

56. Koenig, *Magie et magiciens*, 135 and Donald B. Redford, *Egypt, Canaan, and Israel in Ancient Times* (Princeton: Princeton University Press, 1992), 87–88. Elsewhere in this book, Redford described the prisoner statues as reflecting the motif of the execution of prisoners and linked them with the execration texts (54). Koenig employed an extremely wide

association, which has continued for nearly a century, clearly began with Jéquier's initial arguments and his belief that the Pepi II prisoner statues were precursors of the Middle Kingdom execration figurines, as I mentioned above. As Ritner has noted, the question of intentional versus accidental breakage in regard to the execration figurines affected the interpretation of the broken Old Kingdom prisoner statues.[57]

In comparing the Pepi II prisoner statues and the execration figurines, Jéquier cited an article that George Posener wrote and published in 1939. In this, Posener described several different groups of execration figurines, all of which he dated to the Middle Kingdom.[58] At that time, Hermann Junker had already discovered an Old Kingdom execration deposit at Giza, while George Reisner had uncovered two. However, it was not until years later that these finds were fully published and the Old Kingdom execration figurines became better known.[59] Therefore, although Posener briefly referred to the unpublished figurines that Junker had discovered in his 1939 article, he did not note their Old Kingdom date and instead emphasized the prevalence of execration figurines and this type of magic during the Middle Kingdom.[60]

Execration rituals changed over time, and the Old Kingdom execration figurines were clearly precursors to the Middle Kingdom ones, in contrast to Jéquier's idea that the Middle Kingdom execration figurines developed from the Old Kingdom prisoner statues. Whether or not Jéquier was aware of the Old Kingdom execration figurines, the prisoner statues and the execration figurines coexisted. Yet, while certainly related in terms of theme and subject matter, the two types of objects are different.

Based on the known examples, which I list below, a few overall observations can be made in regard to execration figurines of the Old Kingdom, bearing in mind that these must remain tentative given the fact that some of the material is unprovenanced or unpublished. First, the figurines themselves were highly schematic and abstracted.[61] Second, figurines could be broken, but they did not have to be and there are numerous intact examples. Third, deposits were buried, most frequently in private funerary contexts, though not exclusively. And fourth, dated examples suggest that the use of such figurines did not occur or become widespread until the late Old Kingdom, particularly the Sixth Dynasty. Moreover, there may have been a particular concern with execration figurines and rituals during the reign of Pepi II.

In addition to the three deposits that Junker and Reisner had earlier discovered, in 1955 Abdel Moneim Abu Bakr and the University of Alexandria uncovered a fourth execration deposit at Giza while a fifth deposit from the same site remains unpublished.[62] One of the deposits that Reisner found, east of mastaba

---

definition for execration ("envoûtement") rituals and essentially considered all representations of the triumphant pharaoh or the destruction and containment of chaotic symbols as examples of execration rituals.

57. Ritner, *Mechanics*, 153.

58. This included a number of unprovenanced execration figurines in the Egyptian Museum in Cairo, figurines that Cecil Firth discovered in Saqqara, those that the Metropolitan Museum of Art uncovered in Lisht, and figurines in the Musées Royaux d'Art et d'Histoire in Brussels. See Posener, "Nouvelles listes," 40–46. While Posener did not explicitly date the Brussels figurines to the Middle Kingdom here, he did so in Capart and Posener, "Figurines égyptiennes d'envoûtement," 70–74. See also Posener, *Cinq figurines d'envoûtement*; Georges Posener, "Nouveaux textes hiératiques de proscription," in *Mélanges syriens offerts à monsieur René Dussaud*, vol. 1, Bibliothèque archéologique et historique 30 (Paris: Geuthner, 1939), 313–17; Posener, *Princes et pays*; and Quack, "Some Old Kingdom Execration Figurines."

59. Junker, *Giza VIII*, 30–38 and pls. 6b–7; Georges Posener, "À la recherche de nouveaux textes d'envoutement," in *Proceedings of the Fifth World Congress of Jewish Studies*, vol. 1 (Jerusalem: World Union of Jewish Studies, 1969), 144–49; and Osing, "Ächtungstexte." I describe these in further detail below.

60. Posener, "Nouvelles listes," 44–45.

61. For the form of execration figurines more generally, see Linda Borrmann, "Form Follows Function: Der Zeichencharakter der altägyptischen Ächtungsfiguren," in *Bild: Ästhetik – Medium – Kommunikation; Beiträge des dritten Münchner Arbeitskreiss Junge Ägyptologie (MAJA 3) 7. bis 9.12.2012*, edited by Gregor Neunert, Alexandra Verbovsek, and Kathrin Gabler, GOF 58 (Wiesbaden: Harrassowitz, 2014), 103–17.

62. Abu Bakir and Osing, "Ächtungstexte," 97–133. For the unpublished deposit, which seems to have been similar

Figure 5.3. Execration figurines that Reisner (Harvard University–Boston Museum of Fine Arts Expedition) discovered from Cemetery 2000 (western) in Giza; Sixth Dynasty. Unbaked mud; H. (average) 5.2 cm, W. (average) 2.2 cm, D. (average) 0.55 cm. Boston, MFA 07.1025. Photograph © 2021 Museum of Fine Arts, Boston.

G 7230, came from the eastern cemetery, while all of the other deposits were discovered in the western cemetery. The published deposits all share a number of things in common. Each included highly abstracted clay figurines with long rectangular plaques for bodies, which are inscribed with Egyptian and foreign names, and a pinched triangular protuberance signaling the head (fig. 5.3). Some of these were broken, often snapped roughly in half or at the "neck," while many are intact. The Reisner find from the western cemetery was poorly documented and little can be said concerning its archaeological context. On the other hand, the figurines that Junker and Abu Bakr found, in addition to those that Reisner found in the eastern cemetery, had been put into beer jars, which were subsequently buried. These vessels were inscribed with specific dates referencing an unnamed ruler, who scholars agree is most likely Pepi II.[63] The vessels from the Abu Bakr find and the Reisner deposit in the eastern cemetery also contained a larger clay figurine that was inscribed with differing prototypes of the "rebellion formula," which would become standardized on the execration figurines of the Middle Kingdom; the larger figurine in the Reisner deposit was intact while that in the Abu Bakr deposit was broken into numerous pieces, only some of which were put into the beer jar. Moreover, the Abu Bakr deposit also included an uninscribed, crudely modeled clay figurine of a striding man, who appears to have been broken at the neck, arms, and legs.

Execration figurines have also been unearthed at Saqqara, where an Australian mission discovered a number of very similar small plaque-like figurines in the necropolis next to the pyramid of Teti in an

---

to the other Giza deposits and consists of around 140 figurines that were found in a ceramic vessel, see Rafed El-Sayed, *Afrikanischstämmiger Lehnwortschatz im älteren Ägyptisch: Untersuchungen zur ägyptisch-afrikanischen lexikalischen Interferenz im dritten und zweiten Jahrtausend v. Chr.*, OLA 211 (Leuven: Peeters, 2011), 64 n. 12.

63. This date is based on the inscriptions, but Teodozja Rzeuska also supports it based on the form of the beer jars (Rzeuska, "Execration Again?," 630–31).

unstratified context.⁶⁴ Most of them are intact, but a few were found broken through the middle or at the "neck." Based on their inscriptions, these figurines have been dated to the reign of Pepi I or Pepi II.⁶⁵ More recently, Teodozja Rzeuska published a fragmentary plaque that had been discovered in a secondary context within a tomb shaft from the late Old Kingdom necropolis to the west of the Step Pyramid as an execration figurine.⁶⁶ While its shape does resemble the "bodies" of the other Old Kingdom examples, there is no visible inscription on it. Additionally, according to Harco Willems another deposit of clay execration figurines was discovered in or near the chapel of an Old Kingdom mastaba in Saqqara; this remains unpublished.⁶⁷

There are a handful of unprovenanced execration figurines that closely resemble the larger figurines with early "rebellion formulas" that Abu Bakr and Reisner discovered at Giza; the similarities extend to their shape, contents, and paleography though the formula of the inscriptions differ. These include two fragmentary figurines that are now in Munich and an intact example in Barcelona.⁶⁸ Because of their similarities with the material described above, the Munich and Barcelona figurines likely date to the late Old Kingdom and come from a Memphite cemetery. Their connection to each other and whether they came from a single deposit is unclear.⁶⁹

Not all Old Kingdom execrations figurines came from funerary contexts. Indeed, a French team discovered a fragmentary example, which dates to the Sixth Dynasty, during excavations at the settlement of Ayn Asil, Balat in the Dakhla Oasis.⁷⁰ Its schematic, triangular-shaped body is broken at the waist and is inscribed on both sides. A protuberance, which is broken at the top, extends from this, seemingly indicating a neck or head. Three partially published and slightly later examples, which date to the late Sixth Dynasty or the First Intermediate period, were similarly discovered outside the Memphite region, though they do come from a private cemetery, namely, the northwest cemetery of Elephantine.⁷¹ Additionally, a group of wax enemy figurines, which seem to be execration figurines or related to them, were also found in this same cemetery.⁷²

Finally, some scholars have dated an unprovenanced and intact execration figurine in the Louvre to the late Old Kingdom or the First Intermediate period, though others have preferred to date it to the Middle Kingdom.⁷³ Its form, namely, standing on clearly delineated legs with the arms pulled behind the back,

---

64. Karin Sowada, Tracey Callaghan, and Paul Bentley, *The Teti Cemetery at Saqqara, Volume IV: Minor Burials and Other Material*, RACE 12 (Warminster: Aris & Phillips, 1999), 65 and pls. 19 and 40 and Quack, "Some Old Kingdom Execration Figurines."

65. Quack, 149 and 154 and Theis, *Magie und Raum*, 723.

66. Rzeuska, "Execration Again?"

67. Harco Willems, "The Social and Ritual Context of a Mortuary Liturgy of the Middle Kingdom (CT Spells 30–41)," in *Social Aspects of Funerary Culture in the Egyptian Old and Middle Kingdoms: Proceedings of the International Symposium Held at Leiden University 6–7 June, 1996*, ed. Harco Willems, OLA 103 (Leuven: Peeters, 2001), 319. According to Willems, Jürgen Osing is publishing the find.

68. Munich, Staatliche Museum Ägyptischer Kunst ÄS 7123 and 7124 and Barcelona, Museu Egipci E 619. See Wimmer, "Neue Ächtungstexte," and Diego Espinel, "Newly Identified Old Kingdom Execration Text." For the Munich figurines, see also Étienne, *Heka*, cat. no. 80 and 81 and Theis, *Magie und Raum*, 722–23.

69. Diego Espinel, 27.

70. Grimal, "'Noyés' de Balat."

71. Seidlmayer, "Execration Texts," 487. Linda Borrmann interpreted one of these figurines, with its schematic body, as having hair depicted on its head (Borrmann, "Form Follows Function," 109–10 and Abb. 2).

72. Theis, *Magie und Raum*, 725; Martin Bommas, "Zwei magische Sprüche in einem spätägyptischen Ritualhandbuch (pBM EA 10081): Ein weiterer Fall für die 'Verborgenheit des Mythos,'" *ZÄS* 131 (2004): 98; and Willems, "Social and Ritual Context," 318.

73. Paris, Louvre E 27204. Georges Posener, "Une nouvelle statuette d'envoûtement," in *Studien zu Sprache und Religion*

and its execution, with facial features and incised toes and fingers, is far less rough and schematic than all of the other figurines mentioned above. It also differs in its medium, which is wood, though if the five kneeling bound captives from the tomb chapel of Senedjemib Mehi were in fact execration figurines, as I tentatively suggested in chapter 1.3 and in an earlier publication, there was a precedent for wooden execration figurines in the Old Kingdom (fig. 1.12).[74] At the same time, the Senedjemib Mehi figurines were roughly and schematically carved, and in this way, they are more in keeping with the Old Kingdom clay execration figurines than is the Louvre figurine. The form and execution of the Louvre figurine suggests a post-Old Kingdom date.

Clearly there are significant and notable differences between the Old Kingdom execration figurines and the Pepi I and Pepi II prisoner statues. The most obvious of these is the fact that there are no traces of execration texts anywhere on or near the prisoner statues. Additionally, the prisoner statues were fully executed and are entirely figural, unlike the highly schematic Old Kingdom execration figurines. Their context also differed: the prisoner statues were erected in royal monuments while all of the execration deposits that have been found in situ were discovered in private cemeteries or settlements. Indeed, this highlights another major distinction: the execration figurines were all buried, seemingly as part of the ritual itself. On the other hand, the fragments of the prisoner statues were left above ground and scattered around the pyramid complexes following their mutilation. Moreover, the prisoner statues of Pepi I and Pepi II were consistently broken and damaged, while the execration figurines were not.

Therefore, the prisoner statues did not undergo the same execration rituals that are attested from the Old Kingdom execration figurines, and one should not describe the damage to the prisoner statues as analogous to that of the execration figurines. At the same time, this does not preclude a relationship between the type of ritual activity that was carried out during execration rituals and the destruction of the prisoner statues. In other words, there could have been an execrative nature to the destructive action undertaken on the prisoner statues and/or the damage to the prisoner statues might have been inspired by or related to execration rituals. This is particularly likely for the Pepi II prisoner statues, but before expanding on this, it is necessary to consider how the treatment to the Pepi I and Pepi II prisoner statues was ritualized.

5.4. The Ritualized Context of the Pepi I and Pepi II Prisoner Statues

Egyptologists have identified execration rituals as such because of the contents of the texts, the consistency of the associated objects, and the objects' condition and archaeological context.[75] While the exact nature and processes of these rituals is difficult to reconstruct, the evidence indicates that there were execration rituals. But this touches upon a critical issue: how does one identify rituals in the past? Reconstructing actions and events from archaeological remains is an inevitably problematic and complex endeavor. This is particularly true in regard to ritual. The question of what constitutes ritual and what does not becomes increasingly difficult to identify as one moves back in time, with less and less contextual evidence on which to base one's interpretations.[76] And this question immediately leads to another, equally problematic one: What is ritual? There is no single definition of the term, and scholars continue to debate

---

Ägyptens: Zu Ehren von Wolfhart Westendorf, vol. 1, ed. Friedrich Junge (Göttingen: Hubert & Co., 1984), 613–18; Étienne, *Heka*, 58 and cat. no. 153; and Theis, 724, with further references.

74. Prakash, "Reconsidering," 152–53.

75. See further Ritner, *Mechanics*, 136–80.

76. For discussion of and different approaches to this issue, see further Timothy Insoll, *Archaeology, Ritual, Religion* (London: Routledge, 2004); Evangelos Kyriakidis, ed., *The Archaeology of Ritual*, Cotsen Advanced Seminars 3 (Los Angeles:

what components should be included in any definition of it.[77] There is not even consensus on whether or not a definition of ritual is necessary or possible.

Catherine Bell has argued that it is more productive to consider what ritual does rather than what it is.[78] In regard to the distant past and the fragmentary archaeological record, this practice approach is particularly appropriate and Bell's use of the term ritualization is especially relevant:

> In a very preliminary sense, ritualization is a way of acting that is designed and orchestrated to distinguish and privilege what is being done in comparison, to other, usually more quotidian activities ... a matter of various culturally specific strategies for setting some activities off from others, for creating and privileging a qualitative distinction between the "sacred" and the "profane," and for ascribing such distinctions to realities thought to transcend the powers of human actors.[79]

With this approach, the scholarly focus becomes what people do in ritual and how they do it; what objects do they use and how are these ritualized. Ritualization is a culturally specific phenomenon; rituals are not universal, and one needs to study them contextually in order to recognize and interpret them. By concentrating on the ritualized actions and artifacts within their original context, one can begin to reconstruct their meanings and significance even when one cannot reconstruct the entire ritual itself.

Asking whether the destruction of the Pepi I and Pepi II prisoner statues was a ritual is too simple of a question that fails to elucidate the full complexity of the statues' significance and the activities in which they were instruments. Such a question emphasizes the destructive action itself above all else, which may not have been most important to the Egyptians. Indeed, the significance of violence within a ritual framework is also culturally specific, as recent scholars have argued, and one should not assume that the violent actions were always the foci or critical moment of any ritual activity that involved violence.[80] For this reason, my aim here is to consider the destructive action within the cultural context of the Pepi I and Pepi II prisoner statues and the degree to which this action was ritualized. In the case of Pepi I, the action does not seem to have been especially ritualized; rather the decapitation transformed the statues into offerings for the king, and the primary ritual activities occurred after the destructive action. On the other hand, the destruction of the Pepi II prisoner statues was similar to acts of royal smiting, during which the king executed his enemies, and in this way, the action itself was highly ritualized and paramount.

5.4.1. Pepi I

The decapitation of the Pepi I prisoner statues was methodical; the heads were carefully removed, then beards were chiseled off and remains of the neck possibly polished off the body. This would have been a slow procedure. As I discussed above, the artists must have been responsible for it. This indicates that

---

Cotsen Institute of Archaeology at UCLA, 2007); and Timothy Insoll, ed., *Oxford Handbook of the Archaeology of Ritual and Religion* (Oxford: Oxford University Press, 2011).

77. For a recent discussion on this issue, see Ronald Grimes, *The Craft of Ritual Studies* (Oxford: Oxford University Press, 2014), 189–97. For an archaeological perspective on it, see Evangelos Kyriakidis, "Archaeologies of Ritual," in Kyriakidis, 289–94.

78. Catherine Bell, *Ritual: Perspectives and Dimensions* (Oxford: Oxford University Press, 1997) and Catherine Bell, *Ritual Theory, Ritual Practice* (Oxford: Oxford University Press, 1992).

79. C. Bell, *Ritual Theory, Ritual Practice*, 74.

80. Jennifer Wright Knust and Zsuzsanna Várhelyi, "Introduction: Images, Acts, Meanings and Ancient Mediterranean Sacrifice," in *Ancient Mediterranean Sacrifice*, ed. Jennifer Wright Knust and Zsuzsanna Várhelyi (Oxford: Oxford University Press, 2011), 7–22.

there was a clear concern with how the resulting statues looked and their visual impact. It must have been important that they resembled actual beheaded men, with the heads (including what would naturally remain on them, namely, the beards and necks) fully removed from the torsos. This suggests that the decapitated foreigners, namely, the statue fragments themselves, were significant.

Decapitation in Egypt is attested as far back as the predynastic period.[81] By the time of the Narmer Palette, at the beginning of pharaonic history, it clearly had become associated with the punishment of the king's enemies.[82] During the dynastic period, it seems to have been a punishment that was especially used for non-Egyptian war prisoners or criminals.[83] Similarly, decapitation has been noted in connection with execration magic, such as the Old Kingdom execration figurines that were broken at the "neck," as I mentioned above. Moreover, decapitated bodies were discovered as part of later execration deposits at Mirgissa and possibly Tell el-Dab'a.[84]

Regarding religious beliefs, funerary texts indicate that decapitation was a common form of punishment for enemies of the gods and the deceased, who hoped to join the gods in the afterlife.[85] In the New Kingdom royal tombs, dangerous beings and enemies of the sun god are often depicted decapitated.[86] These creatures also tend to be bound, like the prisoner statues.[87] Contemporary with the prisoner statues, the Pyramid Texts contain multiple verses that describe beheading the enemies of the dead king.[88] For

---

81. Sean P. Dougherty and Renée F. Friedman, "Sacred or Mundane: Scalping and Decapitation at Predynastic Hierakonpolis," in *Egypt at Its Origins 2: Proceedings of the International Conference "Origin of the State, Predynastic and Early Dynastic Egypt,"* ed. Béatrix Midant-Reynes and Yann Tristant, OLA 172 (Leuven: Peeters, 2008), 311–38; Éric Crubézy and Béatrix Midant-Reynes, "Les sacrifices humains à l'époque prédynastique: L'apport de la nécropole d'Adaïma," in *La sacrifice humain: En Égypte ancienne et ailleurs*, ed. Jean-Pierre Albert and Béatrix Midant-Reynes (Paris: Soleb, 2005), 58–81; Bertrand Ludes and Éric Crubézy, "Le sacrifice humain en contexte funéraire: Problèmes poses à l'anthropobiologie et à la médecine légale; L'exemple prédynastique," in Albert and Midant-Reynes, *La sacrifice humain*, 82–95; and Bryan, "Episodes of Iconoclasm," 364–65. See also Xavier Droux, "Une representation de prisonniers décapités en provenance de Hiérakonpolis," *BSEG* 27 (2005–2007): 33–42.

82. Cairo, Egyptian Museum JE 32169; CG 14716. In the case of the Narmer Palette, the phalli of most of the enemies are also severed (William Vivian Davies and Renée Friedman, "The Narmer Palette: An Overlooked Detail," in *Egyptian Museum Collections around the World*, vol. 1, ed. Mamdouh Eldamaty and May Trad [Cairo: Supreme Council of Antiquities, 2002], 243–46).

83. Dougherty and Friedman, "Sacred or Mundane," 333; Nicholas Picardo, "Dealing with Decapitation Diachronically," *Nekhen News* 16 (2004): 13; and Kerry Muhlestein, *Violence in the Service of Order: The Religious Framework for Sanctioned Killing in Ancient Egypt* (Oxford: Archaeopress, 2011), 38–39, 47–48, and 76. However, restoration of the head, during all periods of dynastic history, marked resurrection and had positive associations (Jan Assmann, "Death and Initiation in the Funerary Religion of Ancient Egypt," in Simpson, *Religion and Philosophy*, 137–39 and Christopher Eyre, *The Cannibal Hymn: A Cultural and Literary Study* [Liverpool: Liverpool University Press, 2002], 95–97).

84. Manfred Bietak et al., "Ausgrabungen in dem Palastbezirk von Avaris Vorbericht Tell el-Dab'a/'Ezbet Helmi 1993–2000," *Ägypten und Levante* 11 (2001): 60–64 and 67–74; Étienne, *Heka*, 45; Perla Fuscaldo, "Tell al-Dab'a: Two Execration Pits and a Foundation Deposit," in Hawass, *Egyptology*, 185–88; Janzen, "Iconography of Humiliation," 20–21 and 315–18; Koenig, *Magie et magiciens*, 137–41; Kerry Muhlestein, "Royal Executions: Evidence Bearing on the Subject of Sanctioned Killing in the Middle Kingdom," *JESHO* 51 (2008): 194–96; Ritner, *Mechanics*, 153–80; and Jean Vercoutter, "Textes exécratoires de Mirgissa," *CRAIBL* 107 (1963): 97–102.

85. Eyre, *Cannibal Hymn*, 94–95; Picardo, "Dealing with Decapitation Diachronically," 13; Nicholas Picardo, "'Semantic Homicide' and the So-called Reserve Heads: The Theme of Decapitation in Egyptian Funerary Religion and Some Implications for the Old Kingdom," *JARCE* 43 (2007): 221–24; and Jan Zandee, *Death as an Enemy: According to Ancient Egyptian Conceptions*, trans. W. F. Klasens, Studies in the History of Religions 5 (Leiden: Brill, 1960), 16–17.

86. Erik Hornung, *The Valley of the Kings: Horizon of Eternity*, trans. David Warburton (New York: Timken, 1990), 149–64 and fig. 75 and Picardo, "'Semantic Homicide,'" 224–25.

87. See further Zandee, *Death as an Enemy*, 20–22.

88. Examples include PT 136, PT 273–274, PT 298, PT 367, PT 384–385, PT 477, PT 519, PT 535, and PT 580. For transla-

example, in PT 477 Thoth is called upon to sharpen and use his knife "that removes heads and cuts out hearts, so that it may remove the heads and cut out the hearts of those who would cross me [the deceased king] when I go to you, Osiris, and of those who would impede me [the deceased king] when I go to you, Osiris."[89] In PT 535, Horus is told to punish the followers of Seth: "Seize them, remove their heads, and cut off their forelegs. Gut them, take their hearts, and drink of their blood."[90] Decapitation was greatly feared and possessing one's head was necessary to successfully transition into the afterlife; the deceased king's head is repeatedly described as being tied onto his body in the Pyramid Texts.[91] While receiving the head back following its dislocation and the restoration of it onto the body was a symbol of resurrection, the permanent removal of the head sentenced the victim to complete damnation and thus served as an ultimate form of annihilation.[92] Decapitation was a punishment reserved for the most reprehensible offenders.

Moreover, rebellious enemies and criminals were regularly equated to animals, and the action of decapitating and dismembering a human was often paralleled to the butchering of animals, as the Pyramid Texts demonstrate.[93] Indeed, in PT 535, which I quoted above, Horus is instructed not only to decapitate the miscreants, but also to sever their forelegs and gut them, as one would butcher an ox or bull.[94] The severing of the head occurred after the animal's blood had been drained through the lethal cut in its throat, and although the animal's head does not appear to have regularly been consumed in ancient Egypt, the detached head was frequently depicted on offering tables, serving as a symbol of the slaughtered animal and its meat that was being offered.[95]

In the Cannibal Hymn (PT 273–274) within the Pyramid Texts, gods and people are slaughtered and butchered in the same fashion as an animal for the deceased king to consume.[96] In this way, their powers and magic are transferred to him, and these beings serve to sustain him. Their defeat and his dominance is made complete. The king feeds off of his enemies and those who might stand in his way. Similarly, one could understand bound defeated rebels as symbolic offerings to the king, akin to offerings of meat and other nourishment. Statuary from later periods sometimes made this explicit. For example, bound captive

---

tions, see Allen, *Ancient Egyptian Pyramid Texts*. As I discussed in ch. 2.1, the Pyramid Texts were a collection of religious texts that were inscribed on the walls of the funerary compartments inside late Old Kingdom pyramids beginning with the reign of Unas. Concerning the overall role of enemies in the Pyramid Texts, see Georg Meurer, *Die Feinde des Königs in den Pyramidentexten*, OBO 189 (Göttingen: Vandenhoeck & Ruprecht, 2002).

89. PT 477, § 962–63. Translation based on James P. Allen, *A New Concordance of the Pyramid Texts*, 6 vols. (Providence: Brown University, 2013), 4: https://oi-idb.uchicago.edu/id/55860209-f09f-4b6f-bd3f-40ce4c1a83ab.

90. PT 535, § 1286. Translation based on Allen.

91. For example, PT 254, PT 355, PT 369, and PT 603. See translations in Allen, *Ancient Egyptian Pyramid Texts*.

92. Eyre, *Cannibal Hymn*, 94–95 and Picardo, "'Semantic Homicide,'" 222. See also Zandee, *Death as an Enemy*, 16–17.

93. Eyre, 89–97; Jean Leclant, "La 'mascarade' des boeufs gras et le triomphe de l'Égypte," *MDAIK* 14 (1956): 128–45; Roland Tefnin, *Art et magie au temps des pyramides: L'énigme des têtes dites de "remplacement*,*"* Monumenta Aegyptiaca 5 (Brussels: Fondation égyptologique reine Élisabeth, 1991), 78–80; Jan Assmann, "Spruch 23 der Pyramidentexte und die Ächtung der Feinde Pharaos," in Berger, Clerc, and Grimal, *Hommages à Jean Leclant*, 50–52; Catherine Bouanich, "Mise à mort rituelle de l'animal, offrande carnée dans le temple égyptien," in *La cuisine et l'autel: Les sacrifices en questions dans les sociétés de la Méditerranée ancienne*, ed. Stella Georgoudi, Renée Koch Piettre, and Francis Schmidt, Bibliothèque d'École des hautes études, sciences religieuses 124 (Turnhout: Brepols, 2005), 149–58; Salima Ikram, *Choice Cuts: Meat Production in Ancient Egypt*, OLA 69 (Leuven: Peeters, 1995), 42–43; and Harco Willems, "Crime, Cult and Capital Punishment (Mo'alla Inscription 8)," *JEA* 76 (1990): 27–54. See also Zandee, 22–23.

94. Concerning the process of butchering mammals in ancient Egypt, see Ikram, *Choice Cuts*, 41–54.

95. Eyre, *Cannibal Hymn*, 64 and Ikram, 48–49 and 118–20.

96. These verses have been discussed frequently. Recent analyses and translations, with additional bibliography, include Eyre; Muhlestein, *Violence*, 22–25; Katja Goebs, *Crowns in Egyptian Funerary Literature: Royalty, Rebirth, and Destruction*, Griffith Institute Monographs (Oxford: Griffith Institute, 2008), 205–358; and Meurer, *Feinde des Königs*, 43–51.

imagery can adorn offering tables (fig. 1.10).⁹⁷ In another statue the foreigner himself is the offering: a votive for the governor Khnumemhet features the body of a bound Asiatic on his knees, belly, and chin on top of a base (fig. 5.4).⁹⁸ In this way, the foreigner is visually aligned with a fettered animal offered to a king or god. Both the bound foreigner and the slaughtered animal represent the taming of natural and negative forces and the establishment and maintenance of order over these.⁹⁹ The Breaking the Red Vases ritual further demonstrates the close relationship between the destruction of enemies and offerings.¹⁰⁰ This ritual was an important element of funerary offering rituals and closely associated with the meal that served to sustain and nourish the deceased tomb owner. At the same time, it was clearly linked to execration rituals, which may have developed from it, and the pots symbolized enemies, who were annihilated through their breakage.¹⁰¹

Figure 5.4. Votive statue for the governor Khnumemhet featuring a bound foreign prisoner, probably from Thebes; New Kingdom. Granite; H. 17 cm; W. 21 cm; L. 32 cm. Luxor, Luxor Museum J.906. Photograph: Tara Prakash, Courtesy of the Luxor Museum.

The Pepi I prisoner statues were treated as animals and slaughtered for the king. The decapitation transformed them into beneficial offerings, and the artists took on the role of butchers. Evidence suggests that in most cases the killing of animals intended for offerings was not especially ritualized, even though the animal's death was necessary for offering rituals. Scenes of butchery are extremely common in Old Kingdom tomb chapels and mortuary temples.¹⁰² In most cases, there is nothing to suggest that the butchers themselves were ritualists. Captions often suggest an informal setting.¹⁰³ Priests could accompany and

---

97. Cairo, Egyptian Museum JE 35665 and CG 755/JE 28831. The latter offering table also functioned as a statue base. See Borchardt, *Statuen und Statuetten*, 3:75; Bernard Bruyère, *Rapport sur les fouilles de Deir el Médineh (1935–1940), Quatrième partie, Fascicule II: trouvailles d'objets*, FIFAO 20:2 (Cairo: Institut français d'archéologie orientale, 1952), 58–59 and fig. 3; and Wildung, "König Ägyptens," 112 and Abb. 9.

98. Luxor, Luxor Museum J.906; Previously Cairo, Egyptian Museum TR 14/10/69/3. See Louis Keimer, "Une statue de prisonnier remontant au Nouvel Empire," *ASAE* 49 (1949): 37–39.

99. Salima Ikram, "In Death as in Life, 'You Are What You Eat': Transformation, Mummification and Food Offerings in Ancient Egypt," in *Religion et alimentation en Égypte et Orient anciens*, vol. 2, ed. Marie-Lys Arnette, RAPH 43 (Cairo: Institut français d'archéologie orientale, 2019), 387–413.

100. Concerning this ritual, see further Ritner, *Mechanics*, 144–47; Assmann, "Spruch 23," 50–55; Joachim Friedrich Quack, "Opfermahl und Feindvernichtung im altägyptischen Ritual," *Mitteilungen der Berliner Gesellschaft für Anthropologie, Ethnologie und Urgeschichte* 27 (2006): 67–80; and Julia Budka, "Egyptian Impact on Pot-Breaking Ceremonies at el-Kurru? A Re-Examination," in *The Fourth Cataract and Beyond: Proceedings of the 12th International Conference for Nubian Studies*, ed. Julie R. Anderson and Derek W. Welsby, BMPES 1 (Leuven: Peeters, 2014), 645–47, all with additional bibliography. For archaeological evidence of the ritual from the Old Kingdom, see Miroslav Bárta et al., "'Killed' for Eternity: Artefacts and Ritual Behaviour from a Unique Ceremonial Structure in Abusir South," in Bárta, Coppens, and Krejčí, *Abusir and Saqqara…2015*, 1–21.

101. Dieleman, "Egypt," 103.

102. Ikram, *Choice Cuts*, 41 and table 1.

103. Stefan Grunert, "Die Schächtung im Totenopfer: Ritualbestandteil vs. Reflexion allgemeinen Brauchtums," in *Tierkulte im pharaonischen Ägypten und im Kulturvergleich*, ed. Martin Fitzenreiter (London: Golden House, 2005), 69–82.

oversee the butchery, but it was rare for a priest to be represented conducting the killing and portioning of the animal.[104] Christopher Eyre has suggested that the slaughter was ritualized through the priest's recitations, but at the same time Eyre noted that it is not clear to what extent such recitation accompanied the actual slaughter.[105] In cases where a priest is depicted in an active position, he is carrying the animal's foreleg away.[106] This should be understood as initiating the next phase of the ritual process and distinct from the butchery itself.

Butchering appears to have usually taken place outside of but nearby the tomb chapel or temple offering hall where the processed meat would have been offered.[107] Slaughterhouses definitely were a part of Old Kingdom pyramid complexes. Based on her survey of the available evidence, Salima Ikram concluded that they were usually placed off to one side of the mortuary temple offering hall, often at a north–south axis rather than along the east–west axis of the temple proper, and slaughterhouses had their own entrances.[108] Although the killing took place on temple grounds, it did not occur in the same place as the actual offering and thus appears to have been understood as a separate act. Indeed, Ikram doubted that slaughtering was a sufficiently pure activity to take place inside the heart of the temple.[109]

Eyre described butchery as a key preparatory stage, with core symbolic meanings, but it was not necessarily performed as part of the ritual of the offering hall; the butchery rituals form an independent episode.[110] Similar to Eyre, David Frankfurter argued that the slaughter was peripheral but further suggested that it might have even been understood to be a nonritualized preparatory action.[111] The killing and portioning of the animal, which necessarily included its partial or complete decapitation, was necessary and had symbolic meaning, but it was not explicitly ritualized itself.

There is no reason to assume that every offering ritual was identical. There may have been instances when the slaughter was highly ritualized and performed by priests within a more sacred area of the funerary complex. But in general, the killing and portioning of animals for offerings does not seem to have been especially ritualized even though it occurred in a sacred and religious framework.[112] In this regard, Ronald Grimes's distinction between sacred and ritual objects may be useful.[113] The slaughtered ox might have had sacred value, but the joints of meat did not become ritual objects until they were used in rituals.

The decapitation of the Pepi I prisoner statues should be understood in a similar fashion. Undoubtedly, it was part of a ritualized context. However, the decapitation itself, which the artists would have executed as part of the creation of these statues, does not seem to have been the focal point. This action was symbolic and transformative, but it was likely not a ritual in and of itself. Rather it was an essential step for the broader ritualized sequence. Just as ritualists oversaw the process of butchery, ritualists could have overseen the decapitation of the prisoner statues. It is also possible that some or even all of the artists were

---

104. Fanny Hamonic, "Cérémonial ou céremoniel? Production de viande et pratiques religieuses à l'Ancien Empire," in Arnette, *Religion et alimentation*, 148–52 and Ikram, *Choice Cuts*, 109–11.

105. Eyre, *Cannibal Hymn*, 189.

106. Hamonic, "Cérémonial ou céremoniel," 149–50.

107. A recent study of a New Kingdom slaughterhouse is Mohamed Abuel-Yazid, "Architecture of the Slaughterhouse of the Seti Temple at Abydos," in *Abydos: The Sacred Land at the Western Horizon*, ed. Ilona Regulski, BMPES 8 (Leuven: Peeters, 2019), 7–24, with references to previous studies on slaughterhouses.

108. Ikram, *Choice Cuts*, 88–95.

109. Ikram, 97–98.

110. Eyre, *Cannibal Hymn*, 53 and 139.

111. David Frankfurter, "Egyptian Religion and the Problem of the Category 'Sacrifice,'" in Knust and Várhelyi, *Ancient Mediterannean Sacrifice*, 77.

112. In this regard, see also Hamonic, "Cérémonial ou céremoniel," 141–71.

113. Grimes, *Craft of Ritual Studies*, 267–73.

ritualists themselves to an extent. Indeed, Violaine Chavet has argued that the distinction between craftsmen and ritual agents was fluid during the Old Kingdom.[114] Regardless, the key ritualistic actions, whatever they may have been, likely occurred after the Pepi I prisoner statues had been decapitated, just as the core of the offering ritual consisted of the actual offering of meat rather than the killing of the animal.

The decapitated prisoner statues were left within the pyramid complex for the king's benefit and enjoyment. They served as monumental offerings, similar to the images of food and other offerings that were eternalized in the reliefs. They helped sustain him, as he could perpetually consume his enemies. Moreover, these prisoner statues also served as concrete testaments to his dominance. The complex was filled with the king's annihilated enemies, reminiscent of the headless victims of the gods in the netherworld. Therefore, the decapitated form of the statues was significant for multiple reasons.

The decapitation may have had execrative overtones, and it could have also served to deactivate the statues, just as the removal and damage to the noses might have done. As images, the prisoner statues were inherently powerful and removing their heads might have helped defuse their potency, making the subject matter safer. The action of destroying these statues may have been understood to be apotropaic and intended to further remove and curse any threats to the king and Egypt. But at the pyramid complex of Pepi I, this meaning seems to have been secondary. The artists' meticulous removal of the statues' heads primarily relates to offering rituals for the benefit of the pharaoh and the desire to visualize the annihilated enemies of the king and the gods.

5.4.2. Pepi II

The nature of the prisoner statues' damage changed dramatically at the pyramid complex of Pepi II. The destructive actions were not slow and methodical but violent and haphazard. They did not require any particular expertise, as the decapitation of the Pepi I prisoner statues did. Rather any able-bodied adult could have yielded a weapon against these statues. Moreover, the statues were not carefully treated so that they would look a particular way. In other words, the final appearance of the statue fragments, which were left scattered around the complex, was not a priority. The action itself had more significance.

There are multiple verses in the Pyramid Texts that describe the striking down of the deceased king's enemies, thus demonstrating that this was an appropriate punishment for and way to eradicate negative and threatening beings according to contemporary religious and funerary beliefs.[115] Certainly, the prisoner statues were representative of such beings. Indeed, the Pepi II prisoner statues seem to have been victims of an act that was similar to smiting. The destruction of the Pepi II prisoner statues would have required that a weapon be raised overhead and brought down hard against the statues. The iconic smiting scene represents an extremely similar action: in it, the king strides forward and grasps one or more enemies with one hand as he raises his mace or sword overhead with the other in the act of smiting them (fig. 1.5). The scene is highly symbolic and undoubtedly had multiple layers of meaning, but many scholars have argued that actual smiting did occasionally occur in a ritualized context or as part of certain rituals.[116] The Pepi II prisoner statues seem to have undergone something similar to ritualized smiting, and they were probably

---

114. Violaine Chavet, "Who Did What and Why: The Dynamics of Tomb Preparation," in *Joyful in Thebes: Egyptological Studies in Honor of Betsy M. Bryan*, ed. Richard Jasnow and Kathlyn Cooney, MVCAE 1 (Atlanta: Lockwood, 2015), 63–78.

115. PT 100, PT 105B, PT 251, PT 324, PT 384, PT 580, PT 612, PT 614, PT 663, PT 670, PT 674. For translations, see Allen, *Ancient Egyptian Pyramid Texts*.

116. For further discussion and citation, see Muhlestein, *Violence*, 85–91; Alan Schulman, *Ceremonial Execution and Public Rewards: Some Historical Scenes on New Kingdom Private Stelae*, OBO 75 (Göttingen: Vandenhoeck & Ruprecht, 1988),

attacked as part of a broader ritual sequence or event. In this way, the "smiting" of the Pepi II prisoner statues, namely, the destructive act itself, would have been a highly significant, ritualized event.

The change in the treatment of the Pepi II prisoner statues emphasizes a different aspect of these statues. The fragments were left scattered around this king's pyramid complex, and they may have been understood as offerings to the king, similar to what I have argued was one of the central purposes of the Pepi I prisoner statues. But the Pepi II prisoner statue fragments were not as important as the destructive act itself. Rituals involving smiting were closely tied to kingship, and they had a more overt execrative nature.[117] The victim of the smiting symbolized all negative, rebellious forces that the pharaoh effectively destroyed with his weapon. In this way, smiting was apotropaic. Therefore, while the destruction of the Pepi II prisoner statues was not an execration ritual, it was more closely related to execration than the decapitation of the Pepi I prisoner statues.

It is possible that the change in treatment to the Pepi II prisoner statues was related, perhaps indirectly, to the rise of execration rituals that seems to have occurred during the reign of Pepi II, as I described above. Most of the dated execration deposits come from this king's reign, and it seems likely that these rituals became more widely employed than they had been prior to this time.[118] The consistency and number of execration figurines and the foreign names on them indicate that the state was probably involved in or responsible for their production, despite private influence and local idiosyncrasies.[119] Therefore, the execration figurines must have benefited the king, as the head of the state, in some way even if their original context was quite different from the prisoner statues, whose purpose was undoubtedly to benefit the king in a direct way. I do not think that there is a straightforward link between the contemporary rise in execration figurines and the treatment of the Pepi II prisoner statues because of the important differences between these objects that I described above. But it is conceivable that there was some overall correspondence between them. The increasing prevalence of execration rituals could have inspired or impacted the designers of Pepi II's pyramid complex, including his high officials and even the king himself. Alternatively, the reasons that the state needed/desired more execration figurines, which may have been related to the increasing interactions with Nubia that I discussed in chapter 3, could have been related to the reasons that the treatment of the prisoner statues changed.

The ritualized sequence or event of which the "smiting" of the Pepi II prisoner statues was a part remains unknown and is conjectural. In imagery, the only person shown smiting is the king himself. If Pepi II smashed his own prisoner statues, the act could have somehow been tied to the establishment of his monument or a ritual primarily intended for the living king. Indeed, Sylvia Schoske has argued that smiting rituals occurred as part of the royal *sed* festival.[120] A king could celebrate this festival, which served to

---

8–115; and Anthony Spalinger, *Icons of Power: A Strategy of Reinterpretation* (Prague: Charles University, 2011), 187–89. For a more critical view, see Schoske, "Erschlagen der Feinde," 450–64. I discussed the smiting scene in detail in ch. 1.

117. See sources in the previous footnote.

118. Rzeuska even questioned whether the execration rituals during this time were part of a single initiative or event (Rzeuska, "Execration Again?," 631).

119. Ritner, *Mechanics*, 141–42; Diego Espinel, "Newly Identified Old Kingdom Execration Text," 29–30; Willems, "Social and Ritual Context," 319–20; Quack, "Some Old Kingdom Execration Figurines," 150; and Dieleman, "Egypt," 103–12; cf. John Baines, "Display of Magic in Old Kingdom Egypt," in *Through a Glass Darkly: Magic, Dreams and Prophecy in Ancient Egypt*, ed. Kasia Szpakowska (Swansea: Classical Press of Wales, 2006), 8.

120. Schoske, "Erschlagen der Feinde," 458–63. For the *sed* festival in general, see further Karl Martin, "Sedfest," *LÄ* 5:782–90; Erik Hornung and Elisabeth Staehelin, *Studien zum Sedfest*, AegHelv 1 (Geneva: Edition de Belles Lettres, 1974); and Erik Hornung and Elisabeth Staehelin, *Neue Studien zum Sedfest*, AegHelv 20 (Basel: Schwabe, 2006).

renew his kingship, after thirty years on the throne and subsequently, as frequently as he wanted. With his long reign, Pepi II celebrated at least three *sed* festivals.[121]

In reality, priests, who acted as agents of the king, were responsible for many of the rituals that took place throughout Egypt. The same could be true in regard to the Pepi II prisoner statues. While Pepi II might have carried out some or even all of the destruction, it is equally possible that other sanctioned individuals, such as high-level priests, actually did the "smiting" on the king's behalf.[122] In this case, the destruction could have occurred during the king's life or after his death. In the latter scenario, the ritual might have been meant to provide for and benefit the deceased king. If it occurred following Pepi II's death, there is also a third possibility, namely, that the ritualized destruction could have been related to the coronation of Pepi II's successor, and the new king might have performed the destruction of the prisoner statues.[123] In any case, the ritualized context undoubtedly was multifaceted, and the destruction must have had several meanings and functions. More than one of my proposals could be correct.

5.5. Rituals and Ritualization in the Late Old Kingdom Pyramid Complex

The ritual life of the pyramid complex can productively be understood in terms of ritualization as Bell defined it.[124] Indeed, Nils Billing successfully employed this approach in his study of the complex of Pepi I.[125] This theoretical framework better allows for the complicated overlapping of ritual layers that occurred in these monuments. The monuments were not the sites of a set of rituals that occurred independent from one another. Rather the activities occurred in an overall ritualized context. They intersected and reverberated off one another. Moreover, as Billing has argued, they were monumentalized in the complex itself and in this way they had continual and eternal significance.[126]

The prisoner statues of Pepi I and Pepi II clearly demonstrate this complexity. Their destruction should not be understood as an isolated ritual. Rather it occurred in a broader context and the results of the destruction, namely, the prisoner statue fragments, continued to operate within the ritualization of the pyramid complex. The destructive action was only one layer of this. The scattered prisoner statue fragments eternalized the annihilation of the kings' enemies so that it would perpetually occur, and they served as permanent offerings to the king. This then reinforced other ritual activity that occurred within the complex, all of which served to benefit the king and aid his transition into the afterlife.

The prisoner statues were only one feature of the late Old Kingdom pyramid complex. Consequently, any attempt to reconstruct the ritual life of these monuments cannot be based only or even primarily on them, but rather it would need to take into account the rest of the architecture and decoration. On the other hand, the prisoner statues do have the potential to contribute to such investigations, and here I would like to highlight two observations that can be drawn from my conclusions above.

---

121. See further Darrell Baker, *The Encyclopedia of the Egyptian Pharaohs*, vol. 1 (Oakville: Bannerstone, 2008), 295–97.
122. Depending on when the "smiting" occurred and the age of Pepi II, this might have been necessary.
123. While previous scholars have suggested that smiting rituals may have been part of coronation rituals, Schoske largely dismissed this (Schoske, "Erschlagen der Feinde," 463–64).
124. See ch. 5.4 above.
125. Nils Billing, *The Performative Structure: Ritualizing the Pyramid of Pepy I*, HES 4 (Leiden: Brill, 2018). Katherine Eaton also used Bell's theoretical framework in her study of the depiction of cult rituals on New Kingdom temple walls (Katherine Eaton, *Ancient Egyptian Temple Ritual: Performance, Patterns, and Practice*, Routledge Studies in Egyptology 1 [London: Routledge, 2013]).
126. Billing, *Performative Structure*, 548.

First, the Pepi I and Pepi II prisoner statues demonstrate the difficulties with trying to distinguish rituals for the living king from ones for the deceased ruler and rituals of kingship from mortuary rituals. In his analysis of the Old Kingdom mortuary temple, Billing differentiated between ritualized space and rituals that were intended for the divine ruler and those for the transfigured, deceased ruler.[127] But rituals involving the prisoner statues could have benefited both aspects of the king. This is particularly clear for the prisoner statues of Pepi II. Smiting was closely tied to kingship, and Pepi II or his successor must have at least sanctioned the "smiting" of the prisoner statues, if not performed it. In this way, the "smiting" would have served to benefit the living king and the royal *ka*, and it probably occurred as part of rituals of kingship. Yet, as I described above, the monumentalization of the "smiting" in the form of the annihilated statue fragments enabled the deceased king to perpetually reenact the "smiting." Moreover, the slaughtered remains of his enemies that remained scattered throughout the complex served as magical offerings to him that nourished him and helped him transition to the afterlife. The ritualized context of the Pepi I and Pepi II prisoner statues cannot be understood as solely for the benefit of the living or deceased king or as solely part of royal or mortuary cult. Once again, modern attempts to reconstruct the ritual life need to allow for the overlapping and intertwining of these rituals in regard to their purpose.

This implies that the ritualized space of the pyramid complex cannot be categorized clearly either, as Massimiliano Nuzzolo has also observed.[128] In other words, rituals concerned with specific aspects of the king were not consistently confined to distinct areas. The prisoner statues of Pepi II were set throughout this king's valley temple, mortuary temple, and perhaps even along parts of his causeway, as I argued in chapter 4. Therefore all of these areas were settings for ritualized activity that benefited both the living and deceased king. Scholars have to be wary of assuming that particular parts of each monument, especially everything except the pyramid and royal tomb itself, were only intended for a single aspect of the king or his cult.

Secondly, the change in the treatment of the Pepi I and Pepi II prisoner statues, both in regard to earlier prisoner statues and from the complex of Pepi I to that of Pepi II, demonstrates that the ritual life of the late Old Kingdom pyramid complex was dynamic.[129] Like the decoration and architecture of these monuments, the rituals themselves were not fully standardized but could shift and change to accommodate the needs and desires of their owner. The rituals certainly included particular requirements, and there was continuity from complex to complex, just as the architecture and decoration of the pyramid complex included set elements. But within this larger framework, there seems to have been opportunities for the king and his priests to innovate, reimagine, and experiment with the monument's ritualization in order to better serve the needs of the pharaoh.

The Pyramid Texts also testify to this.[130] The choice of spells, their editing, and their layout changed from complex to complex. The priests, designers, and possibly the king of each monument had a role in this. This should not simply be understood as reflecting changes in pyramid design, but differences in the ritualistic interests inherent within each complex. While the relationship between the Pyramid Texts and

---

127. Billing, 49–52 and 548.

128. Nuzzolo, *Fifth Dynasty Sun Temples*, 23. See also Gerhard Haeny, "New Kingdom 'Mortuary Temples' and 'Mansions of Millions of Years,'" in Shafer, *Temples of Ancient Egypt*, 86–90.

129. Billing made the same observation regarding the Old Kingdom pyramid complex despite arguing that there were distinct patterns in the spatial organization, themes, and activities overall (Billing, *Performative Structure*, 31–32). Concerning ritual dynamism, see C. Bell, *Ritual: Perspectives and Dimensions*, 210–52 and C. Bell, *Ritual Theory, Ritual Practice*, 118–68.

130. The literature on the Pyramid Texts is immense. In addition to Billing, which is cited above, see especially Hays, *Organization* and Allen, *Ancient Egyptian Pyramid Texts*. See also n. 31 in ch. 2.

the ritual life of the monuments is complex and extremely difficult to reconstruct, the changes in the Pyramid Texts, like the changes in the prisoner statues, suggest that the ritualization of each monument was also flexible. Priests and the king may have emphasized some rituals over others, developed new versions or aspects of them, or reused and reinterpreted earlier ones. How the monuments functioned during each king's lifetime and following his death, like its architecture and decoration, was not stagnant or static.

Chapter 6
Conclusion

The prisoner statues were evocative symbols of ancient Egyptian kingship. In their form, they vividly illustrated one of the most important duties of the king, namely, to defeat any and all threats to Egypt and the cosmos. At the same time, the various developments that the genre underwent throughout the late Old Kingdom reflect contemporaneous changes in the conception of kingship. For example, the number of prisoner statues that kings set in their pyramid complexes increased as their role in society shifted. A king's pyramid complex was the primary building project that he commissioned during his reign. Significant resources, labor, and planning went into its execution. As such, it is not surprising that these monuments, and the statuary set inside of them, reveal contemporary concerns. They were not conventional construction projects, but enormous undertakings that were of upmost importance to the king.

The prisoner statues demonstrate how dynamic these monuments were throughout the late Old Kingdom. The architecture, decoration, and ritualization of each complex were distinct and diverse. Today, the scanty archaeological remains can obscure this variability; as piles of stone and rubble lying in the desert and surrounded by varying amounts of debris, the late Old Kingdom pyramid complexes do all look somewhat alike. But enough remains to indicate that back in the Fifth and Sixth Dynasties, when cult was still being performed within the temples, statuary still stood in its original place, and the paint on the walls remained bright, each king's complex was unique and reflected his individual priorities and interests, as well as those of his architects and artists. Some of the variations and changes between pyramid complexes may appear minor through the lens of thousands of years. But this does not mean that they were minor or meaningless to those who initiated them.

For this reason, there is a need for future studies that evaluate each pyramid complex separately, and to fully understand the monument, studies must take into consideration all that remains of the complex's architecture and decoration. Furthermore, the archaeological remains need to be situated against the historical backdrop and what is known about the king who commissioned the monument and the society in which he lived; this approach sheds light on the choices that were made for his funerary complex and the factors that influenced them. The prisoner statues are part of this scholarly endeavor. They were important elements of these monuments, and in this way, they contribute to our understanding of the late Old Kingdom. This volume is only an introduction in this regard; by showing some of the new interpretations of and insight into late Old Kingdom art and culture that the prisoner statues make possible, it aims to initiate future inquiries.

There were major differences between the earliest prisoner statues that were in the pyramid complexes of Niuserre and Djedkare-Isesi and the prisoner statues of Pepi I and Pepi II, who were the last kings to commission prisoner statues. A particularly notable one concerns the backs of the statues. The back pillars of the Niuserre and Djedkare prisoner statues emphasize these statues' close relationship with the two-dimensional decoration of the pyramid complex. When the prisoner statues first appeared in the mid-Fifth Dynasty, they were innovative three-dimensional representations that the artists carved based on a traditional two-dimensional motif, namely, the bound captive. The back pillars emphasized their decorative function within the pyramid complex, and these prisoner statues stood close to reliefs featuring similar themes, namely, the king triumphing over his enemies, in Niuserre's valley temple and in Djedkare's mortuary temple.

Over time, the form of the prisoner statues evolved, and the prisoner statues also took on additional roles within the pyramid complex. While they continued to embellish mortuary temples, they were used in other ways as well, and they developed new meanings. By the reign of Teti, artists were no longer carving back pillars, and throughout the Sixth Dynasty, the artists experimented with ways to better convey the discomfort and pain of the prisoner statues' bound and kneeling position. At the same time, the facial features of the prisoner statues began to show the influence of the expressive Second Style, through attributes like wide eyes, slight smiles, and prominent nasolabial folds. Doing away with the back pillar may also be tied to the Second Style. Statues carved in this style tend to have any stone representing negative space carved away, making the bodies appear more active and lively. While the negative space of the Sixth Dynasty prisoner statues is not carved away, the full carving of their backs may reflect an interest in further freeing the form from the stone, which is consistent with the aims of the Second Style. Additionally, the change in the treatment of the backs could reflect a new position for the statues within the pyramid complex.

By the reign of Pepi I, the back-pillar-less prisoner statues had developed a more active role within the pyramid complex, as they became part of the mortuary temple's ritual life as well as its decoration. The artists decapitated these prisoner statues in order to complete them. The heads and bodies were then ritually offered to the king. In their decapitated form, the Pepi I prisoner statues were also monumental images of the deceased king's annihilated enemies who are frequently referenced in the Pyramid Texts.

This change in the treatment of the prisoner statues coincided with an increase in the number of statues and a change in the representation of their ethnicity; in this way, the reign of Pepi I was a pivotal period for the prisoner statues. As I discussed in chapter 2, Pepi I had at least sixteen to twenty prisoner statues; this is significantly more than the number of statues that his predecessors had. Additionally, the prisoner statues of his predecessors had the stereotypical facial features and hairstyles with which the Egyptians traditionally depicted foreigners.[1] On the other hand, the artists of Pepi I mixed and matched different, non-Egyptian hairstyles and facial features among the heads in order to create a variety of imaginary foreigners. Both in their number and in the treatment of their ethnicity, the Pepi I prisoner statues demonstrate an interest in multiplicity. For the first time at this complex, there was a desire to show many different and distinct enemies of the king. In doing this, the power of the king was also emphasized. Not only had he defeated the known foreign world, which was typically categorized into Nubians, Libyans, and Asiatics, but he also triumphed over all imaginable foreigners.

Indeed, reimaging the ethnicity of the prisoner statues may have also been a way to more comprehensively visualize the king's enemies in this world and the next. These prisoner statues could have simultaneously represented living foreigners and otherworldly rebels and evil beings, such as those who threaten the deceased king in the Pyramid Texts. In this regard, it seems significant that the change in ethnicity first occurred at the same complex in which the prisoner statues were decapitated, namely, the complex of Pepi I. As mentioned above, the decapitation linked these prisoner statues to the deceased kings' enemies who are described in the Pyramid Texts. The statues' ambiguous foreignness, if it symbolized inimical beings in all realms of the cosmos, may have been another way to strengthen this association.

---

1. As I discussed in ch. 3.3, the change in the treatment of the prisoner statues' ethnicity might be evident among Teti's prisoner statues, but this is inconclusive. It is more likely that the new treatment began at the complex of Pepi I.

Yet, the new treatment of ethnicity among the Pepi I prisoner statues primarily was a result of the change in the nature of foreign interactions that occurred during the Sixth Dynasty. The Egyptians, particularly the elite, were more aware of and engaged with foreigners at this time than they had been previously in the Old Kingdom. This impacted conceptions of ethnic and cultural identity, and the generic and imaginary foreignness of the prisoner statues reflects this. The prisoner statues demonstrate the artists' desire to visualize the increasingly broad and culturally complex world in which they lived.

Consequently, the capital must have still been in close contact with the provinces despite the gradual decentralization that occurred during the Sixth Dynasty, as I described in chapter 2. In the Sixth Dynasty, foreign relations were increasingly the purview of the elite, particularly provincial high officials, as I outlined in chapter 3. Yet, the prisoner statues show that the royal artists, who were working and living in the capital, had knowledge of and were affected by events happening in more remote places. Therefore, despite their increasing independence, provincial officials were still communicating with the central administration and regularly traveling to the capital, where they would have shared news of foreign affairs and their experiences with the elite who lived there, including the artists. Indeed, tomb inscriptions directly reference this; for example, the letter from Pepi II that the high official Harkhuf had inscribed in his tomb in Qubbet el-Hawa, near Elephantine, instructs Harkhuf to travel to the capital directly after returning from his expedition to Yam.[2] As discussed in chapter 2, status and power was slowly moving into the hands of high officials in different parts of the country, but this process initially occurred under the direction of the king. The gradual decentralization, which occurred throughout the late Old Kingdom, particularly during the Sixth Dynasty, did not result in the capital's loss of authority until following the reign of Pepi II, and the prisoner statues further testify to this. Even if the king's power was diminishing as his role shifted, the capital was aware of and involved with events happening throughout the country.

The artists of Pepi II's prisoner statues chose to depict the ethnicity of these statues in the same fashion as that of the Pepi I prisoner statues, namely, with mixed and matched hairstyles and facial features in order to portray a large assortment of generic foreigners. Indeed, Pepi II had dozens of prisoner statues, more than any of his predecessors. At the same time, the ritualized context of Pepi II's prisoner statues shifted. These statues, which were set in not only this king's mortuary temple but also his valley temple and possibly parts of his causeway, were not decapitated but instead subjected to something akin to a royal smiting ritual during which they were violently smashed apart. This ritual likely took place as part of a broader ritualized sequence or event, such as one of Pepi II's *sed* festivals. The change in their treatment may demonstrate increasing emphasis on the mundane in regard to the prisoner statues rather than the religious realm, which was so important for Pepi I's prisoner statues. The "smiting" of the Pepi II prisoner statues was apotropaic and had stronger execrative overtones than the decapitation of the Pepi I prisoner statues. Moreover, execration rituals became much more common during the reign of Pepi II than they had been before, as I mentioned in chapter 5. This also seems to be a reflection of the increasingly complex world in which the Egyptians lived, and the growing hostility between them and Nubians living to the south. The prisoner statues, like the execration figurines, testify to a more bellicose environment by the end of the Sixth Dynasty.

***

The prisoner statues reflect the agency of those who were responsible for commissioning, designing, and carving them. They are the products of beliefs, conversations, and decisions that particular ancient Egyptians had and made. It can be easy to overlook this when we study static monuments from the distant past. For example, we may note similarities and differences between pyramid complexes and question their

---

2. Strudwick, *Texts*, 331–33.

significance, but we sometimes forget that people, not time periods or regions or styles, were responsible for the variations. Certainly, time and place, and many other factors, influenced individuals' decisions and choices, but we cannot lose sight of the ancient Egyptians in our analyses of ancient Egypt.

Throughout this volume, I have frequently referred to the artists of the prisoner statues. Although the king was responsible for commissioning the statues and the statues were made for him and to his liking, one should not dismiss the role of the artists in determining how the prisoner statues ultimately looked and functioned inside the pyramid complex. The relationship between the king, the high officials overseeing the monument's construction, the architects and engineers designing and building the monument, and the artists decorating it, would have been complex and multifaceted. Some kings may have been more involved and interested in the process than others. But in all cases, the artists also had a degree of agency as they were the ones who actually carved the statues.[3]

There are certain decisions regarding the prisoner statues that we can conclude, with a relatively strong degree of confidence, the king must have made. For example, the increasing numbers of prisoner statues at the complexes of Pepi I and Pepi II must have been at the request of these kings. More prisoner statues required additional resources, and the king's approval would have been necessary to acquire these. Moreover, the statues were symbols of kingship, and they were a way for Pepi I and Pepi II to emphasize their authority and status visually, ideologically, and magically at a time when this was fading in reality, as I discussed in chapter 2. The fact that the large number of prisoner statues coincided with the change in the nature of foreign interactions that occurred in the Sixth Dynasty may also reflect the king's knowledge of and concern with new foreign threats. Ultimately there were a larger number of prisoner statues at the pyramid complexes of Pepi I and Pepi II than at the complexes of previous kings because Pepi I and Pepi II wanted or felt that they needed more statues.

On the other hand, the artists of Pepi I were responsible for the change in the treatment of ethnicity among these prisoner statues, as I argued in chapter 3, and the artists of Pepi II's prisoner statues chose to employ this same technique rather than using the traditional Old Kingdom foreigner stereotypes. The king probably approved these decisions, either directly or via his high officials who oversaw the monument's construction, but the artists initiated them. And this new technique for depicting foreignness reflected the artists' experiences, particularly the increasingly diverse world in which they, as elite Egyptians, lived, just as the increasing number of prisoner statues were a repercussion of the king's own interests and concerns.

It is more difficult to ascertain who was responsible for the change in the original placement of the prisoner statues over time. One might imagine that the monuments' architects had a say in this, as well as the artists and the kings. Similarly who decided on the treatment of the prisoner statues at the pyramid complexes of Pepi I and Pepi II and developed their ritualistic roles in these monuments? These were major changes; they were much more radical than the change in the method of representing the prisoner statues' ethnicity, which was innovative but did not fundamentally alter the statues since they still depicted foreigners and enemies. Therefore, even though the artists carried out the decapitation of the Pepi I prisoner statues, it seems unlikely that they conceived of it on their own. Ritualists and priests must have been involved, and the king undoubtedly had a say in the matter as well. Indeed, the "smiting" of the Pepi II prisoner statues might be more attributable to the king than the decapitation of the Pepi I prisoner statues

---

3. In regard to the question of tradition and creativity in ancient Egyptian art, which is relevant to my comments here, see Dimitri Laboury, "Tradition and Creativity: Toward a Study of Intericonicity in Ancient Egyptian Art," in *(Re)productive Traditions in Ancient Egypt: Proceedings of the Conference Held at the University of Liège, 6th–8th February 2013*, ed. Todd Gillen, Collection Ægyptiaca Leodiensia 10 (Liège: Presses Universitaires de Liège, 2017), 229–58.

since smiting was a royal prerogative. Regardless, it is perhaps best to understand the change in the treatment of the Pepi I and Pepi II prisoner statues as the result of conversations and collaboration between multiple individuals.

How was knowledge of the prisoner statues passed down from generation to generation? Theories of cultural memory and intericonicity/interpictoriality are significant in this regard, and the prisoner statues deserve further study within these theoretical frameworks than what is possible here.[4] In this book, I have aimed to show that the prisoner statues changed over time and to consider why this was the case by analyzing the larger historical context of these changes. But an additional line of inquiry, which would productively build upon this volume, would be the mechanisms through which these changes occurred. In other words, how did the Egyptians decide what was traditional and what could be changed, and how was this information communicated over time? This question is relevant not only for the prisoner statues but also for the late Old Kingdom pyramid complexes in general. The reign of a king was not a single moment in time. It spanned years, and in the case of particular kings, such as Pepi II who probably reigned for at least sixty years, more than a single generation. When during Pepi II's reign were his prisoner statues carved? Were they all carved at a single time, or did he repeatedly commission prisoner statues? When was the decision to "smite" them made? His sculptors used the technique to depict the statues' foreignness that the sculptors of Pepi I had invented. How did the sculptors of Pepi II know about this technique and how to execute it? Did certain artists work on the prisoner statues of more than one king? Future studies on the identities and working processes of Old Kingdom artists might help answer some of these questions.[5]

In this way, more work remains to be done on the prisoner statues. This book was intended to open doors to this rather than to serve as the final word on the statues. There is no doubt that the prisoner statues were meaningful and important to the late Old Kingdom Egyptians because they dedicated significant labor and resources to carving them and these statues were primary features of the late Old Kingdom pyramid complexes. Consequently, it is only through including the prisoner statues in our analyses of the late Old Kingdom that we will be able to move closer to unraveling this dynamic period of ancient Egyptian history.

---

4. In regard to cultural memory, see further Jan Assmann, *Cultural Memory and Early Civilization: Writing, Remembrance, and Political Imagination*, trans. David Henry Wilson (Cambridge: Cambridge University Press, 2011). For intericonicity and interpictoriality, see recently Laboury, "Tradition and Creativity," 247–54 and Gabriele Pieke, "Lost in Transformation: Artistic Creation between Permanence and Change," in Gillen, *(Re)productive Traditions*, 259–304.

5. Recent studies in this regard for later time periods include Dimitri Laboury, "Designers and Makers of Ancient Egyptian Monumental Epigraphy," in *The Oxford Handbook of Egyptian Epigraphy and Paleography*, ed. Vanesssa Davies and Dimitri Laboury (New York: Oxford University Press, 2020), 85–101 and Gianluca Miniaci et al., ed., *The Arts of Making in Ancient Egypt: Voices, Images, and Objects of Material Producers 2000–1500 BC* (Leiden: Sidestone, 2018).

Appendix
The Unprovenanced Prisoner Statues

In addition to the prisoner statue fragments that archaeologists excavated from the pyramid complexes of Niuserre, Djedkare-Isesi, Unas, Teti, Pepi I, and Pepi II, which are the focus of this volume, there are several unprovenanced examples in museum collections as well as a few statues that are attested only in photographs.[1] Because of their insecure provenance, the limited amount of information available for many of them, and the considerable reconstruction to which three of them were subjected, I discuss them separately here and propose from which complex they most likely came.

A.1. The Prisoner Statues from the Diniacopoulos Collection

Two of the most well known prisoner statues, which happen to be unprovenanced, are in the Metropolitan Museum of Art (New York, MMA 47.2 and 64.260; C.7.3 and C.7.4; figs. 1.2 and 1.4).[2] Both were reconstructed and heavily restored from multiple fragments before the Museum purchased them, with the heads likely being placed onto bodies to which they did not originally belong. Early scholars first dated these statues to the Fifth or Sixth Dynasty.[3] However, after Ahmed Fakhry recognized a similarity between them and the prisoner statues that Hussein had discovered at the pyramid complex of Djedkare-Isesi in the 1940s, Egyptologists began assigning the Met prisoner statues to the Djedkare complex.[4] Marsha Hill then refuted this attribution in 1999 and argued that, based on both stylistic comparison and archival records, they had originally come from the pyramid complex of Pepi II.[5]

---

1. Additionally, I have found entries for a prisoner statue and two prisoner statue heads in auction catalogues (Boisgirard & Associés, *Arts d'Orient*, Hôtel Drouot, Paris, June 16–17, 2005 [Paris: Boisgirard & Associés, 2005], 41, cat. no. 109 and Olivier Coutau-Bégarie, *Archéologie: Egyptienne et Gréco-Romaine*, Drouot Richelieu, Paris, December 1, 1993 [Paris: Olivier Coutau-Bégarie, 1993], 21, cat. no. 157–58). I have not been able to locate any of these objects. However, based on the catalogue entry and photograph of the statue that Boisgirard & Associés listed, there are some stylistic inconsistencies between this and the other prisoner statues. Moreover, its size, which the catalogue lists as 38.2 cm, and its condition, which seems to be complete and largely undamaged, would be highly unusual.

2. I discussed these statues in greater detail in Prakash, "Prisoner Statues." The measurements of MMA 47.2 are H. 88.5 cm; W. 33 cm; D. 49.5 cm, and those of MMA 64.260 are H. 86.7 cm; W. 31.5 cm; D. 40.5 cm.

3. Lansing tentatively dated MMA 47.2 to the reign of Pepi I on stylistic grounds (Lansing, "An Old Kingdom Captive") while Hayes dated it to the Sixth Dynasty (Hayes, *Scepter of Egypt*, 1:115). In 1965, Fischer suggested that both MMA 47.2 and 64.260 had originally stood in one of the royal pyramid temples of the Fifth or early Sixth Dynasty at Saqqara (Fischer, "Egyptian Art," 53).

4. Henry Fischer first published this attribution in *Ancient Egyptian Representations of Turtles*, 18 n. 45. Following that, see Bothmer, "On Realism," 378–79; Lauer, "Recherches...1967–1968 et 1968–1969," 477; Lauer, "Statues de prisonniers," 42; Lauer, "Travaux...1968–1969," 22; PM 3:424; and Verner, "Statuettes de prisonniers," 146–47. See further Prakash, "Prisoner Statues," 203–5.

5. Hill, "173. Kneeling Captive" and Hill, "174. Kneeling Captive."

My research supports Hill's conclusion.[6] Indeed, on stylistic grounds alone, the Djedkare attribution can be solidly dismissed because the Met statues do not have back pillars. Instead these statues share numerous features with the Pepi II prisoner statues, which I list here. First, the Met statues were very well finished with minimal tool marks visible, like the Pepi II prisoner statues. Second, the modeling of the Met statues' chests and backs is also most similar to the Pepi II statues. Third, the Met statues' very large buttocks and thighs, combined with lower legs and feet that are disproportionately small, is most like the two reconstructed Pepi II statues in the Grand Egyptian Museum (GEM 1101; C.6.1; fig. 2.22) and the Suez National Museum (JE 51729; C.6.7; fig. 2.23). Indeed, the treatment of the feet of all four statues is extremely similar; they are small and thin, but fully carved and rounded with three toes carved on the outside of the feet, which are curled underneath the body. Fourth, the shape, finish, and size of the Met bases is analogous to the bases of the reconstructed Pepi II statues. Fifth, the legs of the Met statues are held together, and their arm bonds consist of four strands of rope carved completely around their arms, like the legs and arm bonds of GEM 1101 and JE 51729. Sixth, the strands of rope comprising the lashings of two of the Pepi II prisoner statues, namely, JE 51729 and Cairo, Egyptian Museum JE 45782 (C.6.3), are not completely vertical, in contrast to all of the Pepi I prisoner statues that have lashings with strands of rope, which are vertical; rather, the rope on the backs of JE 51729 and JE 45782 have a slight diagonal toward the left (figs. 2.23 and 2.24). This is exactly the way in which the lashings of MMA 47.2 were carved. Finally, MMA 64.260 has a thumbnail incised on his left hand, and MMA 47.2 has a line denoting the bottom of a thumbnail still visible on his damaged left hand; the only other prisoner statue to have a carved thumbnail is GEM 1101, who has this feature preserved on his right thumb. The left foot of MMA 47.2 also has incised toenails.[7] Overall, this interest in detail is most in keeping with the prisoner statues of Pepi II.

Similarly, the facial features of the Met prisoner statues most closely resemble those of the prisoner statues from the complex of Pepi II.[8] MMA 47.2 has an oval face with fleshy cheeks (Type 2), while MMA 64.260's face is much more tapered with higher cheekbones (Type 4; see table 11). 47.2's eyes are consistent with the "narrow and upward tilt" eye type (Type 2) at the Pepi II complex, while 64.260's eyes are very similar to the "large shape with incised outline" eye type (Type 1; see table 13). Moreover, both of the Met statues have "long" noses (Type 3) and "sharp vermillion borders" mouths (Type 1), types also found among the Pepi II prisoner statues (see tables 14 and 15). In regard to hairstyles, MMA 47.2 wears a plain, helmet-like hairstyle that is similar to that of C.6.9 from the Pepi II complex (fig. 3.19). On the other hand, MMA 64.260's hairstyle is the "wavy" type (Type 1), like Cairo, Egyptian Museum JE 57202 (C.6.4), Cairo, National Military Museum JE 51731 (C.6.6), and C.6.8 from the Pepi II complex (figs. 3.15, 3.17, and 3.18; see table 9). 64.260 also has a triangular beard that is similar to the one that Cairo, Egyptian Museum JE 45781 (C.6.2) wears, although 64.260's beard is slightly more tapered and was better carved (fig. 3.14). Most of MMA 47.2's chin beard is missing, but traces of it remain along his neck and throat.

Archival documents further support this attribution and suggest that the fragments that comprise the statues were unearthed from around the pyramid of Pepi II's queen Oudjebten and had originally been

---

6. Prakash, "Prisoner Statues," 202–6.

7. MMA 47.2's right foot has suffered more damage, and it is not clear whether or not he originally had toenails on this foot as well.

8. Multiple Egyptologists have described the faces of the Met prisoner statues as realistic and expressive (Bothmer, "On Realism," 379; Hayes, *Scepter of Egypt*, 1:115; Lansing, "An Old Kingdom Captive," 152; and Vandier, *Manuel*, 3:138). Yet, for the reasons I outlined in ch. 3, the Met prisoner statues are not portraits, and their expressiveness is due to the late Old Kingdom style. See further Prakash, "The Prisoner Statues," 206–9.

part of prisoner statues that stood in Pepi II's mortuary temple.⁹ Prior to their reconstruction, the fragments had been in the collection of the antiquities dealers, the Khawam brothers.¹⁰ Then in the 1920s, Vincent Diniacopoulos, an antiquities dealer, collector, and restorer, began working with the Khawam brothers.¹¹ Diniacopoulos and the brothers seem to have co-owned the Met prisoner statues, and Diniacopoulos was responsible for their restoration and sale.

Over the course of the twentieth century, Diniacopoulos also restored a third prisoner statue, which he certainly co-owned with the Khawam brothers; this statue is now in the British Museum (BM EA 75198; C.7.2; fig. A.1).¹² As he did for the Met statues, Diniacopoulos seems to have connected a prisoner statue head, which is a much smaller and more poorly preserved fragment than the heads of the Met statues, to a discrete prisoner statue body. Ultimately, there are misleading aspects of Diniacopoulos' restoration for all three statues, and the degree to which he intervened with them is significant.¹³ As a result, scholars need to approach the Met and BM prisoner statues carefully and use them critically when drawing conclusions on the prisoner statues in general.

Although the body and head likely did not originally belong to the same statue, archival documents and stylistic comparison demonstrate that the BM prisoner statue head and body have the same

Figure A.1. Reconstructed prisoner statue probably from the pyramid complex of Pepi II in Saqqara; Sixth Dynasty. London, BM EA 75198. Photograph ©The Trustees of the British Museum, All rights reserved.

---

9. Prakash, "Prisoner Statues," 202–3.

10. Concerning the Khawam brothers, see further Fredrik Norland Hagen and Kim Ryholt, *The Antiquities Trade in Egypt 1880–1930: The H.O. Lange Papers* (Copenhagen: Det Kongelige Danske Videnskabernes Selskab, 2016), 228–29 and Morris Bierbrier, *Who Was Who in Egyptology?*, 4th rev. ed. (London: Egypt Exploration Society, 2012), 294. Concerning the antiquities trade in Egypt during the early twentieth century, see Hagen and Ryholt and Fredrik Norland Hagen and Kim Ryholt, "The Antiquities Trade in Egypt during the Time of Rudolf Mosse," in *Mosse im Museum: Die Stiftungstätigkeit des Berliner Verlegers Rudolf Mosse (1843–1920) für das Ägyptische Museum Berlin*, ed. Jana Helmbold-Doyé and Thomas Gertzen (Berlin: Hentrich & Hentrich, 2017), 59–74.

11. Concerning Diniacopoulos, his family, and their antiquities collection, see further Nadine Blumer, *Finding Home: The Diniacopoulos Family and Collection* (Montreal: Concordia University, 2017); Bierbrier, 154–55; John Fossey and Jane Francis, eds., *The Diniacopoulos Collection in Québec: Greek and Roman Antiquities* (Montreal: Concordia University, 2004); Jane Francis and George Harrison, eds., *Life and Death in Ancient Egypt: The Diniacopoulos Collection* (Montreal: Concordia University, 2011); Hagen and Ryholt, *Antiquities Trade*, 210; and Hagen and Ryholt, "Antiquities Trade," 66.

12. I discussed this statue more fully in Prakash, "Prisoner Statues." The measurements of the reconstructed statue are: H. 86.5 cm; W. 29 cm; D. 41 cm.

13. See Prakash, "Prisoner Statues," 195–98.

provenance as the Met prisoner statues' heads and bodies, namely, the pyramid complex of Pepi II. As for the Met statues, BM EA 75198's overall proportions, with small feet and lower legs in contrast to a thick, heavy buttocks and upper legs, is most similar to the reconstructed Pepi II statues in the Grand Egyptian Museum (GEM 1101; C.6.1; fig. 2.22) and the Suez National Museum (JE 51729; C.6.7; fig. 2.23). His position and well-finished back, with a line down the center emphasizing the tightly pulled back arms, are also most similar to the other Pepi II prisoner statues, as is the shape and size of the base on which he kneels. In regard to his head, his facial features most resemble those of the Pepi II prisoner statues as well. For example, the outer corner of his right eye, which seems to be original, demonstrates that the artists attempted to carve his brow in relief, as they did for JE 57202 (C.6.4; fig. 3.15) and JE 51731 (C.6.6; fig. 3.17; see table 12). His eyes are also most like the "narrow and upward tilt" type (Type 2) that JE 51729 and JE 51731 have (figs. 2.23 and 3.17; see table 13). On the other hand, his mouth, which is somewhat like the "sharp vermillion borders" type (Type 1) that Cairo, National Military Museum JE 51730 (C.6.5), JE 51731 and C.6.9 have, is more unique (figs. 3.16, 3.17, and 3.19; see table 15). It is straight with a very sharp vermillion border, but the vermillion upper and lower lips are flat and taper inwards rather than swell outwards.

The BM prisoner statue clearly demonstrates that there was a range in detail and execution among the prisoner statues from the Pepi II complex; ultimately, this is a characteristic of all of the prisoner statues. For example, BM EA 75198 appears to be less finished than most of the other Pepi II statues: there are no bonds on his upper arms and the back restraint is a plain bar without lashings.[14] Additionally, BM EA 75198's kilt has not been fully carved either. There is no line across his legs to indicate the bottom of the kilt, and instead only the triangle of stone representing negative space between his legs indicates its presence.[15] Finally, the feet of BM EA 75198 curl underneath him and are very similar in shape and size to those of JE 51729 (C.6.7), GEM 1101 (C.6.1), and both Met statues (C.7.3 and C.7.4), but the artists did not depict individual toes on the outside of his feet, as they did for all of the others (figs. 1.2, 1.4, 2.22, and 2.23).

A.2. A Prisoner Statue Head in Brussels

A little known limestone head that is currently in the Musées Royaux d'Art et d'Histoire in Brussels (E.07967; C.7.1) certainly came from a prisoner statue (fig. A.2).[16] Its style, material, condition, and scale suggest this. Moreover, a small portion of the raised left shoulder remains attached to the left side of the head. The position of this shoulder shows that the attached arm had been pulled back, thereby confirming that the Brussels head is indeed the head of a prisoner statue, who would have been kneeling with his arms bound behind his back, and the remains of a chin beard verify that he is a foreigner. Stylistically the Brussels head is comparable to the heads of Sixth Dynasty prisoner statues, and it probably came from the pyramid complex of Pepi II.

---

14. Some of these features, which share the fact that they are less detailed treatments, resemble aspects of certain prisoner statues from the pyramid complex of Pepi I, which were generally less finished than the Pepi II prisoner statues. Yet, for the other reasons I described above regarding the archival records, the amount of material circulating in Cairo from the Pepi II complex during the early twentieth century, and overall stylistic comparison, the body of BM EA 75198 most likely came from the Pepi II complex and was a poorer-quality or less-finished example.

15. Most of this negative space is reconstructed, but a small amount of stone on the inside of BM EA 75198's left thigh proves that the negative space was an original feature.

16. I presented portions of this section in Tara Prakash, "From Saqqara to Brussels: A Head from a Sixth Dynasty Prisoner Statue in the Musées Royaux d'Art et d'Histoire," *CdE* 189 (2020): 5–19, where I discussed this head in greater detail. The dimensions of the head are H. 24 cm; W. 19 cm; D. 20.5 cm.

The face is very badly damaged, a point to which I will return. Thus, all of the facial features are obscured. However, from what remains, it is clear that the head was carved in the late Old Kingdom style, like the heads from the Teti, Pepi I, and Pepi II complexes. He has deeply incised inner canthi that extend diagonally down, and the outer canthus of the right eye also comes to a point and extends out. The eyes appear to be slightly angled, and, based on the better-preserved right eye, at least the lower lid was rimmed in subtle relief. The eyebrows also seem to have been carved in delicate relief. He has a broad nose with a narrow bridge and fleshy nasolabial folds. His small, narrow mouth turns up a bit. All of these features are similar to those of the other Sixth Dynasty prisoner statues, and stylistically, this head could be from the complex of Teti, Pepi I, or Pepi II.

Additional elements support a Sixth Dynasty date for the Brussels head and tentatively point toward the head as originally having been part of a prisoner statue from the pyramid complex of Pepi II. According to the museum records, the head was purchased from the well-known antiquities dealer Phocion Jean Tano in Cairo and registered into the museum collection on November 13, 1954.[17] The sale itself probably occurred in 1952.[18] I have found no indications of when or how Tano acquired the head, and the acquisition history does not rule out any of the Sixth Dynasty pyramid complexes. However, since there were a number of prisoner statue fragments from the complex of Pepi II that were circulating around Cairo and were on the antiquities market in the early twentieth century, as I mentioned above, it seems conceivable that the Brussels head was also from this complex.

Figure A.2. Prisoner statue head probably from the pyramid complex of Pepi II in Saqqara; Sixth Dynasty. Brussels, Musées Royaux d'Art et d'Histoire E.07967. Photograph ©KMKG-MRAH.

The height of the Brussels prisoner statue head is 24 cm. The best preserved Pepi I prisoner statue heads are between 20–21 cm in height. While most of the Pepi II heads are a similar height, the height of JE 45781 (C.6.2)'s head is 26 cm. In contrast, the height of the Teti head (Saqqara, Imhotep Museum JE 40047; C.4.1) is only 14 cm. Therefore the Brussels head fits best among the Pepi II heads, which generally may be slightly taller than the Pepi I heads.

The Brussels head has a tiered hairstyle. This includes a longer top layer with vertical segments that progressively widen toward the bottom. However, rather than meeting on the top of his head, as the segments of the tiered hairstyles of the Pepi I prisoner statues did, the top of this hairstyle is an uncarved, roughly circular area (in the catalogue, compare C.5.16, C.5.19, and C.5.32 with C.7.1).[19] This resembles the heads of GEM 1101 (C.6.1) and JE 51729 (C.6.7) from the Pepi II complex (figs. 2.22 and 2.23). Furthermore, all of the preserved tiered hairstyles from the Pepi I complex have only a single layer at the front of the head, above the forehead. Below the longer top layer, the Brussels head also has a second shorter layer above his forehead. With multiple layers at the front of his head, the Brussels head recalls the "multiple front layers above the forehead" type of tiered hairstyle (Subtype 1) from the Pepi II pyramid complex (see

---

17. Concerning the Tano family, see Hagen and Ryholt, *Antiquities Trade*, 20, 37, 57, 65–76, 118–19, 124, 140, 175, and 265–67; Hagen and Ryholt, "Antiquities Trade," 63 and 69–70; Bierbrier, *Who Was Who*, 533–34; and Robert Merrillees, *The Tano Family: Gifts from the Nile to Cyprus* (Lefkosia: Moufflon, 2003).

18. Luc Delvaux (curator, Musées Royaux d'Art et d'Histoire), pers. comm.

19. https://doi.org/10.5913/2022877

table 10).²⁰ The front of his hairstyle, by the right side of his face, has been fully carved into the appropriate layers and segments, but the front part on the left side of his face was never finished and remains a flat surface. One might compare this to JE 45781 (C.6.2) from the Pepi II complex, whose hairstyle was left uncarved along both sides of his face (fig. 3.14). Overall the Brussels head's hairstyle and facial features most closely resemble those of other Pepi II prisoner statue heads.

The poor condition of the Brussels head, which I referenced above, also suggests an attribution to the Pepi II complex over the Pepi I or Teti complexes. As I described in chapter 5.2.5, the heads from the Pepi II complex are in much worse condition than the heads from any other complex. They may show signs of defacement, and many of the faces are largely obliterated. The condition of the Brussels head, whose left side is mostly gone and whose face is disfigured, is more in keeping with the state of the Pepi II heads than with that of the Pepi I or Teti heads.

It seems relatively certain that the Brussels head dates to the Sixth Dynasty and came from a royal pyramid complex in Saqqara because of its strong late Old Kingdom style attributes. Of the Sixth Dynasty pyramid complexes from which prisoner statues have been excavated, that of Pepi II was most likely the source of the head. The head's size, hairstyle, and condition are more similar to the other known prisoner statue heads from this complex than to the preserved heads from the complexes of Teti and Pepi I.

A.3. Unidentified Prisoner Statues in Egypt

A.3.1. Photographs in the Center of Documentation

In the SCA's Center of Documentation, there are two photographs that document fragments from three different prisoner statues, for which I have found no other attestations or corresponding photographs. This includes two busts (C.7.7 and C.7.8) and the body of a statue (C.7.9). Almost certainly, these photographs record excavated material. Unfortunately, the Center of Documentation no longer has any records of where these photographs were taken, when they were taken, or who took them. But a number of stylistic details suggest that these statues might be from the Pepi II pyramid complex.²¹

One photograph shows the back of C.7.7 and C.7.8. There is nothing else in the photograph, which is set against a black background. The statues appear to be in fairly good condition. C.7.7 consists of two fragments that have been rejoined. A subtle depression runs down the center of his back, emphasizing the pulled-back position of his arms. The arm bonds are damaged, but the back restraint, which has lashings, is preserved. Rather than completely vertical, the rope strands seem to be set at a slight diagonal toward the left. On the other hand, C.7.8 clearly has thick, vertical strands of rope for his lashings and four similarly thick strands of rope wrapped around his left arm above the elbow. C.7.8 may be a single fragment.²² He also has a depression running down the center of his back. The treatment of the backs of these statues, with a depression running down the center, and the diagonal lashings of C.7.7 suggest that C.7.7 and C.7.8

---

20. For this hairstyle, see further ch. 3.1.5.
21. The very limited number of known prisoner statue fragments from the complexes of Unas and Teti complicates stylistic comparison between the statues in these photographs and the prisoner statues of Unas and Teti. For this reason, my attribution of these fragments to the Pepi II complex is tentative, and there is a possibility that these fragments could have been excavated from the complexes of Unas or Teti.
22. There is a barely visible horizontal line below the bottom of the hair that could be from a break, but it could also be a scratch or some other type of mark, or simply a discoloration of the photograph.

are most likely from the complex of Pepi II, where there are fragments that have both of these features (see GEM 1101 and JE 45782; C.6.1 and C.6.3; figs. 2.22 and 2.24).

Unlike the photograph of C.7.7 and C.7.8, there are additional artifacts in the photograph of C.7.9. They are all placed on wooden shelves. Next to C.7.9, there is an upside down fragment of a roughly carved stele. On the upper shelf are three relief fragments.[23] Behind the shelves is a black background, but above them there is a person's left hand.

This large fragment is the nearly complete body of a prisoner statue. He kneels on a thick base that projects on either side of him. His arms are pulled back, and bonds are clear on his right arm on top of the elbow crease. His hands are held in fists on either side of his thighs. The left fist seems to be fully preserved; the thumb was clearly carved as was a depression in the center of his fist. He may also have fingers. His torso was subtly modeled, and he wears a wide, plain belt. His left foot is curled underneath him, and the artists might have carved toes on its front.

Most of C.7.9's details, including the shape and size of the base, his clearly carved belt, and the possible presence of fingers and toes, tentatively point toward an attribution to the complex of Pepi II. Given the size and relative completeness of this fragment it is somewhat surprising that it was not recorded or published elsewhere. However, Jéquier consistently favored the heads that he discovered at the Pepi II complex over the bodies, finding the facial features and hairstyles unusual and noteworthy, unlike the repetitive bodies.[24] Therefore, because C.7.9 does not include a head, Jéquier may have overlooked it.

A.3.2. Prisoner Statues in El-Arish

The Egyptian Museum database includes the records of two prisoner statues that were moved from a Saqqara magazine to the El-Arish National Museum when its collection was being formed in the mid 2000's. AR 48 (C.7.5) is described as a kneeling statue of a captive with the head missing; its magazine registration number was 19. The entry for AR 872 (C.7.6) notes that this is a kneeling statue of a captive on a base; his hands are tied, he is wearing a kilt, his head and right shoulder are missing, and broken parts have been restored. Its magazine registration number was 9. AR 872 is dated to the Sixth Dynasty, though no specific reign is given. AR 48 is designated Old Kingdom but is presumably from the Sixth Dynasty as well because it clearly was moved at the same time and from the same place as AR 872, given the similar registration entries.

The Egyptian Museum database entries do not specify from which magazine both of these statues came. However, the SCA moved PP 10 (C.5.10) from the pyramid complex of Pepi I to their storerooms after its discovery in 1969 and assigned it the registration number FE 19. PP 3 (C.5.3) was also moved and assigned FE 9. It seems likely that PP 10/FE 19 is AR 48 and that PP 3/FE 9 is AR 872. These could have been moved to El-Arish from SCA Saqqara Store Magazine 1, where the Pepi I prisoner statue fragments that are under the direction of the SCA are currently held, or from whatever storeroom the fragments had been at the time of the El-Arish Museum's construction. This conclusion is further supported by the measurements that the Egyptian Museum database provides for AR 48 and AR 872, which are consistent with the size of the Pepi I body fragments.[25] Moreover, PP 3/FE 9 is missing his right shoulder, as is AR 872. Unfortunately,

---

23. Further study of the relief fragments could help to date C.7.9.
24. Jéquier, *Monument funéraire*, 3:27–29 and pls. 47 and 48; Jéquier, *Douze ans*, 64–65; Jéquier, "Planche 22," 22–23; and Jéquier, "Rapport préliminaire…1926–1927," 60.
25. The height of AR 48 is 58 cm, and the height of AR 872 is 60 cm. Compare to ch. 2.2.5.

A.4. A Wrongly Identified Head in Los Angeles

In 1947, the same year that the Metropolitan Museum of Art purchased MMA 47.2 (C.7.3) from Vincent Dinicopoulos, Marguerite and Paul Mallon gifted a limestone statue head to the Los Angeles County Museum of Art (LACMA; fig. A.3).[26] In publishing this, along with several other museum acquisitions, James Henry Breasted Jr., who was the director of the museum at that time, described the head as belonging to a prisoner statue and coming from the Pepi II complex: "It is reported to have come from the Temple of Pepi II (2374–2280 BCE) at South Sakkara, and may have been discovered by Jéquier, who found at this site several half life-size kneeling limestone figures whose heads are similar to the one in Los Angeles."[27] He does not mention from whom or where this report came, and there is no previous history for the piece.

Figure A.3. Limestone head of a late Old Kingdom high official; probably Sixth Dynasty. H. 20 cm, W. 16.5 cm. Los Angeles, LACMA 47.12. Photograph courtesy of LACMA, www.lacma.org.

The head itself is in poor condition. The left side is missing, as is most of the mouth and nose and all of the chin. There is also some damage to the right side and back of the hairstyle. However, the upper right part of the face is well preserved and demonstrates that the head was beautifully carved. His large eyes are delicately rimmed, and he has thick, plastic eyebrows that taper toward the outside. Fleshy nasolabial folds emerge from where his nose was, and the remaining right outer corner of his mouth demonstrates that he had a ridged vermillion border. He wears a short, tiered hairstyle with vertical segments of equal size throughout. There are three homogenous upper layers that run the entire way around his head. Below this are six similar layers, which become slightly shorter toward the bottom, on the sides and back of his head. On the top of his head is a plain, uncarved circle.

Breasted compared the LACMA head to GEM 1101 (C.6.1) and JE 51729 (C.6.7): "The rimming of the eyelids, the pronounced modeling of the cheekbones, the eyebrows in relief, and the details of the wig, all seem very close to the style of the two Cairo captives. Thus, the new head probably is of the same provenance."[28] While he is correct that the Pepi II prisoner statues share some similarities with the LACMA head, the overall execution is significantly different. The hairstyle of LACMA 47.12 is quite similar to GEM 1101 and JE 51729 (figs. 2.22 and 2.23). However, as I described in chapter 3.3, this is not a distinctly foreign wig or hairstyle, and one frequently sees it on contemporary statues of elite male Egyptians. The size and shape of LACMA 47.12's eyes is similar to those of the Pepi II prisoner statues as well, but, unlike the LACMA head, none of the eyes of the Pepi II prisoner statues are rimmed.[29] Although the artists of Pepi I did attempt to rim some of the prisoner statues' eyes, this was not done nearly as effectively as the eyes of

---

26. Los Angeles, LACMA 47.12. Its measurements are H. 20 cm; W. 17.5 cm.
27. James H. Breasted, " Six Pieces of Egyptian Sculpture," *Bulletin of the Art Division of the Los Angeles County Museum* 1:2 (1947): 7.
28. Breasted, "Six Pieces," 7. The head was similarly described in *Illustrated Handbook*, 18.
29. See further ch. 3.1.5.

the LACMA head (see table 4). Similarly, although a few of the Pepi I and Pepi II heads have eyebrows in relief, such as PP 23 (C.5.23) and JE 51731 (C.6.6), these plastic eyebrows were often not fully carved and are in much lower and less rounded relief than what the artists used for the LACMA head (compare figs. A.3 with 3.12 and 3.17). In fact, compared to all of the prisoner statue heads, LACMA 47.12 most closely resembles JE 40047 (C.4.1) from the pyramid complex of Teti, rather than any of the Pepi II heads (fig. 2.6). However, there is a clear disparity in quality between these two heads, with the LACMA head being significantly better executed, and the final impression that each head gives is consequently quite different.

All of the features that Breasted listed in support of the LACMA head being from a prisoner statue are actually characteristics of the late Old Kingdom style, which the Sixth Dynasty prisoner statues also share. Specifically in regard to the LACMA head, this includes its large, rimmed eyes; plastic eyebrows; extended inner canthi; prominent nasolabial folds; lips that sit flat on top of one another, without coming to a point in the corner; and ridged vermillion border. Given the high quality of the head's execution, it is far more likely that LACMA 47.12 is the head of a Sixth Dynasty high official, who was perhaps buried near Pepi II's pyramid complex, if Breasted's information regarding its findspot is correct. It is an excellent example of the "Second Style" in private stone statuary, and there is nothing to support Breasted's argument that it is the head of a prisoner statue.

Bibliography

Archival Sources

Borchardt (Ludwig) Archive, Ägyptisches Museum und Papyrussammlung, Staatliche Museen zu Berlin – PK, Berlin, Germany.
Bothmer (Bernard) Archive, Department of Egyptian, Classical and Ancient Near Eastern Art, The Brooklyn Museum, Brooklyn, New York.
Bothmer (Bernard) Archive, The Institute of Fine Arts, New York University, New York, New York.
Bothmer (Bernard) Collection, Egyptological Library and Archives, Università degli Studi di Milano, Milan, Italy.
Center of Documentation, Supreme Council of Antiquities, Ministry of Tourism and Antiquities, Cairo, Egypt.
Firth (Cecil) fonds, Archives scientifiques, Institut français d'archéologie orientale, Cairo, Egypt.
Image of the Black Archive, Image of the Black Archive & Library at the Hutchins Center, Harvard University, Cambridge, Massachusetts.
Jéquier (Gustave) fonds, Musée d'ethnographie and Archives de l'Etat de Neuchâtel, Neuchâtel, Switzerland.
Mission archéologique française de Saqqâra archives, Mission archéologique franco-suisse de Saqqâra, Paris, France.
Quibell (James) Collection, Egyptological Library and Archives, Università degli Studi di Milano, Milan, Italy.
Varille (Alexandre) Collection, Egyptological Library and Archives, Università degli Studi di Milano, Milan, Italy.

Published Sources

Abu Bakr, Abdel Moneim and Jürgen Osing. "Ächtungstexte aus dem Alten Reich." *MDAIK* 29 (1973): 97–133.
Abuel-Yazid, Mohamed. "Architecture of the Slaughterhouse of the Seti Temple at Abydos." In *Abydos: The Sacred Land at the Western Horizon*, edited by Ilona Regulski, 7–24. BMPES 8. Leuven: Peeters, 2019.
Adams, Matthew J. "Egypt and the Levant in the Early/Middle Bronze Age Transition." In *The Late Third Millennium in the Ancient Near East: Chronology, C14 and Climate Change*, edited by Felix Höflmayer, 493–515. OIS 11. Chicago: Oriental Institute of the University of Chicago, 2017.
Aldred, Cyril. "Some Royal Portraits of the Middle Kingdom in Ancient Egypt." *MMJ* 3 (1970): 27–50.
Allen, James P. *The Ancient Egyptian Pyramid Texts*, 2nd ed. Edited by Peter Der Manuelian. WAW 38. Atlanta: SBL Press, 2015.
———. "The Cosmology of the Pyramid Texts." In *Religion and Philosophy in Ancient Egypt*, edited by William Kelly Simpson, 1–28. New Haven: Yale Egyptological Seminar, 1989.
———. *A New Concordance of the Pyramid Texts*, 6 vols. Providence: Brown University, 2013. Online: https://oi-idb.uchicago.edu.
———. "Reading a Pyramid." In *Hommages à Jean Leclant*, vol. 1, edited by Catherine Berger, Gisèle Clerc, and Nicolas Grimal, 5–28. Cairo: Institut français d'archéologie orientale, 1994.
Altenmüller, Hartwig. "Die 'Abgaben' aus dem 2. Jahr des Userkaf." In *Gedenkschrift für Winfried Barta*, edited by Dieter Kessler and Regine Schulz, 37–48. MÄU 4. Frankfurt am Main: Lang, 1995.
Andrews, Carol. "Pharaoh Trampler of Egypt's Enemies, A New Amuletic Form." In *Ancient Egypt, the Aegean, and the Near East: Studies in Honour of Martha Rhoads Bell*, vol. 1, edited by Jack Phillips, 39–42. San Antonio: Van Siclen, 1997.
Anthony, Flora Brook. *Foreigners in Ancient Egypt: Theban Tomb Paintings from the Early Eighteenth Dynasty (1550–1372 BC)*. London: Bloomsbury, 2017.

Arnold, Dieter. "Architecture: Building for Eternity across Egypt." In *Ancient Egypt Transformed: The Middle Kingdom*, edited by Adela Oppenheim, Dorothea Arnold, Dieter Arnold, and Kei Yamamoto, 10–16. New York: The Metropolitan Museum of Art, 2015.

———. *Building in Egypt: Pharaonic Stone Masonry*. Oxford: Oxford University Press, 1991.

———. *The Encyclopedia of Ancient Egyptian Architecture*. Translated by Sabine H. Gardiner and Helen Strudwick, edited by Nigel Strudwick and Helen Strudwick. Princeton: Princeton University Press, 2003.

———. "Hypostyle Halls of the Old and Middle Kingdom?" In *Studies in Honor of William Kelly Simpson*, vol. 1, edited by Peter Der Manuelian, 39–54. Boston: Museum of Fine Arts, 1996.

———. "Old Kingdom Statues in their Architectural Settings." In *Egyptian Art in the Age of the Pyramids*, edited by Dorothea Arnold, Krzysztof Grzymski, and Christiane Ziegler, 41–49. New York: The Metropolitan Museum of Art, 1999.

———. *The Pyramid of Senwosret I*. MMAEE 22; The South Cemeteries of Lisht 1. New York: The Metropolitan Museum of Art, 1988.

———. "Rituale und Pyramidentempel." *MDAIK* 33 (1977): 1–14.

———. "Royal Cult Complexes of the Old and Middle Kingdoms." In *Temples of Ancient Egypt*, edited by Byron Shafer, 31–85. Ithaca, NY: Cornell University Press, 1997.

Arnold, Dorothea. "Image and Identity: Egypt's Eastern Neighbours, East Delta People and the Hyksos." In *The Second Intermediate Period (Thirteenth–Seventeenth Dynasties): Current Research, Future Prospects*, edited by Marcel Marée, 183–222. OLA 192. Leuven: Peeters, 2010.

———. "Royal Reliefs." In *Egyptian Art in the Age of the Pyramids*, edited by Dorothea Arnold, Krzysztof Grzymski, and Christiane Ziegler, 83–101. New York: The Metropolitan Museum of Art, 1999.

Arnold, Dorothea, Krzysztof Grzymski, and Christiane Ziegler, ed. *Egyptian Art in the Age of the Pyramids*. New York: The Metropolitan Museum of Art, 1999.

Aruz, Joan, Kim Benzel, and Jean M. Evans, ed. *Beyond Babylon: Art, Trade, and Diplomacy in the Second Millennium B.C.* New York: The Metropolitan Museum of Art, 2008.

Ashton, Sally-Ann and Donald Spanel. "Portraiture." In *The Oxford Encyclopedia of Ancient Egypt*, vol. 3, edited by Donald Redford, 55–59. Oxford: Oxford University Press, 2001.

Assmann, Jan. *Cultural Memory and Early Civilization: Writing, Remembrance, and Political Imagination*, translated by David Henry Wilson. Cambridge: Cambridge University Press, 2011.

———. "Death and Initiation in the Funerary Religion of Ancient Egypt." In *Religion and Philosophy in Ancient Egypt*, edited by William Kelly Simpson, 135–59. New Haven: Yale Egyptological Seminar, 1989.

———. "Preservation and Presentation of Self in Ancient Egyptian Portraiture." In *Studies in Honor of William Kelly Simpson*, vol. 1, edited by Peter Der Manuelian, 55–81. Boston: Museum of Fine Arts, 1996.

———. "Spruch 23 der Pyramidentexte und die Ächtung der Feinde Pharaos." In *Hommages à Jean Leclant*, vol. 1, edited by Catherine Berger, Gisèle Clerc, and Nicolas Grimal, 45–59. Cairo: Institut français d'archéologie orientale, 1994.

El Awady, Tarek. "Boat Graves in the Old Kingdom Royal Funerary Complexes." In *The Realm of the Pharaohs: Essays in Honor of Tohfa Handoussa*, edited by Zahi Hawass, Khaled Daoud, and Sawsan Abd El-Fattah, 177–200. CASAE 37. Cairo: Supreme Counsel of Antiquities, 2008.

———. "King Sahura with the Precious Trees from Punt in a Unique Scene!" In *The Old Kingdom Art and Archaeology: Proceedings of the Conference Held in Prague, May 31–June 4, 2004*, edited by Miroslav Bárta, 37–44. Prague: Czech Institute of Egyptology, 2006.

———. *Sahure – The Pyramid Causeway: History and Decoration Program in the Old Kingdom*. Abusir 16. Prague: Charles University, 2009.

Baer, Klaus. *Rank and Title in the Old Kingdom: The Structure of the Egyptian Administration in the Fifth and Sixth Dynasties*. Chicago: University of Chicago Press, 1960.

Baines, John. "Display of Magic in Old Kingdom Egypt." In *Through a Glass Darkly: Magic, Dreams and Prophecy in Ancient Egypt*, edited by Kasia Szpakowska, 1–32. Swansea: Classical Press of Wales, 2006.

———. *High Culture and Experience in Ancient Egypt*. Studies in Egyptology and the Ancient Near East. Bristol: Equinox, 2013.

———. "Kingship before Literature: The World of the King in the Old Kingdom." In *Selbstverständnis und Realität: Akten des Symposiums zur ägyptischen Königsideologie in Mainz 15.–17.6.1995*, edited by Rolf Gundlach and Christine Raedler, 125–74. Wiesbaden: Harrassowitz, 1997.

———. "Kingship, Definition of Culture, and Legitimation." In *Ancient Egyptian Kingship*, edited by David O'Connor and David P. Silverman, 3–47. PAe 9. Leiden: Brill, 1995.

Baker, Darrell. *The Encyclopedia of the Egyptian Pharaohs*, vol. 1. Oakville: Bannerstone, 2008.

Bard, Kathryn and Rodolfo Fattovich. *Seafaring Expeditions to Punt in the Middle Kingdom: Excavations at Mersa/Wadi Gawasis, Egypt.* CHANE 96. Leiden: Brill, 2018.

Bard, Kathryn, Rodolfo Fattovich, and Andrea Manzo. "The Ancient Harbor at Mersa/Wadi Gawasis and How to Get There: New Evidence of Pharaonic Seafaring Expeditions in the Red Sea." In *Desert Road Archaeology in Ancient Egypt and Beyond*, edited by Frank Förster and Heiko Riemer, 533–56. Africa praehistorica 27. Cologne: Heinrich-Barth Institut, 2013.

Barsanti, Alexandre. "Rapports de M. Alexandre Barsanti sur les déblaiements opérés autour de la pyramide d'Ounas pendant les années 1899–1901." *ASAE* 2 (1901): 244–57.

Barsanti, Alexandre and Gaston Maspero. "Fouilles autour de la pyramide d'Ounas." *ASAE* 1 (1901): 150–90.

———. "Fouilles autour de la pyramide d'Ounas (1902–1903)." *ASAE* 5 (1904): 69–83.

Bárta, Miroslav. "'Abusir Paradigm' and the Beginning of the Fifth Dynasty." In *The Pyramids: Between Life and Death; Proceedings of the Workshop Held at Uppsala University, Uppsala, May 31st–June 1st, 2012*, edited by Irmgard Hein, Nils Billing, and Erika Meyer-Dietrich, 51–74. Uppsala: Uppsala University, 2016.

———. *Analyzing Collapse: The Rise and Fall of the Old Kingdom.* Cairo: The American University in Cairo Press, 2019.

———. "Ancient Egyptian History as an Example of Punctuated Equilibrium: An Outline." In *Towards a New History for the Egyptian Old Kingdom: Perspectives on the Pyramid Age*, edited by Peter Der Manuelian and Thomas Schneider, 1–17. HES 1. Leiden: Brill, 2015.

———. "Architectural Innovations in the Development of the Non-Royal Tomb during the Reign of Nyuserra." In *Structure and Significance: Thoughts on Ancient Egyptian Architecture*, edited by Peter Jánosi, 105–25. Vienna: Österreichische Akademie der Wissenschaften, 2005.

———. "Egyptian Kingship during the Old Kingdom." In *Experiencing Power, Generating Authority: Cosmos, Politics, and the Ideology of Kingship in Ancient Egypt and Mesopotamia*, edited by Jane A. Hill, Philip Jones, and Antonio J. Morales, 257–83. Philadelphia: University of Pennsylvania Museum of Archaeology and Anthropology, 2013.

———. "Filling the Chambers, Rising the Status: Sixth Dynasty Context for the Decline of the Old Kingdom." *CRIPEL* 28 (2009–2010): 145–56.

———. "Kings, Viziers, and Courtiers: Executive Power in the Third Millennium B.C." In *Ancient Egyptian Administration*, edited by Juan Carlos Moreno García, 153–75. HdO 104. Leiden: Brill, 2013.

———. "Radiocarbon Dates for the Old Kingdom and their Correspondences." In *Radiocarbon and the Chronologies of Ancient Egypt*, edited by Andrew J. Shortland and C. Bronk Ramsey, 218–23. Oxford: Oxbow, 2013.

———. "Temporary and Permanent: Status Race and the Mechanism of Change in a Complex Civilization: Ancient Egypt in between 2900 and 2120 BC." In *Crisis to Collapse: The Archaeology of Social Breakdown*, edited by Tim Cunningham and Jan Driessen, 277–93. Louvain-la-Neuve: Presses universitaires de Louvain, 2017.

Bárta, Miroslav, Katarína Arias Kytnarová, Martin Odler, and Zdeňka Sůvová. "'Killed' for Eternity: Artefacts and Ritual Behaviour from a Unique Ceremonial Structure in Abusir South." In *Abusir and Saqqara in the Year 2015*, edited by Miroslav Bárta, Filip Coppens, and Jaromír Krejčí, 1–21. Prague: Czech Institute of Egyptology, 2017.

Bárta, Miroslav and Veronika Dulíková. "Divine and Terrestrial: The Rhetoric of Power in Ancient Egypt (The Case of Nyuserra)." In *Royal versus Divine Authority: Acquisition, Legitimization and Renewal of Power*, edited by Filip Coppens, Jiří Janák, and Hana Vymazalová, 31–47. Wiesbaden: Harrassowitz, 2015.

Baud, Michel. *Famille royale et pouvoir sous l'Ancien Empire égyptien*, 2 vols. BiEtud 126. Cairo: Institut français d'archéologique orientale, 1999.

———. "Ménès, la mémoire monarchique et la chronologie du IIIe millénaire." *Archéo-Nil* 9 (1999): 109–47.

———. "The Old Kingdom." In *A Companion to Ancient Egypt*, vol. 1, edited by Alan B. Lloyd, 63–80. Chichester: Wiley-Blackwell, 2010.

———. "The Relative Chronology of Dynasties 6 and 8." In *Ancient Egyptian Chronology*, edited by Erik Hornung, Rolf Krauss, and David A. Warburton, 144–58. HdO 83. Leiden: Brill, 2006.

Baud, Michel and Vassil Dobrev. "De nouvelles annals de l'Ancien Empire égyptien. Une 'Pierre de Palerme' pour la VIe dynastie." *BIFAO* 95 (1995): 23–92.

Beaux, Nathalie. "Enemies étrangers et malfaiteurs egyptiens; la signification du chatiment au pilori." *BIFAO* 91 (1991): 33–53.

Bell, Catherine. *Ritual: Perspectives and Dimensions.* Oxford: Oxford University Press, 1997.

———. *Ritual Theory, Ritual Practice.* Oxford: Oxford University Press, 1992.

Bell, Lanny. "Interpreters and Egyptianized Nubians in Ancient Egyptian Foreign Policy: Aspects of the History of Egypt and Nubia." PhD diss., University of Pennsylvania, 1976.

———. "Luxor Temple and the Cult of the Royal Ka." *JNES* 44 (1985): 251–94.

Ben-Tor, Amnon. "The Early Bronze Age." In *The Archaeology of Ancient Israel*, edited by Amnon Ben-Tor, translated by R. Greenberg, 81–125. New Haven: Yale University Press, 1992.

Benešovská, Hana. "Statues from the Pyramid Complex of King Raneferef." In *The Pyramid Complex of Raneferef: The Archaeology*, edited by Miroslav Verner, 360–437. Abusir 9. Prague: Czech Institute of Egyptology, 2006.

Berger-el Naggar, Catherine and Marie-Noëlle Fraisse. "Béhénou, 'aimée de Pépy,' une nouvelle reine d'Égypte." *BIFAO* 108 (2008): 1–27.

———. "La paroi est de la chamber funéraire de la reine Béhénou." In *The Pyramids: Between Life and Death; Proceedings of the Workshop Held at Uppsala University, Uppsala, May 31st–June 1st, 2012*, edited by Irmgard Hein, Nils Billing and Erika Meyer-Dietrich, 187–206. Uppsala: Uppsala University, 2016.

Berlandini, Jocelyne. "La pyramide "ruinée" de Saqqara-nord et le roi Ikaouhor-Menkaouhor." *RdE* 31 (1979): 3–28.

Bestock, Laurel. *Violence and Power in Ancient Egypt: Image and Ideology before the New Kingdom*. Routledge Studies in Egyptology 5. New York: Routledge, 2018.

Bettum, Anders. "Nesting: The Development and Significance of the 'Yellow Coffin' Ensemble." In *Proceedings First Vatican Coffin Conference 19–22 June 2013*, vol. 1, edited by Alessia Amenta and Hélème Guichard, 71–82. Città del Vaticano: Edizioni Musei Vaticani, 2017.

Bierbrier, Morris. *Who Was Who in Egyptology?*, 4th rev. ed. London: Egypt Exploration Society, 2012.

Bietak, Manfred. "The Early Bronze Age III Temple at Tell Ibrahim Awad and Its Relevance to the Egyptian Old Kingdom." In *Perspectives on Ancient Egypt: Studies in Honor of Edward Brovarski*, edited by Zahi Hawass, Peter Der Manuelian, and Ramadan Hussein, 65–77. ASAE Suppl. 40. Cairo: Supreme Council of Antiquities, 2010.

———. "Saqqara." *AfO* 23 (1970): 205–8.

———. "Zu den nubischen Bogenschützen aus Assiut: Ein Beitrag zur Geschichte der Ersten Zwischenzeit." In *Mélanges Gamal eddin Mokhtar*, vol. 1, edited by Paule Posener-Kriéger, 87–97. BiEtud 97. Cairo: Institut français d'archéologie orientale, 1985.

———. "Zur Marine des Alten Reiches." In *Pyramid Studies and Other Essays Presented to I. E. S. Edwards*, edited by John Baines, T. G. H. James, Anthony Leahy, and A. F. Shore, 35–40. Occasional Publications 7. London: Egypt Exploration Society, 1988.

Bietak, Manfred, Josef Dorner, Peter Jánosi, and Angela von den Driesch. "Ausgrabungen in dem Palastbezirk von Avaris Vorbericht Tell el-Dab'a/'Ezbet Helmi 1993–2000." *Ägypten und Levante* 11 (2001): 27–119.

Billing, Nils. *The Performative Structure: Ritualizing the Pyramid of Pepy I*. HES 4. Leiden: Brill, 2018.

Bissing, F. W. von. *Ägyptische Kunstgeschichte: Von den ältesten Zeiten bis auf die Eroberung durch die Araber*. 3 vols. Berlin: Aegyptologischer Verlag Miron Goldstein, 1934–1938.

Bleiburg, Edward and Stephanie Weissberg. *Striking Power: Iconoclasm in Ancient Egypt*. Brooklyn: Brooklyn Museum, 2019.

Blumer, Nadine. *Finding Home: The Diniacopoulos Family and Collection*. Montreal: Concordia University, 2017.

Bogdanov, Ivan V. "New Relief Fragments from the Tomb of the Seafarer *jnj*." *CdE* 93:186 (2018): 227–47.

Boisgirard & Associés. *Arts d'Orient*, Hôtel Drouot, Paris, June 16–17, 2005. Paris: Boisgirard & Associés, 2005.

Bommas, Martin. "Zwei magische Sprüche in einem spätägyptischen Ritualhandbuch (pBM EA 10081): Ein weiterer Fall für die 'Verborgenheit des Mythos.'" *ZÄS* 131 (2004): 95–113.

Borchardt, Ludwig. "Ausgrabungen der Deutschen Orient-Gesellschaft bei Abusir im Winter 1901-2." *MDOG* 14 (1902): 1–50.

———. "Ausgrabungen der Deutschen Orient-Gesellschaft bei Abusir im Winter 1902-3." *MDOG* 18 (1903): 1–33.

———. "Ausgrabungen der Deutschen Orient-Gesellschaft bei Abusir im Winter 1903-4." *MDOG* 24 (1904): 1–26.

———. *Das Grabdenkmal des Königs Ne-user-re*. Ausgrabungen der Deutschen Orient-Gesellschaft in Abusir 1902–1904 1; WVDOG 7. Leipzig: Hinrichs, 1907.

———. *Das Grabdenkmal des Königs Sahu-re*, 2 vols. Ausgrabungen der Deutschen Orient-Gesellschaft in Abusir 1902–1908 6–7; WVDOG 14, 26. Leipzig: Hinrichs, 1910–1913.

———. *Statuen und Statuetten von Königen und Privatleuten im Museum von Kairo*, 6 vols. CGC. Berlin: Reichdruckerei, 1911–1936.

Borrmann, Linda. "Form Follows Function: Der Zeichencharakter der altägyptischen Ächtungsfiguren." In *Bild: Ästhetik – Medium – Kommunikation; Beiträge des dritten Münchner Arbeitskreiss Junge Ägyptologie (MAJA 3) 7. bis 9.12.2012*, edited by Gregor Neunert, Alexandra Verbovsek, and Kathrin Gabler, 103–17. GOF 58. Wiesbaden: Harrassowitz, 2014.

Bothmer, Bernard. "On Realism in Egyptian Funerary Sculpture of the Old Kingdom." In *Egyptian Art: Selected Writings of Bernard V. Bothmer*, edited by Madeleine Cody, Paul Stanwick, and Marsha Hill, 372–93. New York: Oxford University Press, 2004.

Bouanich, Catherine. "Mise à mort rituelle de l'animal, offrande carnée dans le temple égyptien." In *La cuisine et l'autel: Les sacrifices en questions dans les sociétés de la Méditerranée ancienne*, edited by Stella Georgoudi, Renée Koch Piettre, and Francis Schmidt, 149-158. Bibliothèque d'École des hautes études, sciences religieuses 124. Turnhout: Brepols, 2005.

Brand, Peter. "Ideological Imperatives: Irrational Factors in Egyptian–Hittite Relations under Ramesses II." In *Moving Across Borders: Foreign Relations, Religion and Cultural Interactions in the Ancient Mediterranean*, edited by Panagiotis Kousoulis and Konstantinos Magliveras, 15–33. OLA 159. Leuven: Peeters, 2007.

Breasted, James H. " Six Pieces of Egyptian Sculpture." *Bulletin of the Art Division of the Los Angeles County Museum* 1:2 (1947): 3–11.

Brinks, Jürgen. *Die Entwicklung der königlichen Grabanlagen des Alten Reiches: Eine strukturelle und historische Analyse altägyptischer Architektur*. HÄB 10. Hildesheim: Gerstenberg, 1979.

Brovarski, Edward. "Overseers of Upper Egypt in the Old to Middle Kingdoms." *ZÄS* 140 (2013): 91–111.

———. "A Second Style in Egyptian Relief of the Old Kingdom." In *Egypt and Beyond: Essays Presented to Leonard H. Lesko upon His Retirement from the Wilbour Chair of Egyptology at Brown University June 2005*, edited by Stephen E. Thompson and Peter Der Manuelian, 49–89. Providence: Department of Egyptology and Ancient Western Asian Studies, Brown University, 2008.

———. *The Senedjemib Complex Part I: The Mastabas of Senedjemib Inti (G 2370), Khnumenti (G 2374), and Senedjemib Mehi (G 2378)*. Giza Mastabas 7. Boston: Museum of Fine Arts, 2001.

Bruyère, Bernard. *Rapport sur les fouilles de Deir el Médineh (1935–1940), Quatrième partie, Fascicule II: trouvailles d'objets*. FIFAO 20:2. Cairo: Institut français d'archéologie orientale, 1952.

Bryan, Betsy. "Episodes of Iconoclasm in the Egyptian New Kingdom." In *Iconoclasm and Text Destruction in the Ancient Near East and Beyond*, edited by Natalie Naomi May, 363-94. OIS 8. Chicago: Oriental Institute of the University of Chicago, 2012.

Budka, Julia. "Egyptian Impact on Pot-Breaking Ceremonies at el-Kurru? A Re-Examination." In *The Fourth Cataract and Beyond: Proceedings of the 12th International Conference for Nubian Studies*, edited by Julie R. Anderson and Derek W. Welsby, 641–54. BMPES 1. Leuven: Peeters, 2014.

Burn, John. "An Ecological Approach to Determine the Potential Influence that the Pyramid Texts has upon the Sixth Dynasty Tomb Decorations." In *Abusir and Saqqara in the Year 2010*, vol. 1, edited by Miroslav Bárta, Filip Coppens, and Jaromír Krejčí, 233–45. Prague: Czech Institute of Egyptology, 2011.

Callender, Vivienne Gae. *In Hathor's Image I: The Wives and Mothers of Egyptian Kings from Dynasties I–VI*. Prague: Charles University, 2011.

———. "It's All in the Family: A 6th Dynasty Conundrum." In *Rich and Great: Studies in Honour of Anthony J. Spalinger on the Occasion of His 70th Feast of Thoth*, edited by Renata Landgráfová and Jana Mynářová, 19–27. Prague: Charles University, 2016.

Capart, Jean and Georges Posener. "Figurines égyptiennes d'envoûtement." *CRAIBL* 83 (1939): 66–74.

Chavet, Violaine. "Who Did What and Why: The Dynamics of Tomb Preparation." In *Joyful in Thebes: Egyptological Studies in Honor of Betsy M. Bryan*, edited by Richard Jasnow and Kathlyn Cooney, 63–78. MVCAE 1. Atlanta: Lockwood, 2015.

Cherpion, Nadine. "La statuaire privée d'Ancien Empire: indices de datation." In *Les critères de datation stylistiques à l'Ancien Empire*, edited by Nicolas Grimal, 97–142. BiEtud 120. Cairo: Institut français d'archéologie orientale, 1998.

Cialowicz, Krzysztof M. "The Early Dynastic Administrative-Cultic Centre at Tell el-Farkha." *BMSAES* 13 (2009): 83–123.

———. "The Predynastic/Early Dynastic Period at Tell el-Farkha." In *Before the Pyramids: The Origins of Egyptian Civilization*, edited by Emily Teeter, 55–64. Chicago: The Oriental Institute of the University of Chicago, 2011.

Cinquante années à Saqqarah de Jean-Philippe Lauer: Exposition organisée par le service des musées du Cairo au musée palais du Manial, 13 Avril 1980–15 Mars 1981. Cairo: Organisme Général des Imprimeries Gouvernementales, 1983.

Clayton, Joseph, Aloisia de Trafford, and Mark Borda. "A Hieroglyphic Inscription Found at Jebel Uweinat Mentioning Yam and Tekhebet." *Sahara* 19 (2008): 129–34.

Connor, Simon. "Killing or 'De-Activating' Egyptian Statues: Who Mutilated Them, When, and Why?" In *Statues in Context: Production, Meaning and (Re)uses*, edited by Aurélia Masson-Berghoff, 281–302. BMPES 12. Leuven: Peeters, 2020.

———. "Mutiler, tuer, désactiver les images en Égypte pharaonique." *Perspective* 2 (2018): 147–66.

Cooke, Ashley. *The Architecture of Mastaba Tombs in the Unas Cemetery*. The Munro Archive Project: Studies on the Unas Cemetery in Saqqara 1. Leiden: Sidestone, 2020.

Cooper, Julien. "Reconsidering the Location of Yam." *JARCE* 48 (2012): 1–21.

———. *Toponymy on the Periphery: Placenames of the Eastern Desert, Red Sea, and South Sinai in Egyptian Documents from the Early Dynastic until the End of the New Kingdom*, PAe 39. Boston: Brill, 2020.

Coppens, Filip and Hana Vymazalová. "Long Live the King! Notes on the Renewal of Divine Kingship in the Temple." In *Egypt in Transition: Social and Religious Development of Egypt in the First Millennium BCE*, edited by Ladislav Bareš, Filip Coppens, and Květa Smoláriková, 73–102. Prague: Czech Institute of Egyptology, 2010.

Creasman, Pearce Paul and Richard H. Wilkinson, ed. *Pharaoh's Land and Beyond: Ancient Egypt and its Neighbors*. Oxford: Oxford University Press, 2017.

Crubézy, Éric and Béatrix Midant-Reynes, "Les sacrifices humains à l'époque prédynastique: L'apport de la nécropole d'Adaïma." In *La sacrifice humain: En Égypte ancienne et ailleurs*, edited by Jean-Pierre Albert and Béatrix Midant-Reynes, 58–81. Paris: Soleb, 2005.

Ćwiek, Andrzej. "Relief Decoration in the Royal Funerary Complexes of the Old Kingdom: Studies in the Development, Scene Content and Iconography." PhD diss., Warsaw University, 2003.

Davies, Norman de Garis. *The Tomb of Ken-Amun at Thebes*. MMAEE 5. New York: The Metropolitan Museum of Art, 1930.

Davies, William Vivian and Renée Friedman. "The Narmer Palette: An Overlooked Detail." In *Egyptian Museum Collections around the World*, vol. 1, edited by Mamdouh Eldamaty and May Trad, 243–46. Cairo: Supreme Council of Antiquities, 2002.

Diego Espinel, Andrés. *Abriendo los caminos de Punt: Contactos entre Egipto y el ámbito afroárabe durante la Edad del Bronce (ca. 3000 a.C.–1065 a.C.)*. Barcelona: Bellaterra, 2011.

———. "Bringing Treasures and Placing Fears: Old Kingdom Epithets and Titles Related to Activities Abroad." *Isimu* 18–19 (2015–2016): 103–46.

———. "Egypt and the Levant during the Old Kingdom." Review of *Egypt in the Eastern Mediterranean during the Old Kingdom: An Archaeological Perspective*, by Karin Sowada. *Aula Orientalis* 30 (2012): 359–67.

———. *Etnicidad y territorio en el Egipto del Reino Antiguo*. AulÆg-Stud 6. Bellaterra: Universitat Autònoma de Barcelona, 2006.

———. "A Newly Identified Old Kingdom Execration Text." In *Decorum and Experience: Essays in Ancient Culture for John Baines*, 26–33. Oxford: Griffith Institute, 2013.

———. "The Role of the Temple of Ba'alat Gebal as Intermediary between Egypt and Byblos during the Old Kingdom." *SAK* 30 (2002): 103–19.

———. "The Scents of Punt (and Elsewhere): Trade and Functions of *sntr* and *ꜥntw* during the Old Kingdom." In *Flora Trade between Egypt and Africa in Antiquity: Proceedings of a Conference Held in Naples, Italy, 13 April 2015*, edited by Ilaria Incordino and Pearce Paul Creasman, 21–48. Oxford: Oxbow, 2017.

———. "Surveyors, Guides and Other Officials in the Egyptian and Nubian Deserts: Epigraphic and Historical Remarks on Some Old Kingdom Graffiti." *RdE* 65 (2014): 29–48.

———. "'Unusual Herders': Iconographic Development, Diffusion and Meanings of Dwarves, Boys and Lame and Emaciated People as Drovers from the Old Kingdom to the Early Middle Kingdom." In *Old Kingdom Art and Archaeology 7: Proceedings of the International Conference; Università degli studi di Milano 3–7 July 2017*, edited by Patrizia Piacentini and Alessio Delli Castelli, 418–35. *Egyptian & Egyptological Documents, Archives, Libraries* 6. Milan: Pontremoli, 2019.

Dieleman, Jacco. "Egypt." In *Guide to the Study of Ancient Magic*, edited by David Frankfurter, 87–114. RGRW 189. Leiden: Brill, 2019.

Dobrev, Vassil. "The South Saqqara Stone and the Sarcophagus of Queen Mother Ankhesenpepy (JE 65908)." In *Abusir and Saqqara in the Year 2000*, edited by Miroslav Bárta and Jaromír Krejčí, 381–96. Prague: Oriental Institute of the Academy of Sciences of the Czech Republic, 2000.

Dohrmann, Karin. "Arbeitsorganisation, Produktionsverfahren und Werktechnik – eine Analyse der Sitzstatuen Sesostris' I. aus Lischt." PhD diss., Georg-August-Universität Göttingen, 2004.

Dougherty, Sean P. and Renée F. Friedman. "Sacred or Mundane: Scalping and Decapitation at Predynastic Hierakonpolis." In *Egypt at Its Origins 2: Proceedings of the International Conference "Origin of the State, Predynastic and Early Dynastic Egypt,"* edited by Béatrix Midant-Reynes and Yann Tristant, 311–38. OLA 172. Leuven: Peeters, 2008.

Drioton, Étienne and Jean-Philippe Lauer. "Une inscription de Khamouas sur la face sud de la pyramide d'Ounas à Saqqarah." *ASAE* 37 (1937): 201–11.

Droux, Xavier. "Une representation de prisonniers décapités en provenance de Hiérakonpolis." *BSEG* 27 (2005–2007): 33–42.

Eaton, Katherine. *Ancient Egyptian Temple Ritual: Performance, Patterns, and Practice*. Routledge Studies in Egyptology 1. London: Routledge, 2013.

Eaton-Krauss, Marianne. "The Location of Inscriptions on Statues of the Old Kingdom." In *Sitting beside Lepsius: Studies in Honour of Jaromir Malek at the Griffith Institute*, edited by Diana Magee, Janine Bourriau, and Stephen Quirke, 129–53. Leuven: Peeters, 2009.

———. "Non-Royal Pre-Canonical Statuary." In *Les critères de datation stylistiques à l'Ancien Empire*, edited by Nicolas Grimal, 209–25. BiEtud 120. Cairo: Institut français d'archéologie orientale, 1998.

———. *The Representations of Statuary in Private Tombs of the Old Kingdom*. ÄgAbh 39. Wiesbaden: Harrassowitz, 1984.

Edel, Elmar. "Studien zu den Relieffragmenten aus dem Taltempel des Königs Snofru." In *Studies in Honor of William Kelly Simpson*, vol. 1, edited by Peter Der Manuelian, 199–208. Boston: Museum of Fine Arts, 1996.

Edwards, I. E. S. *The Pyramids of Egypt*. London: Penguin, 1947.

Eichler, Eckhard. *Untersuchungen zum Expeditionswesen des ägyptischen Alten Reiches*. GOF 26. Wiesbaden: Harrassowitz, 1993.

Emery, Walter B. and L. P. Kirwan. *The Excavations and Survey between Wadi es-Sebua and Adindan 1929–1931*, 2 vols. Mission archéologique de Nubie, 1929–1934. Cairo: Service des antiquités de l'Égypte, 1935.

Étienne, Marc. *Heka: Magie et envoûtement dans l'Égypte ancienne*. Paris: Éditions de la Réunion des musées nationaux, 2000.

Evers, Hans Gerhard. *Staat aus dem Stein: Denkmäler, Geschichte und Bedeutung der ägyptischen Plastik während des Mittleren Reichs*. Munich: Bruckmann, 1929.

Eyre, Christopher. *The Cannibal Hymn: A Cultural and Literary Study*. Liverpool: Liverpool University Press, 2002.

———. "Weni's Career and Old Kingdom Historiography." In *The Unbroken Reed: Studies in the Culture and Heritage of Ancient Egypt in Honour of A. F. Shore*, edited by Christopher Eyre, Anthony Leahy, and Lisa Montagno Leahy, 107–24. London: Egypt Exploration Society, 1994.

Fakhry, Ahmed. *The Bent Pyramid*. The Monuments of Sneferu at Dahshur 1. Cairo: Antiquities Department, 1959.

———. *The Pyramids*. Chicago: University of Chicago Press, 1961.

Fay, Biri. *The Louvre Sphinx and Royal Sculpture from the Reign of Amenemhat II*. Mainz: von Zabern, 1996.

Firth, Cecil. "Preliminary Report on the Excavations at Saqqara (1925–1926)." *ASAE* 26 (1926): 97–101.

———. "Report on the Excavations of the Department of Antiquities at Saqqara (November, 1929–April, 1930)." *ASAE* 30 (1930): 185–89.

Firth, Cecil and Battiscombe Gunn. *Teti Pyramid Cemeteries*. SAE. Cairo: Institut français d'archéologie orientale, 1926.

Firth, Cecil and James Quibell. *The Step Pyramid*, 2 vols. Excavations at Saqqara. Cairo: Institut français d'archéologie orientale, 1935.

Fischer, Henry. *Ancient Egyptian Representations of Turtles*. New York: The Metropolitan Museum of Art, 1968.

———. "Egyptian Art." *BMMA* 24 (1965): 52–54.

———. "An Elusive Shape within the Fisted Hands of Egyptian Statues." *MMJ* 10 (1975): 9–21.

———. "The Nubian Mercenaries of Gebelein during the First Intermediate Period." *Kush* 9 (1961): 44–80.

———. "A Scribe of the Army in a Saqqara Mastaba of the Early Fifth Dynasty." *JNES* 18 (1959): 233–72.

———. *Varia*. Egyptian Studies 1. New York: The Metropolitan Museum of Art, 1976.

Förster, Frank. *Der Abu Ballas-Weg: Eine pharaonische Karawanenroute durch die Libysche Wüste*. Africa praehistorica 28. Cologne: Heinrich-Barth Institut, 2015.

———. "Beyond Dakhla: The Abu Ballas Trail in the Libyan Desert (SW Egypt)." In *Desert Road Archaeology in Ancient Egypt and Beyond*, edited by Frank Förster and Heiko Riemer, 297–337. Africa praehistorica 27. Cologne: Heinrich-Barth Institut, 2013.

———. "With Donkeys, Jars and Water Bags into the Libyan Desert: The Abu Ballas Trail in the Late Old Kingdom/First Intermediate Period." *BMSAES* 7 (2007): 1–36.

Forstner-Müller, Irene and Dietrich Raue. "Contacts between Egypt and the Levant in the 3rd Millennium BC." In *Egypt and the Southern Levant in the Early Bronze Age*, edited by Felix Höflmayer and Ricardo Eichmann, 57–67. Orient-Archäologie 31. Rahden: Leidorf, 2014.

———. "Elephantine and the Levant." In *Zeichen aus dem Sand: Streiflichter aus Ägyptens Geschichte zu Ehren von Günter Dreyer*, edited by Eva-Maria Engel, Vera Müller, and Ulrich Hartung, 127–48. Menes 5. Wiesbaden: Harrassowitz, 2008.

Fossey, John and Jane Francis, eds. *The Diniacopoulos Collection in Québec: Greek and Roman Antiquities*. Montreal: Concordia University, 2004.

Francis, Jane and George Harrison, eds. *Life and Death in Ancient Egypt: The Diniacopoulos Collection*. Montreal: Concordia University, 2011.

Frankfurter, David. "Egyptian Religion and the Problem of the Category 'Sacrifice.'" In *Ancient Mediterannean Sacrifice*, edited by Jennifer Wright Knust and Zsuzsanna Várhelyi, 75–93. Oxford: Oxford University Press, 2011.

———. "The Vitality of Egyptian Images in Late Antiquity: Christian Memory and Response." In *The Sculptural Environment of the Roman Near East: Reflections on Culture, Ideology, and Power*, edited by Yaron Z. Eliav, Elise A. Friedland, and Sharon Herbert, 659–78. Interdisciplinary Studies in Ancient Culture and Religion 9. Leuven: Peeters, 2008.

Freed, Rita. "Sculpture of the Middle Kingdom." In *A Companion to Ancient Egypt*, vol. 2, edited by Alan B. Lloyd, 882–912. Chichester: Wiley-Blackwell, 2010.

———. "Stela Workshops of Early Dynasty 12." In *Studies in Honor of William Kelly Simpson*, vol. 1, edited by Peter Der Manuelian, 297–336. Boston: Museum of Fine Arts, 1996.

Fuscaldo, Perla. "Tell al-Dab'a: Two Execration Pits and a Foundation Deposit." In *Egyptology at the Dawn of the Twenty-First Century: Proceedings of the Eighth International Congress of Egyptologists, Cairo, 2000*, vol. 1, edited by Zahi Hawass, 185–88. Cairo: The American University in Cairo Press, 2003.

Gardiner, Alan. *Egyptian Grammar*, 3rd rev. ed. Oxford: Griffith Institute, 1957.

Giddy, Lisa. *Egyptian Oases*. Warminster: Aris & Phillips, 1987.

Goebs, Katja. *Crowns in Egyptian Funerary Literature: Royalty, Rebirth, and Destruction*. Griffith Institute Monographs. Oxford: Griffith Institute, 2008.

Gourdon, Yannis. "Le nom des épouses abydéniennes de Pépy Ier et la formule de serment à la fin de l'Ancien Empire." *BIFAO* 106 (2006): 89–104.

Gratien, Brigitte. "La Basse Nubie à l'Ancien Empire: Egyptiens et autochtones." *JEA* 81 (1995): 43–56.

Greenberg, Raphael. "No Collapse: Transmutations of Early Bronze Age Urbanism in the Southern Levant." In *The Late Third Millennium in the Ancient Near East: Chronology, C14 and Climate Change*, edited by Felix Höflmayer, 31–58. OIS 11. Chicago: Oriental Institute of the University of Chicago, 2017.

Grimal, Nicolas. "Les 'noyés' de Balat." In *Melanges offerts à Jean Vercoutter*, edited by Francis Geus and Florence Thill, 111–21. Paris: Editions Recherche sur les Civilisations, 1985.

Grimes, Ronald. *The Craft of Ritual Studies*. Oxford: Oxford University Press, 2014.

Grunert, Stefan. "Die Schächtung im Totenopfer: Ritualbestandteil vs. Reflexion allgemeinen Brauchtums." In *Tierkulte im pharaonischen Ägypten und im Kulturvergleich*, edited by Martin Fitzenreiter, 69–82. London: Golden House, 2005.

Gundacker, Roman. "The Significance of Foreign Toponyms and Ethnonyms in Old Kingdom Text Sources." In *The Late Third Millennium in the Ancient Near East: Chronology, C14 and Climate Change*, edited by Felix Höflmayer, 333–426. OIS 11. Chicago: Oriental Institute of the University of Chicago, 2017.

Haeny, Gerhard. "New Kingdom 'Mortuary Temples' and 'Mansions of Millions of Years.'" In *Temples of Ancient Egypt*, edited by Byron Shafer, 86–126. Ithaca, NY: Cornell University Press, 1997.

Hagen, Fredrik Norland and Kim Ryholt. *The Antiquities Trade in Egypt 1880–1930: The H.O. Lange Papers*. Copenhagen: Det Kongelige Danske Videnskabernes Selskab, 2016.

———. "The Antiquities Trade in Egypt during the Time of Rudolf Mosse." In *Mosse im Museum: Die Stiftungstätigkeit des Berliner Verlegers Rudolf Mosse (1843–1920) für das Ägyptische Museum Berlin*, edited by Jana Helmbold-Doyé and Thomas Gertzen, 59–74. Berlin: Hentrich & Hentrich, 2017.

Hall, Emma Swan. *The Pharaoh Smites His Enemy: A Comparative Study*. MÄS 44. Munich: Deutscher Kunstverlag, 1986.

Hamonic, Fanny. "Cérémonial ou cérémoniel? Production de viande et pratiques religieuses à l'Ancien Empire." In *Religion et alimentation en Égypte et Orient anciens*, vol. 1, edited by Marie-Lys Arnette, 141–71. RAPH 43. Cairo: Institut français d'archéologie orientale, 2019.

Harvey, Julia C. *Wooden Statues of the Old Kingdom: A Typological Study*. Egyptological Memoirs 2. Leiden: Brill, 2001.

Hassan, Selim. "The Causeway of Wnis at Sakkara." *ZÄS* 80 (1955): 136–39.

———. "Excavations at Saqqara 1937–1938." *ASAE* 38 (1938): 518–21.

Hawass, Zahi. "Five Old Kingdom Sphinxes Found at Saqqara." In *Millions of Jubilees: Studies in Honor of David P. Silverman*, edited by Zahi Hawass and Jennifer Houser Wegner, 205–25. CASAE 39. Cairo: Supreme Council of Antiquities, 2010.

Hawass, Zahi and Miroslav Verner. "Newly Discovered Blocks from the Causeway of Sahure (Archaeological Report)." *MDAIK* 52 (1996): 177–86.

Hayes, William C. *The Scepter of Egypt: A Background for the Study of the Egyptian Antiquities in The Metropolitan Museum of Art*, 2 vols. New York: The Metropolitan Museum of Art, 1953–1978.

Hays, Harold M. "The Death of the Democratisation of the Afterlife." In *Old Kingdom, New Perspectives: Egyptian Art and Archaeology 2750–2150 BC*, edited by Nigel Strudwick and Helen Strudwick, 115–30. Oxford: Oxbow, 2011.

———. "The Entextualization of the Pyramid Texts and the Religious History of the Old Kingdom." In *Towards a New History for the Egyptian Old Kingdom: Perspectives on the Pyramid Age*, edited by Peter Der Manuelian and Thomas Schneider, 200–226. HES 1. Leiden: Brill, 2015.

———. *The Organization of the Pyramid Texts: Typology and Disposition*. PAe 31. Leiden: Brill, 2012.

———. "Unreading the Pyramids." *BIFAO* 109 (2009): 195–220.

Helck, Wolfgang. "Die Bedeutung der Felsinschriften J. Lopez, Inscripciones rupestres Nr. 27 und 28." *SAK* 1 (1974): 215–25.

Hendrickx, Stan, Frank Förster, and Merel Eyckerman. "The Pharaonic Pottery of the Abu Ballas Trail: 'Filling Stations' along a Desert Highway in Southwestern Egypt." In *Desert Road Archaeology in Ancient Egypt and Beyond*, edited by Frank Förster and Heiko Riemer, 339–79. Africa praehistorica 27. Cologne: Heinrich-Barth Institut, 2013.

Hill, Marsha. "170. Pepi I Kneeling." In *Egyptian Art in the Age of the Pyramids*, edited by Dorothea Arnold, Krzysztof Grzymski, and Christiane Ziegler, 434–35, cat. no. 170. New York: The Metropolitan Museum of Art, 1999.

———. "173. Kneeling Captive." In *Egyptian Art in the Age of the Pyramids*, edited by Dorothea Arnold, Krzysztof Grzymski, and Christiane Ziegler, 440–41. New York: The Metropolitan Museum of Art, 1999.

———. "174. Kneeling Captive." In *Egyptian Art in the Age of the Pyramids*, edited by Dorothea Arnold, Krzysztof Grzymski, and Christiane Ziegler, 441. New York: The Metropolitan Museum of Art, 1999.

———. *Royal Bronze Statuary from Ancient Egypt: With Special Attention to the Kneeling Pose*. Egyptological Memoirs 3. Leiden: Brill, 2004.

Höflmayer, Felix. "Egypt and the Southern Levant in the Late Early Bronze Age." In *Egypt and the Southern Levant in the Early Bronze Age*, edited by Felix Höflmayer and Ricardo Eichmann, 135–48. Orient-Archäologie 31. Rahden: Leidorf, 2014.

Hölscher, Uvo. *Das Hohe Tor von Medinet Habu: Eine Baugeschichtliche Untersuchung*. WVDOG 12. Leipzig: Hinrichs, 1910.

———. *The Mortuary Temple of Ramses III*, part 1. Translated by Diederika Seele. The Excavation of Medinet Habu 3; OIP 54. Chicago: University of Chicago Press, 1941.

———. *The Mortuary Temple of Ramses III*, part 2. Translated by Elizabeth Hauser. The Excavation of Medinet Habu 4; OIP 55. Chicago: University of Chicago Press, 1951.

Hope, Colin. "Egypt and 'Libya' to the End of the Old Kingdom: A View from Dakhleh Oasis." In *The Archaeology and Art of Ancient Egypt: Essays in Honor of David B. O'Connor*, vol. 1, edited by Zahi Hawass and Janet Richards, 399–415. CASAE 36. Cairo: Supreme Council of Antiquities, 2007.

Hornung, Erik. *The Valley of the Kings: Horizon of Eternity*, translated by David Warburton. New York: Timken, 1990.

Hornung, Erik and Elisabeth Staehelin. *Neue Studien zum Sedfest*. AegHelv 20. Basel: Schwabe, 2006.

———. *Studien zum Sedfest*. AegHelv 1. Geneva: Edition de Belles Lettres, 1974.

Hornung, Erik, Rolf Krauss, and David A. Warburton, ed. *Ancient Egyptian Chronology*. HdO 83. Leiden: Brill, 2006.

Hussein, Abd-el-Salam Mohamed. "Fouilles sur la chaussee d'Ounas (1941–1943)." *ASAE* 43 (1943): 439–42.

Ibrahim, Moustafa Rezk and Pierre Tallet. "Trois bas-reliefs de l'époque thinite au Ouadi el-Humur: aux origins de l'exploitation du Sud-Sinaï par les Égyptiens." *RdE* 59 (2008): 155–80.

Ikram, Salima. *Choice Cuts: Meat Production in Ancient Egypt*. OLA 69. Leuven: Peeters, 1995.

———. "In Death as in Life, 'You Are What You Eat': Transformation, Mummification and Food Offerings in Ancient Egypt." In *Religion et alimentation en Égypte et Orient anciens*, vol. 2, edited by Marie-Lys Arnette, 387–413. RAPH 43. Cairo: Institut français d'archéologie orientale, 2019.

Illustrated Handbook of the Los Angeles County Museum of Art. Los Angeles: Los Angeles County Museum of Art, 1965.

Insoll, Timothy. *Archaeology, Ritual, Religion*. London: Routledge, 2004.

———, ed. *Oxford Handbook of the Archaeology of Ritual and Religion*. Oxford: Oxford University Press, 2011.

Jánosi, Peter. "Bemerkungen zu den Nordkapellen des Alten Reiches." *SAK* 22 (1995): 145–68.

———. "Die Entwicklung und Deutung des Totenopferraumes in den Pyramidentempeln des Alten Reiches." In *Ägyptische Tempel – Struktur, Funktion und Programm (Akten der Ägyptologischen Tempeltagungen in Gosen 1990 und in Mainz 1992)*, edited by Rolf Gundlach and Matthias Rochholz, 143–63. HÄB 37. Hildesheim: Gerstenberg, 1994.

———. "Die Pyramiden der Könige der 5. Dynastie." In *Die Pyramiden Ägyptens: Monumente der Ewigkeit*, edited by Christian Hölzl, Martin Fitzenreiter, Regina Hölzl, Wilfried Seipel, and Schloss Schallaburg, 85–99. Wien: Brandstätter, 2004.

———. "Die Pyramidenanlage der "anonymen Königin" des Djedkare-Isesi." *MDAIK* 45 (1989): 187–202.

———. *Die Pyramidenanlagen der Königinnen: Untersuchungen zu einem Grabtyp des Alten und Mittleren Reiches*. DÖAWW 13; Untersuchungen der Zweigstelle Kairo des Österreichischen Archäologischen Institutes 13. Vienna: Verlag der Österreichischen Akademie der Wissenschaften, 1996.

———. "The Reconstruction and Evaluation of the Pyramid Complex of Queen Khentkaus." In *The Pyramid Complex of Khentkaus*, edited by Miroslav Verner, 143–64. Abusir 3. Prague: Czech Institute of Egyptology, 1995.

———. "The Tombs of Officials: Houses of Eternity." In *Egyptian Art in the Age of the Pyramids*, edited by Dorothea Arnold, Krzysztof Grzymski, and Christiane Ziegler, 27–39. New York: The Metropolitan Museum of Art, 1999.

Jánosi, Peter and Mohamed Megahed. "Eine fast vergessene Pyramidenanlage." *Antike Welt* 46:2 (2015): 51–60.

Janzen, Mark. "The Iconography of Humiliation: The Depiction and Treatment of the Bound Foreigner in New Kingdom Egypt." PhD diss, University of Memphis, 2013.
Jéquier, Gustave. *Douze ans de fouilles dans la nécropole memphite: 1924–1956*. Neuchâtel: Université de Neuchâtel, 1940.
———. *Le monument funéraire de Pépi II*, 3 vols. FouillesSaqq. Cairo: Institut français d'archéologie orientale, 1936–1940.
———. "Planche 22." In *Documents pour servir à l'étude de l'art égyptien*, vol. 2, by Jean Capart, 21–23. Paris: Les Éditions du Pégase, 1931.
———. "Rapport préliminaire sur les fouilles exécutées en 1926–1927 dans la partie méridionale de la nécropole memphite." *ASAE* 27 (1927): 49–61.
———. "Rapport préliminaire sur les fouilles exécutées en 1929–1930 dans la partie méridionale de la nécropole memphite." *ASAE* 30 (1930): 105–16.
Jeuthe, Clara. "Initial Results: The Sheikh Muftah Occupation at Balat North/1 (Dakhla Oasis)." *Archéo-Nil* 24 (2014): 103–14.
Junker, Hermann. *Giza VIII: Der Ostabschnitt des Westfriedhofs*. AAWWien 81. Vienna: Akademie der Wissenschaften, 1947.
Just, Bryan R. "Modifications of Ancient Maya Sculpture." *RES: Anthropology and Aesthetics* 48 (2005): 69–82.
Kanawati, Naguib. *Conspiracies in the Egyptian Palace: Unis to Pepy I*. London: Routledge, 2003.
———. *The Egyptian Administration in the Old Kingdom: Evidence on Its Economic Decline*. Warminster: Aris & Phillips, 1977.
———. *Governmental Reforms in Old Kingdom Egypt*. Warminster: Aris & Phillips, 1980.
———. "The Vizier Nebet and the Royal Women of the Sixth Dynasty." In *Thebes and Beyond: Studies in Honour of Kent R. Weeks*, edited by Zahi Hawass and Salima Ikram, 115–25. Cairo: Supreme Council of Antiquities, 2010.
Kanawati, Naguib and Ann McFarlane. *Deshasha: The Tombs of Inti, Shedu and Others*. RACE 5. Sydney: The Australian Centre for Egyptology, 1993.
Kanawati, Naguib and Joyce Swinton. *Egypt in the Sixth Dynasty: Challenges and Responses*. Wallasey: Abercromby Press, 2018.
Kaper, Olaf and Harco Willems. "Policing the Desert: Old Kingdom Activity around the Dakhleh Oasis." In *Egypt and Nubia: Gifts of the Desert*, edited by Renée Friedman, 79–94. London: British Museum Press, 2002.
Keimer, Louis. "Notes de lecture." *BIFAO* 56 (1957): 97–120.
———. "Une statue de prisonnier remontant au Nouvel Empire." *ASAE* 49 (1949): 37–39.
Kemp, Barry. "Old Kingdom, Middle Kingdom, and Second Intermediate Period c. 2686–1552 BC." In *Ancient Egypt: A Social History*, 71–182. Cambridge: Cambridge University Press, 1983.
Klemm, Dietrich and Rosemarie Klemm. *The Stones of the Pyramids: Provenance of the Building Stones of the Old Kingdom Pyramids of Egypt*. Berlin: de Gruyter, 2010.
Kloth, Nicole. *Die (auto-) biographischen Inschriften des ägyptischen Alten Reiches: Untersuchungen zu Phraseologie und Entwicklung*. Hamburg: Buske, 2002.
Knust, Jennifer Wright and Zsuzsanna Várhelyi. "Introduction: Images, Acts, Meanings and Ancient Mediterranean Sacrifice." In *Ancient Mediterranean Sacrifice*, edited by Jennifer Wright Knust and Zsuzsanna Várhelyi, 3–31. Oxford: Oxford University Press, 2011.
Kockelmann, Holger. "Die Fremdvölkerlisten in den Soubassements der ptolemäisch-römischen Heiligtümer: Feindnamen und Feindvernichtungsrituale im Tempel zwischen Tradition und Wandel." In *Von Meroe bis Indien: Fremdvölkerlisten und nubische Gabenträger in den griechisch-römischen Tempeln*, edited by Holger Kockelmann and Alexa Rickert, 3–141. Wiesbaden: Harrassowitz, 2015.
Koenig, Yvan. "The Image of the Foreigner in the Magical Texts of Ancient Egypt." In *Moving Across Borders: Foreign Relations, Religion and Cultural Interactions in the Ancient Mediterranean*, edited by Panagiotis Kousoulis and Konstantinos Magliveras, 223–38. OLA 159. Leuven: Peeters, 2007.
———. *Magie et magiciens dans l'Égypte ancienne*. Paris: Pygmalion, 1994.
Köhler, E. Christiana and Jean-Paul Thalmann. "Synchronising Early Egyptian Chronologies and the Northern Levant." In *Egypt and the Southern Levant in the Early Bronze Age*, edited by Felix Höflmayer and Ricardo Eichmann, 181–206. Orient-Archäologie 31. Rahden: Leidorf, 2014.
Krejčí, Jaromír. *The Architecture of the Mastaba of Ptahshepses*. Abusir 11. Prague: Czech Institute of Egyptology, 2009.
———. "Nyuserra Revisited." In *Abusir and Saqqara in the Year 2010*, vol. 2, edited by Miroslav Bárta, Filip Coppens, and Jaromír Krejčí, 518–29. Prague: Czech Institute of Egyptology, 2011.
Kuhlmann, Klaus Peter. "The 'Oasis Bypath' or the Issue of Desert Trade in Pharaonic Times." In *Tides of the Desert – Gezeiten der Wüste: Contributions to the Archaeology and Environmental History of Africa in Honour of Rudolph Kuper*, edited by Jennerstrasse 8, 125–70. Cologne: Heinrich-Barth Institut, 2002.
———. "Der 'Wasserberg des Djedefre' (Chufu 01/1): Ein Lagerplatz mit Expeditionsinschriften der 4. Dynastie im Raum der Oase Dachla." *MDAIK* 61 (2005): 244–89.

Kuraszkiewicz, Kamil O. "The Tomb of Ikhi/Mery in Saqqara and Royal Expeditions during the Sixth Dynasty." *Études et Travaux* 27 (2014): 202–16.

Kusber, Eberhard. "Der altägyptische Ka – 'Seele' oder 'Persönlichkeit'?" PhD Diss., University of Tübingen, 2005.

Kyriakidis, Evangelos. "Archaeologies of Ritual." In *The Archaeology of Ritual*, ed. Evangelos Kyriakidis, 289–308. Cotsen Advanced Seminars 3. Los Angeles: Cotsen Institute of Archaeology at UCLA, 2007.

———, ed. *The Archaeology of Ritual*. Cotsen Advanced Seminars 3. Los Angeles: Cotsen Institute of Archaeology at UCLA, 2007.

Laboury, Dimitri. "Designers and Makers of Ancient Egyptian Monumental Epigraphy." In *The Oxford Handbook of Egyptian Epigraphy and Paleography*, edited by Vanesssa Davies and Dimitri Laboury, 85–101. New York: Oxford University Press, 2020.

———. "Portrait versus Ideal Image." *UCLA Encyclopedia of Egyptology*, edited by Willeke Wendrich. Los Angeles: UCLA, 2010. http://digital2.library.ucla.edu/viewItem.do?ark=21198/zz0025jjv0.

———. "Tradition and Creativity: Toward a Study of Intericonicity in Ancient Egyptian Art." In *(Re)productive Traditions in Ancient Egypt: Proceedings of the Conference Held at the University of Liège, 6th–8th February 2013*, edited by Todd Gillen, 229–58. Collection Ægyptiaca Leodiensia 10. Liège: Presses Universitaires de Liège, 2017.

Labrousse, Audran. *L'architecture des pyramides à textes*, 2 vols. MAFS 3; BiEtud 114 and 131. Cairo: Institut français d'archéologique orientale, 1996–2000.

———. "Les complexes funéraires du roi Pépi Ier et de trois reines." *Les dossiers d'archéologie* 146–147 (1990): 80–87.

———. "Une épouse du roi Mérenrê Ier: La reine Ânkhesenpépy II." In *Abusir and Saqqara in the Year 2000*, edited by Miroslav Bárta and Jaromír Krejčí, 485–90. Prague: Oriental Institute of the Academy of Sciences of the Czech Republic, 2000.

———. "Huit épouses du roi Pepy Ier." In *Egyptian Culture and Society: Studies in Honour of Naguib Kanawati*, edited by Alexandra Woods, Ann McFarlane, and Susanne Binder, 297–314. Cairo: Supreme Council of Antiquities, 2010.

———. "The Pyramids of the Sixth Dynasty." In *The Treasures of the Pyramids*, edited by Zahi Hawass, 264–81. Cairo: The American University in Cairo Press, 2003.

———. "Le temple funéraire de Pépi I au Nouvel Empire." In *Memphis et ses nécropoles au Nouvel Empire: Novelles données, nouvelles questions,* edited by Alain-Pierre Zivie, 67–68. Paris: Éditions du Centre National de la Recherche Scientifique, 1988.

———. *Le temple funéraire du roi Pépy Ier: Le temps de la construction*. MAFS 6; MIFAO 137. Cairo: Institut français d'archéologie orientale, 2019.

Labrousse, Audran and Ahmed Moussa. *La chaussée du complexe funéraire du roi Ounas*. BiEtud 134. Cairo: Institut français d'archéologie orientale, 2002.

———. *Le temple d'accueil du complexe funéraire du roi Ounas*. BiEtud 111. Cairo: Institut français d'archéologie orientale, 1996.

Labrousse, Audran and Jean-Philippe Lauer. *Les complexes funéraires d'Ouserkaf et de Néferhétepès*. BiEtud 130. Cairo: Institut français d'archéologie orientale, 2000.

Labrousse, Audran, Jean-Philippe Lauer, and Jean Leclant. *Le temple haut de complexe funéraire du roi Ounas*. MAFS 2; BiEtud 73. Cairo: Institut français d'archéologie orientale, 1977.

Landgráfová, Renata. *Faience Inlays from the Funerary Temple of King Raneferef: Ranferef's Substitute Decoration Programme*. Abusir 14. Prague: Czech Institute of Egyptology, 2006.

———. "The Function of the Faience Inlays in the Funerary Temple of Raneferef at Abusir." In *The Old Kingdom Art and Archaeology: Proceedings of the Conference Held in Prague, May 31–June 4, 2004*, edited by Miroslav Bárta, 203–8. Prague: Czech Institute of Egyptology, 2006.

Lansing, Ambrose. "An Old Kingdom Captive." *BMMA* 5 (1947): 149–52.

Lauer, Jean-Philippe. "Cinquante années de recherches et travaux aux pyramides de Saqqarah." *CRAIBL* 124 (1980): 536–67.

———. "Fouilles du Service des Antiquites à Saqqarah." *ASAE* 39 (1939): 447–67.

———. *Le mystere de pyramides*. Paris: Presses de la Cité, 1988.

———. "Note sur divers travaux effectues à Saqqarah en 1936 et 1937." *ASAE* 37 (1937): 103–15.

———. "Rapport sur les travaux à Saqqarah (26 Novembre 1969–25 Mars 1970)." *ASAE* 62 (1977): 201–5.

———. "Recherches et travaux à Saqqarah (campagnes 1967-1968 et 1968–1969)." *CRAIBL* 113 (1969): 460–79.

———. "Recherches et travaux à Saqqarah (campagne 1969–1970)." *CRAIBL* 114 (1970): 484–503.

———. "Recherches et travaux à Saqqarah: campagnes 1970–1971 et 1971–1972." *CRAIBL* 116 (1972): 577–600.

———. "Recherches et travaux à Saqqarah (campagnes 1972–1973)." *CRAIBL* 117 (1973): 323–40.

———. *Saqqara: The Royal Cemetery of Memphis*. New York: Scribner's Sons, 1976.

———. "Les statues de prisonniers du complexe funeraire de Pepi Ier." *BIE* 51 (1969–1970): 37–45.

———. "Travaux à Saqqarah (campagne 1976–1977)." *ASAE* 65 (1983): 79–82.

———. "Travaux aux pyramids de Saqqarah et à leurs complexes monumentaux." *BIE* 60 and 61 (1978–1979, 1979–1980): 95–132.

———. "Travaux d'anastylose et nouvelles recherches sur les pyramides et leurs complexes à Saqqarah." *CRAIBL* 110 (1966): 453–69.

———. "Travaux dans la necropole de Saqqarah (campagne 1965–1966)." *BSFE* 47 (1966): 20–35.

———. "Travaux effectués à Saqqarah de fin Novembre 1975 au 20 Mars 1976." *ASAE* 64 (1981): 149–53.

———. "Travaux et découvertes à Saqqarah (1970–1971)." *BSFE* 62 (1971): 30–48.

———. "Travaux et découvertes à Saqqarah (campagne 1968–1969)." *BSFE* 56 (1969): 11–24.

———. "Travaux et recherches à Saqqarah (15 Décembre 1974–28 Mars 1975)." *ASAE* 63 (1979): 137–42.

Lauer, Jean-Philippe and Jean Leclant. "Découverte de statues de prisonniers au temple de la pyramide de Pépi I." *RdE* 21 (1969): 56–62.

———. *Le temple haut du complexe funéraire du roi Teti*. MAFS 1; BiEtud 51. Cairo: Institut français d'archéologie orientale, 1972.

Lebedev, Maksim. "Exploiting the Southern Lands: Ancient Egyptian Quarrying, Mining, and Trade Missions to Nubia and Punt during the Old Kingdom." In *Nubian Archaeology in the XXIst Century: Proceedings of the Thirteenth International Conference for Nubian Studies, Neuchâtel, 1st–6th September 2014*, edited by Matthieu Honegger, 277–91. OLA 273; Publications de la Mission archéologique suisse à Kerma 1. Leuven: Peeters, 2018.

Leclant, Jean. "La 'famille libyenne' au temple haut de Pépi Ier." In *Livre du centenaire: 1880–1980*, edited by Jean Vercoutter, 49–54. MIFAO 104. Cairo: Institut français d'archéologie orientale, 1980.

———. "Fouilles et travaux en Égypte, 1952–1953." *Orientalia* 23 (1954): 64–79.

———. "Fouilles et travaux en Égypte et au Soudan, 1968–1969." *Orientalia* 39 (1970): 320–74.

———. "Fouilles et travaux en Égypte et au Soudan, 1969–1970." *Orientalia* 40 (1971): 224–66.

———. "Fouilles et travaux en Égypte et au Soudan, 1972–1973." *Orientalia* 43 (1974): 171–227.

———. "Fouilles et travaux en Égypte et au Soudan, 1973–1974." *Orientalia* 44 (1975): 200–244.

———. "Fouilles et travaux en Égypte et au Soudan, 1974–1975." *Orientalia* 45 (1976): 275–314.

———. "Fouilles et travaux en Égypte et au Soudan, 1975–1976." *Orientalia* 46 (1977): 233–99.

———. "Fouilles et travaux en Égypte et au Soudan, 1976–1977." *Orientalia* 47 (1978): 266–320.

———. "Fouilles et travaux en Égypte et au Soudan, 1977–1978." *Orientalia* 48 (1979): 340–412.

———. "Fouilles et travaux en Égypte et au Soudan, 1979–1980." *Orientalia* 51 (1982): 49–122.

———. "Fouilles et travaux en Égypte et au Soudan, 1981–1982." *Orientalia* 52 (1983): 461–542.

———. "Fouilles et travaux en Égypte et au Soudan, 1982–1983." *Orientalia* 53 (1984): 350–416.

———. "La 'mascarade' des boeufs gras et le triomphe de l'Égypte." *MDAIK* 14 (1956): 128–45.

———. "Récentes recherches à la pyramide de Téti, à Saqqarah." *BIE* 47 (1969): 53–63.

———. "Récentes recherches à la pyramide de Téti à Saqqarah." *BSFE* 46 (1966): 9–16.

———. *Recherches dans la pyramide et au temple haut du pharaon Pepi Ier, à Saqqarah*. Leiden: Nederland Instituut voor het Nabije Oosten, 1979.

———. "Travaux de la Mission archéologique française de Saqqarah (campagne 1980)." *ASAE* 68 (1982): 55–61.

Leclant, Jean and Audran Labrousse. "Découvertes récentes de la Mission archéologique française à Saqqâra (campagnes 2001–2005)." *CRAIBL* 150 (2006): 103–20.

———. "Les reines Ankhnespépy II et III (fin de l'Ancien Empire): campagnes 1999 et 2000 de la MAFS." *CRAIBL* 145 (2001): 367–84.

Leclant, Jean and Gisèle Clerc. "Fouilles et travaux en Égypte et au Soudan, 1983–1984." *Orientalia* 54 (1985): 337–415.

———. "Fouilles et travaux en Égypte et au Soudan, 1984–1985." *Orientalia* 55 (1986): 236–319.

———. "Fouilles et travaux en Égypte et au Soudan, 1985–1986." *Orientalia* 56 (1987): 292–389.

Legros, Rémi, ed. *Cinquante ans d'éternité: jubilé de la Mission archéologique française de Saqqâra*. MAFS 5, BiEtud 162. Cairo: Institut français d'archéologie orientale, 2015.

———. "Inhumations privées dans la nécropole de Pépy Ier." In *Abusir and Saqqara in the Year 2015*, edited by Miroslav Bárta, Filip Coppens, and Jaromír Krejčí, 211–18. Prague: Czech Institute of Egyptology, 2017.

Lehner, Mark. *The Complete Pyramids*. London: Thames & Hudson, 2008.

Lepsius, C. R. *Denkmäler aus Ägypten und Äthiopien*, 7 vols. Reprint on reduced scale. Geneva: Éditions de Belles-Lettres, 1972–1973.

Lichtheim, Miriam. *Ancient Egyptian Literature: A Book of Readings*, vol. 2. Berkeley: University of California Press, 1976.

Liverani, Mario. *Prestige and Interest: International Relations in the Near East ca. 1600–1100 B.C.* Padua: Sargon, 1990.

Lopez, Jesus. "Inscriptions de l'Ancien Empire à Khor el-Aquiba." *RdE* 19 (1967): 51–66.

Loprieno, Antonio. *Topos und Mimesis: Zum Ausländer in der ägyptischen Literatur.* ÄgAbh 48. Wiesbaden: Harrassowitz, 1988.

Ludes, Bertrand and Éric Crubézy. "Le sacrifice humain en contexte funéraire problèmes poses à l'anthropobiologie et à la médecine légale: L'exemple prédynastique." In *La sacrifice humain: En Égypte ancienne et ailleurs*, edited by Jean-Pierre Albert and Béatrix Midant-Reynes, 82–95. Paris: Soleb, 2005.

McFarlane, Ann. *Mastabas at Saqqara: Kaiemhest, Kaipunesut, Kaiemsenu, Sehetepu and Others.* RACE 20. Oxford: Aris & Phillips, 2003.

Malek, Jaromir. *In the Shadow of the Pyramids: Egypt during the Old Kingdom.* Norman: University of Oklahoma Press, 1986.

Maragioglio, Vito and Celeste Ambrogio Rinaldi. *L'Architettura della Piramidi Menfite*, vol. 8, translated by Alfred Ernest Howell. Rapallo: Officine Grafiche Canessa, 1975.

Marcolin, Michele. "*Iny*, a Much-Traveled Official of the Sixth Dynasty: Unpublished Reliefs in Japan." In *Abusir and Saqqara in the Year 2005*, edited by Miroslav Bárta, Filips Coppens, and Jaromir Krejčí, 282–310. Prague: Czech Institute of Egyptology, 2006.

Marcolin, Michele and Andrés Diego Espinel. "The Sixth Dynasty Biographic Inscriptions of Iny: More Pieces to the Puzzle." In *Abusir and Saqqara in the Year 2010*, vol. 2, edited by Miroslav Bárta, Filips Coppens, and Jaromir Krejčí, 570–615. Prague: Czech Institute of Egyptology, 2011.

Martin, Karl. "Sedfest." *LÄ* 5 (1984): 782–90.

Martin-Pardey, Eva. *Untersuchungen zur ägyptischen Provinzialverwaltung bis zum Ende des Alten Reiches.* Hildesheim: Gerstenberg, 1976.

Mathieu, Bernard. "Mais qui est donc Osiris? Ou la politique sous le linceul de la religion (enquêtes dans les Textes des Pyramides, 3)." *ENiM* 3 (2010): 77–107.

Matić, Uroš. *Ethnic Identities in the Land of the Pharaohs: Past and Present Approaches in Egyptology.* Cambridge Elements. Cambridge: Cambridge University Press, 2020.

———. "'Her Striking but Cold Beauty': Gender and Violence in Depictions of Queen Nefertiti Smiting the Enemies." In *Archaeologies of Gender and Violence*, edited by Uroš Matić and Bo Jensen, 103–21. Oxford: Oxbow, 2017.

Megahed, Mohamed. "The Altar of Djedkare's Funerary Temple from South Saqqara." In *Cult and Belief in Ancient Egypt: Proceedings of the Fourth International Congress for Young Egyptologists*, edited by Teodor Lekov and Emil Buzov, 56–62. Sofia: East West, 2014.

———. "The *Antichambre Carrée* in the Old Kingdom. Decoration and Function." In *Rich and Great: Studies in Honour of Anthony J. Spalinger on the Occasion of His 70th Feast of Thoth*, edited by Renata Landgráfová and Jana Mynářová, 239–58. Prague: Charles University, 2016.

———. "Neue Forschungen im Grabbezirk des Djedkare-Isesi." *Sokar* 22 (2011): 24–35.

———. "The Pyramid Complex of 'Djedkare's Queen' in South Saqqara: Preliminary Report 2010." In *Abusir and Saqqara in the Year 2010*, vol. 2, edited by Miroslav Bárta, Filip Coppens, and Jaromír Krejčí, 616–34. Prague: Czech Institute of Egyptology, 2011.

———. "Sculptures from the Pyramid Complex of Djedkare Isesi at South Saqqara: A Preliminary Report." *Prague Egyptological Studies* 17 (2016): 24–33.

———. "Die Wiederentdeckung des Pyramindenbezirks des Djedkare-Isesi in Sakkara-Sud." *Sokar* 15 (2014): 6–19.

Megahed, Mohamed and Hana Vymazalová. "Neues zum Pyramidenbezirk der Königin Setibhor, der Gemahlin des Djedkare-Isesi." Translated by Christine Mende. *Sokar* 39 (2020): 64–79.

———. "Notes on the Newly Discovered Name of Djedkare's Queen." In *Guardian of Ancient Egypt: Studies in Honor of Zahi Hawass*, vol. 2, edited by Janice Kamrin, Miroslav Bárta, Salima Ikram, Mark Lehner, and Mohamed Megahed, 1023–41. Prague: Charles University, Faculty of Arts, 2020.

Megahed, Mohamed and Peter Jánosi. "The Pyramid Complex of Djedkare at Saqqara-South: Recent Results and Future Prospects." In *Abusir and Saqqara in the Year 2015*, edited by Miroslav Bárta, Filip Coppens, and Jaromír Krejčí, 237–56. Prague: Faculty of the Arts, Charles University, 2017.

Megahed, Mohamed, Peter Jánosi, and Hana Vymazalová. "Neues von der Pyramidenanlage des Djedkare-Isesi: Grabungs- und Forschungsergebnisse 2015–2016." *Sokar* 34:1 (2017): 36–63.

Merrillees, Robert. *The Tano Family: Gifts from the Nile to Cyprus.* Lefkosia: Moufflon, 2003.

Meurer, Georg. *Die Feinde des Königs in den Pyramidentexten.* OBO 189. Göttingen: Vandenhoeck & Ruprecht, 2002.

———. *Nubier in Ägypten bis zum beginn des Neuen Reiches: Zur Bedeutung der Stele Berlin 14753.* Berlin: Achet, 1996.

Miniaci, Gianluca, Juan Carlos Moreno García, Stephen Quirke, and Andréas Stauder, eds. *The Arts of Making in Ancient Egypt: Voices, Images, and Objects of Material Producers 2000–1500 BC*. Leiden: Sidestone, 2018.

de Miroschedji, Pierre. "Les Égyptiens au Sinaï du nord et en Palestine au Bronze Ancien." In *Le Sinaï durant l'antiquité et le Moyen Âge: 4000 ans d'histoire pour un desert*, edited by Dominique Valbelle and Charles Bonnet, 20–32. Paris: Editions Errance, 1998.

———. "The Socio-Political Dynamics of Egyptian–Canaanite Interaction in the Early Bronze Age." In *Egypt and the Levant: Interrelations from the 4th through the Early 3rd Millennium BCE*, edited by Edwin C. M. van den Brink and Thomas E. Levy, 39–57. London: Leicester University Press, 2002.

Moers, Gerald. "'Unter den Sohlen Pharaos': Fremdheit und Alterität im pharaonischen Ägypten." In *Abgrenzung, Eingrenzung: Komparatistische Studien zur Dialektik kultureller Identitätsbildung*, edited by Frank Lauterbach, Fritz Paul, and Ulrike-Christine Sander, 81–160. Göttingen: Vandenhoeck & Ruprecht, 2004.

———. "The World and the Geography of Otherness in Pharaonic Egypt." In *Geography and Ethnography: Perceptions of the World in Pre-Modern Societies*, edited by Kurt Raaflaub and Richard Talbert, 169–81. Malden, MA: Wiley-Blackwell, 2010.

Montet, M. Pierre. *Les constructions et les tombeau de Chéchanq III à Tanis*. La nécropole royale de Tanis 3; Fouilles de Tanis. Paris: Typographie Protat Frères, 1960.

———. "Les fouilles de Tanis: En 1933 et 1934." *Kemi* 5 (1935–1937): 1–18.

Morales, Antonio J. "From Voice to Papyrus to Wall: *Verschriftung* and *Verschriftlichung* in the Old Kingdom Pyramid Texts." In *Understanding Material Text Cultures*, edited by Markus Hilgert, 69–130. Berlin: de Gruyter, 2016.

———. "Traces of Official and Popular Veneration to Nyuserra Iny at Abusir, Late Fifth Dynasty to the Middle Kingdom." In *Abusir and Saqqara in the Year 2005*, edited by Miroslav Bárta, Filip Coppens, and Jaromír Krejčí, 311–41. Prague: Czech Institute of Egyptology, 2006.

Moreno García, Juan Carlos. "Building the Pharaonic State: Territory, Elite, and Power in Ancient Egypt in the 3rd Millennium." In *Experiencing Power, Generating Authority: Cosmos, Politics and the Ideology of Kingship in Ancient Egypt and Mesopotamia*, edited by Jane Hill, Philip Jones, and Antonio Morales, 185–217. Philadelphia: University of Pennsylvania Museum of Archaeology and Anthropology, 2013.

———. "The 'Other' Administration: Patronage, Factions, and Informal Networks of Power in Ancient Egypt." In *Ancient Egyptian Administration*, edited by Juan Carlos Moreno García, 1029–65. HdO 104. Leiden: Brill, 2013.

———. "The Territorial Administration of the Kingdom in the Third Millennium." In *Ancient Egyptian Administration*, edited by Juan Carlos Moreno García, 85–152. HdO 104. Leiden: Brill, 2013.

———. "War in Old Kingdom Egypt (2686–2125 BCE)." In *Studies on War in the Ancient Near East: Collected Essays on Military History*, edited by Jordi Vidal, 5–41. AOAT 372. Münster: Ugarit-Verlag, 2010.

Morris, Ellen. "Ancient Egyptian Exceptionalism: Fragility, Flexibility and the Art of Not Collapsing." In *The Evolution of Fragility: Setting the Terms*, edited by Norman Yoffee, 61–88. Cambridge: McDonald Institute for Archaeological Research, 2019.

———. *Ancient Egyptian Imperialism*. Hoboken, NJ: Wiley-Blackwell, 2018.

Mourad, Anna-Latifa. "The Asiatic $sṯt$ and $sṯtyw$ from the Early Dynastic Period to the Middle Kingdom." In *The Cultural Manifestations of Religious Experience: Studies in Honour of Boyo G. Ockinga*, edited by Camilla Di Biase-Dyson and Leonie Donovan, 297–310. ÄAT 85. Münster: Ugarit-Verlag, 2017.

———. "Siege Scenes of the Old Kingdom." *BACE* 22 (2011): 135–58.

Moursi, Mohamed. "Die Ausgrabungen in der Gegend um die Pyramide des $ḏd-k3-rʿ$ 'issj' bei Saqqara." *ASAE* 71 (1987): 185–93.

Muhlestein, Kerry. "Royal Executions: Evidence Bearing on the Subject of Sanctioned Killing in the Middle Kingdom." *JESHO* 51 (2008): 181–208.

———. *Violence in the Service of Order: The Religious Framework for Sanctioned Killing in Ancient Egypt*. Oxford: Archaeopress, 2011.

Müller-Wollerman, Renate. "Krisenfaktoren im ägyptischen Staat des Ausgehenden Alten Reichs." PhD diss., University of Tübingen, 1986.

Mumford, Gregory. "Ras Budran and the Old Kingdom Trade in Red Sea Shells and Other Exotica." *BMSAES* 18 (2012): 107–45.

———. "Tell Ras Budran (Site 345): Defining Egypt's Eastern Frontier and Mining Operations in South Sinai during the Late Old Kingdom (Early EB IV/MB I)." *BASOR* 342 (2006): 13–67.

Murnane, William J. "Imperial Egypt and the Limits of Power." In *Amarna Diplomacy: The Beginnings of International Relations*, edited by Raymond Cohen and Raymond Westbrook, 101–11. Baltimore: Johns Hopkins University Press, 2000.

Myśliwiec, Karol. "A Contribution to the Second Style in Old Kingdom Art." In *Servant of Mut: Studies in Honor of Richard A. Fazzini*, edited by Sue D'Auria, 170–78. Leiden: Brill, 2008.

Na'aman, Nadav. "The Egyptian–Canaanite Correspondence." In *Amarna Diplomacy: The Beginnings of International Relations*, edited by Raymond Cohen and Raymond Westbrook, 125–38. Baltimore: Johns Hopkins University Press, 2000.

Näser, Claudia. "Structures and Realities of Egyptian–Nubian Interactions from the Late Old Kingdom to the Early New Kingdom." In *The First Cataract of the Nile: One Region – Diverse Perspectives*, edited by Dietrich Raue, Stephen Seidlmayer, and Philipp Speiser, 135–48. SDAIK 36. Berlin: de Gruyter, 2013.

Nuzzolo, Massimiliano. *The Fifth Dynasty Sun Temples: Kingship, Architecture and Religion in Third Millennium BC Egypt*. Prague: Charles University, 2018.

———. "Royal Architecture and Pyramid Texts: Some Remarks on 'Kingship' in the III Millennium B.C." In *Recent Discoveries and Latest Researches in Egyptology: Proceedings of the First Neapolitan Congress of Egyptology, Naples, June 18th–20th 2008*, edited by Francesco Raffaele, Massimiliano Nuzzolo, and Ilaria Incordino, 177–97. Wiesbaden: Harrassowitz, 2010.

———. "The Sun Temples of the Vth Dynasty: A Reassessment." *SAK* 36 (2007): 217–47.

Obsomer, Claude. "Les expeditions d'Herkhouf (VIe dynastie) et la localization de Iam." In *Pharaons noirs: Sur la piste des quarante jours*, edited by Marie-Cécile Bruwier, 39–52. Mariemont: Musée Royal de Mariemont, 2007.

O'Connor, David. "Egypt's Views of 'Others'." In *"Never Had the Like Occurred": Egypt's View of Its Past*, edited by John Tait, 155–85. London: UCL Press, 2003.

———. "The Interpretation of the Old Kingdom Pyramid Complex." In *Stationen: Beiträge zur Kulturgeschichte Ägyptens, Rainer Stadelmann gewidmet*, edited by Heike Guksch and Daniel Polz, 135–44. Mainz: von Zabern, 1998.

———. "The Locations of Yam and Kush and Their Historical Implications." *JARCE* 23 (1986): 27–50.

———. *The Old Kingdom Town at Buhen*. MEES 106. London: Egypt Exploration Society, 2014.

O'Connor, David and David P. Silverman, ed. *Ancient Egyptian Kingship*. PAe 9. Leiden: Brill, 1995.

O'Connor, David and Stephen Quirke. "Introduction: Mapping the Unknown in Ancient Egypt." In *Mysterious Lands*, edited by David O'Connor and Stephen Quirke, 1–21. London: UCL Press, 2003.

Olivier Coutau-Bégarie. *Archéologie: Egyptienne et Gréco-Romaine*, Drouot Richelieu, Paris, December 1, 1993. Paris: Olivier Coutau-Bégarie, 1993.

Orsenigo, Christian. "Digging at Sakkara in Milan: The James E. Quibell Archive." *KMT* 27.4 (Winter 2016–2017): 32–44.

———. "James E. Quibell Records on Saqqara in the Archives of Alexandre Varille." In *Abusir and Saqqara in the Year 2015*, edited by Miroslav Bárta, Filip Coppens, and Jaromír Krejčí, 675–84. Prague: Faculty of the Arts, Charles University, 2017.

Osing, Jürgen. "Ächtungstexte aus dem Alten Reich (II)." *MDAIK* 32 (1976): 133–85.

Page, Anthea. *Egyptian Sculpture: Archaic to Saite, From the Petrie Collection*. Warminster: Aris & Phillips, 1976.

Pantalacci, Laure. "Balat: A Frontier Town and Its Archive." In *Ancient Egyptian Administration*, edited by Juan Carlos Moreno García, 197–214. HdO 104. Leiden: Brill, 2013.

———. "Broadening Horizons: Distant Places and Travels in Dakhla and the Western Desert at the End of the 3rd Millennium." In *Desert Road Archaeology in Ancient Egypt and Beyond*, edited by Frank Förster and Heiko Riemer, 283–96. Africa praehistorica 27. Cologne: Heinrich-Barth Institut, 2013.

Papazian, Hratch. *Domain of Pharaoh: The Structure and Components of the Economy of Old Kingdom Egypt*. HÄB 52. Hildesheim: Gerstenberg, 2012.

———. "Perspectives on the Cult of Pharaoh during the Third Millennium BC: A Chronological Overview." In *Chronology and Archaeology in Ancient Egypt (The Third Millennium B.C.)*, edited by Hana Vymazalová and Miroslav Bártá, 61–80. Prague: Czech Institute of Egyptology, 2008.

———. "The State of Egypt in the Eighth Dynasty." In *Towards a New History for the Egyptian Old Kingdom: Perspectives on the Pyramid Age*, edited by Peter Der Manuelian and Thomas Schneider, 393–428. HES 1. Leiden: Brill, 2015.

Parcak, Sarah. "Egypt's Old Kingdom 'Empire' (?): A Case Study Focusing on South Sinai." In *Egypt, Israel, and the Ancient Mediterranean World: Studies in Honor of Donald B. Redford*, edited by Gary Knoppers and Antoine Hirsch, 41–60. PAe 20. Leiden: Brill, 2004.

Patch, Diana Craig. *Dawn of Egyptian Art*. New York: The Metropolitan Museum of Art, 2011.

Piacentini, Patrizia. "Excavating the Egyptological Archives of the Università degli Studi di Milano: The Varille Documentation on the Pyramid Complex of Djedkare-Izezi at Saqqara." In *Abusir and Saqqara in the Year 2015*, edited by Miroslav Bárta, Filip Coppens, and Jaromír Krejčí, 355–68. Prague: Faculty of Arts, Charles University, 2017.

———. "The Preservation of Antiquities: Creation of Museums in Egypt during the Nineteenth Century." In *Egypt and the Pharaohs: Pharaonic Egypt in the Archives and Libraries of the Università degli Studi di Milano*, vol. 2, edited by Patrizia Piacentini, 5–44. Milan: Università degli Studi di Milano, 2011.

Picardo, Nicholas. "Dealing with Decapitation Diachronically." *Nekhen News* 16 (2004): 13–14.

———. "'Semantic Homicide' and the So-called Reserve Heads: The Theme of Decapitation in Egyptian Funerary Religion and Some Implications for the Old Kingdom." *JARCE* 43 (2007): 221–52.

Pieke, Gabriele. "Lost in Transformation: Artistic Creation between Permanence and Change." In *(Re)productive Traditions in Ancient Egypt: Proceedings of the Conference Held at the University of Liège, 6th–8th Feburary 2013*, edited by Todd Gillen, 259–304. Collection Ægyptiaca Leodiensia 10. Liège: Presses Universitaires de Liège, 2017.

Pinch, Geraldine. *Magic in Ancient Egypt*. London: British Museum Press, 1994.

Porter, Bertha, Rosalind L. B. Moss, Ethel W. Burney, and Jaromír Málek. *Topographical Bibliography of Ancient Egyptian Hieroglyphic Texts, Reliefs, and Paintings*, 8 vols. Oxford: Clarendon, 1960–.

Posener, Georges. "À la recherche de nouveaux textes d'envoûtement." In *Proceedings of the Fifth World Congress of Jewish Studies*, vol. 1, 144–49. Jerusalem: World Union of Jewish Studies, 1969.

———. *Cinq figurines d'envoûtement*. BiEtud 101. Cairo: Institut français d'archéologie orientale, 1987.

———. "Les empreintes magiques de Gizeh et les morts dangereux." *MDAIK* 16 (1958): 252–70.

———. "Nouveaux textes hiératiques de proscription." In *Mélanges syriens offerts à monsieur Rene Dussaud*, vol. 1, 313–17. Bibliothèque archéologique et historique 30. Paris: Geuthner, 1939.

———. "Une nouvelle statuette d'envoûtement." In *Studien zu Sprache und Religion Ägyptens: Zu Ehren von Wolfhart Westendorf*, vol. 1, edited by Friedrich Junge, 613–18. Göttingen: Hubert & Co., 1984.

———. "Nouvelles listes de proscription (Ächtungstexte) datant du Moyen Empire." *CdE* 14:27 (1939): 39–46.

———. *Princes et pays d'Asie et de Nubie: Textes hiératiques sur des figurines d'envoûtement du Moyen Empire*. Brussels: Fondation égyptologique reine Élisabeth, 1940.

Posener-Kriéger, Paule. *Les archives du temple funéraire de Néferirkarê-Kakai (Les Papyrus d'Abousir)*. BiEtud 65. Cairo: Institut français d'archéologie orientale, 1976.

Posener-Kriéger, Paule and Jean Louis de Cenival. *The Abu Sir Papyri*. London: Trustees of the British Museum, 1968.

Posener-Kriéger, Paule, Miroslav Verner, and Hana Vymazalová. *The Pyramid Complex of Raneferef: The Papyrus Archive*. Abusir 10. Prague: Czech Institute of Egyptology, 2006.

Prakash, Tara. "Bruised, Beaten, and Broken: Interpreting and Misinterpreting the Pain of Foreigners in Ancient Egyptian Art." In *Visualiser les émotions dans l'Égypte ancienne: Images et textes*, edited by Rania Merzeban, Marie-Lys Arnette, Dimitri Laboury, and Cédric Larcher. BiEtud. Cairo: Institute français d'archéologie orientale, forthcoming.

———. "Depictions of Defeated Foreigners in the Late Old Kingdom Pyramid Complex: A Mythological Interpretation." In *Old Kingdom Art and Archaeology 7: Proceedings of the International Conference; Università degli studi di Milano 3–7 July 2017*, edited by Patrizia Piacentini and Alessio Delli Castelli, 454–65. Egyptian & Egyptological Documents, Archives, Libraries 6. Milan: Pontremoli, 2019.

———. "Depictions of the Foreign 'Other': The Old Kingdom Prisoner Statues." PhD diss., Institute of Fine Arts, New York University, 2017.

———. "Enemies of the State: The Old Kingdom Prisoner Statues and Three-Dimensional Representations of Foreigners." *Bulletin of the American Research Center in Egypt* 208 (2016): 55–59.

———. "From Saqqara to Brussels: A Head from a Sixth Dynasty Prisoner Statue in the Musées Royaux d'Art et d'Histoire." *CdE* 189 (2020): 5–19.

———. "The Prisoner Statue 'Fragments' in Milano." *Egyptian & Egyptological Documents, Archives, Libraries* 5 (2015/2016): 17–27.

———. "The Prisoner Statues in the Metropolitan Museum of Art and the British Museum: From the Late Old Kingdom to Today." *SAK* 49 (2020): 197–221.

———. "Reconsidering the Bound Captive Statuary from the Pyramid Complex of Raneferef." *JARCE* 54 (2018): 137–59.

Quack, Joachim Friedrich. "Opfermahl und Feindvernichtung im altägyptischen Ritual." *Mitteilungen der Berliner Gesellschaft für Anthropologie, Ethnologie und Urgeschichte* 27 (2006): 67–80.

———. "Some Old Kingdom Execration Figurines from the Teti Cemetery." *BACE* 13 (2002): 149–60.

Quibell, James. *Excavations at Saqqara, 1906–1907*. SAE. Cairo: Institut français d'archéologie orientale, 1908.

———. *Excavations at Saqqara, 1907–1908*. SAE. Cairo: Institut français d'archéologie orientale, 1909.

———. *Hierakonpolis*, part 1. ERA 4. London: Quaritch, 1900.
Quibell, James and F. W. Green. *Hierakonpolis*, part 2. ERA 5. London: Quaritch, 1900.
Quirke, Stephen. *The Cult of Ra: Sun-Worship in Ancient Egypt*. London: Thames & Hudson, 2001.
Raslan, Mohamed Awad M. "The Causeway of Ounas Pyramid." *ASAE* 61 (1973): 151–69.
Raue, Dietrich. "Centre and Periphery: Elephantine and Its Surroundings in the Third Millennium BC." In *The First Cataract of the Nile: One Region – Diverse Perspectives*, edited by Dietrich Raue, Stephen Seidlmayer, and Philipp Speiser, 149–55. SDAIK 36. Berlin: de Gruyter, 2013.
Abd el-Razek, Essam M. "A Note on the Difference between Execration Statues and Prisoners Statues." *GM* 147 (1995): 7–8.
Redford, Donald B. "Egypt and Western Asia in the Old Kingdom." *JARCE* 23 (1986): 125–43.
———. *Egypt, Canaan, and Israel in Ancient Times*. Princeton: Princeton University Press, 1992.
Refai, Hosam. *Untersuchungen zum Bildprogramm der großen Säulensäle in den thebanischen Tempeln des Neuen Reiches*. BeitrÄg 18. Vienna: Afro-Pub, 2000.
Regev, Johanna, Pierre de Miroschedji, Raphael Greenberg, Eliot Braun, Zvi Greenhut, and Elisabetta Boaretto. "Chronology of the Early Bronze Age in the Southern Levant: New Analysis for a High Chronology." *Radiocarbon* 54 (2012): 525–66.
Reisner, George A. "New Acquisitions of the Egyptian Department: A Family of Builders of the Sixth Dynasty, about 2600 B. C." *Museum of Fine Arts Bulletin* 11 (1913): 53–66.
Revez, Jean. "Le traitement iconographique des prisonniers étrangers dans l'art pharaonique à travers une pièce de la collection Diniacopoulos." In *Life and Death in Ancient Egypt: The Diniacopoulos Collection*, edited by Jane E. Francis and George W. M. Harrison, 41–49. Montreal: Concordia University, 2011.
Richards, Janet. "Kingship and Legitimation." In *Egyptian Archaeology*, edited by Willeke Wendrich, 55–84. Chichester: Wiley-Blackwell, 2010.
———. "Text and Context in Late Old Kingdom Egypt: The Archaeology and Historiography of Weni the Elder." *JARCE* 39 (2002): 75–102.
Ricke, Herbert. "Bemerkungen zur ägyptischen Baukunst des Alten Reiches 2." In *Beiträge zur ägyptischen Bauforschung und Altertumskunde*, vol. 5, edited by Herbert Ricke, 1–128. Cairo: Schweizerisches Institut für ägyptische Bauforschung und Altertumsunde, 1950.
Riemer, Heiko. "Lessons in Landscape Learning: The Dawn of Long-Distance Travel and Navigation in Egypt's Western Desert from Prehistoric to Old Kingdom Times." In *Desert Road Archaeology in Ancient Egypt and Beyond*, edited by Frank Förster and Heiko Riemer, 77–106. Africa praehistorica 27. Cologne: Heinrich-Barth Institut, 2013.
Ritner, Robert. "Killing the Image, Killing the Essence: The Destruction of Text and Figures in Ancient Egyptian Thought, Ritual, and 'Ritualized History.'" In *Iconoclasm and Text Destruction in the Ancient Near East and Beyond*, edited by Natalie Naomi May, 395–405. OIS 8. Chicago: Oriental Institute of the University of Chicago, 2012.
———. *The Mechanics of Ancient Egyptian Magical Practice*. SAOC 54. Chicago: Oriental Institute of the University of Chicago, 1993.
Roberson, Joshua A. "The Trampled Foe: Two New Examples of a Rare Amuletic Form." *JEA* 96 (2010): 119–22.
Robins, Gay. *The Art of Ancient Egypt*. Cambridge: Harvard University Press, 1997.
Rochholz, Matthias. "Sedfest, Sonnenheiligtum, und Pyramidenbezirk: Zur Deutung der Grabanlagen der Könige der 5. und 6. Dynastie." In *Ägyptische Tempel: Struktur, Funktion und Programm (Akten der Ägyptologischen Tempeltagungen in Gosen 1990 und in Mainz 1992)*, edited by Rolf Gundlach and Matthias Rochholz, 255–80. HÄB 37. Hildesheim: Gerstenberg, 1994.
Roehrig, Catharine H. "125. Pair Statue of Demedji and Henutsen." In *Egyptian Art in the Age of the Pyramids*, edited by Dorothea Arnold, Krzysztof Grzymski, and Christiane Ziegler, 365–67, cat. no. 125. New York: The Metropolitan Museum of Art, 1999.
Romano, James F. "Sixth Dynasty Royal Sculpture." In *Les critères de datation stylistiques à l'Ancien Empire*, edited by Nicolas Grimal, 235–304. BiEtud 120. Cairo: Institut français d'archéologie orientale, 1998.
Roth, Ann Macy. "The Meaning of Menial Labor: 'Servant Statues' in the Old Kingdom Serdabs." *JARCE* 39 (2002): 103–21.
———. "Representing the Other: Non-Egyptians in Pharaonic Iconography." In *A Companion to Ancient Egyptian Art*, edited by Melinda Hartwig, 155–74. Chichester: Wiley-Blackwell, 2014.
Russmann, Edna R. *Egyptian Sculpture: Cairo and Luxor*. Austin: University of Texas Press, 1989.
———. *Eternal Egypt: Masterworks of Ancient Art from the British Museum*. Berkeley: University of California Press, 2001.
———. "A Second Style in Egyptian Art of the Old Kingdom." *MDAIK* 51 (1995): 269–79.

Rzepka, Slawomir. "Methods of Optimizing Sculptor's Work during the Old Kingdom." In *Egyptology at the Dawn of the Twenty-First Century: Proceedings of the Eighth International Congress of Egyptologists Cairo, 2000*, vol. 2, edited by Zahi Hawass, 467–73. Cairo: The American University in Cairo Press, 2003.

Rzeuska, Teodozja. "Execration Again? Remarks on an Old Kingdom Ritual." *Polish Archaeology in the Mediterranean* 22 (2013): 627–34.

Säve-Söderbergh, Torgny. *The Navy of the Eighteenth Egyptian Dynasty*. UUÅ 6. Uppsala: Lundequistska Bokhandeln, 1946.

El-Sayed, Rafed. *Afrikanischstämmiger Lehnwortschatz im älteren Ägyptisch: Untersuchungen zur ägyptisch-afrikanischen lexikalischen Interferenz im dritten und zweiten Jahrtausend v. Chr*. OLA 211. Leuven: Peeters, 2011.

Scandone Matthiae, Gabriella. "Les rapports entre Ebla et l'Égypte à l'Ancien et au Moyen Empire." In *Egyptology at the Dawn of the Twenty-First Century: Proceedings of the Eighth International Congress of Egyptologists Cairo, 2000*, vol. 2, edited by Zahi Hawass, 487–93. Cairo: The American University in Cairo Press, 2003.

Schäfer, Heinrich. *Ein Bruchstück altägyptischer Annalen*. Berlin: Verlag der Königl. Akademie der Wissenschaften, 1902.

———. "Neue Alterümer der 'new race' aus Negadeh." *ZÄS* 34 (1896): 158–61.

Scharff, Alexander. *Die Altertümer der Vor- und Frühzeit Ägyptens*, vol. 2. Berlin: Curtius, 1929.

Schlögl, Hermann A. "1. Mann mit auf dem Rücken gefesselten Armen." In *Höhenflug und Absturz: Wilhelm Dieudonné Stieler (1888–1912), Ägyptenreisender, Sammler und Luftfahrtpionier*, edited by Noëlle Gmür Brianza and Elisabeth Staehelin, cat. no. 1. Basel: Stiftung fur ein Schweizerisches Orient-Museum, 2006.

Schneider, Thomas. *Ausländer in Ägypten: Während des Mittleren Reiches und der Hyksoszeit*, 2 vols. ÄAT 42. Wiesbaden: Harrassowitz, 1998.

———. "Foreigners in Egypt: Archaeological Evidence and Cultural Context." In *Egyptian Archaeology*, edited by Willeke Wendrich, 143–63. Chichester: Wiley-Blackwell, 2010.

———. "The Old Kingdom Abroad: An Epistemological Perspective; With Remarks on the Biography of Iny and the Kingdom of Dugurasu." In *Towards a New History for the Egyptian Old Kingdom: Perspectives on the Pyramid Age*, edited by Peter Der Manuelian and Thomas Schneider, 429–55. HES 1. Leiden: Brill, 2015.

Schoske, Sylvia. "Das Erschlagen der Feinde: Ikonographie und Stilistik der Feindvernichtung im alten Ägypten." PhD diss., University of Heidelberg, 1994.

Schoske, Sylvia and Dietrich Wildung. *Gott und Götter im alten Ägypten*. Mainz am Rhein: von Zabern, 1993.

Schott, Siegfried. "Bermerkungen zum ägyptischen Pyramidenkult." In *Beiträge zur ägyptischen Bauforschung und Altertumskunde*, vol. 5, edited by Herbert Ricke, 131–252. Cairo: Schweizerisches Institut für ägyptische Bauforschung und Altertumsunde, 1950.

Schulman, Alan. *Ceremonial Execution and Public Rewards: Some Historical Scenes on New Kingdom Private Stelae*. OBO 75. Göttingen: Vandenhoeck & Ruprecht, 1988.

Seidlmayer, Stephan. "Beispiele nubischer Keramik aus Kontexten des Hohen Alten Reiches aus Elephantine." In *Ägypten im afro-orientalischen Kontext – Gedenkschrift Peter Behrens*, edited by Daniela Mendel and Ulrike Claudi, 337–50. Afrikanistische Arbeitspapiere Sondernummer. Cologne: Universität zu Köln, 1991.

———. "Execration Texts." In *The Oxford Encyclopedia of Ancient Egypt*, vol. 1, edited by Donald Redford, 487–89. Oxford: Oxford University Press, 2001.

———. "Town and State in the Early Old Kingdom: A View from Elephantine." In *Aspects of Early Egypt*, edited by Jeffrey Spencer, 108–27. London: British Museum Press, 1996.

Shalomi-Hen, Racheli. "The Dawn of Osiris and the Dusk of the Sun-Temples: Religious History at the End of the Fifth Dynasty." In *Towards a New History for the Egyptian Old Kingdom: Perspectives on the Pyramid Age*, edited by Peter Der Manuelian and Thomas Schneider, 456–69. HES 1. Leiden: Brill, 2015.

Shaw, Ian. "Egypt and the Outside World." In *The Oxford History of Ancient Egypt*, edited by Ian Shaw, 308–23. Oxford: Oxford University Press, 2000.

———. "Exploiting the Desert Frontiers: The Logistics and Politics of Ancient Egyptian Mining Expeditions." In *Social Approaches to an Industrial Past: The Archaeology and Anthropology of Mining*, edited by Bernard Knapp, Vincent Pigott, and Eugenia Herbert, 242–58. London: Routledge, 1998.

———. "Pharaonic Quarrying and Mining: Settlement and Procurement in Egypt's Marginal Regions." *Antiquity* 68 (1994): 108–19.

Simpson, William Kelly. "Egyptian Sculpture and Two-Dimensional Representation as Propaganda." *JEA* 68 (1982): 266–71.

———, ed. *The Literature of Ancient Egypt: An Anthology of Stories, Instructions, Stelae, Autobiographies, and Poetry*, 3rd ed. New Haven: Yale University Press, 2003.

Smith, Harry S. and Lisa L. Giddy. "Nubia and Dakhla Oasis in the Late Third Millennium B.C.: The Present Balance of Textual and Archaeological Evidence." In *Mélanges offerts à Jean Vercoutter*, edited by Francis Geus and Florence Thill, 317–30. Paris: Éditions Recherche sur les Civilisations, 1985.

Smith, Mark. *Following Osiris: Perspectives on the Osirian Afterlife from Four Millennia*. Oxford: Oxford University Press, 2017.

Smith, Stuart Tyson. "Ethnicity and Culture." In *The Egyptian World*, edited by Toby Wilkinson, 218–41. London: Routledge, 2007.

———. *Wretched Kush: Ethnic Identities and Boundaries in Egypt's Nubian Empire*. London: Routledge, 2003.

Smith, William Stevenson. *Ancient Egypt as Represented in the Museum of Fine Arts, Boston*. Boston: Museum of Fine Arts, 1960.

———. *A History of Egyptian Sculpture and Painting in the Old Kingdom*. New York: Hacker Art Books, 1978.

Soukiassian, Georges, Michel Wuttmann, and Laure Pantalacci. *Le palais des gouverneurs de l'époque de Pépy II: Les sanctuaires de ka et leurs dépendances*. Balat 6; FIFAO 46. Cairo: Institut français d'archéologie orientale, 2002.

Sourouzian, Hourig. "L'apparition du pylône." *BIFAO* 81 (1981): 141–51.

———. "Concordances et écarts: Entre statuaire et représentations à deux dimensions des particuliers de l'époque archaïque." In *Les critères de datation stylistiques à l'Ancien Empire*, edited by Nicolas Grimal, 305–52. BiEtud 120. Cairo: Institut français d'archéologie orientale, 1998.

———. "Old Kingdom Sculpture." In *A Companion to Ancient Egypt*, vol. 2, edited by Alan B. Lloyd, 853–81. Chichester: Wiley-Blackwell, 2010.

Souza, Aaron de. Review of *Ethnic Identities in the Land of the Pharaohs: Past and Present Approaches in Egyptology*, by Uroš Matić. *JARCE* 57 (2021): 347–51.

Sowada, Karin. *Egypt in the Eastern Mediterranean during the Old Kingdom: An Archaeological Perspective*. OBO 237. Fribourg: Academic Press, 2009.

———. "Never the Twain Shall Meet? Synchronising Egyptian and Levantine Chronologies in the 3rd Millennium BC." In *Egypt and the Southern Levant in the Early Bronze Age*, edited by Felix Höflmayer and Ricardo Eichmann, 293–313. Orient-Archäologie 31. Rahden: Leidorf, 2014.

Sowada, Karin, Tracey Callaghan, and Paul Bentley. *The Teti Cemetery at Saqqara, Volume IV: Minor Burials and Other Material*. RACE 12. Warminster: Aris & Phillips, 1999.

Spalinger, Anthony. *Icons of Power: A Strategy of Reinterpretation*. Prague: Charles University, 2011.

Spanel, Donald. *Through Ancient Eyes: Egyptian Portraiture*. Birmingham: Birmingham Museum of Art, 1988.

Stadelmann, Rainer. *Die ägyptischen Pyramiden: Vom Ziegelbau zum Weltwunder*, 3rd ed. KAW 30. Mainz: von Zabern, 1997.

Staehelin, Elisabeth. *Untersuchungen zur ägyptischen Tracht im Alten Reich*. MÄS 8. Berlin: Hessling, 1966.

Stewart, Peter. "The Destruction of Statues in Late Antiquity." In *Constructing Identities in Late Antiquity*, edited by Richard Miles, 159–89. London: Routledge, 1999.

Stockfisch, Dagmar. *Untersuchungen zum Totenkult des ägyptischen Königs im Alten Reich: Die Dekoration der königlichen Totenkultanlagen*. Hamburg: Kovač, 2003.

Strudwick, Nigel. *The Administration of Egypt in the Old Kingdom: The Highest Titles and Their Holders*. London: KPI, 1985.

———. *Texts from the Pyramid Age*, edited by Ronald Leprohon. WAW 16. Atlanta: Society of Biblical Literature, 2005.

Szpakowska, Kasia and Richard Johnston. "Snake Busters: Experiments in Fracture Patterns of Ritual Figurines." In *Mummies, Magic and Medicine in Ancient Egypt: Multidisciplinary Essays for Rosalie David*, edited by Campbell Price, Roger Forshaw, Andrew Chamberlain, and Paul Nicholson, 459–73. Manchester: Manchester University Press, 2016.

Tallet, Pierre. "Ayn Sukhna and Wadi el-Jarf: Two Newly Discovered Pharaonic Harbours on the Suez Gulf." *BMSAES* 18 (2012): 147–68.

Tallet, Pierre and Damien Laisney. "Iry-Hor et Narmer au Sud-Sinaï (Ouadi 'Ameyra): Un complément à la chronologie des expéditions minières égyptiennes." *BIFAO* 112 (2012): 381–98.

Tallet, Pierre and Gregory Marouard. "The Harbor Facilities of King Khufu on the Red Sea Shore: The Wadi al-Jarf/Tell Ras Budran System." *JARCE* 52 (2016): 135–77.

———. "The Harbor of Khufu on the Red Sea Coast at Wadi al-Jarf, Egypt." *NEA* 77 (2014): 4–14.

Taylor, John H. "Patterns of Colouring on Ancient Egyptian Coffins from the New Kingdom to the Twenty-Sixth Dynasty: An Overview." In *Colour and Painting in Ancient Egypt*, edited by William Vivian Davies, 164–81. London: British Museum Press, 2001.

Tefnin, Roland. *Art et magie au temps des pyramides: L'énigme des têtes dites de "remplacement."* Monumenta Aegyptiaca 5. Brussels: Fondation égyptologique reine Élisabeth, 1991.

Terrace, Edward L. B. and Henry G. Fischer. *Treasures of Egyptian Art from the Cairo Museum.* London: Thames & Hudson, 1970.
Theis, Christoffer. "Ächtungstexte." *Das Wissenschaftliche Bibellexikon im Internet,* Deutsche Bibel Gesellschaft, http://www.bibelwissenschaft.de/stichwort/12613.
———. *Magie und Raum: Der magische Schutz ausgewählter Räume im alten Ägypten nebst einem Vergleich zu angrenzenden Kulturbereichen.* Oriental Religions in Antiquity 13. Tübingen: Mohr Siebeck, 2014.
Török, László. *Between Two Worlds: The Frontier Region between Ancient Nubia and Egypt 3700 BC–500 AD.* PAe 29. Leiden: Brill, 2009.
Uphill, Eric. "The Nine Bows." *Jaarbericht van het Vooraziatisch-Egyptisch Genootschap Ex Oriente Lux* 19 (1965–1966): 393–420.
Valbelle, Dominique. "L'égyptien en Nubie." In *Études nubiennes: Conférence de Genève, actes du VIIe Congrès international d'études nubiennes 3–8 septembre 1990,* vol. 1, edited by Charles Bonnet, 359–62. Geneva: Bonnet, 1992.
Vandenbeusch, Marie. "Statue of a Prisoner." In *Pharaoh: King of Ancient Egypt,* edited by Marie Vandenbeusch, Aude Semat, and Margaret Maitland, 122–23. Cleveland, The Cleveland Museum of Art, 2016.
Vandersleyen, Claude. "Porträt." *LÄ* 4 (1982): 1074–80.
Vandier, Jacques. *Manuel d'archéologie égyptienne,* 6 vols. Paris: Picard, 1952–1978.
Varille, Alexandre. *À propos des pyramides de Snefrou.* Cairo: Imprimerie Schindler, 1947.
Vercoutter, Jean. "The Iconography of the Black in Ancient Egypt: From the Beginnings to the 25th Dynasty," translated by William Granger Ryan. In *The Image of the Black in Western Art,* vol. 1, rev. ed., edited by David Bindman and Henry Louis Gates, 41–94. Cambridge: Belknap Press of Harvard University Press, 2010.
———. "Textes exécratoires de Mirgissa." *CRAIBL* 107 (1963): 97–102.
Verner, Miroslav. *Abusir: The Necropolis of the Sons of the Sun.* Cairo: American University in Cairo, 2017.
———. "The Columns of Abusir." In *The Old Kingdom Art and Archaeology: Proceedings of the Conference Held in Prague, May 31–June 4, 2004,* edited by Miroslav Bárta, 343–55. Prague: Czech Institute of Egyptology, 2006.
———. "*Pr-twt*: The Cult Place of Raneferef's Statues." In *Rich and Great: Studies in Honour of Anthony J. Spalinger on the Occasion of His 70th Feast of Thoth,* edited by Renata Landgráfová and Jana Mynářová, 325–30. Prague: Charles University, 2016.
———. *The Pyramid Complex of Khentkaus.* Abusir 3. Prague: Charles University, 1995.
———, ed. *The Pyramid Complex of Raneferef: The Archaeology.* Abusir 9. Prague: Czech Institute of Egyptology, 2006.
———. *The Pyramids.* Translated by Steven Randall. Cairo: American University of Cairo Press, 2001.
———. "Several Thoughts on the Old Kingdom Residence." In *Studies Dedicated to the Memory of Eva Pardey,* edited by Miroslav Bárta and Hella Küllmer, 119–22. Prague: Charles University, 2013.
———. *Sons of the Sun: Rise and Decline of the Fifth Dynasty.* Prague: Czech Institute of Egyptology, 2014.
———. *The Statues of Raneferef and the Royal Sculpture of the Fifth Dynasty.* Abusir 28. Prague: Charles University, 2017.
———. "Les statuettes de prisonniers en bois d'Abousir." *RdE* 36 (1985): 145–52.
———. "The System of Dating in the Old Kingdom." In *Chronology and Archaeology in Ancient Egypt (The Third Millennium B.C.),* edited by Hana Vymazalová and Miroslav Bárta, 23–43. Prague: Czech Institute of Egyptology, 2008.
———. "Who Was Shepseskare, and When Did He Reign?" In *Abusir and Saqqara in the Year 2000,* edited by Miroslav Bárta and Jaromír Krejčí, 581–602. Prague: Oriental Institute of the Academy of Sciences of the Czech Republic, 2000.
Vischak, Deborah. *Community and Identity in Ancient Egypt: The Old Kingdom Cemetery at Qubbet el-Hawa.* Cambridge: Cambridge University Press, 2015.
Vymazalová, Hana. "The Administration of the Royal Funerary Complexes." In *Ancient Egyptian Administration,* edited by Juan Carlos Moreno García, 177–95. HdO 104. Leiden: Brill, 2013.
———. "The Economic Connection between the Royal Cult in the Pyramid Temples and the Sun Temples in Abusir." In *Old Kingdom, New Perspectives: Egyptian Art and Archaeology 2750-2150 BC,* edited by Nigel Strudwick and Helen Strudwick, 295–303. Oxford: Oxbow, 2011.
Vymazalová, Hana and Filip Coppens. "Statues and Rituals for Khentkaus II: A Reconsideration of Some Papyrus Fragments from the Queen's Funerary Complex." In *Abusir and Saqqara in the Year 2010,* vol. 2, edited by Miroslav Bárta, Filip Coppens, and Jaromír Krejčí, 785–99. Prague: Charles University, 2011.
Walle, Baudouin van de. "Rückenpfeiler." *LÄ* 5 (1984): 315–18.
Warden, Leslie Anne. "Centralized Taxation during the Old Kingdom." In *Towards a New History for the Egyptian Old Kingdom: Perspectives on the Pyramid Age,* edited by Peter Der Manuelian and Thomas Schneider, 470–95. HES 1. Leiden: Brill, 2015.

Welsby, Derek. "Kerma Ancien Cemeteries: From the Batn el-Hajar to the Fourth Cataract." In *Nubian Archaeology in the XXIst Century: Proceedings of the Thirteenth International Conference for Nubian Studies, Neuchâtel, 1st–6th September 2014*, edited by Matthieu Honegger, 35–63. OLA 273; Publications de la Mission archéologique suisse à Kerma 1. Leuven: Peeters, 2018.

Wendrich, Willeke. "Identity and Personhood." In *Egyptian Archaeology*, edited by Willeke Wendrich, 200–219. Chichester: Wiley-Blackwell, 2010.

Wildung, Dietrich. "4. Gefangenenköpfe." In *Götter Pharaonen*, edited by Dietrich Wildung and Günter Grimm, cat. no. 4. Essen: Villa Hügel e. V., 1978.

——. "The Image of the Nubian in Egyptian Art." In *Sudan: Ancient Kingdoms of the Nile*, edited by Dietrich Wildung, translated by Peter Der Manuelian and Kathleen Guillaume, 143–57. Paris: Flammarion, 1997.

——. "Der König Ägyptens als Herr der Welt? Ein seltener ikonographischer Typus der Königsplastik des Neuen Reiches." *AfO* 24 (1973): 108–16.

Wilkinson, Richard. *The Complete Gods and Goddesses of Ancient Egypt*. London: Thames & Hudson, 2003.

Wilkinson, Toby, ed. *The Egyptian World*. London: Routledge, 2007.

——. *Royal Annals of Ancient Egypt: The Palermo Stone and Its Associated Fragments*. London: Kegan Paul International, 2000.

Willems, Harco. "Crime, Cult and Capital Punishment (Mo'alla Inscription 8)." *JEA* 76 (1990): 27–54.

——. "The Social and Ritual Context of a Mortuary Liturgy of the Middle Kingdom (CT Spells 30–41)." In *Social Aspects of Funerary Culture in the Egyptian Old and Middle Kingdoms: Proceedings of the International Symposium Held at Leiden University 6–7 June, 1996*, edited by Harco Willems, 253–372. OLA 103. Leuven: Peeters, 2001.

Wimmer, Stefan. "Neue Ächtungstexte aus dem Alten Reich." *BN* 67 (1993): 87–100.

Winnerman, Jonathan. "Rethinking the Royal *Ka*." PhD Diss., University of Chicago, 2018.

Wuttmann, Michel. "La restauration des appartements funéraires de la pyramide de Pépy Ier à Saqqâra." In *Études sur l'Ancien Empire et la nécropole de Saqqâra dédiées à Jean-Philippe Lauer*, edited by Catherine Berger and Bernard Mathieu, 449–60. OrMonsp 9. Montpellier: Université Paul Valéry, 1997.

Zandee, Jan. *Death as an Enemy: According to Ancient Egyptian Conceptions*. Translated by W. F. Klasens. Studies in the History of Religions 5. Leiden: Brill, 1960.

Zibelius-Chen, Karola. *Afrikanische Orts- und Völkernamen in hieroglyphischen und hieratischen Texten*. Wiesbaden: Reichert, 1972.

——. *Die ägyptische Expansion nach Nubien: Eine Darlegung der Grundfaktoren*. Wiesbaden: Reichert, 1988.

Ziegler, Christiane. "135. Snefru-nefer Standing." In *Egyptian Art in the Age of the Pyramids*, edited by Dorothea Arnold, Krzysztof Grzymski, and Christiane Ziegler, 384–85, cat. no. 135. New York: The Metropolitan Museum of Art, 1999.

——. "Nonroyal Statuary." In *Egyptian Art in the Age of the Pyramids*, edited by Dorothea Arnold, Krzysztof Grzymski, and Christiane Ziegler, 57–71. New York: The Metropolitan Museum of Art, 1999.

——. "Nouveaux témoignages du 'Second Style' de l'Ancien Empire." In *Perspectives on Ancient Egypt: Studies in Honor of Edward Brovarski*, edited by Zahi Hawass, Peter Der Manuelian, and Ramadan B. Hussein, 459–74. ASAE-Suppl. 40. Cairo: Supreme Council of Antiquities, 2010.

Zivie, Alain-Pierre. *Decouverte à Saqqarah: Le vizir oublié*. Paris: Seuil, 1990.

Subject Index

Abu Ballas Trail, 101
Abu Ghurob, 4n7, 24–25
Abusir, 4, 4n7, 24–25, 27
Abusir papyri, 107n7, 135
Abydos, 13n45, 30–31
administration, 3–4, 23–26, 29–31, 56–59, 99, 107n6, 142
alabaster, 2, 110, 136
apotropaic, 9–10, 43, 161, 171–72, 179
architects, 7, 21, 105–6, 110, 112, 128, 142, 177, 180
artists, 2, 7, 10, 84–86, 104–6, 128, 142, 150, 177, 180–81. *See also under* prisoner statue(s)
Asiatics. *See under* foreigners
autobiography. *See under* high official(s)
Ayn Soukhna, 94

basalt, 1, 110, 136–37
beards, 84–86, 89n89. *See also under* prisoner statue(s)
bound captive motif, 7–9, 12–13, 16–19, 83, 128–33, 135, 138–39, 145, 159, 161, 168–69, 177
Buhen, 94, 97, 99
butchering, 132, 145–46, 168–71
Byblos, 95, 97, 99, 101

capital. *See* Memphis
captive. *See* bound captive motif; prisoner statue(s)
causeway, 5, 105–8, 110, 141
 Djedkare-Isesi, 114–15
 Niuserre, 111–12, 130, 133, 139
 Pepi I, 121, 123, 141
 Pepi II, 111, 121, 124–27, 132–33, 140, 159, 174, 179
 relief(s), 6, 95, 97, 110, 112, 118, 128–33, 139–40
 Sahure, 95, 109–10, 128n86, 130–31, 133
 Teti, 119, 141
 Unas, 97, 100n134, 117–18, 128n86, 131, 133
consort. *See* queen(s)
criminals, 8, 10, 61–62, 83–84, 167–69, 171, 178

cult. *See* ritual

Dakhla Oasis, 96–98, 100–101, 103, 164
decapitation, 20, 145, 153, 155–56, 160, 166–72, 178–80
demon, 8
Diniacopoulos, Vincent, 185, 190
Djedkare-Isesi, 25–28, 95, 136, 138. *See also under* causeway; mortuary temple; pyramid; pyramid complex; valley temple
 prisoner statue(s), 4, 23, 35–38, 46–48, 53–56, 64–65, 81, 86–87, 89, 115–16, 139–40, 150–52, 159, 177–78, 183
Djoser, 14, 24, 27, 29

Early Dynastic period, 92–93, 95–96, 95n111, 150
Eighth Dynasty, 3n1, 30n49
Elephantine, 94, 99, 164, 179. *See also* Qubbet el-Hawa
elite. *See* high official(s). *See also under* statuary
enemy. *See* criminals; foreigners
ethnicity, 10, 85–86, 102–3. *See also under* prisoner statue(s)
execration figurine(s), 18–19, 101–2, 145–47, 161–65, 167, 172, 179
execration ritual. *See under* ritual
experimentation, 17, 20, 54, 57, 81, 90, 103–5, 137–38, 141–43, 178

Fifth Dynasty, 1–4, 12, 16–18, 23–28, 31, 33, 55, 57, 62, 78–81, 83, 86–87, 88n84, 92, 94–99, 102–3, 105–6, 119, 121n61, 128, 132, 135–38, 141–42, 150, 159, 177, 183
First Intermediate period, 3n1, 7n22, 89, 101, 122n66, 125, 148n16, 159, 164
foreigners, 146–47. *See also* mining; prisoners of war; trade
 Asiatics, 11, 85–90, 85n69, 97, 103–4, 131, 169, 178

foreigners, *continued*
   depictions of, 2, 10–11, 12n38, 13–19, 57, 81–87, 89–90, 97, 103–4, 128–34, 139, 142, 150n19, 159, 178. *See also* bound captive motif
   Egyptian interactions with, 10–11, 19, 59, 62, 90–104, 172, 179–80
   ideology of, 7–11, 61–62, 83, 103–4, 128–30, 138, 145, 161, 169
   Libyans, 11, 85–90, 85n69, 97, 97n122, 101n138, 101n143, 103–4, 130–32, 131n100, 142, 178
   Nubians, 10–11, 83, 85–90, 85n69, 98, 101–4, 131–32, 178–79
Fourth Dynasty, 1–3, 6, 14n49, 18n60, 28, 57, 92–98, 106, 121n61, 135, 137
funerary cult. *See* mortuary cult
funerary literature and texts, 145, 167. *See also* Pyramid Texts
funerary monument, nonroyal. *See* high officials: tomb; tomb
funerary monument, royal, 1, 6, 12, 26, 57, 138, 142–43, 165. *See also* pyramid complex
funerary temple. *See* mortuary temple

Giza, 1-2, 3, 18, 137, 162–64
granite, 110–11, 113, 115, 117–19, 121, 136–37, 150

harbor, 109, 111, 118, 124, 141. *See also* Wadi el-Jarf; Ayn Soukhna; Mersa Gewasis
Heliopolis, 29
Hierakonpolis, 13, 13n45, 17, 54
high official(s), 2–4, 7, 12n39, 20–21, 23–33, 56–58, 62, 83–84, 86, 90–92, 98–104, 152–53, 172, 179–80, 191. *See also* nomarch; priest; vizier
   autobiography, 26, 31, 98–102
   tomb, 3–4, 18, 25–26, 28–29, 31–32, 57, 84, 88, 98, 99n134, 137n128, 142, 169–70, 179
hunting scenes, 128–33, 139

identity, 11, 20, 179. *See also* ethnicity

ka, 6
   chapels, 29, 100
   royal, 6, 107, 140n145, 146, 174
Khafre, 1, 94, 96n112, 135–36
Khawam brothers, 185
Khufu, 1, 5n12, 14n49, 18, 96

kingship, 6–7, 20, 23–24, 29, 32–33, 107, 109, 113, 128, 135, 137–38, 140, 172–74. *See also under* prisoner statue(s); ritual

late Old Kingdom style. *See* Second Style
Late period, 54
Levant, 11, 95, 99, 100n134. *See also* foreigners: Asiatics
limekiln, 122–23, 122n66, 147–48, 149n16, 151, 153–56, 153n28, 158
limestone, 17, 42n102, 120–21, 124, 137, 139–40, 147, 150, 152n25, 153n28, 190. *See also under* prisoner statue(s)
Libyans. *See under* foreigners

magic, 9–10, 12, 18, 83, 101, 146–47, 161–62, 167–68, 174, 180
Mastabat Faraon, 125
Memphis, 3–4, 3n1, 25, 29, 31–32, 56–58, 62n6, 99, 102–3, 164, 179
Menkauhor, 4n10, 26, 28, 136n122
Menkaure, 1, 135
Merenre, 4n10, 30–32, 58, 101, 132n108, 138n136
Mersa Gewasis, 94
Middle Kingdom, 12–13, 12n38, 88, 92, 142, 146, 148n16, 162–64
mining, 90–92, 94, 96
mortuary cult, 4, 107, 146, 148n16, 174
mortuary literature. *See* funerary literature and texts
mortuary monument. *See* funerary monument
mortuary temple, 5, 105–8, 110–11, 113, 127, 132, 141, 143, 152, 170, 174, 178
   decoration of, 1–2, 135, 178
   Djedkare-Isesi, 28, 114–17, 119, 136–40, 178
   Niuserre, 25, 89, 111–13, 115, 130–31, 136–37
   Pepi I, 12n39, 41, 121–24, 131, 132n108, 133–34, 139–42, 147, 148n16, 154n35, 155, 155n36, 178
   Pepi II, 59, 111, 119n52, 124, 126–27, 132–34, 140, 142, 142n149, 179, 185
   Raneferef, 17, 17n57, 136–37
   relief(s), 6, 41n101, 59, 110, 128–34, 139–40, 143, 169
   ritual(s). *See under* pyramid complex
   Sahure, 59, 89, 97n122, 109–10, 112, 128n86, 130, 131n100, 136–37, 140

Teti, 119–21, 132n108, 136, 139–42, 153n28
Unas, 116–19, 131, 137, 139, 152n25

Neferirkare, 16, 24, 24n8, 111–12. *See also under* pyramid complex
New Kingdom, 8n24, 10–11, 10n30, 14n49, 16n53, 34, 92, 148n16, 167, 170n107, 173n125
Niuserre, 16–17, 23–26, 56–57, 136, 138, 142–43. *See also under* causeway; mortuary temple; pyramid; pyramid complex; statuary; sun temple; valley temple
    prisoner statue(s), 3–4, 23, 33–34, 38, 46, 53–57, 63, 80–81, 83, 86, 110–12, 127, 138–40, 150–52, 159, 177–78
nomarch, 3n1, 31–32, 57, 100
Nubia, 10–11, 99, 172. *See also* Buhen; Yam
    Lower, 93–94, 98–101
    Nubians. *See under* foreigners
    Upper, 93n100, 94, 101

Old Kingdom
    chronology, 3n1
    collapse of, 3n1, 56–59, 179
Osiris, 27–29, 135, 168

Palermo Stone, 93, 95, 97
Pepi I, 29–32, 57, 96n112, 101, 153, 160, 164. *See also under* causeway; mortuary temple; pyramid complex; statuary; valley temple
    prisoner statue(s), 4, 11, 20, 23, 41–51, 53–57, 59, 61–63, 65–71, 74–79, 81–83, 87–90, 92, 98, 102–4, 120–23, 139–40, 143, 145–48, 153–56, 159–61, 165–74, 177–81, 184, 186n14, 187–91
Pepi II, 3n1, 30–31, 57, 59, 81, 99–101, 136, 140, 162–64, 172–73, 179, 181. *See also under* causeway; mortuary temple; pyramid complex; valley temple
    prisoner statue(s), 4, 11, 20, 23, 38n90, 44n111, 50–57, 59, 61–63, 65, 73–78, 81–84, 87–90, 92, 98, 102–4, 111, 116, 124–27, 140, 143, 145–47, 156–62, 165–66, 171–74, 177, 179–81, 184–91
portrait, 20, 61, 80, 83, 87, 184n8
predynastic period, 13, 54, 96, 167
priest, 146, 148n16, 169–70, 173–75, 180

prisoners of war, 92, 167
prisoner statue(s). *See also under* Djedkare-Isesi; Niuserre; Pepi I; Pepi II; Teti; Unas
    artists, 21, 23, 45, 47–48, 51, 53–56, 62, 73, 78, 82–83, 88–90, 92, 102–4, 137–38, 140, 145, 150, 152, 160, 166, 169–71, 178–81, 189–90
    back pillar, 20, 23, 33–36, 38, 40, 54–55, 63–64, 87, 138–39, 150–52, 159, 177–78, 184
    base, 46–49, 53–56, 120, 127, 184, 186, 189
    beards, 63, 65–66, 70–71, 77, 84–88, 90, 154–55, 160, 166–67, 184, 186
    bonds, 23, 33–35, 38–40, 46, 48, 51–55, 63, 184, 186, 188–89
    clothing, 7, 35–37, 47–48, 53, 55, 86–87, 89, 186, 189
    condition of, 20, 145–61, 165, 186, 188
    decoration, as, 2, 12, 20, 54, 135, 141–43, 159, 177–78
    emotion, 20, 61–62, 78–79, 82
    ethnicity, 2, 11, 20–21, 42, 61–63, 66, 78, 78n34, 83–90, 92, 98, 102–4, 143, 178–80
    expressiveness, 20, 23, 54–55, 61–63, 78–82, 102, 152, 178, 184n8
    facial features, 7, 20, 38, 55, 62–83, 86–88, 90, 102–3, 151–54, 156n37, 157, 160, 171, 178–79, 184, 186–91
    hairstyles, 7, 20, 35–36, 38, 55, 63–68, 71, 74, 78, 83–84, 86–88, 90, 103, 153, 156n37, 160, 178–79, 184, 187–90
    kingship, and, 2, 4, 56–59, 177, 180
    limestone, 1, 7, 42, 64, 68n22, 121, 148, 160
    number of, 4, 20–21, 23, 29, 41, 50, 55, 57, 59, 87n77, 89, 103–4, 127, 138–40, 143, 156, 177–80
    paint, 42–44, 66, 88–89
    placement of, 19–21, 47, 56, 105–6, 110–12, 116, 123–24, 127–28, 138–41, 143, 152, 178–80
    ritual(s) and, 20–21, 145–75, 178–80
    size of, 7, 20, 37, 41, 49, 53, 56, 120, 127, 187–89
    treatment of, 19–21, 143, 145–75, 178–81
protodynastic period, 13
provinces, 4, 24–27, 29–32, 56–58, 62n6, 99–102, 179
Ptolemaic period, 149n16, 154n35
Punt, 94–95, 97
pylon, 114, 117n49, 130n96

pyramid, 5, 28, 106, 142, 174
    Djedkare-Isesi, 114–15
    Niuserre, 113
    Sahure, 109–10
    satellite, 6, 25, 107
    size, 1, 106–7
    Teti, 119, 163
    Unas, 119n53
pyramid complex, 1–2, 4, 105–43, 170, 177, 179–81, 188. *See also* causeway; mortuary temple; pyramid; valley temple
    architecture, 6–7, 57, 105–6, 108, 110–30, 135, 140–42, 146, 173–75, 177
    decoration of, 6–7, 10, 12, 20, 57, 105–6, 134–35, 137–43, 146, 159, 173–75, 177. *See also under* mortuary temple
    Djedkare-Isesi, 27, 35, 114–16, 141n148, 151, 183–84
    interpretation of, 107–9, 141–43
    Neferirkare, 24–25, 111–12, 135, 141
    Niuserre, 17, 33, 111–14, 137, 151
    parts of, 5–6, 105–8, 146
    Pepi I, 29, 41, 121–23, 131, 133, 156, 165, 171, 173, 187
    Pepi II, 31, 53, 116, 121n61, 124–28, 131, 133, 136, 140, 161, 165, 171, 174, 183, 186–91
    preservation of, 106, 121, 136, 148–51
    queen(s), 29–30, 32, 107, 115, 126, 184–85
    Raneferef, 16–17, 24–25, 84n68, 86–87, 89, 141
    relief program, 105–6, 108, 110, 128–35, 138–43, 171, 177–78
    ritual(s), 6–7, 21, 107–10, 134–35, 141n148, 143, 146, 156, 173–75, 177–78
    Sahure, 4, 24, 38n91, 97, 105–6, 109–10, 130, 142
    sculptural program, 106, 110, 134–38, 141–143
    Teti, 29, 38–40, 119–21, 131, 137–38, 187
    Unas, 27, 29, 37, 116–19, 131, 138
    Userkaf, 24, 29, 137
pyramid temple. *See* mortuary temple
Pyramid Texts, 27–28, 32, 58–59, 119n53, 167–68, 171, 174–75, 178

quarrying. *See* mining
quartzite, 118–19, 124
Qubbet el-Hawa, 99, 179

queen(s), 8n24, 28–30, 32, 57–59. *See also under* pyramid complex
    Ankhnespepi II, 30–32

Raneferef, 16, 24, 136, 138. *See also under* mortuary temple; pyramid complex
Re. *See* sun god
rebels. *See* criminals
regent, 30–32
relief(s), 2, 12, 14, 20, 26, 38n91, 79n41, 83–87, 89, 97, 99n134, 104, 137, 169, 189. *See also under* causeway; mortuary temple; pyramid complex; valley temple
ritual, 19, 28, 148, 165–66, 173. *See also* mortuary cult; prisoner statue(s): ritual(s); pyramid complex: ritual(s); statuary: cult
    Breaking the Red Vases, 169
    execration, 18–19, 145, 161–62, 165, 167, 169, 171–72, 179. *See also* execration figurine(s)
    kingship, 146, 174
    offering, 168–74, 178
    smiting, 146, 166, 171–72, 174, 179, 181
    triumph, 146
royal family, 3, 7, 24, 27. *See also* queen(s)
royal *ka*. See under *ka*

Sahure, 24, 95, 136, 138, 143. *See also under* causeway; mortuary temple; pyramid; pyramid complex; valley temple
Saqqara, 4, 24, 27, 29, 42n102, 50, 79, 163–64, 188–90
    South, 27, 29, 31, 41
Second Intermediate period, 148n16
Second Style, 20, 62, 79–82, 85–86, 90, 102–4, 152, 178, 184n8, 187–88, 191
sed festival, 108, 113, 132, 172–73, 179
Seventh Dynasty, 3n1
Shepseskare, 24, 24n6, 26n24
Sinai, 91, 95–96, 100n134
Sixth Dynasty, 1–2, 4, 11–12, 20, 23, 26, 28–33, 54–59, 62, 79–80, 82–83, 90, 92, 95, 98–107, 119, 128, 132n108, 138–39, 141–43, 159, 162, 164, 177–80, 183, 186–89, 191
smiting scene, 8–10, 34, 89, 91, 128–33, 132n108, 139–40, 142, 171–72. *See also under* ritual
Sneferu, 93, 94n106, 96
sphinx. *See* statuary: animal

statuary, 44–45, 78–79, 81, 150. *See also* bound captive motif; execration figurines; foreigners: depictions of; prisoner statue(s)
    animal, 113, 135, 137–39, 143
    cult, 26, 107, 110, 135
    elite, 79–81, 83–84, 150, 190–91
    king's, 2, 14–17, 34, 107, 110–12, 120, 135–38, 154n33
    Maya, 160
    mutilation and damage, 148, 151, 153, 154n33, 160
    Niuserre, 80
    Pepi I, 81–82, 138n136
    serving, 84n67, 150
sun god, 4, 24, 27–29, 119n53, 167
sun temple, 4, 24–27
    Niuserre, 4n7, 24–25
    Userkaf, 24

Tano, Phocion Jean, 187
Teti, 29, 31, 57, 101, 136, 141, 152–53. *See also under* causeway; mortuary temple; pyramid; pyramid complex; valley temple
    prisoner statue(s), 4, 23, 38–41, 46, 53–56, 64, 81, 87, 89n90, 102, 120–21, 139–40, 152–53, 159, 178, 178n1, 187–88, 188n20, 191
Third Dynasty, 3, 4n1, 12n38, 14, 17, 91–93, 95–98
Third Intermediate period, 149n16, 154n35, 155n36
tomb, 4, 7, 125, 159, 164, 167. *See also* high official(s): tomb; pyramid
trade, 90–95, 98–103
trampling scene, 9–10, 128–30, 132–33, 137, 139–40
triumph scene, 41n101, 103, 131n100, 140, 142, 178. *See also* smiting scene; trampling scene

Unas, 18, 27–29, 79. *See also under* causeway; mortuary temple; pyramid; pyramid complex; valley temple
    prisoner statue(s), 4, 23, 34, 37–40, 46, 53–56, 90n90, 116–17, 139, 151–52, 159, 188n20
Userkaf, 4n7, 24, 138. *See also under* pyramid complex; sun temple
Userkare, 29

valley temple, 5, 105–8, 141, 143
    Djedkare-Isesi, 114, 116
    Niuserre, 110–11, 118–19, 127, 130, 139, 141, 178
    Pepi I, 121
    Pepi II, 111, 124, 126–27, 131–32, 140–41, 174, 179
    relief(s), 6, 110, 128–33, 139–40
    ritual(s). *See under* pyramid complex
    Sahure, 109–11, 118, 130, 141
    Teti, 119–20
    Unas, 117–19, 137, 141
vizier, 30
    Abd'el, 10
    Ptahshepses, 26, 28, 57
    Senedjemib Mehi, 18, 165
    Weni, 31, 99n134, 101

Wadi el-Jarf, 94, 96
Wadi Maghara, 91, 96
Western Desert, 11, 96–97, 100, 103
wood, 17, 86, 136, 165

Yam, 101, 179